MILDREDS
THE COOKBOOK

MILDREDS
THE COOKBOOK

DELICIOUS VEGETARIAN RECIPES
FOR SIMPLY EVERYONE

PHOTOGRAPHY BY JONATHAN GREGSON

MITCHELL BEAZLEY

This book is dedicated to everyone who has been involved in Mildreds—you all helped make it what it is today.

"When baking, follow instructions; when cooking, go by your own taste."
LAIKO BAHRS

An Hachette UK Company
www.hachette.co.uk

First published in Great Britain in 2015 by Mitchell Beazley, a division of Octopus Publishing Group Ltd, Carmelite House, 50 Victoria Embankment, London EC4Y 0DZ
www.octopusbooks.co.uk
www.octopusbooksusa.com

Design & layout copyright © Octopus Publishing Group Ltd 2015
Text copyright © Mildreds Limited 2015
Photography copyright © Jonathan Gregson 2015

Distributed in the US by Hachette Book Group, 1290 Avenue of the Americas, 4th and 5th Floors, New York, NY 10020

Distributed in Canada by Canadian Manda Group, 664 Annette St., Toronto, Ontario, Canada M6S 2C8

All rights reserved. No part of this work may be reproduced or utilized in any form or by any means, electronic or mechanical, including photocopying, recording, or by any information storage and retrieval system, without the prior written permission of the publisher.

The authors assert the moral right to be identified as the authors of this work.

ISBN 978-1-78472-030-8

Printed and bound in China

10 9 8 7 6 5 4 3 2 1

Recipe Writers: Daniel Acevedo & Sarah Wasserman
Commissioning Editor: Eleanor Maxfield
Senior Editor: Leanne Bryan
Copy Editor: Simon Davis
Proofreader: Clare Sayer
Indexer: Helen Snaith
Americanizer: Constance Novis
Deputy Art Director: Yasia Williams-Leedham
Designer: Patrick Budge
Illustrator: Kirsti-Lee Poulter
Photographer: Jonathan Gregson
Home Economist: Annie Rigg
Prop Stylist & Art Director: Tabitha Hawkins
Assistant Production Manager: Caroline Alberti

CONTENTS

Introduction 6

Soups 14
Appetizers 30
  Mezze 60
Salads 80
Mains 104
  Burgers 138
  Pasta 144
  Latin 158
Sides 180
Desserts 200
Dips, Sauces & Dressings 224

Gluten-free Menu Ideas 244
Vegan Menu Ideas 246
Suppliers 248
Index 250
Acknowledgments 256

INTRODUCTION

In 1988, when London's Soho was still edgy, Diane Thomas and I took the plunge and opened Mildreds on Greek Street, right in the heart of the West End.

Back then, vegetarian restaurants still had that sixties hippy vibe—doling out "worthy" brown food into earthenware pottery placed on pine tables. The whole thing felt dated, or so it seemed to us. Our aim was to open a restaurant serving good value, fresh, and colorful international vegetarian food. Armed with the supreme confidence of youth (and little else) we took the lease on a small café that, in its former life, had been a seedy sex club, complete with an S&M padded cell in the basement!

At that time our porn baron landlords would come to collect their extortionate rent in person, usually with a glamorous brunette or blonde—wrapped in fur and wearing large, dangly earrings—in tow. After invariably asking for a bacon sandwich, they would slip the envelopes of cash into the inside pockets of their cashmere coats and head out for a "real meal," as they put it.

The word on the street was that we would last six months.

Yet, despite the prophecies, it turned out that there were people out there who did want to eat the sort of food we were cooking, and we soon became a popular fixture in Soho. With main courses priced at £2.95 (about $4.50), we also pretty quickly figured out that we needed to turn those tables to cover the overheads, and so we made the unusual decision (at that time) not to take reservations. Our clientele had nowhere to wait, so we would spend a lot of each night running back and forth across the road to the pub, shouting out the names of waiting customers above the pumping rock music.

After 12 years, the opportunity to move to a larger premises—with a proper kitchen, a bar, and a private dining room—arose. From inauspicious beginnings, Mildreds had grown up.

Diane Thomas sadly passed away in 2001 but is with us in spirit always.

Many people ask how the name "Mildreds" came about. I had been waitressing at the impossibly cool 192 in Notting Hill before opening Mildreds and wanted a name that stood on its own without reference to wholefoods or vegetarianism. A friend started calling me "Mildred" after the lead character from the great film noir *Mildred Pierce*, starring Joan Crawford. For those who don't know, she was a downtrodden waitress who managed to open a chain of successful restaurants despite being hampered by a scheming social-climbing daughter and a double-crossing playboy lover. The name seemed perfect.

Obviously the food, the service, the ambience, and the profit margins are important, but that's only a small part of running a restaurant. There's more. The people who bring the place alive are the staff.

The past 26 years have gone by in the blink of an eye and during that time we have had our fair share of ups and downs. There has been the joy of birth, and the sadness of death and illness. We have risen again after fire, flood, and pestilence (the less said about the latter, the better). We have fallen in love, built lasting friendships, suffered breakups and divorce, and weathered recessions (it's been touch and go at times). Yet through it all we've forged ahead together with pride, ambition, ideas, hopes, dreams, laughs, and drama (the notorious incident of the missing chef found slumped in the walk-in fridge comes to mind!). We've worked hard to still be here, and now it's better than ever, with more to come. I embrace it all. It's my life. It's what makes me tick.

We still have the same values, integrity, and love for what we do that we've had from the very start. Even though over the years the food scene has changed, a lot of these changes—such as the move toward using independent suppliers and organic, ethically sourced produce—reflect the way we have always done things.

Daniel, the head chef, and Sarah, our chef extraordinaire, have been the backbone of the Mildreds team for the past ten years. What follows is the culmination of their hard work and talent. They are the real heros of this book.

This book has been a long time coming. We hope you enjoy it.

JANE MUIR

DANIEL ACEVEDO

I always knew I wanted to be a chef. When I was young, I loved being in the kitchen. I remember coming home from school, grabbing my mother's copy of *Cookery the Australian Way* and baking Anzac cookies and scones. I must have been about nine or ten years old at the time.

I started cooking professionally in 1997 at the age of 17 and trained in various restaurants in and around Melbourne, working mainly with Italian, Greek, and pan-Asian cuisines, before deciding in 2005 to move to London to expand my knowledge and further my career as a chef. One of the first jobs that I applied for was at Mildreds. I had never worked in a vegetarian restaurant and jumped at the chance to work somewhere where there would be a strong emphasis on the use of herbs and spices (which has always been the most exciting part of cooking for me).

Over the next couple of years I moved up to the sous chef position within the kitchen and soon after that I took over as head chef.

Working at Mildreds has given—and keeps on giving me—new opportunities, both personally and professionally. I love my job and my team of chefs in the kitchen and would like to thank them for the hard work they have put in over the years that I have been nagging, pushing, and encouraging them to deliver the best of themselves into the food we make at the restaurant. It simply wouldn't be possible to do what we do without such a strong team.

In October 2010, fellow chef Sarah Wasserman and I started a food blog for Mildreds, primarily with the aim of giving us a platform to experiment and share some of our recipes and daily specials from the restaurant with the blogging community. We always felt, though, that this vegetarian institution deserved a cookbook in its own right, and our blog turned out to be a first step on the road toward accomplishing this.

Many of the restaurant's best-known dishes are featured in this book, along with my favorites, and I love and am very proud of the variety of internationally inspired recipes we have created. Working with Sarah is always a joy and I feel we have really pushed each other to achieve a wonderful book for the restaurant. What a great food adventure it has been!

SARAH WASSERMAN

I have always worked with food, from my first job in a health food store deli in North Carolina, to my time spent hitchhiking across America and my return to London and employment in an eclectic range of busy restaurants. Having misspent my youth at various wonderful London Art colleges, I'm lucky that I had this equal passion, which, unlike my art education, meant I could always put bread on the table!

During my postgrad at the Royal Academy of Art, I would often pass Mildreds and always thought it would be a lovely place to work. Daniel and I started at Mildreds a few days apart and have been friends and collaborators ever since. We started the Mildreds blog together—coming up with recipes, interviewing suppliers, and photographing the food in our spare time—so when we got the chance to write the book we jumped at it. I've read cookbooks for fun since primary school and have been known to lug a hardback copy of Claudia Roden's Jewish Food around for a month to read on the subway. The idea of writing a book of our own was wonderful.

Even though we are sometimes insanely busy at Mildreds, we never rest on our laurels. Jane is always looking for ways in which we can improve, and that drives us as chefs to keep looking for new dishes. The menu is international because we find it really helpful to look to other cultures for vegetarian inspiration. Asian recipes are great for vegan ideas because they contain little or no dairy; the Middle East is good for salads and side dishes because foods from that region are often meat-free; Passover recipes can be excellent for gluten-free ideas, while, of course, India is a fantastic source of vegetarian food. There is always a new avenue to explore, which is what makes cooking vegetarian food so interesting.

One of the things I like about working at Mildreds is that, although we cater for a wide range of vegetarian diets, nothing is on the menu simply because it fits a particular dietary choice—everything is there on merit. So, if we put a new brownie on the menu it's because we think it's a brilliant brownie. The fact that it's gluten-free and vegan just happens to be the icing on the cake, if you'll forgive the expression.

MILDREDS AT HOME

 VEGAN

 GLUTEN-FREE

HOW TO USE THIS BOOK

People who choose a vegetarian restaurant may do so for any number of reasons, be they moral, religious, dietary, environmental, or just for a change. Nowadays, vegetarian cooking really is for everyone, whether you still enjoy tucking into a steak, or prefer a completely vegetarian diet. Vegetables, fruit, legumes, nuts, and seeds have now taken their rightful place in the kitchen and have stolen the limelight.

Although this book is organized by course, you'll find a number of dishes that can be beefed up to become a main meal or combined with other dishes to share. Look for notes at the end of some recipes giving tips for dietary requirements, creative variations, flavor twists, or recommendations for dishes that go particularly well together.

You'll also find stamps, like the ones on the left, at the top of many of the recipes to indicate dishes that are vegan and gluten-free. Of course, recipes can also be amended to suit your particular diet. For example, if you want to cook a gluten-free pasta dish, just choose gluten-free pasta instead of the regular kind. Likewise, gluten-free flour can be substituted for regular flour in most instances. Gluten-free vegetable bouillon powder is also a must for gluten-free options.

A NOTE ON COOKING FOR FRIENDS

If only *all* you had to fret about when throwing a dinner party was to pull off a meal that left your satisfied guests begging for your recipes. These days you are also likely to be catering for people with specific dietary preferences, including vegetarians, vegans, and guests who are wheat-intolerant. Your meal should be full of dishes that everyone can enjoy. Putting a different plate of food in front of someone who can't eat the same food as the other guests will only give them the feeling that they have inconvenienced you.

For that reason, there are also some great ideas for gluten-free and vegan dinner menus at the back of the book (*see* pages 244–5 and 246–7). We've also included Middle Eastern mezze and Latin features in the book (*see* pages 60–79 and 158–79), which should give you tons of ideas about which dishes go together.

SOUPS

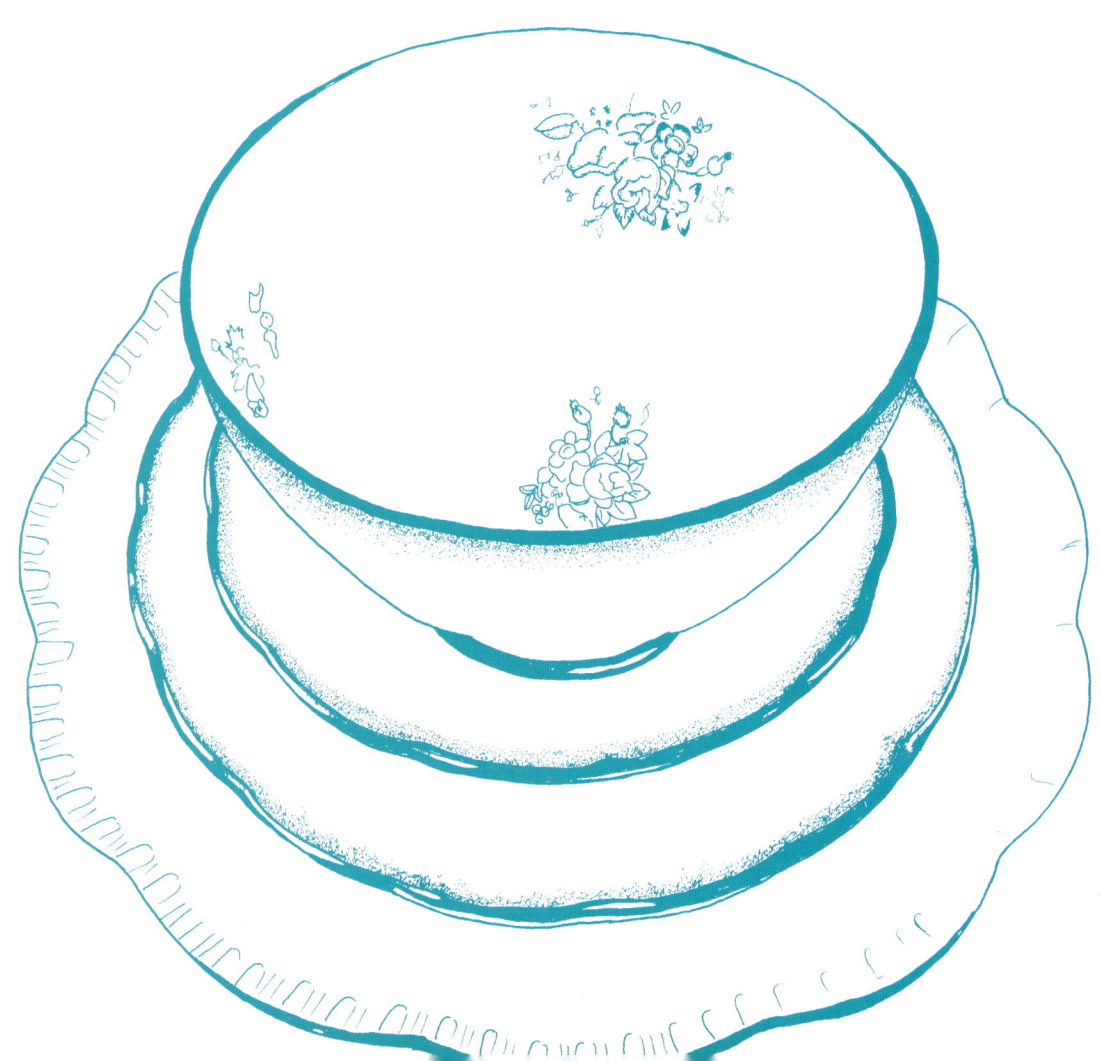

In this rich, creamy, and colorful soup the subtle flavor of the lime leaves complements the sweet potato nicely. We use fresh lime leaves when we cook this in the restaurant, but if you're having trouble getting hold of these the dried ones are fine too—just soak them in warm water for a few minutes to rehydrate before using.

THAI-SPICED ROASTED RED BELL PEPPER, SWEET POTATO, GINGER & COCONUT MILK SOUP

SERVES 4 TO 5

6 lime leaves
olive oil
1 small white onion, diced
1 red chile, trimmed and diced
3 garlic cloves, chopped
1½-inch piece of fresh ginger root, peeled and chopped
1lb 10oz sweet potatoes, peeled and cut into 2-inch chunks
2 x 14fl oz cans coconut milk
1 cup water
7oz roasted piquillo peppers or other roasted red bell peppers in oil, drained and chopped
salt and pepper
hunks of crusty bread, to serve (optional)

Cut the tough central veins out of the lime leaves and discard. Finely slice the remaining lime leaves. Set aside.

Heat a splash of oil in a large saucepan set over medium heat. Add the onion, chile, garlic, and ginger and cook, stirring, for 8 to 10 minutes, or until the onion softens and starts to color. Add the lime leaf slices and sweet potatoes. Sauté for another 2 to 3 minutes.

Add the coconut milk and water, stir in the piquillo peppers, and bring to a simmer. Let cook for 30 minutes, or until the sweet potato chunks are soft. At this stage you can add some more water to achieve the desired consistency for your soup, and check the seasoning to see if salt or pepper is needed.

Purée the soup in a food processor or with a stick blender until smooth and creamy. Serve with hunks of crusty bread, if you like.

This soup makes a nice appetizer before a noodle-based main, such as **Mee Goreng** (*see* page 156) or **Tempura Vegetables with Noodle, Mango & Cucumber Salad and Chile Dipping Sauce** (*see* page 56).

If you can't find fresh or dried lime leaves, just add an extra squeeze of **lime juice** and some **fresh cilantro** before blending.

If roasted piquillo peppers prove elusive, just roast some **fresh red bell peppers** instead (*see* page 66).

This is a lovely fresh soup for spring. Blending in the fresh herbs gives it a vibrant green color, which contrasts nicely with the bright yellow rice. The mascarpone can be omitted, or replaced with soy cream, to make this suitable for vegans.

MINESTRONE VERDE WITH SAFFRON ARBORIO RICE

SERVES 6 TO 8

olive oil
1 white onion, diced
3 garlic cloves, minced
1 teaspoon fennel seeds, toasted and crushed
2 small leeks, trimmed, cleaned, and finely diced
1 fennel bulb, trimmed and finely diced
½ cup white wine
1½ to 2 pints vegetable stock
1½ cups baby peas
1 zucchini, finely diced
3½oz green string beans, trimmed and finely chopped
1 bunch of basil
1 bunch of mint
grated zest of ½ lemon
salt and pepper

For the Saffron Arborio Rice
2 cups vegetable stock
small pinch of saffron threads
olive oil
1 cup arborio rice
⅔ cup white wine

To serve
6 to 8 teaspoons mascarpone cheese, divided
breadsticks (optional)

For the rice, bring the stock to a simmer in a saucepan, add the saffron, and let it infuse. Heat a splash of oil in a separate saucepan, add the rice, and cook, stirring, for a minute. Pour in the wine and let it bubble to reduce down until the pan is quite dry. Gradually add the stock a ladleful at a time, stirring frequently, until the rice is cooked but still firm.

Meanwhile, heat a separate large saucepan and splash in a little oil. Add the onion and garlic and cook, stirring, for a few minutes until the onion is translucent. Add the fennel seeds, leeks, and fennel bulb and cook, stirring frequently, for 5 minutes, or until the vegetables soften. Add the wine and reduce until almost evaporated. Pour in the stock and bring to a simmer. Finally add the peas, zucchini, and string beans and let simmer 2–3 minutes.

Remove 2 cups of the soup and blend together with the herbs and grated lemon zest in a food processor or in a bowl with a stick blender until smooth. Pour the mixture back into the soup, stir, and adjust the seasoning to taste. Add the rice and heat through.

Ladle the hot soup into bowls, adding a spoonful of mascarpone to the center of each. Serve immediately, with breadsticks, if liked.

A surprisingly creamy soup with a smoky chile flavor, this is a real favorite among the staff at Mildreds. The pico de gallo (or tomato salsa) adds a nice fresh finish and a flash of color.

CRANBERRY BEAN SOUP
WITH SMOKED TOFU & PICO DE GALLO

SERVES 6 TO 8

olive oil
1 onion, diced
1 red chile, trimmed, seeded, and minced
3 garlic cloves, minced
1 celery stalk, trimmed, peeled, and diced
1 carrot, diced
1 leek, trimmed, cleaned, and diced
2 thyme sprigs
1 tablespoon smoked paprika
1 tablespoon ground coriander
2 x 14oz cans cranberry beans, drained and rinsed, divided
1 teaspoon brown sugar
grated zest and juice of ½ lime
2 pints water
7½oz smoked tofu
salt and pepper

For the Pico de Gallo
1 chile, trimmed
4 scallions, trimmed
handful of cilantro leaves
2 tomatoes, flesh and seeds removed and reserved for the soup
grated zest and juice of 1 lime

Heat a splash of oil in a large saucepan set over medium heat. Add the onion and cook, stirring, for 8 to 10 minutes, or until soft and translucent. Then add the chile and garlic and cook for another 2 minutes. Add the celery, carrot, leek, thyme, and the reserved tomato flesh and seeds from the *pico de gallo* and cook, stirring, over low heat for 5 minutes, or until the vegetables start to soften. Add the paprika and ground coriander and sauté for a further 2 minutes to allow the flavors to infuse.

Add three-quarters of the cranberry beans, the sugar, and the grated lime zest and juice. Pour in the water and bring to a simmer. Cook, stirring regularly, for 20 minutes, or until the beans are beginning to break down.

While the beans are cooking, make the *pico de gallo*. Finely chop the chile, scallions, cilantro, and tomato skins, add to a bowl, and mix together with the lime juice and grated zest. Taste and adjust the seasoning if necessary.

Purée the soup in a food processor or with a stick blender until smooth and creamy. Return to the pan, add the remaining beans and the smoked tofu, and warm through over very low heat. Season with salt and pepper to taste.

Ladle into bowls and serve topped with a spoonful of *pico de gallo*.

This Korean-inspired dish is really more of a broth than a soup, but can be bulked up further with the addition of some cooked noodles or vegetable dumplings if you'd like to serve it as a main course. The recipe calls for Korean chili powder, but regular chili powder works fine, too. And if you like a tangy finish, just add a little more tamarind paste.

KOREAN HOT & SOUR SOUP

SERVES 6 TO 8

light oil (such as canola, peanut, or sunflower)
1 onion, diced
4 garlic cloves, minced
1-inch piece of fresh ginger root, peeled and minced
1 red chile, trimmed and finely sliced
2 teaspoons Korean chili powder
2 quarts vegetable stock
13oz can diced tomatoes
⅓ cup tamarind paste
2 tablespoons superfine sugar
½ Chinese leaf cabbage, shredded
3 cups shredded bok choy

To garnish
1 cup bean sprouts
4 scallions, finely sliced
handful of cilantro sprigs

In a large saucepan, heat a splash of oil and sauté the onion, garlic, ginger, and chile for 5 to 8 minutes, or until the onion is translucent. Add the chili powder and cook, stirring, for another minute or so, then add the vegetable stock, tomatoes, tamarind paste, and sugar. Bring to a boil, reduce the heat, and simmer for 15 to 20 minutes to allow the flavors to meld together.

When the broth is cooked, increase the heat, stir in the cabbage and bok choy, and cook for 2 to 3 minutes, or until the vegetables are tender. Ladle into bowls and garnish with the bean sprouts, scallions, and cilantro to serve.

This tangy Thai soup is absolutely delicious and so good for colds it should be prescribed as medicine. We usually make it with cremino mushrooms, but button or oyster mushrooms would work equally well. If you can't get hold of jaggery (also known as palm sugar), just use dark brown sugar instead.

TOMATO & MUSHROOM TOM YUM

SERVES 6 TO 8

7 tomatoes, quartered
sesame oil or other light cooking oil (such as canola, peanut, or sunflower)
1 white onion, coarsely chopped
3 garlic cloves, coarsely chopped
2 bird's-eye chiles, trimmed and coarsely chopped
2½-inch piece of peeled fresh galangal or ginger root, coarsely chopped
3 lemon grass stalks, bashed with a rolling pin and cut into pieces 1½ inches long
1 bunch of cilantro, leaves and stalks separated
10 lime leaves
2 tablespoons tamarind paste
½ cup jaggery (palm sugar) or dark brown sugar
2 tablespoons tomato paste
2 quarts vegetable stock
1lb cremino mushrooms, trimmed and halved
juice of 2 limes
salt and pepper

Using a spoon, scrape the seeds out of the tomato quarters. Reserve the seeds and then coarsely chop the flesh and reserve it, too.

Warm a splash of sesame oil in a large saucepan. Add the onion, garlic, chiles, and galangal or ginger to the pan and cook, stirring, for 2 to 3 minutes, or until the onion has softened slightly. Add the lemon grass pieces, reserved tomato seeds, cilantro stalks, and lime leaves and sauté for 5 minutes, or until fragrant.

Add the tamarind paste, sugar, and tomato paste to the pan and give everything a good stir before adding the stock. Bring to a boil and then reduce the heat and simmer gently for at least 20 minutes to allow the flavors to infuse. Season to taste with salt and pepper.

In another saucepan, heat a splash of oil over medium heat, add the mushrooms, and cook until just tender.

Strain the broth through a sieve, add the cooked mushrooms, chopped tomato flesh, cilantro leaves, and lime juice and ladle into bowls. Serve immediately.

With its ribbons of red cabbage and generous chunks of vegetables and apples, this sweet and sour eastern European classic is almost more of a stew than a broth. Serve it with some delicious rye bread for a hearty winter's lunch. The sour cream can be omitted, or replaced with soy cream, to make this vegan.

BEET, APPLE & RED CABBAGE BORSCHT

SERVES 6 TO 8

2 celery stalks, trimmed
1 carrot, peeled
1 white potato, peeled
1 leek, trimmed and cleaned
2 large beets, peeled
1 apple, peeled and cored
light oil (such as canola, peanut, or sunflower)
1 large white onion, finely diced
½ red chile, trimmed and minced
1-inch piece of fresh ginger root, minced
5 garlic cloves, minced
1 teaspoon ground fennel seeds
1 teaspoon ground caraway seeds
3 cups sliced red cabbage, cut lengthwise into strands ⅛ inch long
2 star anise
3 tablespoons tomato paste
2 tablespoons balsamic vinegar
3¼ cups apple juice
2 pints vegetable stock
salt and white pepper

To serve
1 bunch of dill leaves, chopped
¼ to ½ cup sour cream

Cut the celery, carrot, potato, leek, beets, and apple into cubes about ½ inch in size, and set aside.

Splash a little oil into a large saucepan over medium heat, add the onion, and sauté for 5 to 8 minutes, or until clear and translucent. Add the chile, ginger, and garlic to the pan and sauté for 2 minutes, then add the carrot, leek, beets, ground fennel, and caraway seeds and cook, stirring, for a further 15 minutes, or until the beet cubes are beginning to lose their bite.

Add the red cabbage and cook, stirring, for 2 to 3 minutes, or until the cabbage has begun to soften. Then add the star anise, tomato paste, and balsamic vinegar along with the cubed celery, potato, and apple. Pour in the apple juice and stock, bring to a simmer, and cook gently for 45 minutes, or until the beets are cooked through. Season to taste with salt and pepper.

Ladle the soup into bowls, scatter with the dill leaves, and serve with the sour cream alongside for adding a dollop on top of each serving.

This simple winter soup is all about its three main ingredients, so it's important to get the best quality you can find. We use fantastic Spanish haricot beans and they really are worth seeking out for the smooth creamy texture they impart. A dense, sweet variety of pumpkin is perfect for this soup. If all you can find are the more watery varieties, however, use a butternut squash instead.

PUMPKIN, CAVALO NERO & HARICOT BEAN BROTH

SERVES 6 TO 8

olive oil
1¾lb pumpkin or butternut squash, peeled and cut into 1-inch cubes
1 white onion, finely diced
1-inch piece of fresh ginger root, peeled and chopped
3 garlic cloves, chopped
3 celery stalks, peeled and minced
1 leek, trimmed, cleaned, and finely diced
1 tablespoon chopped rosemary
1 tablespoon chopped thyme
1¼ cups white wine
2 teaspoons sugar
2 quarts vegetable stock
15oz can haricot beans, drained and rinsed
1 head of cavolo nero, stalks removed, chopped into bite-size pieces
salt

Preheat the oven to 375°F.

Drizzle a little oil into a roasting pan. Add the pumpkin pieces, season with salt, and toss together thoroughly to coat. Roast for 15 minutes, or until cooked through. Set aside.

Heat a splash of oil in a large saucepan over low heat, add the onion, ginger, and garlic and cook gently, stirring, for 8 minutes, or until the onion has begun to soften. Add the celery, leek, and herbs and cook, stirring, for another 2 minutes. Then add the wine and sugar and let simmer for 15 to 20 minutes until the liquid has reduced by two-thirds.

Pour in the stock and bring to a boil. Reduce to a simmer and cook for 10 minutes, stirring occasionally. Add the beans and simmer for another 10 minutes until the flavors have melded together. Stir in the roasted pumpkin and cavolo nero and simmer for another 2 to 3 minutes, or until the cavolo nero is tender. Remove from the heat, ladle into bowls, and serve.

A great soup for beating the heat on a summer's day, this has been given a slight twist on the usual with the addition of chopped cilantro. To enjoy it at its refreshing best, be sure to let the soup cool down sufficiently before serving. And if the day is really hot, try adding a few ice cubes to each bowl to chill it further still.

GAZPACHO

SERVES 4 TO 6

3 x 14oz cans diced tomatoes
½ cup light olive oil
1 small red onion, minced
1 small red bell pepper, cored, seeded, and finely diced
1 small yellow bell pepper, cored, seeded, and finely diced
handful of cilantro, leaves picked and chopped
1 small cucumber, peeled, seeded, and finely diced
2 celery stalks, trimmed and finely diced
2 cups water
3 tablespoons vegetarian Worcestershire sauce
4 garlic cloves, minced
salt and pepper

Add the tomatoes to a food processor with the olive oil and blend together until smooth, or place in a bowl and use a stick blender. Pass the mixture through a sieve to remove the seeds.

Put the diced onion, peppers, cilantro, cucumber, celery, and puréed tomato mixture into a large container, add the water, vegetarian Worcestershire sauce, and garlic and season to taste with salt and pepper. Stir together well.

Transfer to the refrigerator and let chill for at least 1 hour so the flavors can develop. Check the seasoning and adjust if necessary before serving.

APPETIZERS

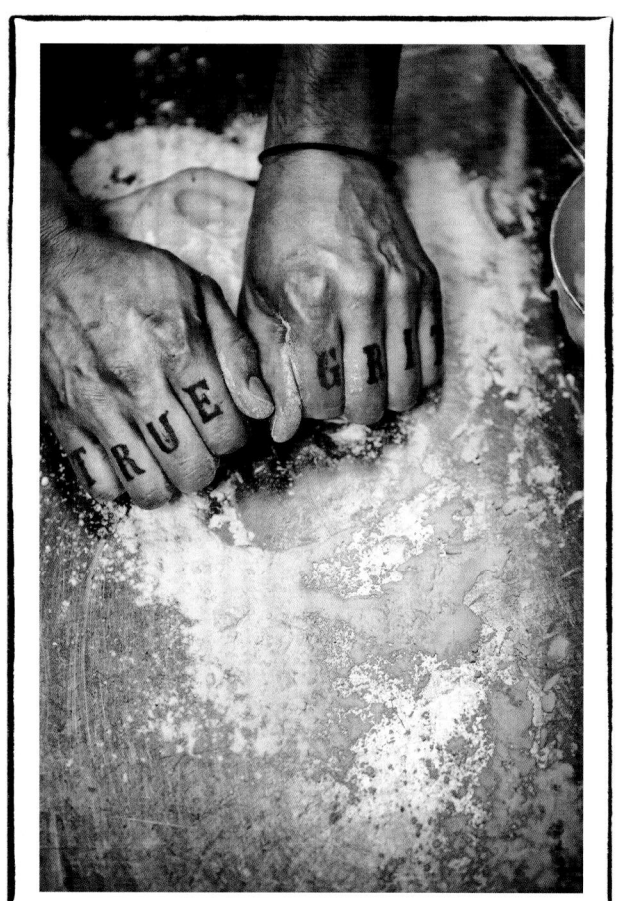

Arancini are a great way to use up leftover risotto. They are lovely served with lemon wedges for squeezing over, though here they are partnered with a warm grilled eggplant and zucchini salad for something more substantial. The balsamic pickled onions in this salad are available in most supermarkets, but if you're struggling to find them then use regular pickled onions instead. To make this recipe gluten-free, simply coat the arancini with gluten-free breadcrumbs.

SUN-DRIED TOMATO & MOZZARELLA ARANCINI WITH WARM GRILLED EGGPLANT & ZUCCHINI SALAD

SERVES 8

2 pints vegetable stock
olive oil
1 onion, diced
6 garlic cloves, crushed
5oz sun-dried tomatoes in oil, drained and coarsely chopped
1 teaspoon dried basil
2 cups arborio rice
handful of fresh basil leaves, chopped
7oz bocconcini cheese
2¼ cups dried bread crumbs
lemon wedges, to serve

For the Warm Grilled Eggplant & Zucchini Salad

4 zucchini, cut diagonally into ½-inch slices
2 large eggplants, cut into round disks ¾ inch thick
¼ cup light olive oil
2 garlic cloves, minced
8 balsamic pickled onions, quartered, plus 2 tablespoons of pickling juice
handful of flat-leaf parsley leaves, chopped
2 tablespoons extra virgin olive oil
1 tablespoon good-quality aged balsamic vinegar or balsamic glaze
sea salt flakes

Bring the stock to a simmer in a saucepan. Heat a splash of oil in a separate saucepan, add the onion and garlic, and cook, stirring, for 2 to 3 minutes, or until the onion has started to soften. Add the tomatoes, dried basil, and rice and sauté for another 2 minutes.

Gradually add the stock to the rice a ladleful at a time, stirring frequently, until the rice is cooked but still firm. Remove from the heat and transfer to a small tray or large plate and let cool for 10 minutes, then refrigerate for another 15 to 20 minutes.

Meanwhile, make the salad. Heat a ridged grill pan or large heavy skillet over medium heat. Mix the zucchini and eggplant slices with the oil and garlic in a mixing bowl, add to the pan, and cook until tender; about 1 to 2 minutes on each side for the zucchini and at least 2 to 3 minutes on each side for the eggplant. Remove from the heat and return to the bowl along with the pickled onions, pickling juice, chopped parsley, extra virgin olive oil, and balsamic vinegar. Season with sea salt flakes and stir to combine. Set aside.

Remove the cooled rice from the refrigerator, add the chopped fresh basil to the rice, and stir to combine. Shape into 1¾-inch balls, pushing a piece of bocconcini into the center of each with your thumb. Roll the *arancini* in the bread crumbs. Heat a thin layer of olive oil in a skillet. Add the *arancini* and fry for 2 to 3 minutes on each side until golden brown. Serve with the warm grilled eggplant and zucchini salad, and the lemon wedges, for squeezing over.

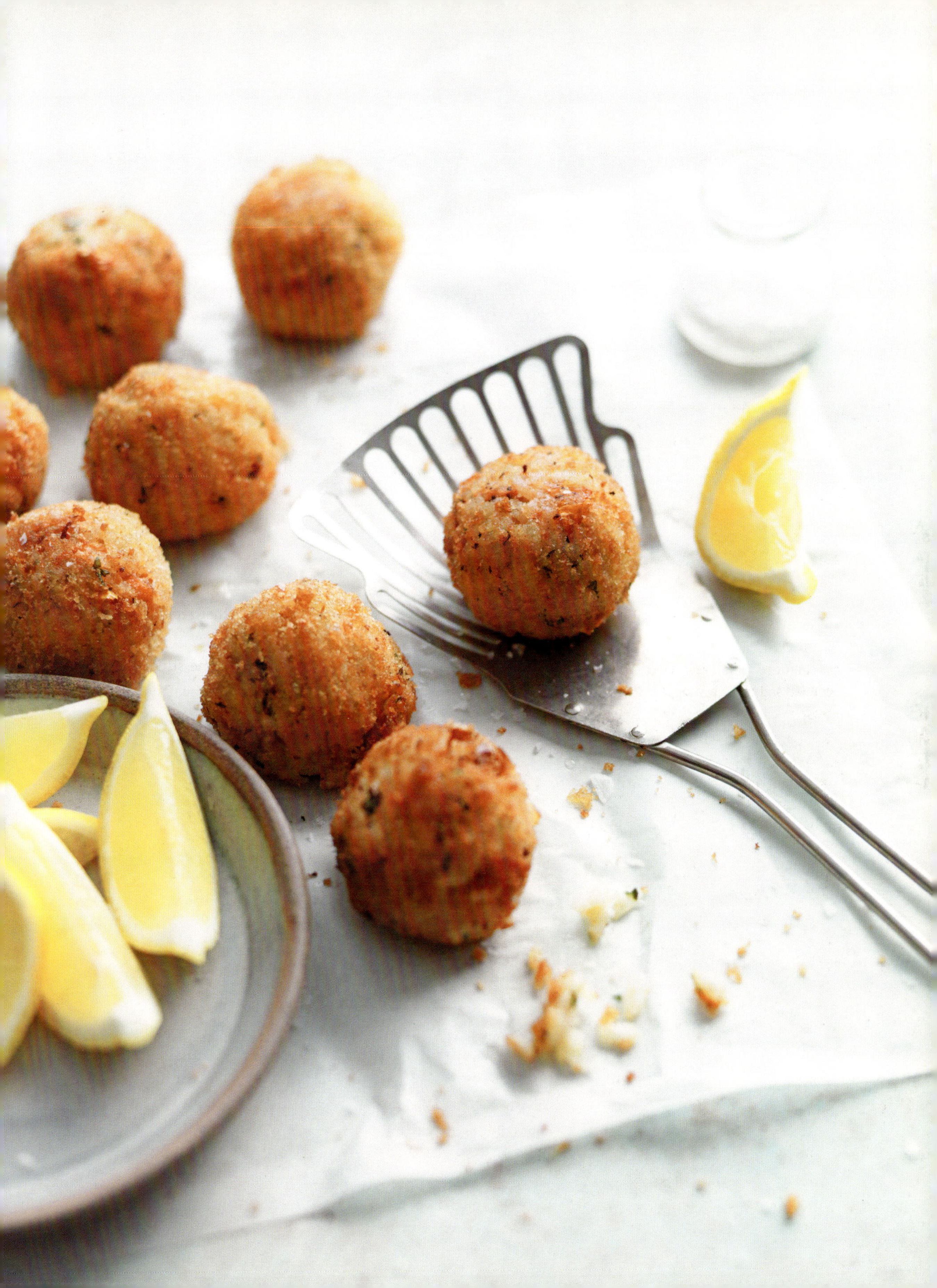

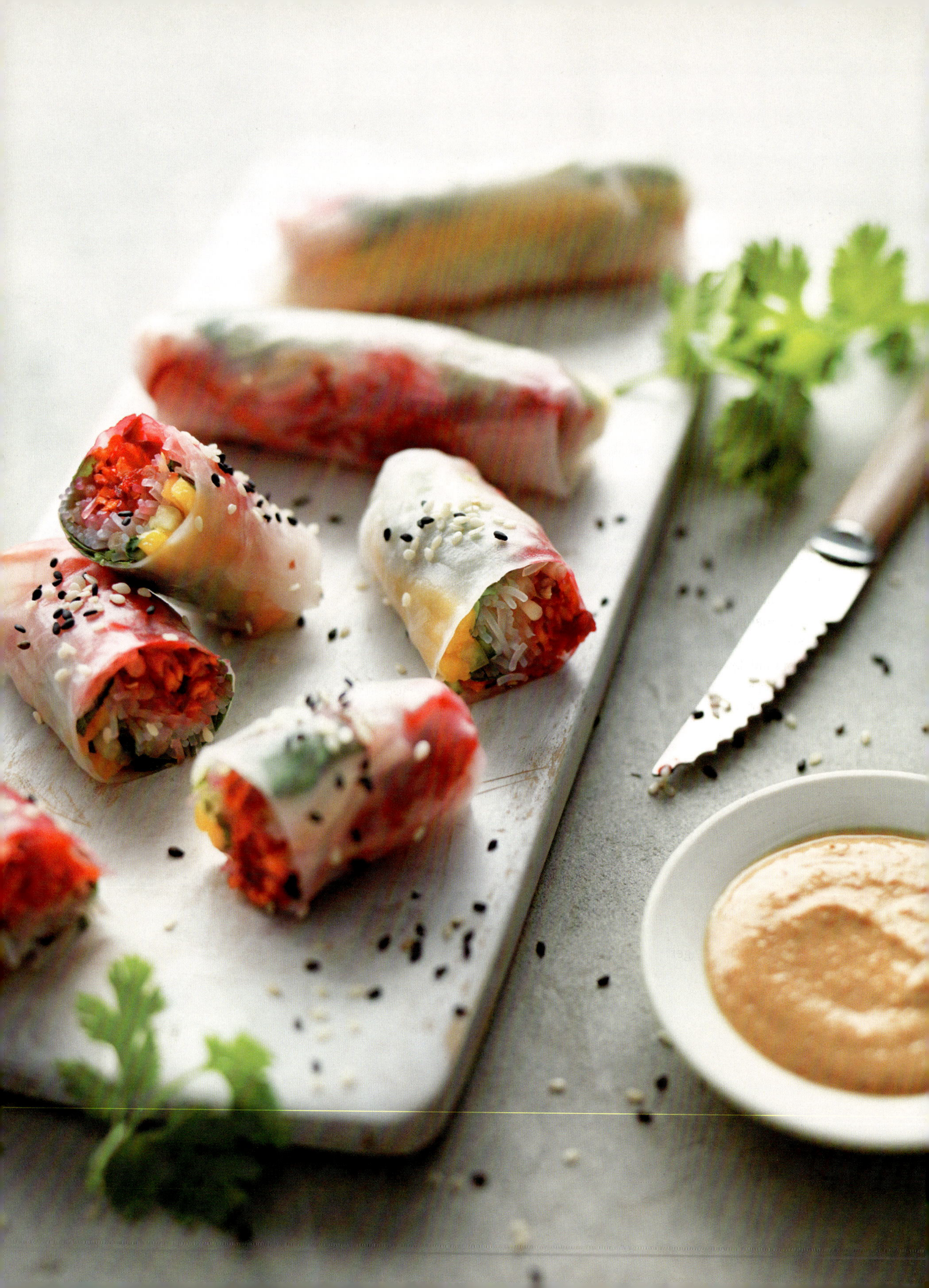

Summer rolls have proved to be a very popular addition to our menu. Gluten-free, vegan, and very light, they make a great snack on a hot day. They are really simple to make but you may have to go to an Asian supermarket or look online to find the rice paper wrappers.

MANGO SUMMER ROLLS WITH SPICY PEANUT SAUCE

SERVES 4 TO 6

3oz vermicelli rice noodles
½ cup bean sprouts
1 large red chile, trimmed and diced
grated zest of 2 limes
9-inch square rice paper wrappers
½ cucumber, seeded and cut into batons ¼ inch thick
1 small ripe mango, peeled and cut into batons ¼ inch thick
handful of mint, leaves picked
handful of fresh cilantro, leaves picked, plus extra to garnish
1 medium beet, coarsely grated
1 large carrot, coarsely grated

For the Spicy Peanut Sauce
¾ cup crunchy peanut butter
1 cup water
1 red chile, trimmed and minced
juice of 2 limes
1 tablespoon dark brown sugar
4 garlic cloves, minced
¾-inch piece of fresh ginger root, peeled and minced

Cook or soak the rice noodles in boiling water following the package instructions then drain them well. Once cool, add them to a bowl with the bean sprouts, chile, and grated lime zest. Mix together well.

Wet a rice paper wrapper by dipping it into a bowl of water for 15 to 20 seconds. When it starts to soften and become pliable, place it on a clean work surface. Set a few batons of cucumber and mango across the center of the wrapper, leaving a gap of 1½ to 2 inches on either side for folding. Add a few mint and cilantro leaves and then a small handful of the noodle mixture and grated vegetables.

Bring the bottom and top edges of the wrapper tightly up over the filling then fold the sides in over it. Continue to roll it up tightly and place on a plate. Repeat this process with the remaining rolls and filling ingredients.

To make the sauce, put all the ingredients into a bowl and beat together until smooth.

Serve the rolls accompanied by the spicy peanut sauce and garnished with cilantro leaves.

What more can we say? When asparagus comes into season for those short few weeks in late spring and early summer there's nothing better to eat, particularly when paired with freshly poached eggs and a generous serving of hollandaise sauce. In this hollandaise we have used orange juice instead of lemon juice to give it a sweeter, fruitier tang.

ROASTED ASPARAGUS WITH POACHED EGGS & ORANGE HOLLANDAISE

SERVES 4 TO 6

16 asparagus spears
sea salt flakes
¼ cup olive oil
2 tablespoons apple cider vinegar or white wine vinegar
4 to 6 eggs

For the Orange Hollandaise
2 egg yolks
1 tablespoon apple cider vinegar
4 sticks butter, melted, divided
juice of ½ small orange
salt and pepper

Preheat the oven to 375°F. Line a cookie sheet with nonstick parchment paper.

To prepare the asparagus, snap off the woody base of the stalks. Place the asparagus on the prepared cookie sheet, sprinkle with sea salt flakes, and drizzle with the olive oil. Roast for 10 minutes, or until the asparagus spears are tender but still firm.

Meanwhile prepare your hollandaise sauce by beating the yolks and vinegar in a bowl set over a pan of gently simmering water until the yolks are thick, pale, and tripled in volume. Remove from the heat and beat in three-quarters of the butter, continuing to beat until the sauce is thick and shiny. Beat in the orange juice and the remaining butter, leaving out the pale white milk solids that will have formed when the butter melted. Season with salt and pepper and cover with a dish towel to keep warm until needed.

Bring a large saucepan of water to a boil and lower the heat to bring it to a rolling simmer. Add the vinegar and give the water a light clockwise swirl with a spoon. Crack one of the eggs into a cup and pour it into the water. Repeat with the remaining eggs and poach for approximately 2 to 3 minutes, or until the whites are set but the yolks are still soft. Lift out the eggs with a slotted spoon and set them on a clean dish towel to drain.

Divide the asparagus spears between plates, drizzle them with the hollandaise sauce, and place an egg on top of each serving. Garnish with freshly ground black pepper and serve.

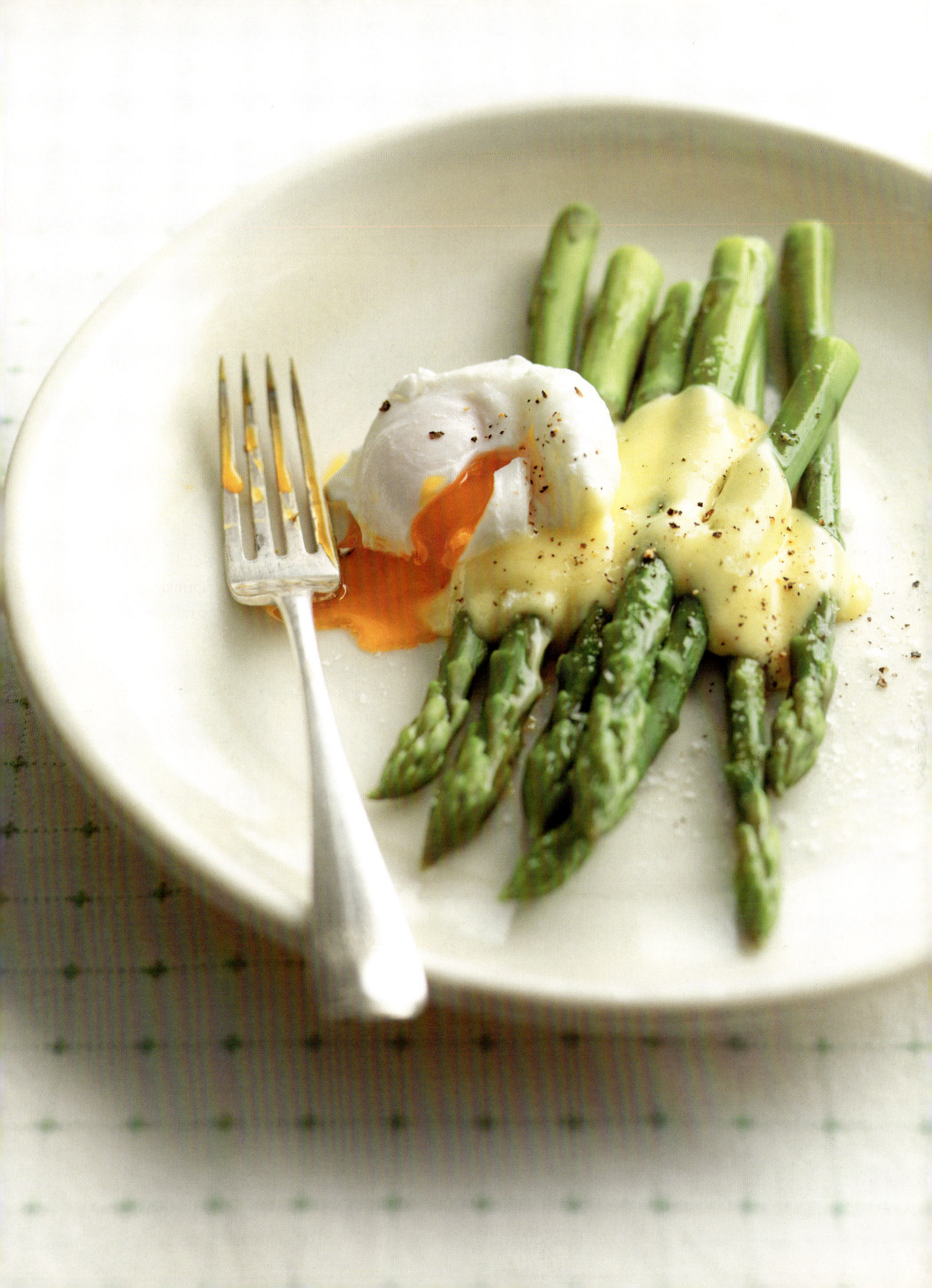

These delicious cakes would make a perfect Christmas Day appetizer, or a Boxing Day lunch using the leftover roasted vegetables from the big meal itself. The gooey melted rarebit in the center of the cakes transforms the bubble and squeak into something quite special.

BUBBLE & SQUEAK CAKES
FILLED WITH WELSH RAREBIT

SERVES 6 TO 8

olive oil
2lb potatoes, peeled and cut into 1½-inch chunks
2 carrots, peeled, halved, and cut into 2-inch pieces
2 parsnips, peeled and cut into 1½-inch chunks
½ small onion, chopped
3¼ cups cabbage, chopped
1 rosemary sprig
1 thyme sprig
¼ cup peas, defrosted if frozen
5 scallions, trimmed and finely sliced
salt

For the Welsh Rarebit
3½ tablespoons butter
3 tablespoons gluten-free all-purpose flour (or regular all-purpose flour, for non gluten-free)
⅔ cup gluten-free ale (or regular ale, for non gluten-free)
8oz smoked Cheddar or regular sharp Cheddar cheese
2 teaspoons Dijon mustard
1 teaspoon vegetarian Worcestershire sauce
3 tablespoons sour cream

To serve
2 cups watercress leaves
½ cup cranberry sauce

Preheat the oven to 400°F.

For the rarebit, melt the butter in a saucepan over low heat, add the flour, and cook, stirring, for 1 minute. Add the ale, cheese, mustard, relish, and sour cream and cook, stirring, until the cheese has melted and the sauce is thick. Spoon into a container and chill in the freezer for 15 to 20 minutes, or until the rarebit is cold but still pliable. Once chilled, divide the mixture into 12 to 16 pieces and roll them into balls. Flatten the balls slightly to finish, and return them to the freezer until needed.

Splash a little oil into a roasting pan, add the potatoes, carrots, and parsnips, season with salt, and mix together thoroughly to coat. Roast for 20 to 25 minutes, or until the vegetables are golden brown at the edges. Set aside to cool.

Heat a drizzle of oil in a skillet, add the onion, and sauté for 8 to 10 minutes, or until translucent. Add the cabbage and herbs and cook, stirring, for 3 to 4 minutes, or until tender. Set aside.

Add the roasted vegetables to a bowl along with the peas and coarsely mash them together. Add the onion, cabbage, and scallions and mix together with your hands. Take a scoop of the mixture and flatten it to just bigger than the size of your palm. Place a rarebit ball in the center and fold the mixture around it to form a cake. Repeat with the remaining bubble and squeak and rarebit balls.

Add a layer of olive oil to a large nonstick skillet over medium heat. Set the potato cakes in the skillet and fry for 4 minutes on each side until brown and crisp. Serve with watercress and cranberry sauce.

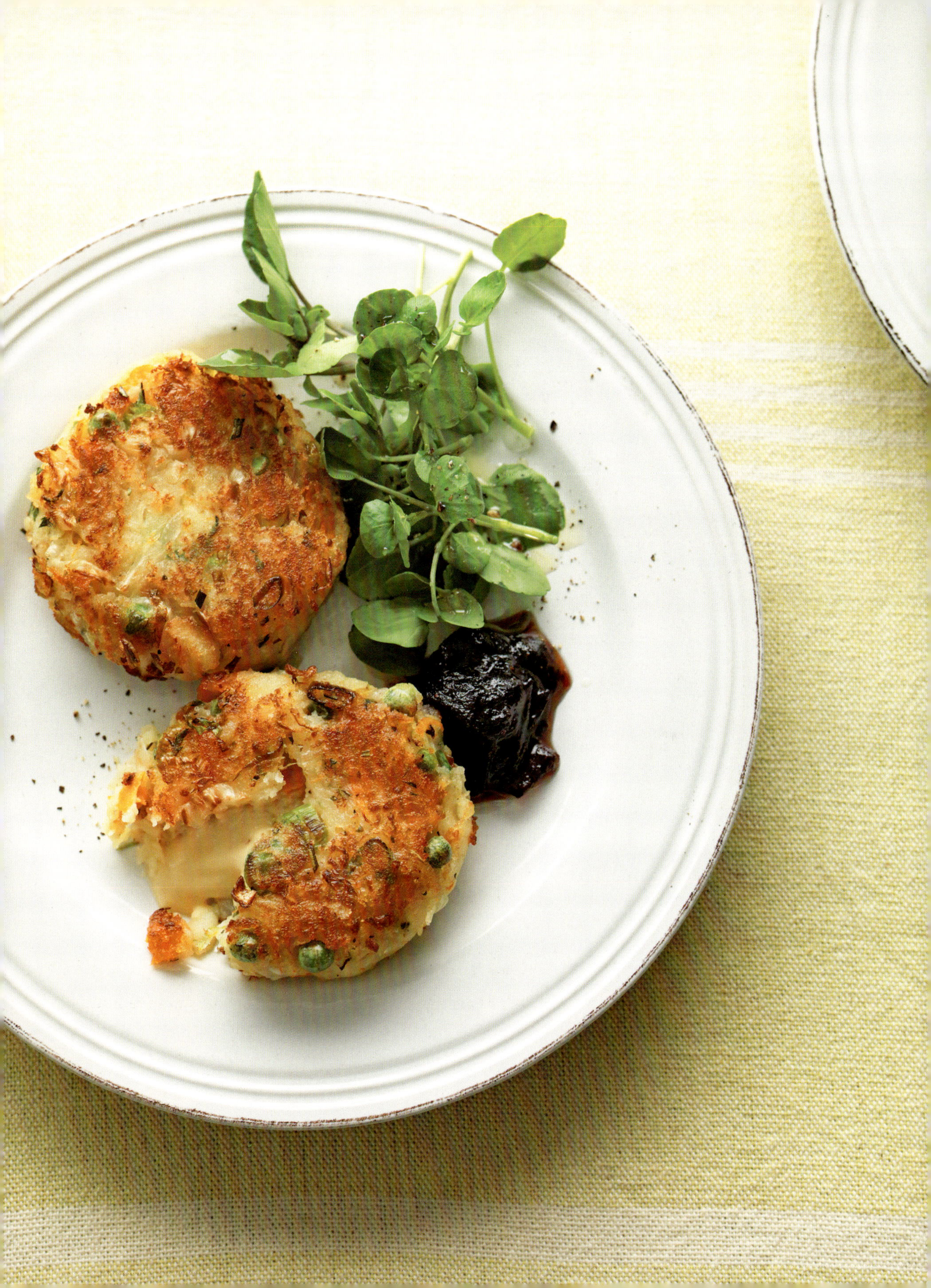

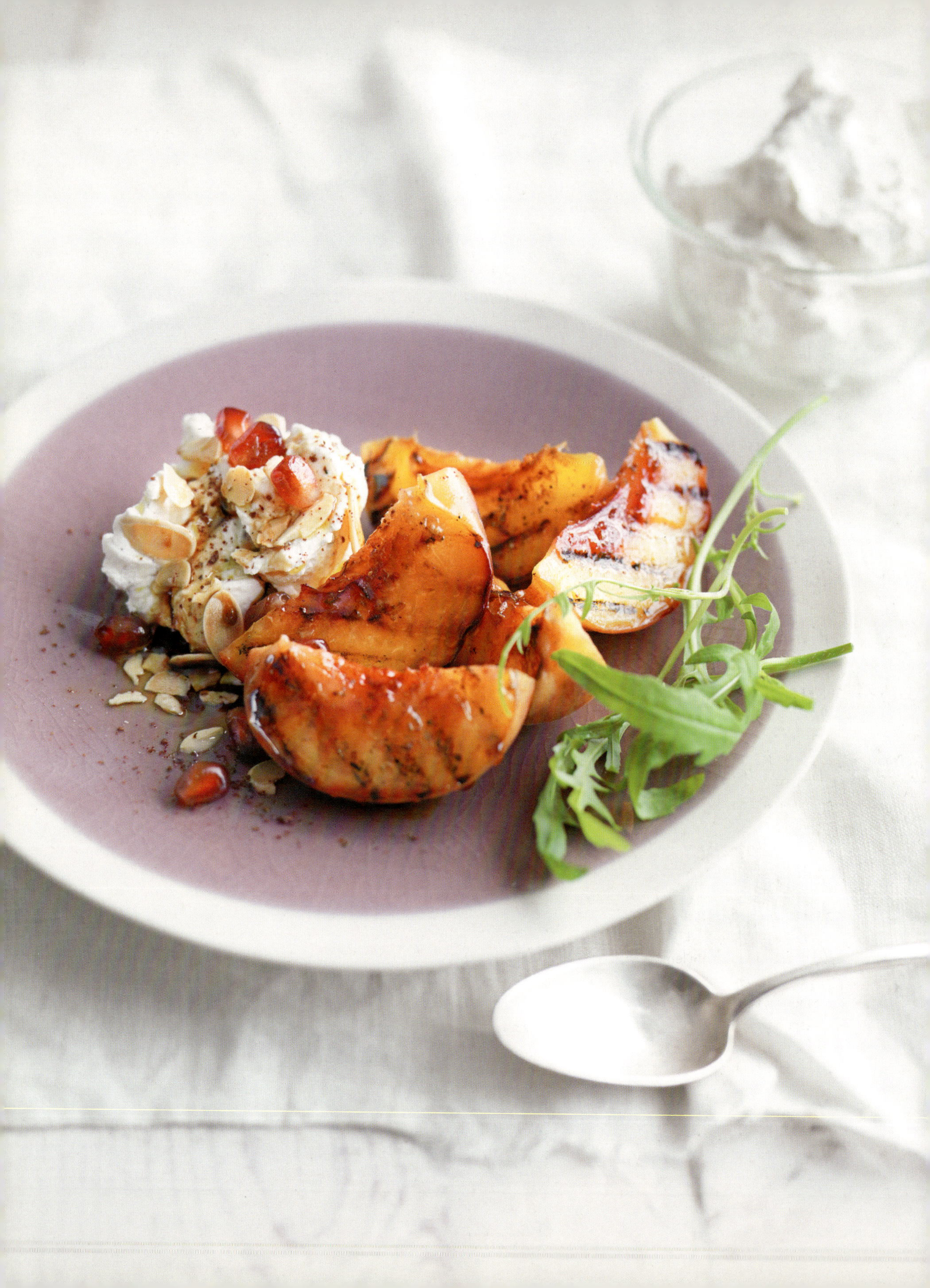

The stunning colors in this simple appetizer bring summer to the table. If you can't find peaches, nectarines are a good substitute. The trick with this is to serve it right away while the peaches are still warm so that the labneh softens alongside. The pomegranate molasses, which can be found in delicatessens and now in some supermarkets, adds a wonderful sweet and sour finish.

Labneh is a delicious, creamy Middle Eastern cheese made with yogurt. If you've never made cheese before don't worry, it couldn't be easier. The recipe makes more than you will need and the cheese is lovely in salad or dolloped on top of stews, tagines, or soups. The spices in this recipe are just a suggestion. Use whatever you prefer.

HOMEMADE LABNEH CHEESE WITH GRILLED PEACHES, ALMONDS, ARUGULA & POMEGRANATE MOLASSES

SERVES 6

5 peaches
3½oz arugula
⅔ cup toasted sliced almonds
1 pomegranate, seeds removed (optional)
⅓ cup extra virgin olive oil
⅓ cup pomegranate molasses

For the Homemade Labneh Cheese
2 cups Greek-style yogurt
grated zest and juice of 1 lemon
1 garlic clove, minced
1 teaspoon sumac
½ teaspoon chili flakes
½ teaspoon ground cumin
1½ teaspoons salt

To make the labneh, mix all the ingredients together in a bowl. Line a sieve with cheesecloth, set it over a separate bowl, and then pour the cheese mixture into the lined sieve. Tie the opposite ends of the cheesecloth together before tying the ends around a wooden spoon. Suspend above a container deep enough to ensure the cloth clears the bottom by at least 4 inches. Transfer to the refrigerator and let drain for 24 to 48 hours, depending on your preferred consistency. (After 24 hours the cheese will be soft and creamy whereas 48 hours will yield a firmer cheese like a full-fat cream cheese.)

To make the salad, cut the peaches in half along the seam, twist to open, and prise out the pits. Heat a large ridged grill pan until hot, add the peach halves flesh-side down, and cook for around 5 minutes, or until nicely blackened and charred. Turn them over and cook for 1 minute on the skin side until tender.

Slice each peach half into three pieces and divide among plates with the arugula. Top each salad with a tablespoon of labneh and scatter with the flaked almonds and pomegranate seeds, if using. Drizzle with the oil and pomegranate molasses and serve immediately.

This very simple appetizer is perfect for the fall when figs are at their best. It's one of those great dishes that looks like it takes ages to make but is actually whipped up in minutes. We also like to serve it with homemade Polenta Crackers (see opposite), and they are well worth putting in the extra effort on those occasions when time is not an issue. The biscuits can be omitted, or replaced with gluten-free crackers, to make this recipe gluten-free.

FIGS WITH BLUE CHEESE
MOUSSE & ROASTED HAZELNUTS

SERVES 4

12 ripe fresh figs
5oz watercress
½ cup roasted hazelnuts
3 tablespoons extra virgin olive oil
Polenta Crackers, to serve (*see* opposite)

For the Blue Cheese Mousse
½ cup heavy cream
3½oz blue cheese
3½oz cream cheese
1 small rosemary sprig, leaves picked and coarsely chopped
1 teaspoon Dijon mustard
salt and pepper

To make the mousse, lightly whip the heavy cream in a bowl. Coarsely dice the blue cheese and add to a food processor along with the cream cheese, rosemary, and mustard. Blend until smooth. Remove from the food processor and fold into the whipped cream using a spatula. Season to taste with salt and pepper.

Make two crossways cuts three-quarters of the way down each fig and squeeze the sides to open them up like flowers. Divide between plates with the watercress and serve with a dollop of the mousse, a scattering of roasted hazelnuts, and a drizzle of olive oil. Serve with Polenta Crackers, if desired.

These lovely, crunchy polenta crackers are great with cheese. We also like to serve them with our Figs with Blue Cheese Mousse & Roasted Hazelnuts appetizer (see opposite).

POLENTA CRACKERS

MAKES 8 TO 10 CRACKERS

3½ tablespoons butter
1 tablespoon superfine sugar
½ cup instant polenta
½ cup all-purpose flour, plus extra for dusting
2 to 3 tablespoons water

Beat together the butter and sugar in a mixing bowl until pale and creamy. Add the dry ingredients and mix well, gradually adding the water to form a smooth, firm dough. Shape into a ball, seal in plastic wrap, and refrigerate for 15 to 20 minutes.

Preheat the oven to 375°F. Line a large cookie sheet with nonstick parchment paper.

Remove the dough from the refrigerator. On a lightly floured surface, roll out the dough into a circle with a thickness of ¼ inch. Slice into 8 to 10 triangular pieces, as if slicing a pie, and arrange the pieces on the prepared cookie sheet. Bake for 20 to 25 minutes, or until golden brown. Transfer to a wire rack to cool.

For a savory option, add **fresh thyme** or **rosemary** to the recipe along with some **freshly cracked black pepper**.

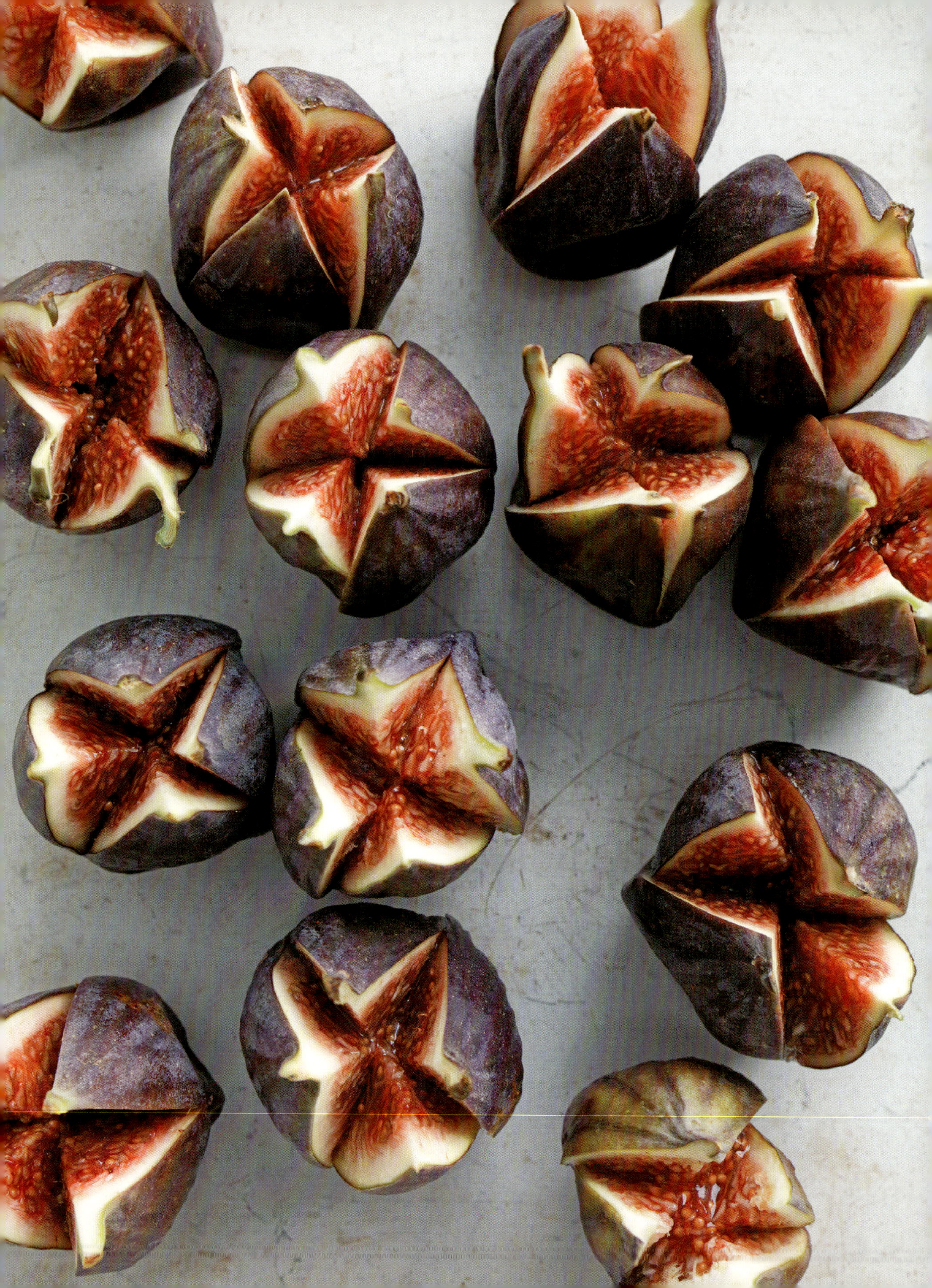

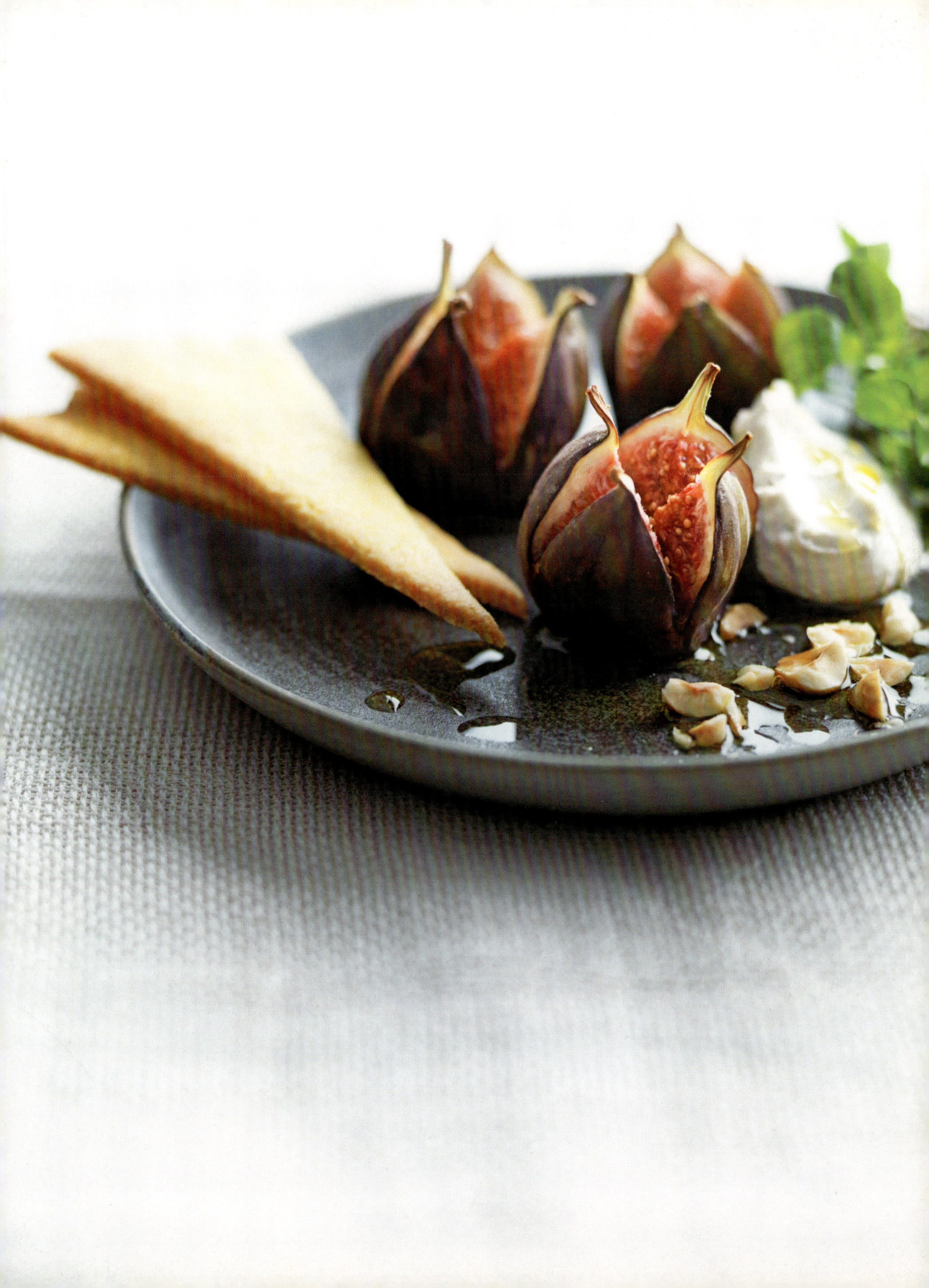

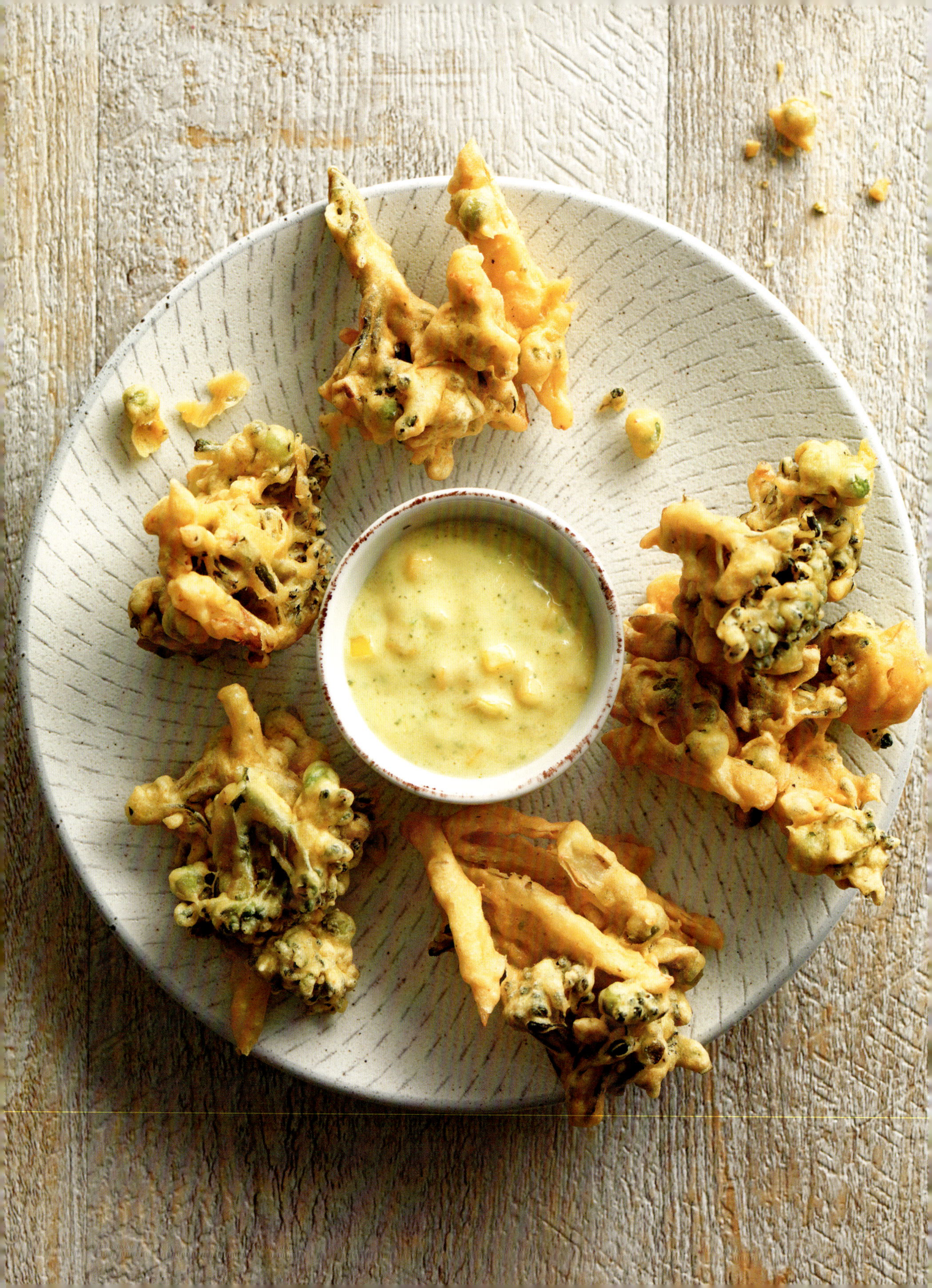

The spring vegetables and fresh mint give these pakora a very light, delicate finish that works well with our creamy mango yogurt dip. For a vegan option, substitute vegan yogurt in the Mango Yogurt Dip. These are at their best served straight out of the pan while still crisp and hot.

SPRING VEGETABLE PAKORA
WITH MANGO YOGURT DIP

SERVES 4 TO 5

½lb long-stem broccoli, trimmed
½lb fennel bulb, trimmed
½ white onion
⅔ cup peas, defrosted if frozen
10 mint leaves
vegetable oil, for deep-frying

For the Mango Yogurt Dip
½lb mango, peeled and chopped, divided
1 green chile, trimmed
grated zest of ½ lime plus juice of 1 lime
10 mint leaves
1 cup yogurt

For the batter
2¾ cups besan (gram flour)
½ cup gluten-free self-rising flour (or regular self-rising flour, for non gluten-free)
1 teaspoon curry powder
1 tablespoon lemon juice
1 green chile, trimmed and minced

Slice the broccoli spears in half, cut out the tough central cores from the bottom of the fennel and onion bulbs, and cut the remainder into slices ½ inch thick. Put them in a bowl with the peas and mint leaves and mix together well with your hands.

For the mango yogurt dip, put two-thirds of the mango and all the remaining ingredients into a blender and blend until smooth. Stir in the remaining mango to finish.

Half-fill a large saucepan or deep-fryer with vegetable oil and heat to 350°F, or until a cube of bread added to the oil browns in 30 seconds.

While the oil is heating, make the batter. Combine the besan, self-rising flour, and curry powder together in a large bowl. Add the lemon juice and green chile and gradually pour in enough water to give the mixture the consistency of heavy cream, beating constantly to remove any lumps.

Take a few small handfuls of the vegetable mixture and dip them into the batter to coat evenly. Deep-fry the pakora in batches for 5 to 6 minutes, or until they are crisp and golden, then transfer to some paper towels to drain off any excess oil. Serve immediately with the mango yogurt dip.

These surprisingly light and fluffy, blinis are filled with sweet potato and coconut, giving them a pleasantly sweet flavor that balances well with the peppery Caribbean spices of the okra and jerk dressing.

SWEET POTATO & COCONUT BLINIS
WITH PAN-FRIED OKRA & JERK DRESSING

SERVES 6 TO 8

2 tablespoons light olive oil or other light cooking oil (such as canola, peanut, or sunflower), plus extra for frying
1½lb sweet potatoes, peeled and cut into 1¼-inch chunks
½ red chile, trimmed and chopped
1½oz creamed coconut
1 cup coconut milk
pinch of ground cinnamon
pinch of paprika
½ cup wheat-free all-purpose flour
2 large eggs, separated
1lb okra, trimmed
salt and pepper

For the Jerk Dressing
1 teaspoon coriander seeds
1 allspice berry
½-inch piece of fresh ginger root, peeled
2 red chiles, trimmed and chopped
1 good handful of cilantro leaves
grated zest and juice of 1 lime
½ cup light oil (such as canola, peanut, or sunflower)
3 garlic cloves

Preheat the oven to 400°F. Drizzle the oil into a roasting pan. Add the sweet potato pieces and chopped chile, season with salt, and mix everything together thoroughly to coat. Roast for 15 to 20 minutes, or until the sweet potato is cooked. Set aside to cool.

Gently warm the creamed coconut in a microwave or a small saucepan over low heat to soften it, then add it to a food processor with the sweet potato pieces, coconut milk, cinnamon, paprika, and flour. Season to taste with salt and pepper and blend until smooth. Transfer to a large bowl and stir in the egg yolks. Whip the egg whites in a separate bowl until soft peaks form, and then carefully fold into the blini mixture.

Warm a splash of oil in a nonstick skillet over low heat. Drop spoonfuls of the mixture into the pan and cook for 3 minutes on each side, or until golden brown, turning carefully. Continue until you have used up all the mixture. Keep the fritters warm in a low oven.

For the jerk dressing, toast the coriander seeds and allspice berry in a dry skillet over medium heat for a minute until fragrant. Using a mortar and pestle, grind the spices together, and then add them to a bowl with the remaining ingredients. Blend everything together using a stick blender or in a food processor to form a thick, spiced oil.

Heat a drizzle of oil in a wok or large skillet over medium heat. Put the okra into a sieve and rinse under running water. Add the okra to the wok and cook, stirring, for about 5 minutes, or until the okra has puffed up and softened slightly. Add 2 to 3 tablespoons of the jerk dressing and cook, stirring, for another minute. Then remove it from the heat. Arrange the blini on a serving platter, top with the okra, and drizzle the remaining jerk dressing around the plate to finish.

Latkes are eastern European or Russian rösti pancakes that are usually made with potatoes and served with apple sauce. Our recipe borrows a lot of flavors from the cuisine of India, so this unlikely combination works really well to lighten up what can typically be a somewhat heavy dish. For best results, serve the latkes immediately, fresh from the pan.

SPICED CARROT, APPLE & PARSNIP LATKES
WITH CUCUMBER RIBBON SALAD

SERVES 6 TO 8

3 carrots, peeled
2 parsnips, peeled
1 apple, peeled and cored
1-inch piece of fresh ginger root, peeled
1 white onion, very finely diced
1 teaspoon coriander seeds
1 teaspoon cumin seeds
½ teaspoon chili powder
1 teaspoon turmeric powder
2 eggs, lightly beaten
2 tablespoons finely ground cornmeal
1 tablespoon gluten-free all-purpose flour (or regular all-purpose flour, for non gluten-free)
light cooking oil (such as canola, peanut, or sunflower)
Mango Yogurt Dip (*see* page 49), to serve

For the Cucumber Ribbon Salad
2 cucumbers, peeled
1 green chile, trimmed, seeded, and minced
grated zest and juice of 1 lime
8 mint leaves
4 scallions, trimmed and chopped

Coarsely grate the carrots, parsnips, and apple into a mixing bowl. Finely grate the ginger and add it to the bowl along with the onion. Mix everything together well and set aside.

Toast the coriander and cumin seeds in a dry skillet over medium heat for about a minute until fragrant. Using a mortar and pestle, grind the toasted spices together with the chili powder and turmeric. Add the spice mixture to the bowl with the vegetables, and then add the beaten egg, polenta, and flour. Mix together well to combine.

For the cucumber ribbon salad, shave the cucumber into wide ribbons with a vegetable peeler. Combine with the other salad ingredients in a bowl. Set aside.

Heat a thin layer of oil in a wide skillet. You will need to fry the latkes in batches: drop several spoonfuls of the mixture into the pan, spacing them well apart, and fry for 2 to 3 minutes on each side, or until golden and cooked through. Transfer to a warm plate lined with paper towels and keep warm while you cook the rest (there should be enough mixture for 6 to 8 fritters).

Divide the latkes between plates, top with the cucumber salad, and serve immediately accompanied by the Mango Yogurt Dip.

This very simple appetizer has proved perennially popular at Mildreds. To make it work you do need to use good-quality artichokes, though. Look for the tender ones with the long stems that are preserved in oil (the ones in vacuum packs rather than cans are worth hunting down since they taste better and are fresher). You can find them in any decent Italian delicatessen or other Mediterranean food store.

ARTICHOKE CROSTINI
WITH ROAST GARLIC & LEMON AIOLI

SERVES 4

8 focaccia or sourdough bread slices
6 to 8 good-quality artichoke hearts in oil, drained
3oz mixed baby leaf lettuce
¼ cup Roast Garlic & Lemon Aïoli (*see* page 234)

Heat a ridged grill pan or heavy skillet over high heat. Add the bread slices and toast them for 1½ to 2 minutes on each side until they are nicely charred.

Slice the artichokes in half lengthwise. Add to the pan and grill for 1 to 2 minutes on each side. Divide the artichokes, toasted bread slices, and lettuce leaves between plates and serve with Roast Garlic & Lemon Aïoli.

If you would like to make this vegan, substitute our **Vegan Basil Mayonnaise** (*see* page 232).

This is a nice appetizer to precede an Italian main such as the **Long-stem Broccoli & Asparagus White Lasagne** (*see* page 112).

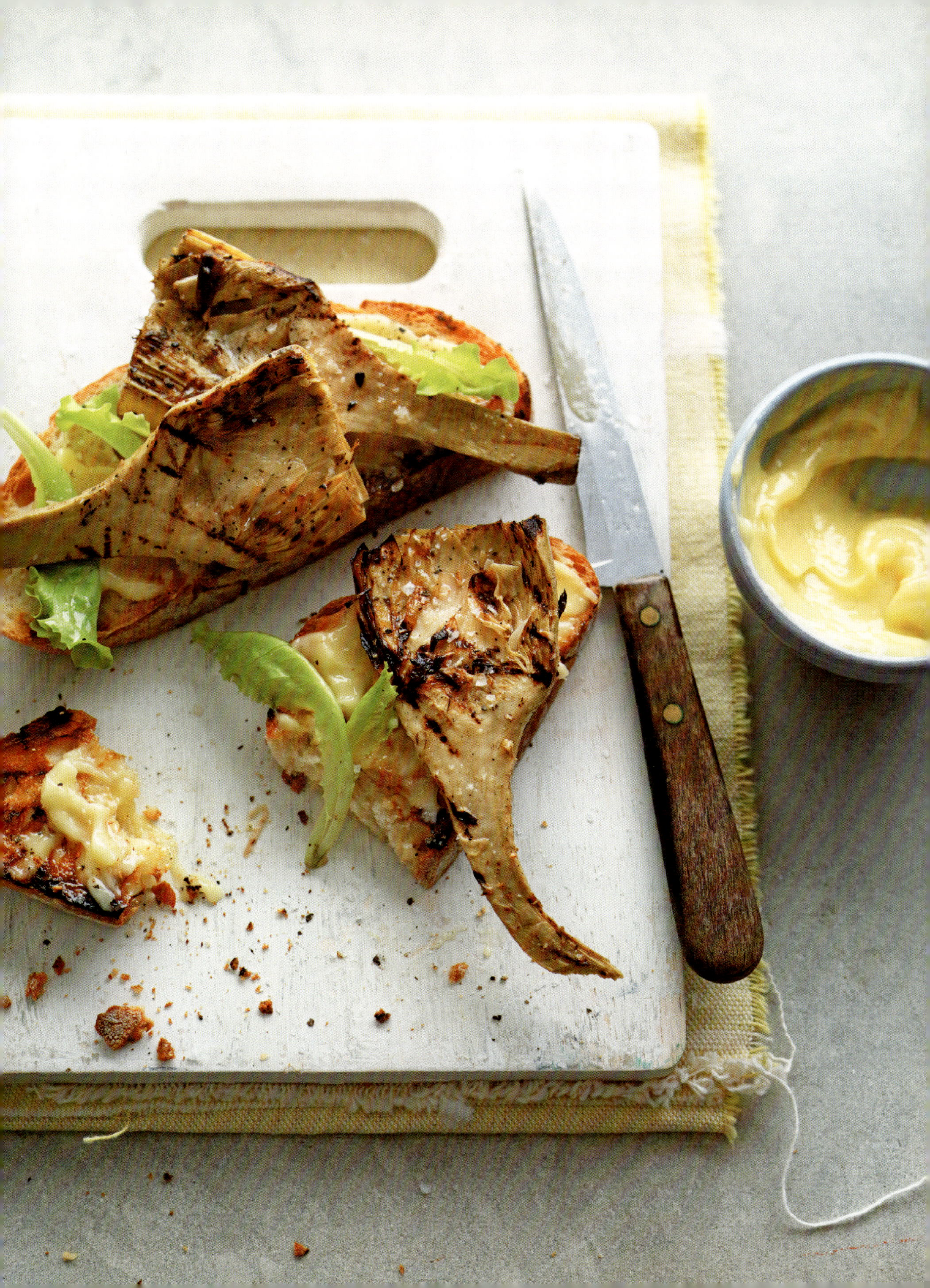

These popular filled pancakes from eastern Europe, known as blintzes in the Ashkenazi Jewish community, are often made with fruit and served as a brunch dish or for dessert. This savory version makes an elegant dinner party appetizer. They may seem a little labor-intensive, but everything is very straightforward, while the pancakes can be prepared in advance of the final filling and cooking stages. Serve with a lightly dressed green salad.

SAVORY HAZELNUT PANCAKES FILLED WITH CHANTERELLE MUSHROOMS & MASCARPONE

MAKES 8 TO 10 PANCAKES

¾ cup blanched hazelnuts
¾ cup all-purpose flour
2 eggs
1 tablespoon melted butter, plus extra for frying
1 cup milk, plus extra if needed
light oil (such as canola, peanut, or sunflower)

For the filling
light oil (such as canola, peanut, or sunflower)
1 small onion, minced
3 garlic cloves, minced
1 leek, trimmed, cleaned, and finely sliced
½–1 chanterelle and/or black trumpet mushrooms, trimmed and torn into ½-inch strips
1 tablespoon white wine (optional)
grated zest of ½ lemon
10oz mascarpone or cream cheese
handful of chives, snipped

To make the pancake batter, blend the hazelnuts and flour together in a food processor. Add the eggs and melted butter and pulse, adding the milk in a steady stream, until it achieves the consistency of heavy cream (if it is looking too thick, add a little more milk). Transfer to a bowl, cover with plastic wrap, and let chill in the refrigerator for 20 minutes.

Prepare a skillet by heating it well and wiping it with oil. Pour in enough batter to thinly coat the bottom and cook until bubbles begin to form in the center. Flip the pancake over with a spatula or lifter and cook the other side until brown. Transfer the pancake to a plate and make the remaining pancakes. Set aside until needed.

For the filling, heat a splash of oil in a skillet over medium heat, add the onion, and sauté for 8 to 10 minutes until translucent. Add the garlic, leek, mushrooms, and a splash of white wine, if using, and cook, stirring, for 3 to 4 minutes, or until the mushrooms have softened. Remove from the heat and stir in the grated lemon zest, mascarpone, and chives.

Divide the filling mixture evenly between the pancakes. Fold each end and then the sides to meet in the middle to form rectangular parcels. Warm a little butter in a skillet and fry the filled pancakes for 2 to 3 minutes on each side until golden brown. Serve immediately.

This is a lovely rustic pie that makes great use of the delicate sweet flesh of fall pumpkins or squash. It has been on the menu at Mildreds in the past but here we've adjusted it for making at home. We like to keep it a little messy, too, not worrying about trimming the crust or glazing the top. If you like a shine on your pie, however, simply brush the top with a little beaten egg or soy cream before baking.

PUMPKIN, FETA & PIQUILLO PEPPER PIE

SERVES 8 TO 10

2 tablespoons olive oil
2lb pumpkin or butternut squash, peeled, seeded, and cut into 1-inch chunks
4 small rosemary sprigs, leaves picked and coarsely chopped
4 garlic cloves, finely sliced
1 red chile, trimmed and minced
6 roasted piquillo peppers or other roasted red peppers in oil, drained and sliced
7oz feta cheese
sea salt flakes

For the pie crust
3¼ cups all-purpose flour, plus extra to dust
1¾ sticks butter (cubed and cold)
1 tablespoon chopped fresh herbs (such as oregano, sage, or thyme)
1 egg yolk
ice-cold water

Preheat the oven to 375°F.

For the pie crust, place the flour in a bowl, add the butter, and rub it in with your fingertips until the mixture resembles fine bread crumbs. Add the herbs, egg yolk, and enough ice-cold water to make a firm dough. Knead together briefly, seal with plastic wrap, and let rest in the refrigerator for 15 minutes.

Meanwhile, prepare your filling. Drizzle the oil into a roasting pan, add the pumpkin pieces, rosemary, garlic, and chile, and season with sea salt flakes. Toss everything thoroughly to coat. Roast in the oven for 25 to 30 minutes, or until the pumpkin is very soft and almost collapsing on itself. Set aside to cool, then add to a bowl with the piquillo peppers. Crumble over the feta cheese and mix together well.

Take two-thirds of the dough and, on a lightly floured surface, roll it out to a thickness of ¼ inch and use it to line a 9-inch pie plate. Spoon the filling into the lined pie plate, spreading it evenly. Roll out the remaining dough to a thickness of ¼ inch and drape it on top of the pie, folding and crimping the edges to seal.

Bake in the oven for 30 to 40 minutes, or until golden brown. Cut into slices and serve.

This is one of our favorite dishes for the warmer months. It's full of lovely fresh flavors and is great when mangoes are at their best. You can use any type of wheat or rice noodle here; just avoid egg noodles because these are best eaten hot.

TEMPURA VEGETABLES WITH NOODLE, MANGO & CUCUMBER SALAD & CHILE DIPPING SAUCE

SERVES 4 TO 6

For the dressing
½ cup mirin
juice of 2 limes
2 green chiles, seeded and finely diced
2 tablespoons Japanese rice vinegar
¼ cup soy sauce
½ teaspoon brown sugar

For the noodles
8oz soba noodles or rice noodles
light oil
1 cucumber, finely diced
1 mango, peeled and finely diced
1 red chile, seeded and chopped
½ small red onion, minced
handful of cilantro leaves, chopped
handful of mint leaves, chopped

For the tempura vegetables
sunflower oil for deep-frying
1½ cups ice-cold sparkling water
1½ cups all-purpose flour, plus extra for dusting
2 eggs
½ teaspoon baking powder
2½ tablespoons each black and white sesame seeds, toasted
2 zucchini, quartered and cut into 4-inch batons
1 red bell pepper, cored, seeded, and cut into 4-inch batons
1 yellow pepper, cored, seeded and cut into 4-inch batons
2 carrots, thinly sliced

To make the dressing, put all the ingredients into a mixing bowl and mix together well.

Cook the noodles in a pan of boiling water following the package instructions. Transfer to a sieve and cool under running water, drain, and then stir in a drop or two of oil to prevent them from sticking together. Add to a mixing bowl with the cucumber, mango, chile, onion, herbs, and 3 tablespoons of the dressing. Mix well, then set aside.

For the tempura vegetables, fill a large saucepan or deep-fryer with the sunflower oil and heat to 350°F, or until a cube of bread added to the oil browns in 30 seconds.

Put the water, flour, eggs, baking powder, and sesame seeds in a bowl and beat together briefly to form a batter (don't overwork this; it's fine if it is slightly lumpy). Working in batches, lightly dust a handful of the vegetables with flour and then dip them into the batter. Fry the vegetables for about 3 to 4 minutes, or until lightly golden, remove from the pan, and transfer to paper towels to allow the excess oil to drain off. Repeat with the remaining vegetables, being sure to remove any excess batter from the pan before frying the next batch.

Serve the tempura vegetables alongside the noodle salad, with the remainder of the dressing in a bowl as a dipping sauce.

If you would like to make this gluten-free, substitute **gluten-free all-purpose flour** for the **regular all-purpose flour** used here. However, note that you may need to use a little more of it to achieve the desired thickness of batter.

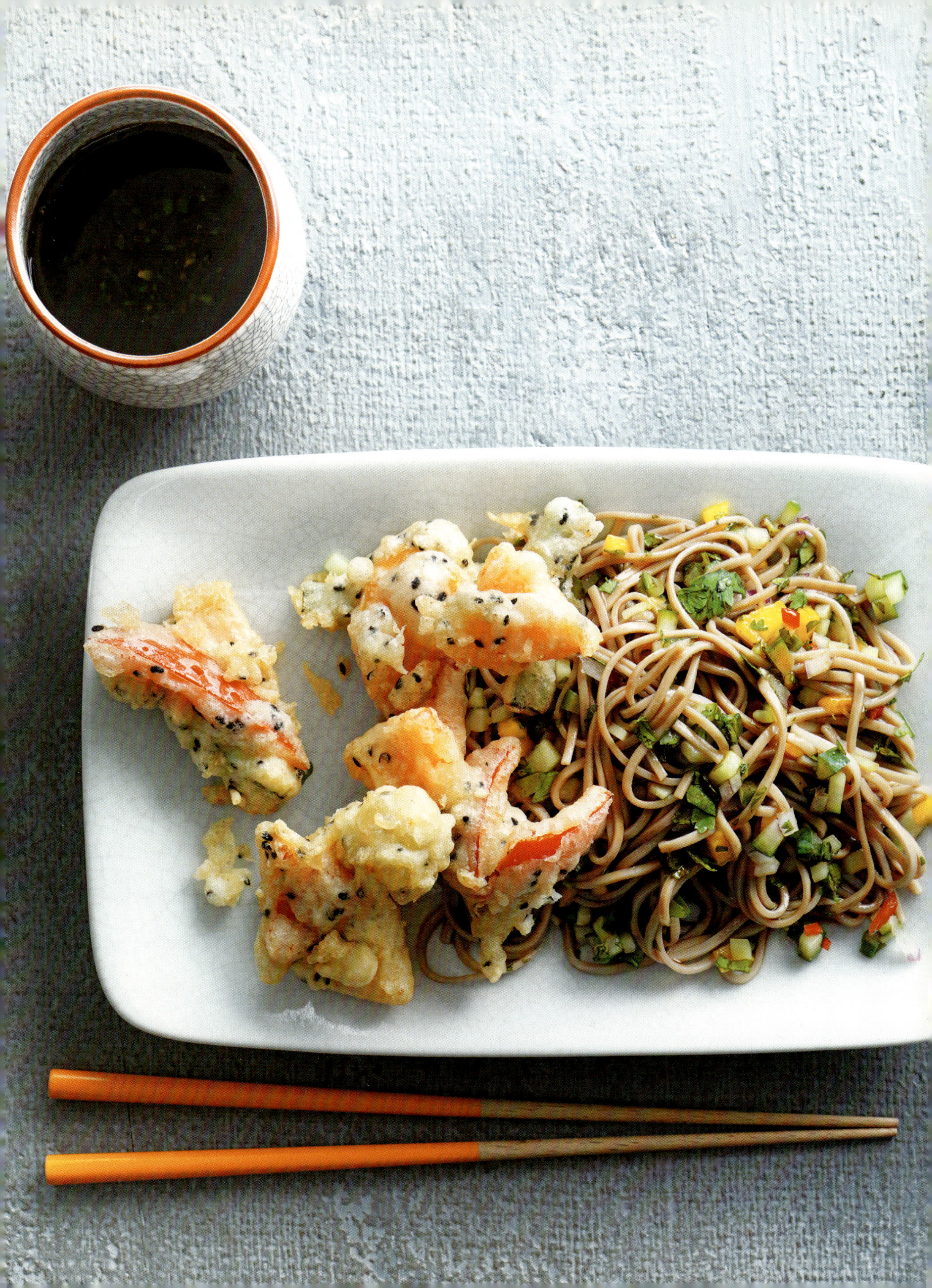

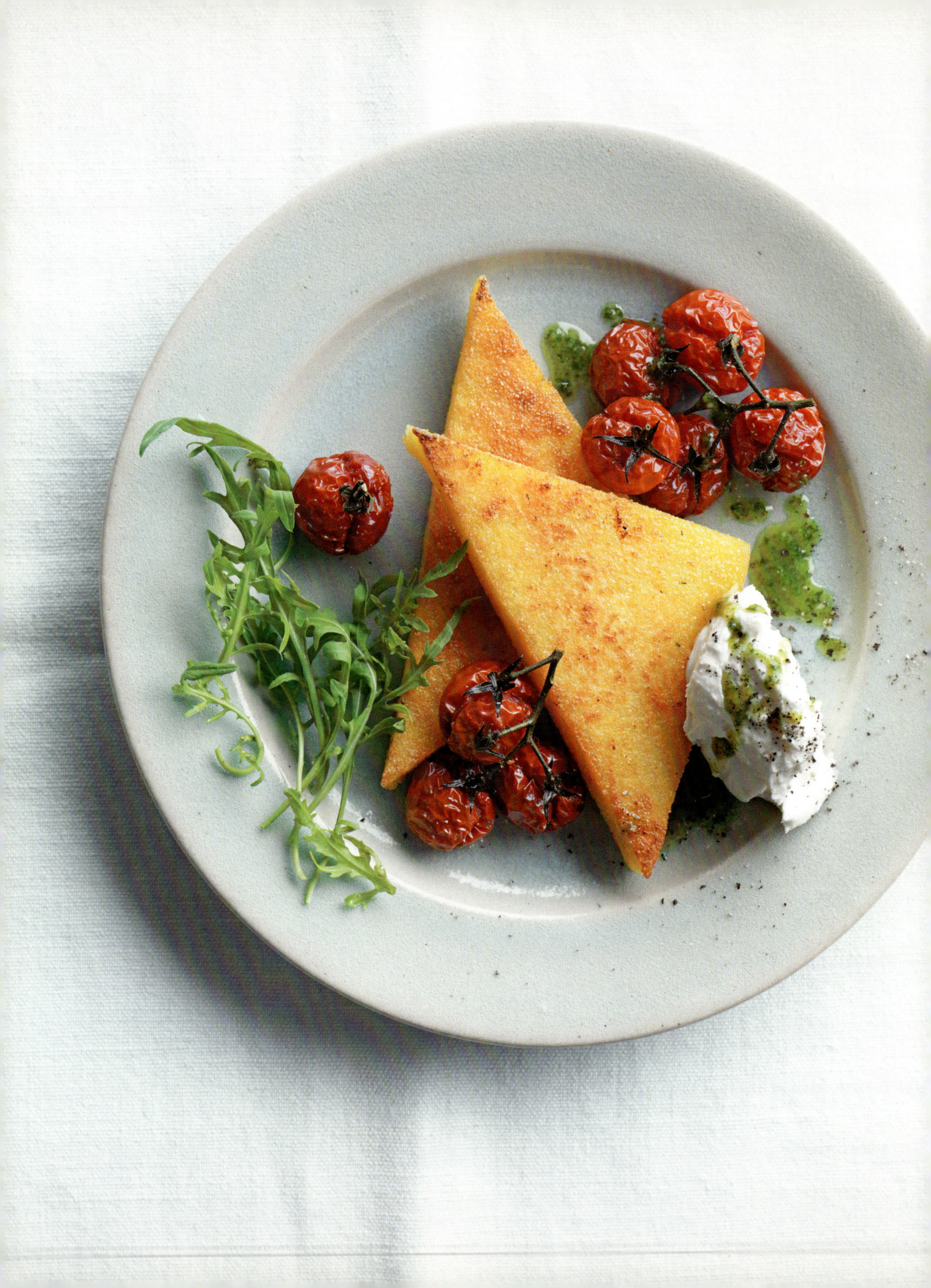

This appetizer is all about textures, with the crispy polenta making a great crunchy contrast to the creamy mascarpone and sharp, juicy tomatoes. Cooked like this, polenta also makes a wonderful side dish for slow-cooked vegetable dishes, such as caponata or ratatouille.

CRISPY POLENTA WITH SLOW-ROAST CHERRY TOMATOES & LEMON MASCARPONE

SERVES 6

14½oz cherry tomatoes, preferably on the vine
2 tablespoons olive oil, plus extra for oiling
pinch of dried oregano
3½ cups vegetable stock
1¾ cups instant polenta
½ cup vegetable oil
sea salt flakes

For the Lemon Mascarpone
zest of 1 lemon, finely chopped, plus 1 tablespoon lemon juice
1lb mascarpone
salt

To serve
2½oz arugula
½ cup Wild Garlic Pesto (*see* page 147) or Purple Basil Oil (*see* page 238)

Preheat the oven to 225°F. Line a cookie sheet with nonstick parchment paper.

Place the tomatoes on the prepared cookie sheet, drizzle over the olive oil, and sprinkle with the oregano and a pinch of sea salt flakes. Bake in the oven for about 2 hours, or until the tomatoes are wrinkled and have begun to dry out and intensified in flavor.

Meanwhile, prepare the polenta. Pour the stock into a medium saucepan, salt lightly, and bring to a boil. Add the polenta and cook following the package instructions, beating the mixture thoroughly to avoid any lumps, until the polenta thickens and all the stock has been absorbed.

Pour the polenta onto a lightly oiled 10-inch pie plate. Using a spatula, smooth the polenta evenly to a thickness of 1 inch. Refrigerate for 15 to 20 minutes to cool and set.

To make the lemon mascarpone, put the lemon zest, lemon juice, and mascarpone in a bowl. Season with salt and mix together well.

Heat the vegetable oil in a small skillet over medium heat. Cut the polenta into 4-inch triangles, add to the pan, and cook for about 2 minutes on each side, or until golden brown.

To serve, place the polenta slices on plates and arrange the arugula and slow-roasted tomatoes alongside. Drizzle with the Wild Garlic Pesto or Purple Basil Oil plus a generous dollop of lemon mascarpone.

MEZZE

Mediterranean and Middle Eastern cuisines are so rich in vegetarian and vegan dishes that we found putting together this banquet of mezze dishes a breeze. In fact, the hard part was knowing where to stop, with so many dishes to choose from, many of them boasting beautiful colors as well as flavors. You may find a few things here that you haven't tried before, or come across some new takes on old favorites. Either way, this collection of small plates is ideal when you want your table to be a feast for the eyes as well as the palate.

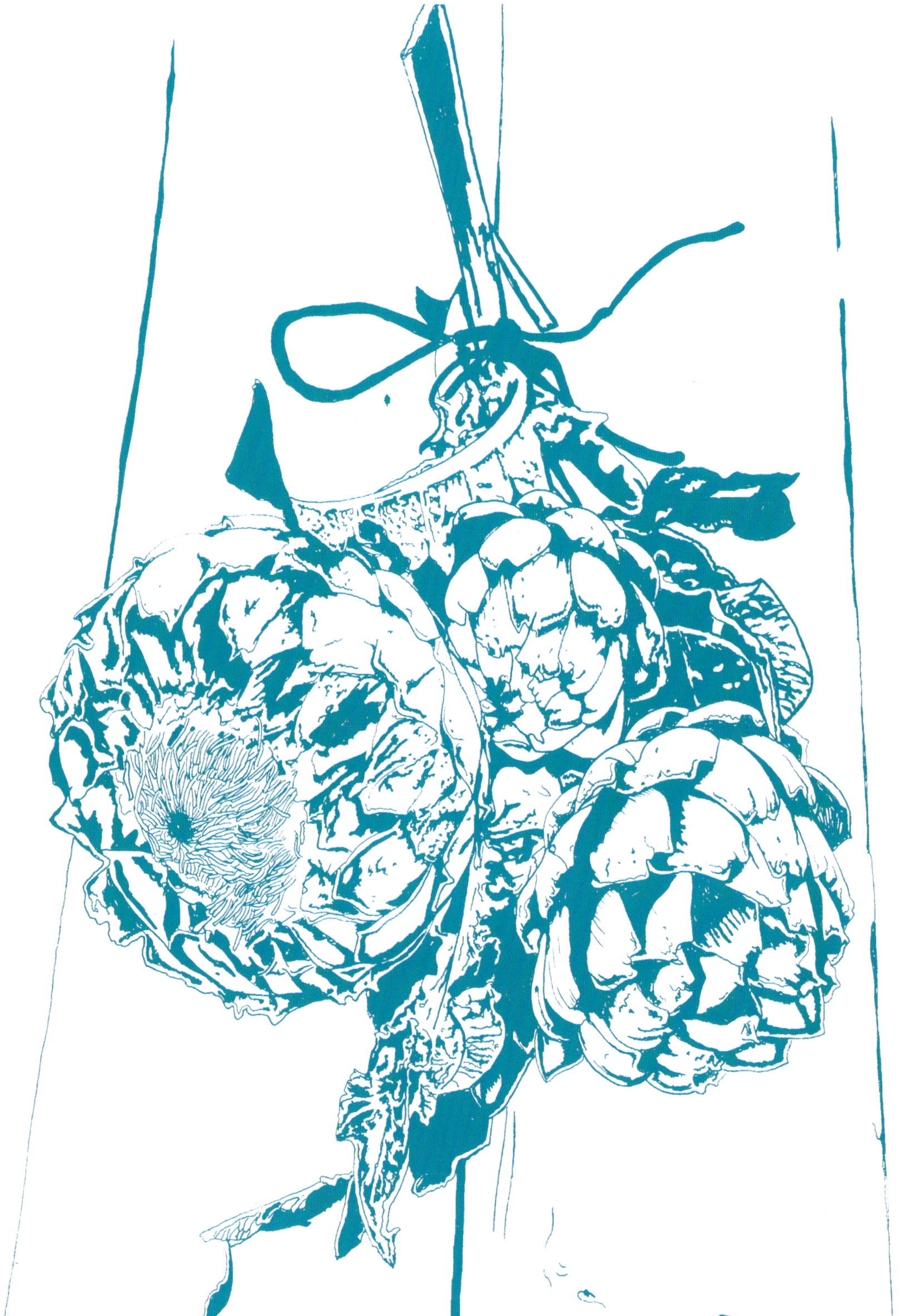

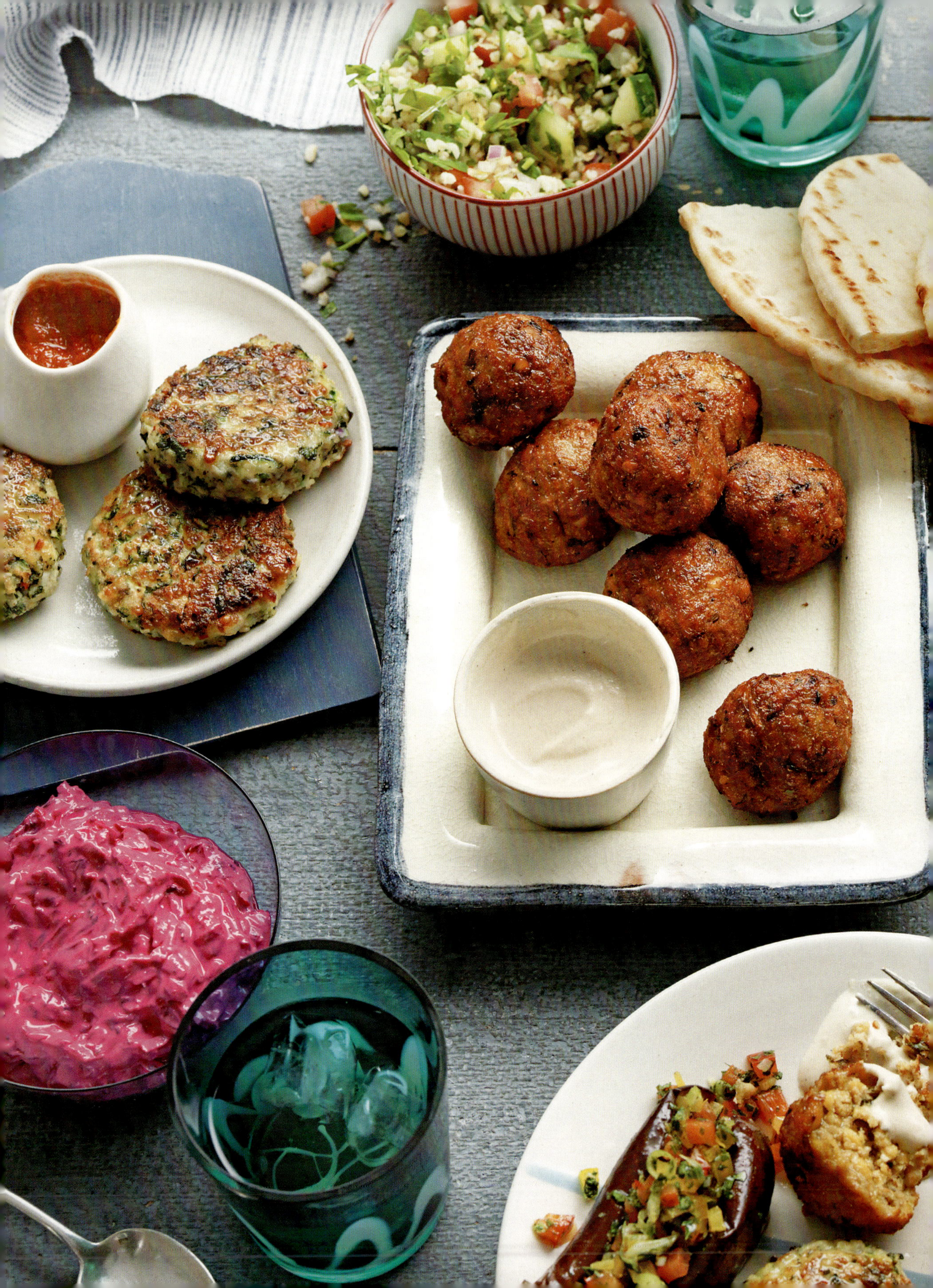

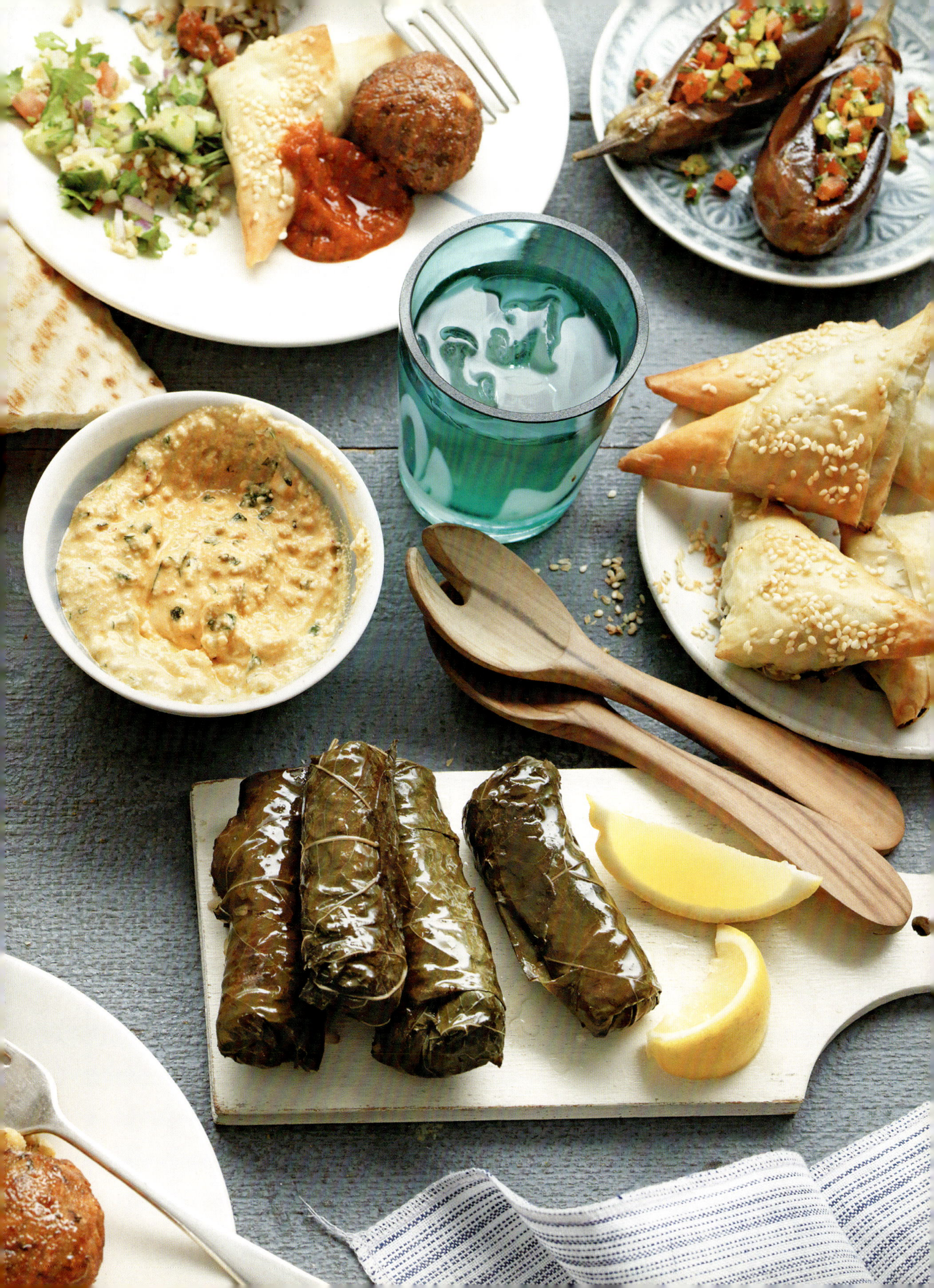

Combining gooey cheese with crunchy zucchini, these fritters make for an utterly irresistible mouthful and are at their best straight from the skillet. Pair them with Harissa (see page 228) and Cucumber Ribbon Salad (see page 51) for a great appetizer.

HALOUMI, ZUCCHINI & MINT FRITTERS

SERVES 6 TO 8 AS PART OF A MEZZE PLATTER

8oz haloumi cheese, coarsely shredded
½ red onion, minced
1 large chile, trimmed and minced
3 garlic cloves, minced
1 small bunch of mint, finely chopped
grated zest of 1 lemon
2 zucchini, coarsely grated
3 eggs, lightly beaten
2 to 3 cups fresh white bread crumbs
2 tablespoons all-purpose flour, for coating
light cooking oil (such as canola, peanut, or sunflower)

To serve
Harissa (*see* page 228)
lemon wedges

Put the grated haloumi into a bowl with the onion, chile, garlic, mint, and grated lemon zest and stir to combine.

Wrap the zucchini in a clean dish towel and squeeze to remove any excess liquid. Add to the bowl along with the eggs and just enough of the bread crumbs to hold everything together. Cover with plastic wrap and let stand in the refrigerator for at least 10 minutes.

Using your hands, shape the mixture into egg-sized patties, adding more bread crumbs if the mixture is very sticky. Toss the fritters lightly in the flour to coat, shaking off any excess.

Warm a splash of oil in a skillet over medium heat. Cook the fritters in batches for 2 to 3 minutes on each side until golden brown. Serve immediately with Harissa, and lemon wedges for squeezing over.

For a gluten-free option, make the **bread crumbs** with a **gluten-free bread**.

For a main course, serve the fritters wrapped in a **thin flatbread**, accompanied by our **Ruby Jeweled Tabbouleh** (*see* page 96) or our **Wild Rice Salad with Peas, Pea Shoots & Green Harissa** (*see* page 84).

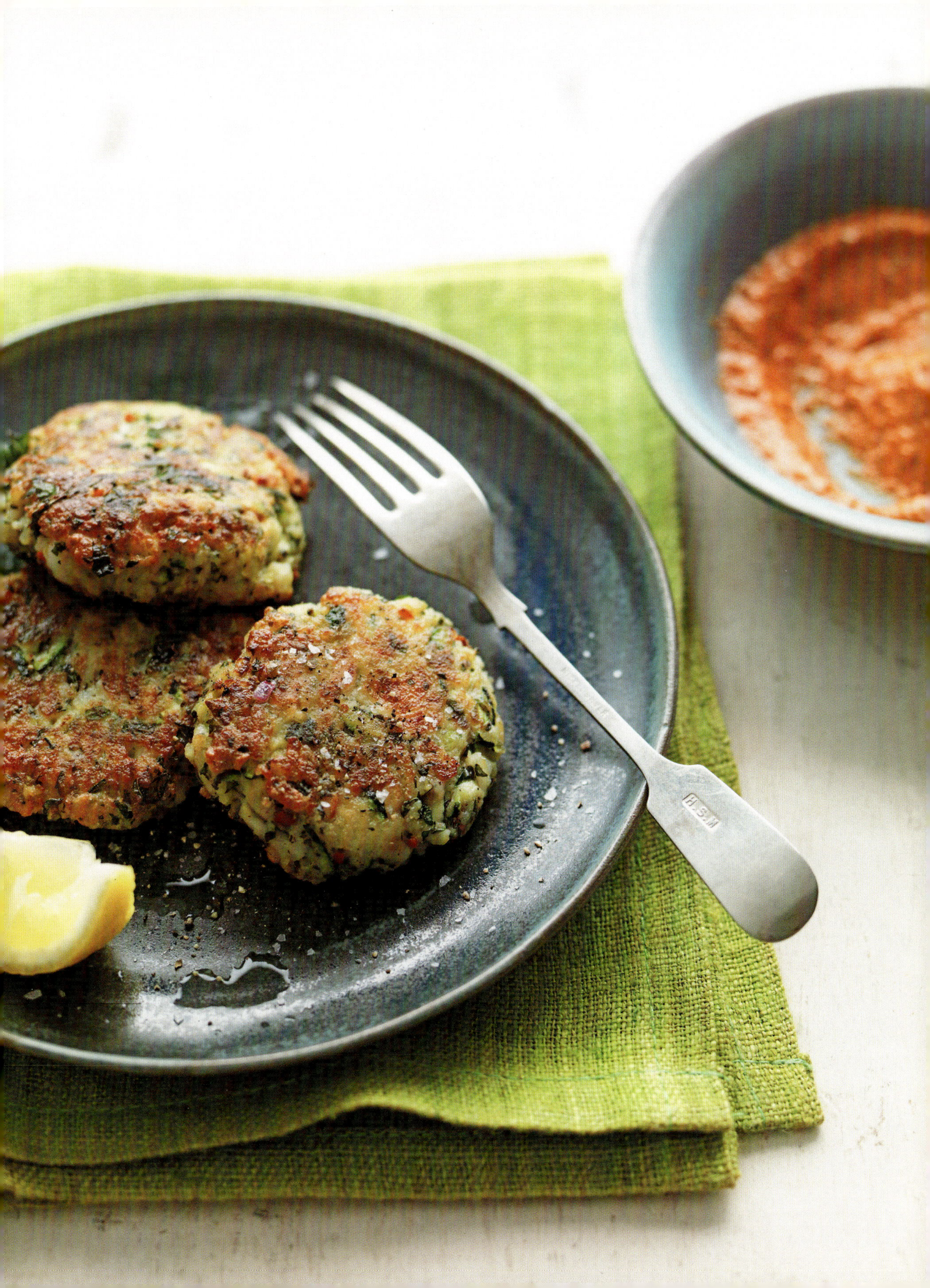

These little flatbreads are often called Turkish pizzas, though they are popular right across the Middle East. The name translates as "meat on dough" in Arabic, so ours is a loose interpretation. We have tried to maintain the richness of the typical topping while adding a little tang using tomato and tamarind. Another diversion from tradition is that these are party-sized (just make them twice the size for a main course). Enjoy them warm, smothered with hummus and salad, or just on their own fresh from the oven.

ROAST PEPPER & BLACK OLIVE LAHMACUNS

SERVES 6 TO 8 AS PART OF A MEZZE PLATTER

For the dough
½ cup warm water
2 tablespoons olive oil
½ teaspoon superfine sugar
¼oz sachet quick-rising dry yeast
2 cups strong white bread flour, plus extra for dusting
1 teaspoon salt

For the topping
2 tablespoons olive oil
3 red bell peppers
1 garlic clove, chopped
2 tablespoons tomato paste
1 teaspoon tamarind paste
1 teaspoon soft brown sugar
1 cup coarsely chopped kalamata olives
3 tablespoons chopped flat-leaf parsley
1 tablespoon chopped mint leaves

Preheat the oven to 425°F. Oil a cookie sheet.

For the dough, put the warm water, olive oil, and sugar in a bowl and stir together until the sugar is dissolved. Add the yeast and let stand for about 5 to 10 minutes to activate.

Add the flour and salt to a separate bowl. Create a well in the center and pour in the yeast liquid. Incorporate it into the flour with a spoon until a sticky dough is formed. Turn out onto a floured surface and knead until smooth and elastic. Return the dough to the bowl and let stand in a bowl in a warm place for about 30 minutes, or until doubled in size.

Meanwhile, prepare the topping. Pour the olive oil into a roasting pan, add the bell peppers, and toss thoroughly to coat. Roast the bell peppers for 10 to 15 minutes, or until they start to collapse, then remove them from the oven, add them to a bowl, and cover with plastic wrap. When cool enough to handle, peel off the skins and discard the cores and seeds. Coarsely chop the bell pepper flesh and mix together with the other topping ingredients in a bowl.

Increase the oven heat to 475°F. Divide the dough into egg-sized balls, then roll each out on a lightly floured work surface into a circle around ¼ inch thick. Place the dough circles on the prepared cookie sheet and spread the topping evenly over each one, all the way out to the edges. Bake for 10 to 15 minutes, or until lightly golden. Serve immediately.

Introduced to us by one of our chefs Nasaralla Soliman, this recipe is an adaptation of a typical dish from his home country of Egypt. It's great served as a cold appetizer with an arugula salad or as a side dish in a mezze platter like this.

STUFFED BABY EGGPLANTS

SERVES 8 TO 10 AS PART OF A MEZZE PLATTER

24 baby eggplants
light olive oil
1 red bell pepper, cored, seeded, and finely diced
1 yellow bell pepper, cored, seeded, and finely diced
½ red chile, trimmed, seeded, and minced
handful of cilantro leaves, finely chopped
handful of flat-leaf parsley leaves, finely chopped
2 scallions, trimmed and minced
1 garlic clove, minced
grated zest of ½ lemon and juice of 1 lemon
salt and pepper

Preheat the oven to 400°F.

Using a sharp knife, make an incision about ½ inch deep into each eggplant lengthwise. Place the eggplants on a baking pan, drizzle with a little olive oil, and roast for 15 to 20 minutes, or until the eggplants are soft but still retain their shape. Let cool.

Put all the remaining ingredients in a mixing bowl, mix together well, and season with salt and pepper to taste. Spoon the stuffing into the holes in each eggplant. Cover with plastic wrap and let chill in the refrigerator until needed. Serve cold.

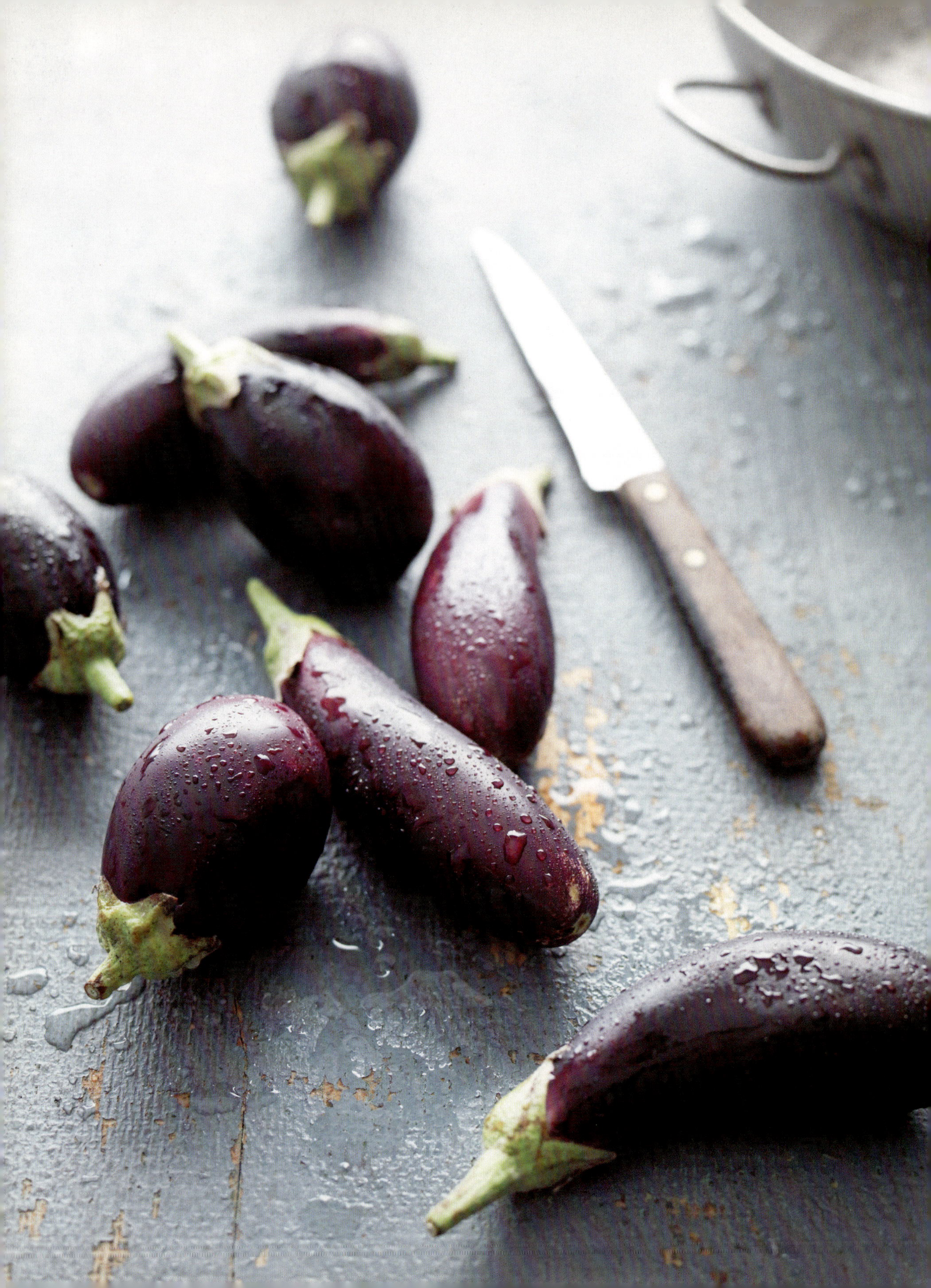

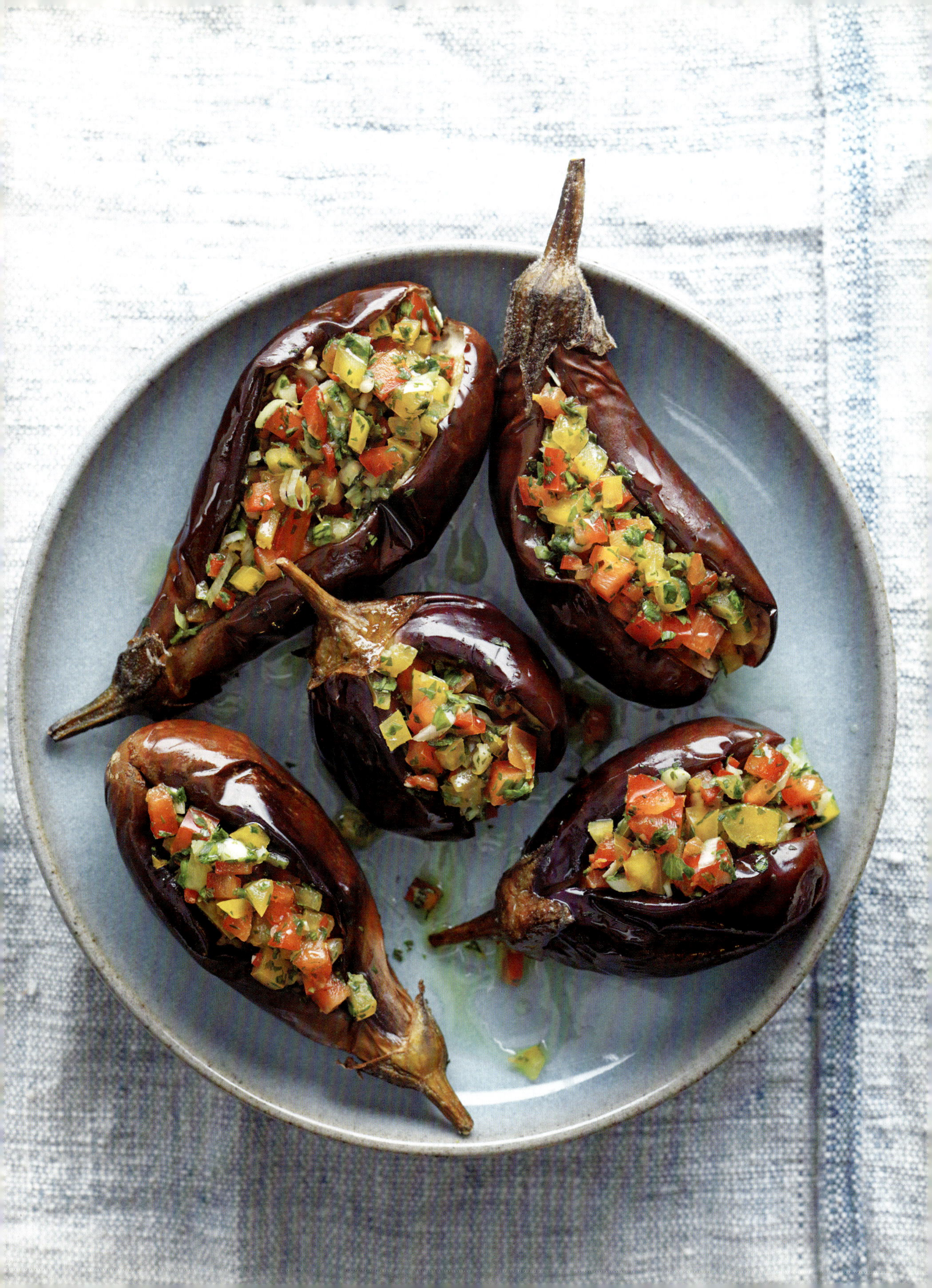

Our version of this traditional Greek home-style recipe has been adapted slightly over the years to include caramelized onions. We have also tried making it with a variety of feta cheeses, finding it to be particularly good when made with a soft, almost creamy feta. Filo can be tricky to use because it tears easily and dries out quickly—just remember to keep any unused sheets covered with plastic wrap or parchment paper and place a damp dish towel on the top. If you tear a piece, simply patch it up with another, gluing them together with a little melted butter. This will won't show in the final product.

SPANAKOPITA

MAKES 24 INDIVIDUAL SPANAKOPITA

13oz package filo pastry, defrosted, if frozen
1 stick butter, melted
2 teaspoons sesame seeds

For the filling
olive oil
2 large onions, finely sliced
1 teaspoon superfine sugar
1 teaspoon salt
1lb spinach, rinsed and drained
2 garlic cloves, minced
4oz feta cheese, crumbled
1 bunch of dill leaves, chopped
3 tablespoons pine nuts, lightly toasted
¼ teaspoon grated nutmeg
pinch of black pepper

Preheat the oven to 375°F. Line a cookie sheet with nonstick parchment paper. For the filling, heat a splash of olive oil in a pan, add the onions, sugar, and salt and cook over medium heat, stirring occasionally, for 15 minutes, or until the onions are caramelized and golden brown. Remove from the heat and set aside.

Cook the spinach in a pan of boiling water for 1 minute, or until tender. Strain and let cool, then squeeze out any excess liquid with your hands. Coarsely chop the spinach and place in a mixing bowl with the caramelized onion and the rest of the filling ingredients. Mix together well.

Cut the filo pastry sheets lengthwise into 4 even strips about 3 inches wide. Brush an individual strip with melted butter, place a small spoonful of the mixture toward one end of the strip and fold the corner of the pastry over it to form a triangle. Continue to fold the pastry strip over itself at right angles, making sure you brush it with more melted butter once more before you make the last fold to ensure it sticks together well. Place the triangle seam-side down on the prepared cookie sheet. Repeat with the remaining strips.

Brush the tops of the prepared spanakopita with the remaining melted butter and sprinkle with the sesame seeds. Bake for 30 to 40 minutes, or until golden brown. Serve warm.

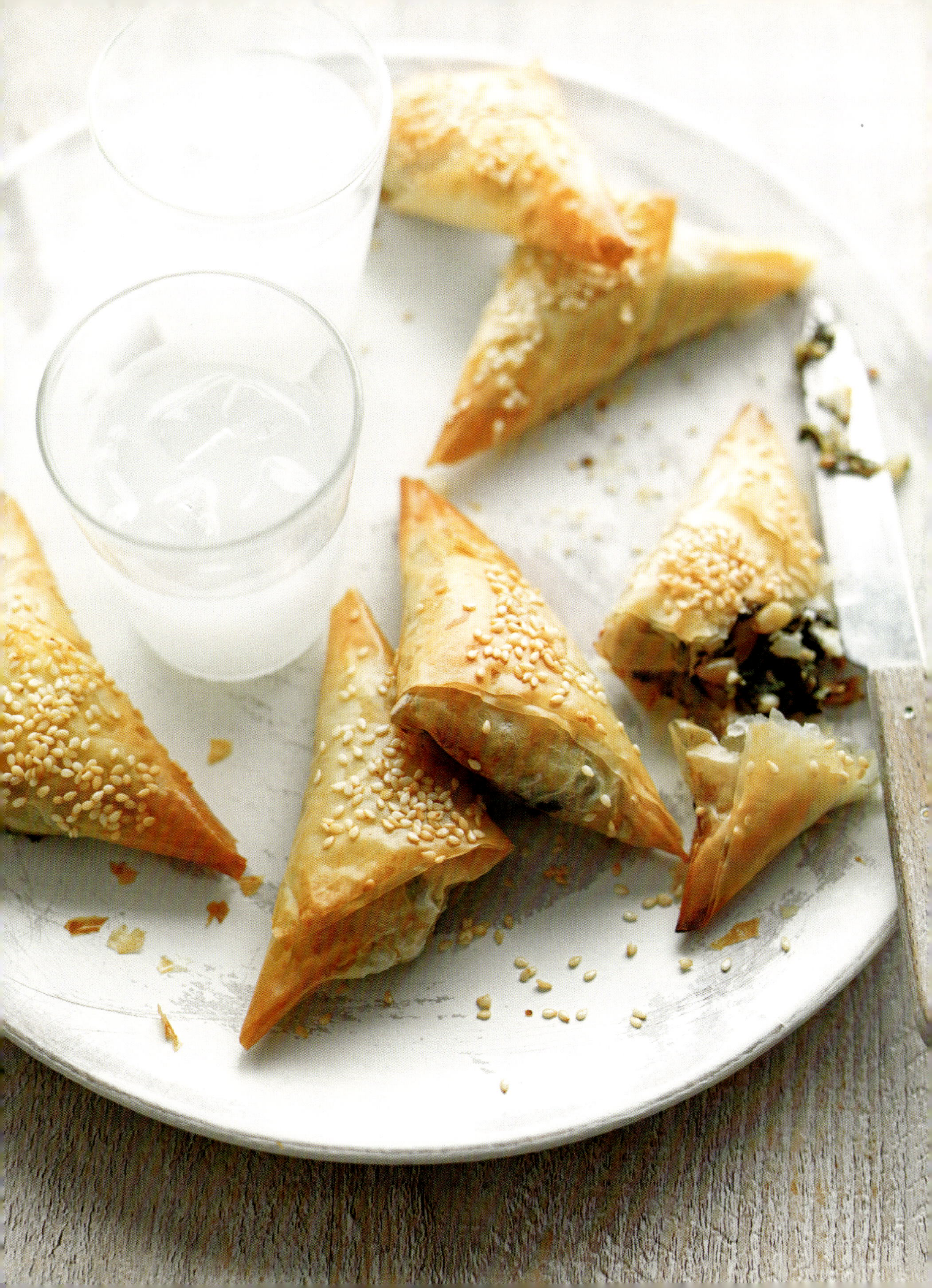

We find using dried fava beans makes all the difference as they give the falafel a lighter texture. Just remember to start soaking them the day before you want to make the recipe. Dried chickpeas can also be used, giving a heavier texture. Serve these Falafel with Tahini Dressing (see page 100) and Ruby Jeweled Tabbouleh (see page 96) as an appetizer, or wrap them up in pitta bread with shredded lettuce, tomato, tahini, and Harissa (see page 228) for a filling lunch.

FALAFEL

MAKES APPROXIMATELY 20 FALAFEL

1½ cups dried fava beans
1 small potato, peeled
½ onion, diced
1 garlic clove, minced
2 teaspoons ground coriander
1 teaspoon ground cumin
pinch of cayenne pepper
2 tablespoons all-purpose or wheat-free flour, plus extra for dusting
2 tablespoons lemon juice
handful of cilantro leaves
sunflower oil, for deep-frying
salt and pepper

Put the fava beans into a bowl, cover with plenty of water, and let soak for at least 24 hours.

The next day, put the whole peeled potato in a saucepan of boiling salted water and cook for 10 to 15 minutes, or until tender and cooked through. Drain, mash, and set aside.

Drain the soaked beans and add them to a food processor. Blend them together to your preferred consistency, either leaving the mixture slightly coarse (this will give the falafels more bite) or continuing to blend it until it resembles fine bread crumbs.

Add the onion, garlic, spices, flour, lemon juice, and cilantro leaves to the beans, season with salt and pepper, and blend together to combine. Add the mixture to a bowl, and then add the potato. Mix together well using your hands. Roll the falafel mixture into bite-size pieces on a lightly floured work surface.

Fill a large saucepan or deep-fryer with the sunflower oil and heat to 350°F, or until a cube of bread added to the oil browns in 30 seconds. Deep-fry the falafel in batches in the hot oil for about 3 to 4 minutes, or until golden brown all over. Remove with a slotted spoon and let drain on paper towels. Serve.

It's best to make these marinated beauties in advance to allow the flavors plenty of time to develop. They will keep really well in the refrigerator for a week or so.

MARINATED MUSHROOMS

MAKES 2½ CUPS

½lb cremino mushrooms
½lb button mushrooms
2 bay leaves
1 small cinnamon stick
4 thyme sprigs
2½ tablespoons turbinado sugar
1 cup balsamic vinegar
2 cups water

To serve
1 tablespoon extra virgin olive oil
1 tablespoon chopped parsley leaves

Wash the mushrooms thoroughly, trimming the ends if necessary to make sure they are free from dirt.

Put the cleaned mushrooms in a small saucepan along with the remaining ingredients. Bring to a simmer, cover with a plate small enough to fit inside the pan (this will weigh down on the mushrooms and help them absorb more of the juices), and let them cook for 15 to 20 minutes.

Remove from the heat and set aside to cool, then add to a suitable airtight container and refrigerate for at least 12 hours. Drizzle with a little olive oil and scatter with some chopped parsley before serving.

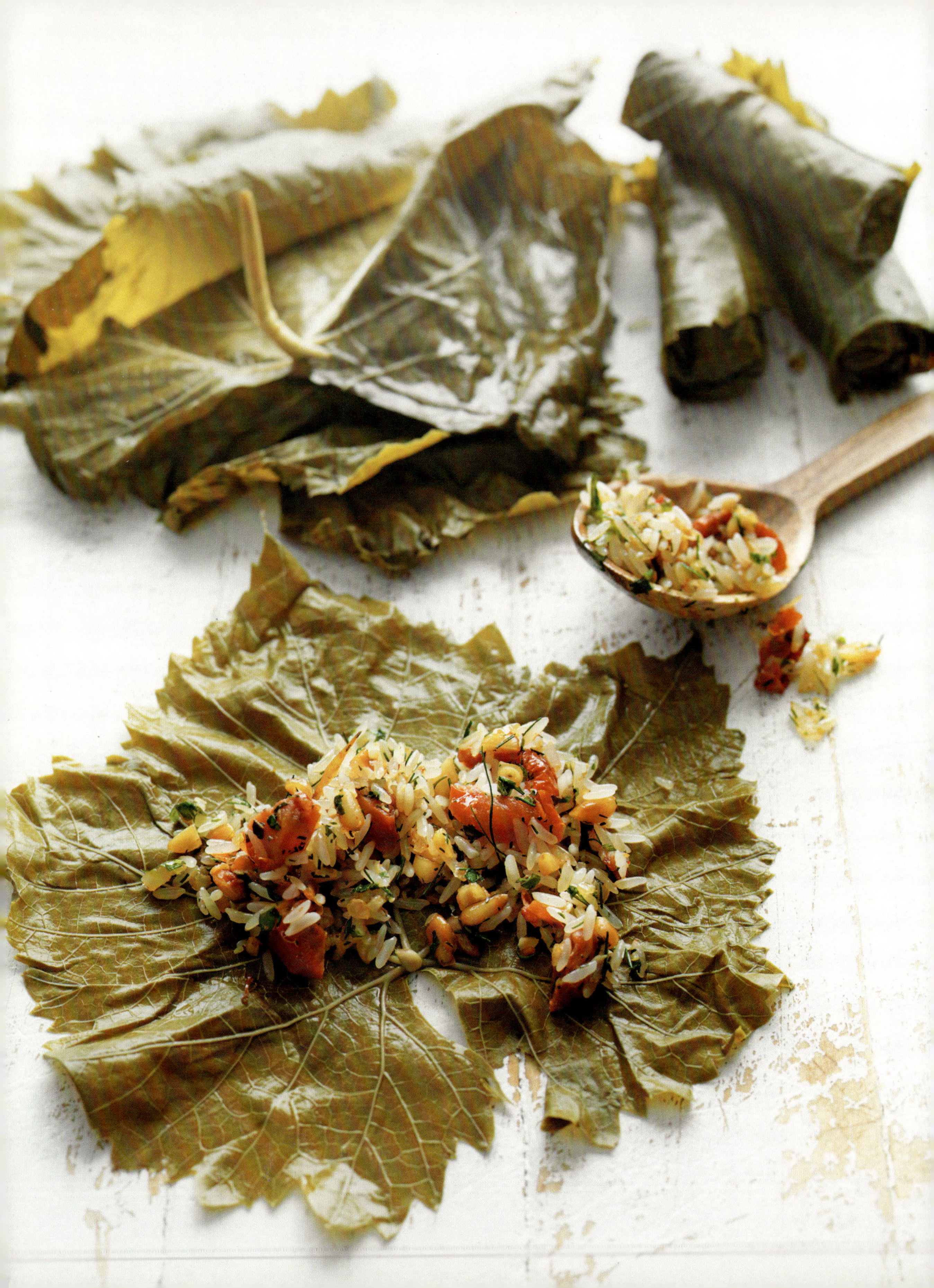

If you've only ever had cold stuffed grape leaves from the supermarket or, heaven forbid, the mushy canned variety, then you need to try these because they are totally delicious. Although they are best served warm you can make them in advance, refrigerate them, and then let them come up to room temperature. Just don't serve them straight from the fridge because the rice will be hard. You can use a ceramic baking dish for this recipe. However, because it is helpful to be able to see the water level through the dish, a Pyrex dish is recommended.

SUN-DRIED TOMATO
& PINE-NUT STUFFED GRAPE LEAVES

SERVES 8 TO 10 AS PART OF A MEZZE PLATTER

30 to 35 grape leaves in brine
2 tablespoons olive oil
1 large white onion, finely diced
4 garlic cloves, minced
¼ teaspoon ground cumin
8oz sun-dried tomatoes in oil, drained and chopped, oil reserved
1⅔ cups long-grain white rice, rinsed and drained
2 tablespoons chopped flat-leaf parsley leaves
2 tablespoons chopped dill leaves
½ cup pine nuts, lightly toasted and coarsely chopped
grated zest of ½ lemon

Preheat the oven to 375°F. Soak the grape leaves in boiling water and drain them following the package instructions.

Heat the oil in a pan, add the onion, garlic, and cumin and cook over very low heat, stirring, for 5 to 8 minutes, or until the onions are soft and translucent. Add the sun-dried tomatoes and cook for another minute or so, then remove from the heat and stir in the rice, herbs, nuts, and grated lemon zest.

Spread out the grape leaves, trimming off the stalk at the base of each with a pair of scissors. Spoon a tablespoon or so of the filling into the center of each, fold the ends over, and roll the leaves up, pressing the mixture into a sausage shape as you go. Arrange the rolls seam-side down in a 9 x 13-inch baking dish, packing them together as tightly as possible to stop them from moving around while cooking. The dish must be tightly packed or the grape leaves will fall apart. If you find you have any empty space left in the dish, pack it with balls of crunched-up parchment paper.

Pour enough water over the grape leaves to cover them by about ⅛ inch and drizzle them with the oil from the sun-dried tomatoes. Cover with nonstick parchment paper and weigh down with a smaller baking dish or a couple of plates to stop the grape leaves from floating around. Bake for 1 hour, adding extra water halfway through cooking if the grape leaves are starting to dry out. Serve warm.

If you're in a rush, you can use ready-cooked beets here, but the flavor, color, and texture is much better if you cook the beets yourself.

BEET & DILL DIP

SERVES 4 TO 6

13oz beets
1 cup Greek yogurt
handful of chopped dill leaves
grated zest and juice of ½ lemon
salt and white pepper

Put the beets into a large saucepan, cover with water, and bring to a boil. Reduce to a simmer and cook for 20 to 30 minutes over medium heat until tender enough for a knife to pierce the center of each beet easily. Drain and let cool.

Grate the cooled cooked beets into a mixing bowl, add the yogurt, dill leaves, and grated lemon zest and juice. Stir together well. Season to taste with salt and white pepper and serve.

V **GF**

The amount of lemon juice and tahini used when making hummus is quite personal, so if you feel the need to adjust the amounts to suit your taste, please do so. The key factor to getting a superior hummus is finding first-rate ingredients, so it's definitely worth hunting for good-quality chickpeas to give the hummus a smooth texture and great taste.

HUMMUS

SERVES 6 TO 8

2 x 14oz cans chickpeas
juice of 1 small lemon
3 tablespoons light tahini paste
¼ teaspoon ground cumin
1 small garlic clove, minced
1¼ cups light olive oil
salt and white pepper

Add the chickpeas to a food processor and briefly pulse. Then add the remaining ingredients and season with salt and white pepper. Blend until smooth, taste, and adjust the seasoning if necessary. Serve with warm flatbread or as part of a mezze platter.

If you prefer not to use chickpeas, use white beans such as **lima beans** or **haricot beans** in this recipe.

Adapt your hummus by spicing it up with some minced **chile** and **cilantro** or sweetening it with some **roast bell pepper**.

To give your hummus an impressive finishing touch, top it with a few reserved chickpeas mixed with a drizzle of olive oil, some chili flakes, and toasted cumin seeds.

Using an electric stand mixer to make this dip gives it a light, moussy texture that cannot be achieved with a stick blender because the air is needed to give it a creamier finish. If you don't have a stand mixer, beat all the ingredients together in a bowl with an electric hand-held beater for a similar effect.

CHILI FLAKE & FETA DIP

SERVES 4

11½oz feta cheese
pinch of dried chili flakes
pinch of cayenne pepper
pinch of sweet paprika
1 small garlic clove, minced
1 tablespoon chopped flat-leaf parsley
½ cup olive oil
warmed flatbread, to serve

Put all the ingredients in the bowl of a stand mixer. Using the beater attachment, mix together for 5 minutes on a slow speed to combine, then mix together for another 20–25 minutes until the dip is light and mousse-like. Serve with warm flatbread.

Give more of a kick to this dip by adding **extra chili** or **cayenne pepper**.

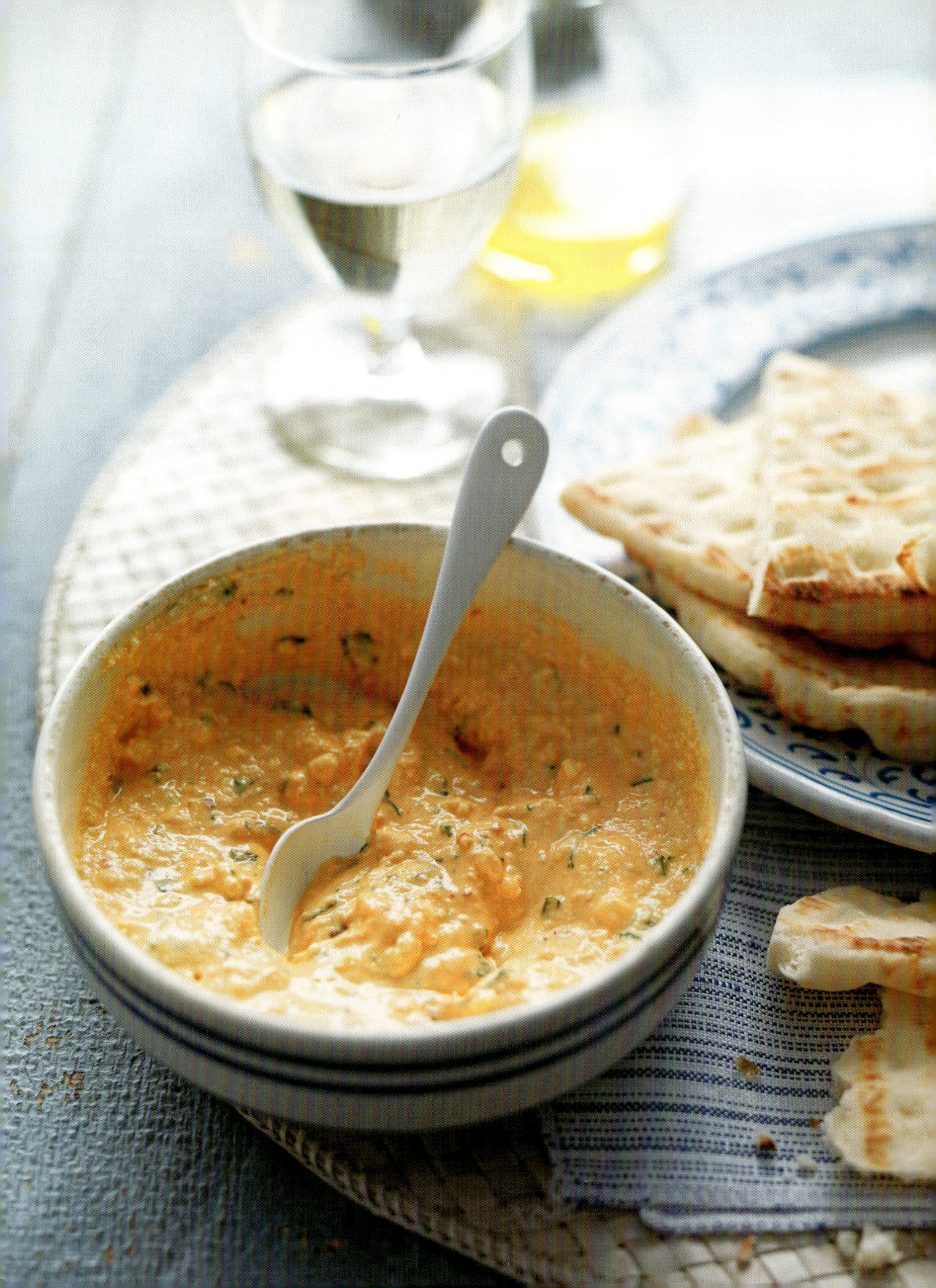

SALADS

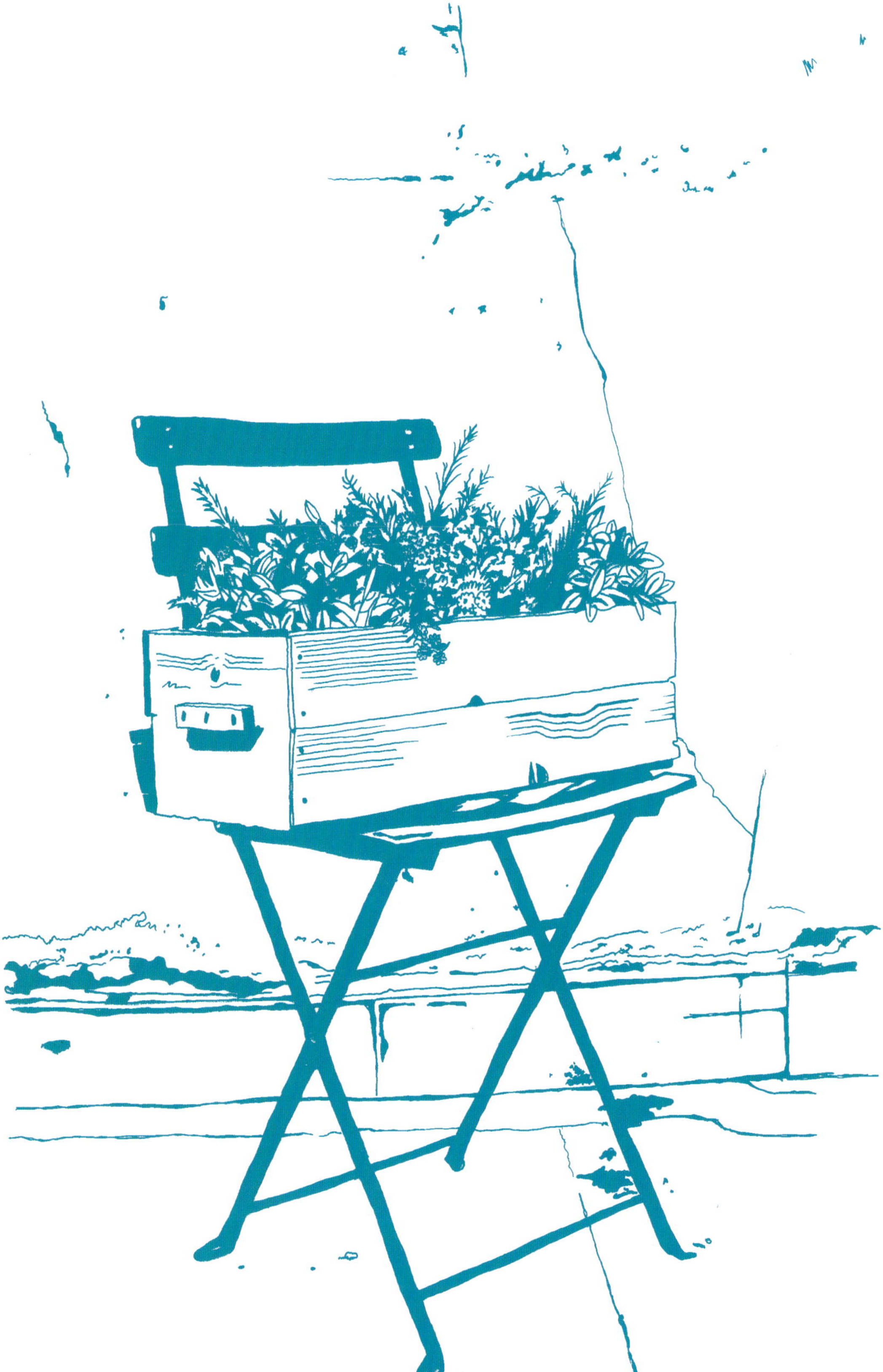

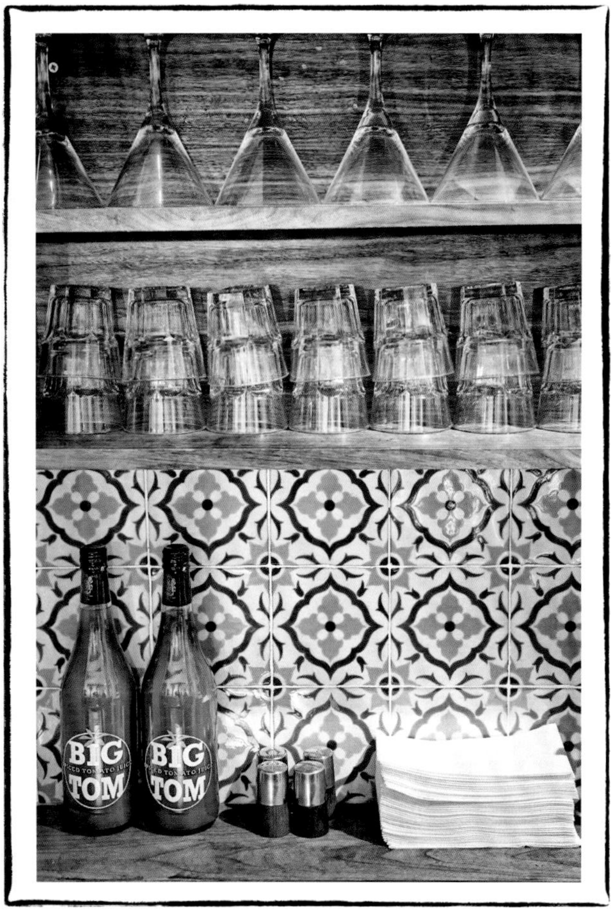
BIG
TOM
BIG
TOM

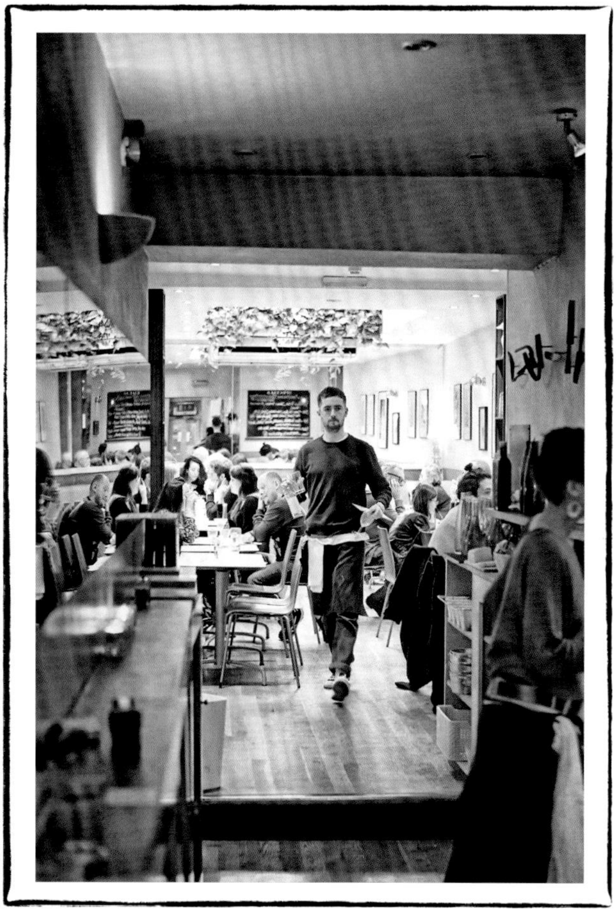

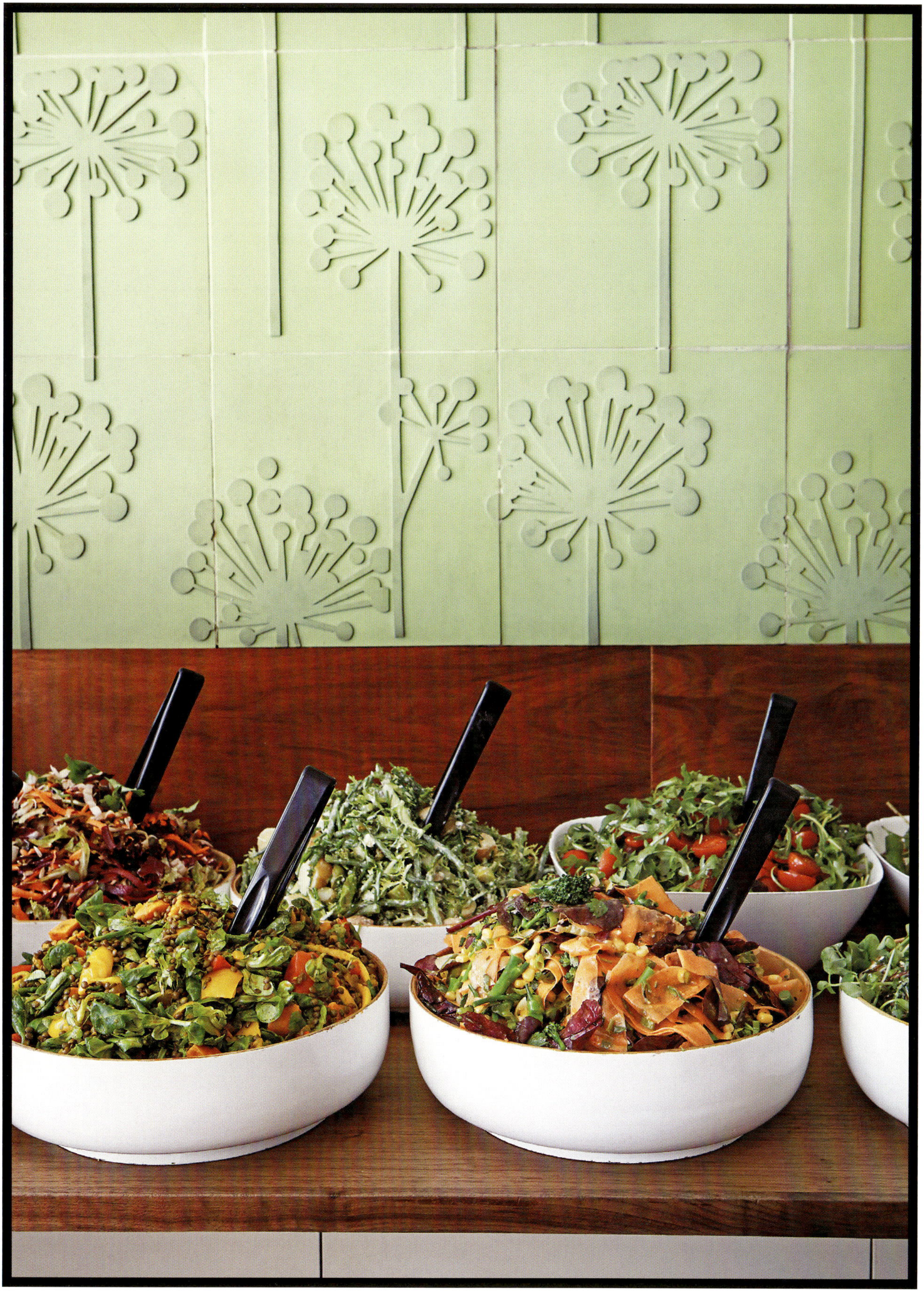

A delicious, summery salad full of fresh green flavors and contrasting textures. If you eat dairy and would like to have this as a main course, top it with a little grilled or fried halloumi cheese. For a vegan option, this makes a wonderful accompaniment to homemade Falafel (see page 72).

WILD RICE SALAD WITH PEAS, PEA SHOOTS & GREEN HARISSA

SERVES 6 TO 8 AS AN APPETIZER

2 cups wild rice
6 scallions, trimmed
1 cucumber
1 handful of flat-leaf parsley leaves
1 handful of cilantro leaves
1 handful of mint leaves
2 green chiles, trimmed
1 cup frozen baby peas, defrosted
½ cup Green Harissa (*see* page 229)
grated zest and juice of 1 lemon
salt
2oz pea shoots or watercress, to garnish

Bring a saucepan of salted water to a boil. Add the rice, lower the heat to a simmer, and cook for 20 to 30 minutes, or until the rice is tender. Drain the rice and let cool.

While the rice is cooling, thinly slice the scallions and coarsely chop the cucumber and herbs. Finely chop the chiles and add to a bowl with the chopped herbs, cucumber, scallion slices, peas, and cooled rice. Toss together with the green harissa, grated lemon zest, and lemon juice. Garnish with the pea shoots or watercress to serve.

If you eat dairy then this salad is great with **feta** or **grilled halloumi**.

If you would like to save time, dress this salad with **lemon juice** and **olive oil** rather than **Green Harissa**.

To make in advance, layer all the ingredients except the lemon juice and zest on top of the rice in the serving bowl then just toss before serving, adding the lemon juice and zest at this stage. This will ensure that the colors stay vibrant.

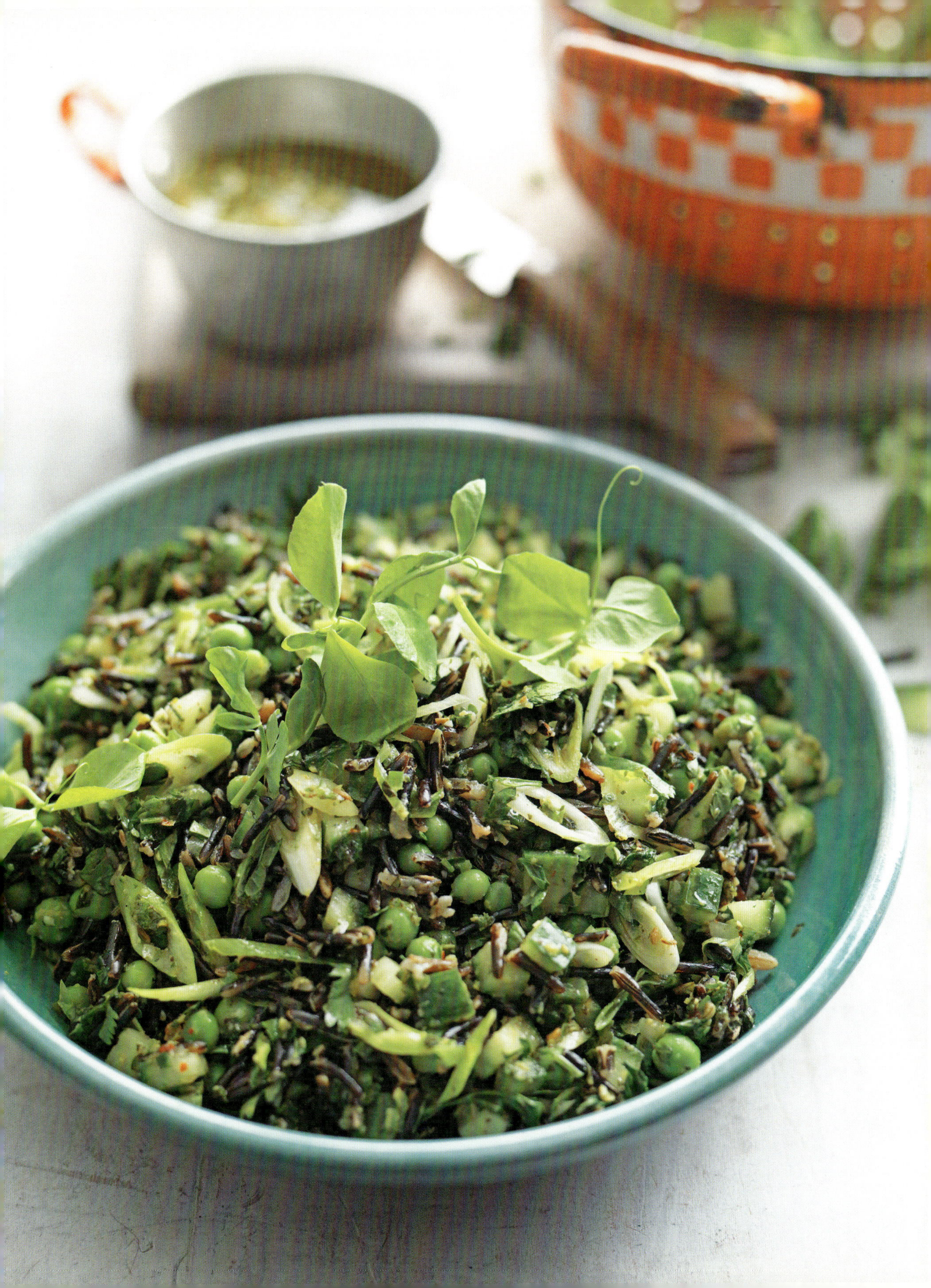

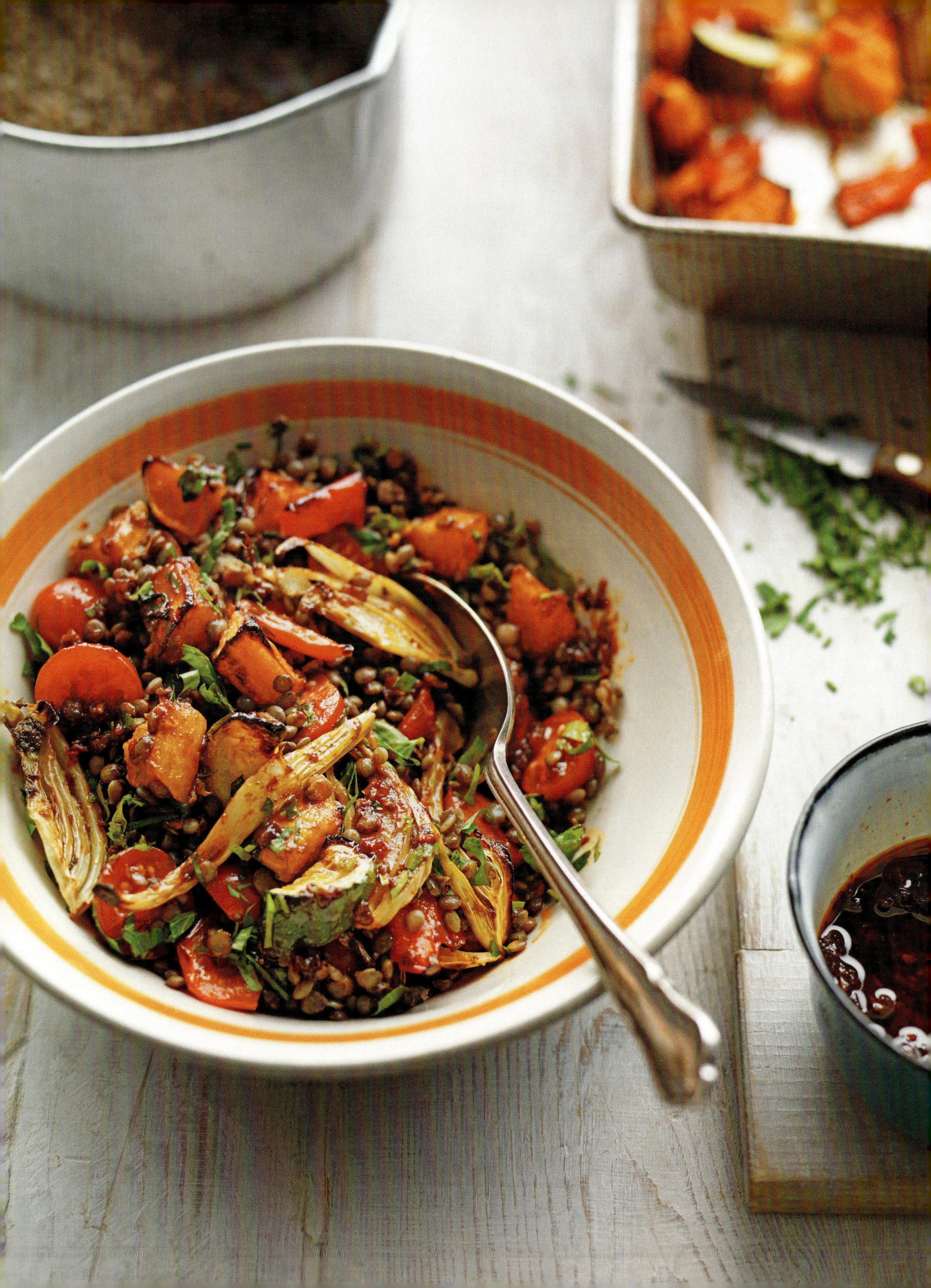

Yes, yes, we know, lentil salad may seem a bit clichéd, but this is so tangy and irresistible we couldn't possibly leave it out. It's great either warm or cold and, if you don't mind a little dairy, works brilliantly with goat cheese, too. You can substitute any other vegetables you like for the ones used here—just try to stick to vegetables that will hold their shape when mixed together with the lentils.

PUY LENTIL SALAD
WITH ROASTED VEGETABLES

SERVES 6 TO 8 AS AN APPETIZER

1 cup Puy lentils
1 red onion, very finely diced
⅓ cup olive oil
⅓ cup balsamic vinegar
1 red chile, trimmed and chopped
3 garlic cloves, chopped
2 tablespoons dark brown sugar
3 tablespoons tomato paste
1 tablespoon fennel seeds, toasted and lightly crushed
handful of flat-leaf parsley leaves
3oz baby spinach, red chard, or bull's blood beet leaves
salt

For the roasted vegetables
olive oil
10oz pumpkin or butternut squash, peeled and cut into wedges ¾ inch thick
½ fennel bulb, trimmed and cut into wedges ½ inch thick
1 cup cherry tomatoes
1 zucchini, cut into wedges ½ inch thick
2 red or yellow bell peppers, cored, seeded, and cut into wedges ½ inch thick wedges

Preheat the oven to 400°F.

Bring a saucepan of salted water to a boil and add the lentils. Lower the heat and simmer for 15 to 20 minutes, or until tender. Drain and put into a large salad bowl.

Add the onion, olive oil, balsamic vinegar, chile, garlic, sugar, tomato paste, and crushed fennel seeds to a small saucepan. Bring to a simmer and cook gently, stirring frequently, for 4 to 5 minutes, or until the sugar has dissolved. Spoon the warm dressing over the lentils and let cool.

For the roasted vegetables, drizzle a little oil into a roasting pan. Add the pumpkin or squash pieces, season with salt and toss together to coat. Roast for 10 minutes. Toss the fennel and whole tomatoes in a little oil, add to the pan, and roast for another 10 minutes. Finally, toss the zucchini and bell peppers in a little oil, add to the pan, and roast for another 10 minutes. By now the vegetables should all be tender and cooked through. Set aside to cool slightly.

Coarsely chop the parsley and add to the salad bowl along with the salad leaves and roasted vegetables. Mix everything together well and serve.

Quinoa is an ancient, Incan grainlike crop grown for its seeds, which are boiled or steamed until they have a texture something like couscous. Unlike couscous, though, quinoa is both amazingly nutritious—full of protein, iron, and magnesium, among other things—and gluten-free. Here it is combined with kidney beans and bell peppers and covered in our chipotle lime dressing to create a zingy, chunky salad full of flavor and texture.

PERUVIAN QUINOA SALAD WITH KIDNEY BEANS, BELL PEPPERS & CHIPOTLE LIME DRESSING

SERVES 6 TO 8 AS AN APPETIZER

1 ¾ cups white, red, or black quinoa grains
1 sweet potato, peeled and cut into 1-inch cubes
olive oil
1 large red bell pepper, cored, seeded, and cut into 1-inch chunks
1 large yellow bell pepper, cored, seeded, and cut into 1-inch chunks
grated zest and juice of 1 lime
1 bunch of cilantro, leaves picked and coarsely chopped
3 red chiles, trimmed and minced
2 red onions, finely diced
13oz can kidney beans, drained and rinsed
3oz bull's-blood beet leaves, red chard, or baby spinach
½ cup Chipotle Lime Dressing (*see* page 240)
salt and pepper

Preheat the oven to 375°F. Line a cookie sheet with nonstick parchment paper.

Cook the quinoa in boiling water following the package instructions and then drain well and let cool. Season with salt and pepper.

Toss the sweet potato pieces in a little oil, arrange on the prepared cookie sheet, and roast in the oven for 15 to 20 minutes or so, until just starting to soften. Toss the bell peppers in a little oil, add them to the cookie sheet with the sweet potatoes, and roast for a further 10 minutes or so, until tender. Let cool on the sheet, then add to a large salad bowl with the quinoa and all the remaining ingredients. Mix everything together well to serve.

This salad has been a staple on our menu for many, many years. It is 100 percent organic in the restaurant because we use only organic fruit and vegetables to prepare it; if you're making it at home then the choice is entirely up to you. For those of you who own a mandoline, use it here to cut your fennel into perfect paper-thin slices. Just watch your fingers!

DETOX SALAD

SERVES 6 TO 8 AS AN APPETIZER

6 carrots, peeled and grated
3 medium beets, peeled and grated
1 small fennel bulb, very finely sliced
½ cup mixed bean sprouts
⅔ cup golden raisins
3 tablespoons sunflower seeds, toasted
3 tablespoons pumpkin seeds, toasted
3 tablespoons extra virgin olive oil
handful of cilantro leaves, to garnish

For the dressing
½-inch piece of fresh ginger root
juice of 2 large oranges
¼ cup nonpasteurized apple juice
2 tablespoons lime juice

To make the dressing, peel and finely dice the ginger. Using the flat side of your knife, press down on the ginger pieces to release any excess juice. (Alternatively, if you have a juicing machine, peel and juice the ginger.) Put the diced or juiced ginger into a small jar along with the remainder of the dressing ingredients, screw the lid on securely, and shake well.

Assemble all the salad ingredients in a large mixing bowl and toss together well. Drizzle with the dressing and serve, garnished with cilantro leaves.

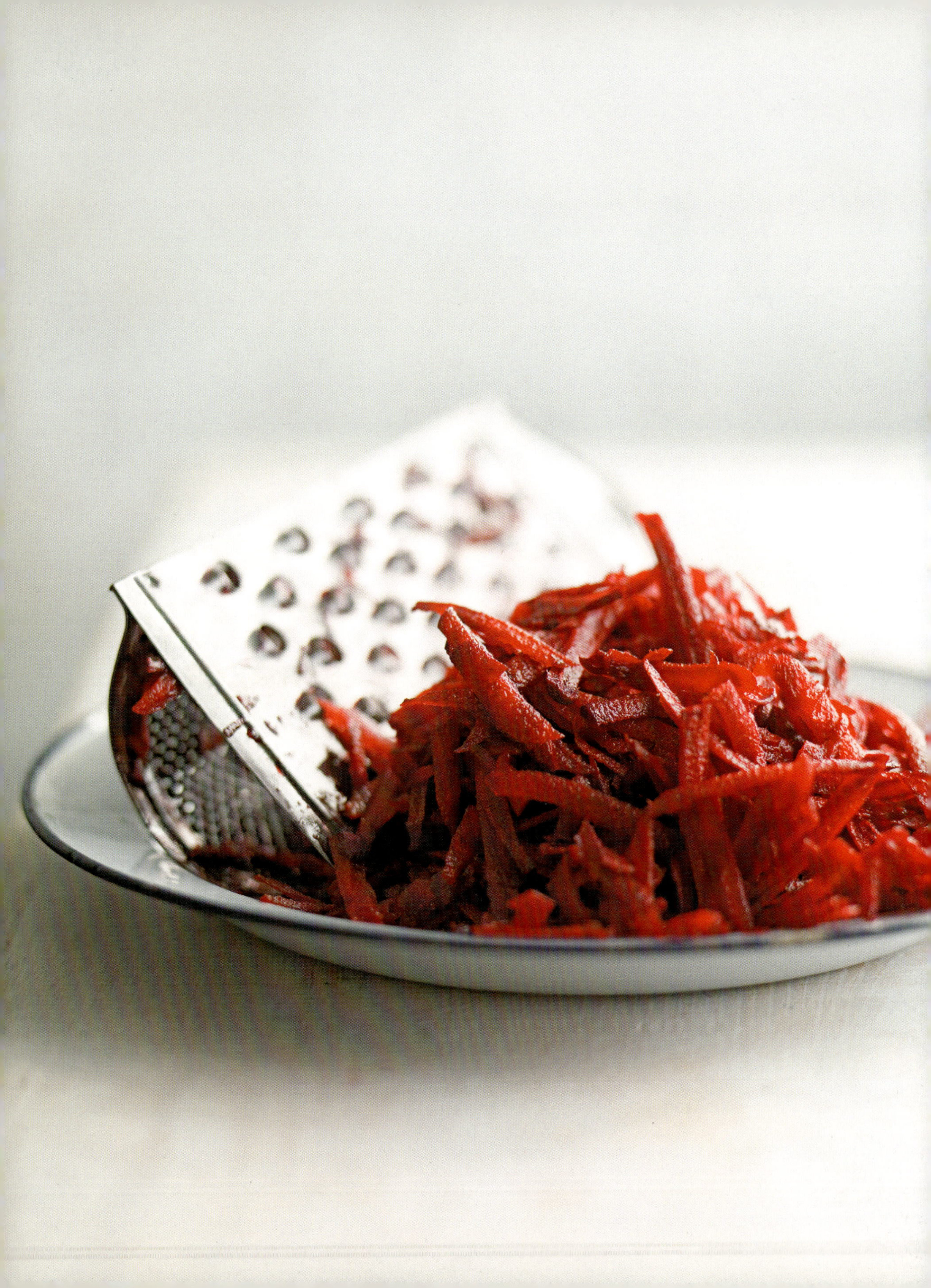

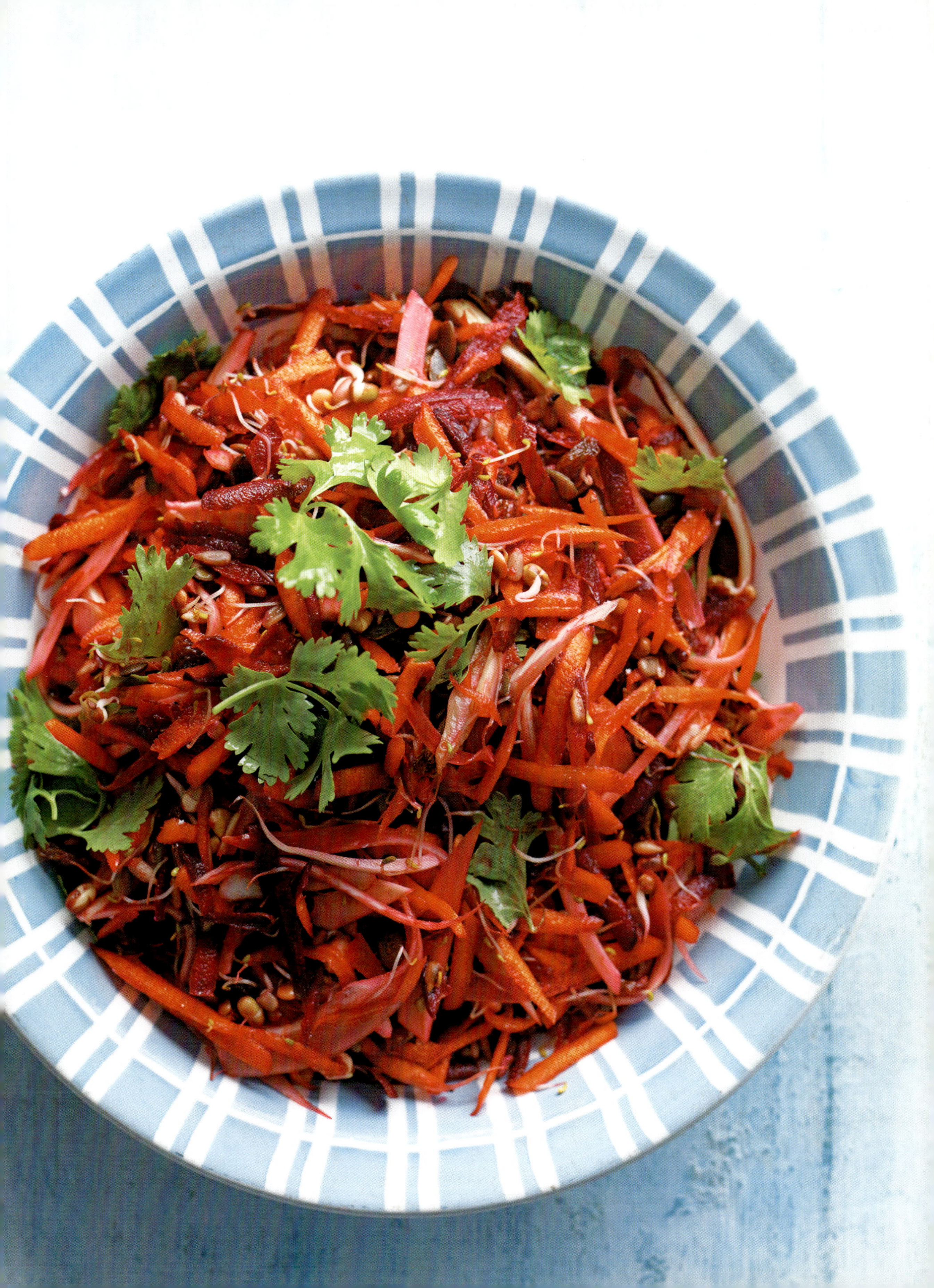

GF

This salad is a riot of fantastic, jewel-like colors and bright, fresh flavors. It's becoming easier to find golden and striped varieties of beets at the supermarkets, but if you are having trouble sourcing them don't worry too much; normal red beets won't make any difference in terms of flavor (though they won't look quite as pretty). Likewise, if blood oranges are out of season, simply use regular oranges in their place.

WARM RUBY & GOLDEN BEET SALAD
WITH ROAST HAZELNUTS, BLOOD ORANGES & LABNEH

SERVES 6 TO 8 AS AN APPETIZER

3lb mixed beets (such as Chioggia, Bull's Blood, and Golden)
⅓ cup olive oil
⅓ cup date syrup
1 cup skinned hazelnuts
5 blood oranges
3½oz baby spinach
13oz Homemade Labneh Cheese (*see* page 43)
sea salt flakes

Preheat the oven to 375°F. Line 2 cookie sheets with nonstick parchment paper.

Bring a large saucepan of water to a boil, add the beets, and boil until they are beginning to soften (about 20 to 30 minutes for medium beets and 40 minutes for large—you'll know they are ready when a knife stuck into them comes out pretty easily). Drain and let cool, then peel, cut in half, and slice into half moons about ½ inch thick.

Arrange the beet slices on one of the cookie sheets, drizzle them with the olive oil and date syrup, and sprinkle with sea salt flakes. Roast for 15 minutes, until golden brown at the edges.

Meanwhile, spread the hazelnuts out on the other cookie sheet and roast for 5 minutes, or until lightly golden. Remove from the oven and let cool slightly.

Cut the skins and pith off of the oranges and slice the orange flesh horizontally into thin strips. Put in a salad bowl and toss together with the beets, hazelnuts, and spinach leaves. Spoon the Homemade Labneh Cheese over the salad and serve.

It's great to see that heirloom potatoes are becoming more widely available. There are some wonderful old varieties out there, many of which both look and taste fantastic. This salad celebrates them, and we like to make it with a mixture of violet, ruby, and new potatoes. If you're struggling to find heirloom potatoes, just use new potatoes instead.

HEIRLOOM POTATO & ROAST ASPARAGUS
SALAD WITH TRUFFLE MAYONNAISE

SERVES 6 TO 8 AS AN APPETIZER

1lb mixed heirloom potatoes (such as Bliss' Triumph, Vermont Champion, or Garnet Chile)
1lb new potatoes
16 asparagus spears
olive oil
6 scallions, trimmed and sliced
1 bunch of chives, finely snipped, plus a few extra to garnish
3oz watercress, plus a few extra leaves to garnish
grated zest of ½ lemon
½ cup Truffle Mayonnaise (*see* page 235)
sea salt flakes

Preheat the oven to 400°F. Line a cookie sheet with nonstick parchment paper.

Bring a saucepan of salted water to a boil, add the potatoes, and cook for 20 to 30 minutes until tender. Drain and cut into bite-size pieces.

To prepare the asparagus, snap off the woody base of the stalks. Place the spears on the prepared cookie sheet, sprinkle with sea salt flakes, and drizzle with a little olive oil. Roast for 5 to 10 minutes, or until tender but still firm. Let cool, then slice into thirds.

Put the potatoes and asparagus in a large salad bowl with the scallions, chives, watercress, and grated lemon zest. Add the Truffle Mayonnaise and toss well to coat. Scatter with a few extra watercress leaves and chives to finish, and serve.

While pasta salad might seem a little old-fashioned, this simple, sophisticated dish is full of beautiful flavors and colors. It's worth hunting down purple basil leaves (also sometimes confusingly called red basil) to use here because they will give the oil and salad a lovely dark pink color. For an extra mushroomy hit, add a few drops of truffle oil to taste when mixing your ingredients together before serving.

OYSTER MUSHROOM FUSILLI SALAD
WITH PURPLE BROCCOLI, BASIL & PINE NUTS

SERVES 6 TO 8 AS AN APPETIZER

10oz fusilli
10oz purple sprouting broccoli
2 tablespoons olive oil
3 garlic cloves, chopped
½lb oyster mushrooms, trimmed and coarsely shredded
½ cup Purple Basil Oil (*see* page 238)
3½ tablespoons toasted pine nuts
grated zest of ½ lemon
10 purple basil leaves
salt

Add the pasta to a large saucepan of boiling salted water and cook following the package instructions until al dente. Drain and set aside. In another saucepan, blanch the broccoli for 2 to 3 minutes in boiling salted water until tender. Set aside.

Heat the olive oil in a wok or skillet over medium–high heat, add the garlic, and cook, stirring, for 1 minute. Add the oyster mushrooms and cook for 2 to 3 minutes, or until they are beginning to brown. Remove from the heat. If the mushrooms have released a lot of liquid while cooking, drain in a colander.

Chop the broccoli into ½-inch pieces, add them to a large salad bowl, and toss together with the Purple Basil Oil, mushrooms, pasta, pine nuts and grated lemon zest. Tear the basil leaves into strips, toss them through the salad, and serve.

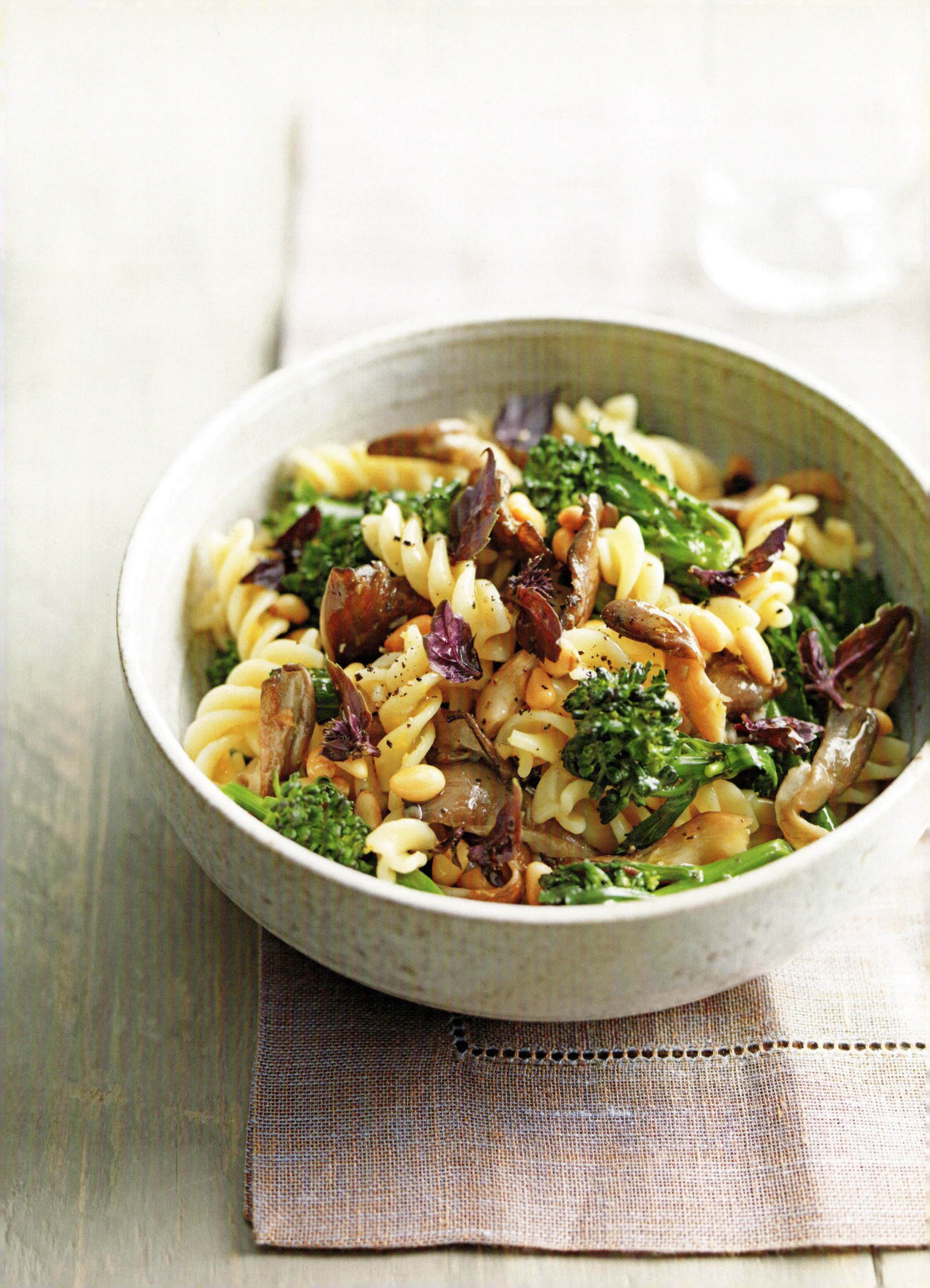

This ruby tabbouleh is a beautiful twist on the traditional bulgur wheat salad, its vibrant colors and fresh, herby flavors providing the perfect antidote to a dull fall or winter's day. If you feel like giving the salad a little more substance, the grassy herbs and sweet fruit go very well with the sharp tang of feta cheese.

RUBY JEWELED TABBOULEH

SERVES 6 TO 8 AS AN APPETIZER

2 cups bulgur wheat
1 large bunch of flat-leaf parsley, leaves picked
1 large bunch of mint, leaves picked
grated zest and juice of 2 oranges
grated zest and juice of 1 lemon
2 red chiles, trimmed and minced
3 red onions, finely chopped
3 large beef tomatoes or 8 vine tomatoes, seeded and finely diced
3 tablespoons olive oil
¼ teaspoon sumac
pinch of ground cinnamon
pinch of ground cumin
1¼ lb red seedless grapes, cut in half
2 cups pomegranate seeds
1 cup pistachios, toasted and lightly crushed
salt

Rinse the bulgur wheat thoroughly and drain in a fine sieve.

Bring a large saucepan of salted water to a boil. Add the bulgur wheat, reduce the heat to a simmer, and cook for 10 to 15 minutes, or until the bulgur wheat is tender but still retains a bite. Remove from the heat and let the grains to steam in the pan for 2 to 3 minutes then add to a fine sieve, rinse with cold water, and let drain.

Meanwhile, coarsely chop the parsley and mint leaves, and add to a salad bowl with the remaining ingredients. Add the drained bulgur wheat, toss everything together well to mix, and serve.

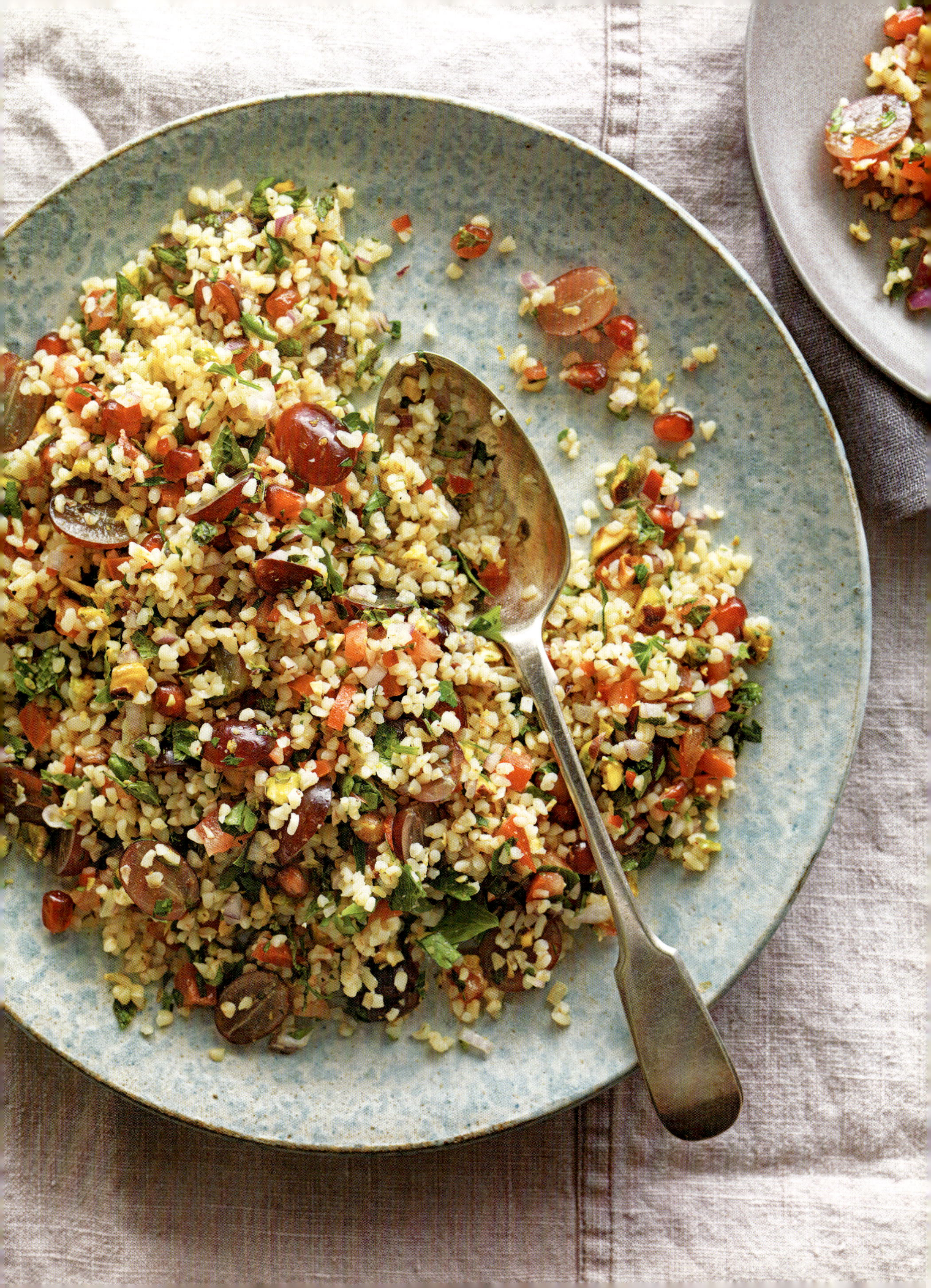

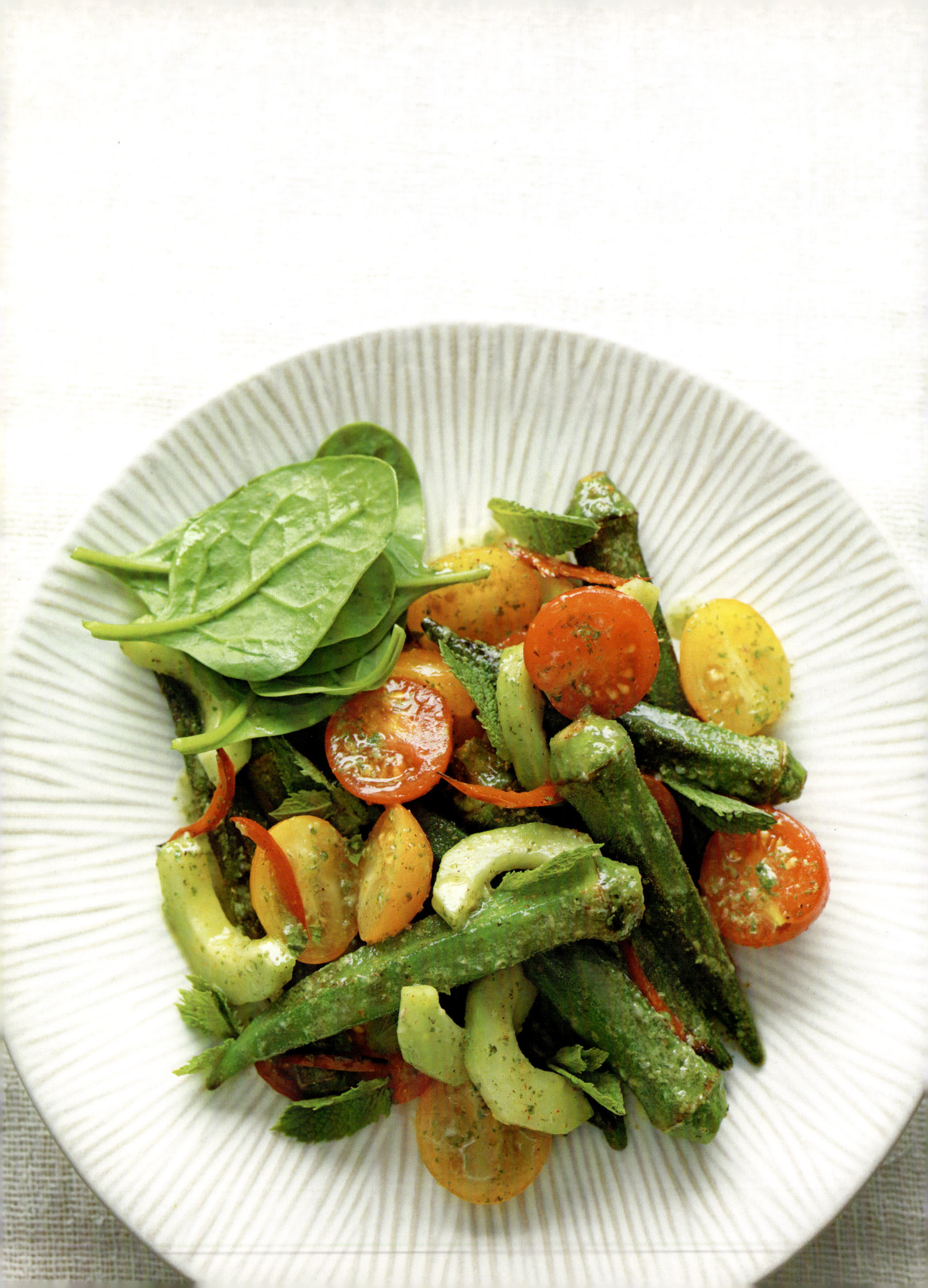

A lot of people don't like okra but that's probably because they've either only had the stringy old stuff, or it's been overcooked. When buying okra, be picky and only select the smaller green fingers. To prepare, just remove the stem rather than cutting off the entire top to stop the okra from releasing liquid while frying. Finally, make sure you wash your okra just before you use it and no earlier—if it sits around in water it will quickly discolor and become gluey.

SPICED OKRA WITH CHERRY TOMATOES, BABY SPINACH & MINT

SERVES 6 TO 8 AS AN APPETIZER

light oil (such as canola, peanut, or sunflower)
10oz okra, stems removed
1 teaspoon medium Madras curry powder
2 cups mixed red and yellow cherry tomatoes, halved
½ cucumber, peeled, seeded, and cut into ½-inch slices
4 scallions, trimmed and thinly sliced
handful of mint leaves
2 red chiles, trimmed and thinly sliced
2oz baby spinach or baby chard
2 to 3 tablespoons Lemon Mint Dressing (*see* page 242)
sea salt flakes

Heat a drizzle of light oil in a wok or large skillet over medium heat. Wash the okra, drain briefly, and put in the hot pan still slightly wet. Cook, stirring, for 5 minutes, or until the okra has puffed up and is beginning to collapse. Add the curry powder and cook for another 30 seconds or so. Remove from the heat.

Add a large pinch of sea salt flakes to the okra and let cool slightly, then pour it into a large salad bowl and toss together with the other ingredients. Serve.

This is a nice simple salad full of chunky vegetables and Middle Eastern flavors. The black skins of the eggplant provide a wonderful contrast to the red of the tomatoes and the green of the cucumbers. We like to use baby plum tomatoes here for their richer, sweeter flavor but, if you can get hold of them, good ripe cherry tomatoes will work well, too.

ROAST EGGPLANT, CUCUMBER & BABY PLUM TOMATO SALAD WITH TAHINI DRESSING

2 large eggplants
½ teaspoon smoked paprika
½ teaspoon ground cumin
2 to 3 tablespoons olive oil
1 bunch of flat-leaf parsley, leaves picked and coarsely chopped
handful of mint leaves, coarsely chopped
2 bunches of scallions, trimmed and sliced
1 large cucumber, seeded and cut into 1-inch cubes
1½lb baby plum tomatoes, cut in half
3oz baby spinach
grated zest of ½ lemon
salt and pepper
Tahini Dressing (*see* page 243), to serve

Cut the eggplants into 1-inch cubes, sprinkle with salt, and let stand in a colander set over a bowl for 20 minutes (this will remove any bitter juices and stop the eggplant from absorbing as much oil during cooking).

Preheat the oven to 400°F. Line two cookie sheets with nonstick parchment paper.

Rinse the eggplants to remove the salt and add them to a bowl along with the paprika, cumin, and olive oil. Mix together well. Spoon them out evenly onto the prepared cookie sheets. Roast for 15 to 20 minutes, or until the eggplants are soft but not mushy. Set aside to cool.

Once cool, add the eggplants to a large bowl and combine with the remaining salad ingredients. Season to taste with salt and pepper. Drizzle the dressing over the salad and serve.

This is an absolute classic and still one of our most popular salads. The homemade croutons toasted in our herb oil elevate it to special status. We like to use day-old sourdough bread to make our croutons, but it's worth playing around and using whatever leftover loaf you have on hand (you can even use gluten-free bread if you like); just bear in mind that an airy bread with a lot of texture will give the best results.

CAESAR SALAD WITH AVOCADO & GREEN STRING BEANS

SERVES 6 TO 8 AS AN APPETIZER

4 eggs
7oz green string beans, trimmed
2 romaine or 4 baby gem lettuces, trimmed
2 ripe avocados, peeled and sliced
3½oz vegetarian Parmesan-style hard cheese, shaved
1 cup Vegetarian Dressing (*see* page 240)
salt

For the croutons
7oz sourdough bread
½ cup Herb Oil (*see* page 238)
large pinch of sea salt flakes

Preheat the oven to 350°F.

For the croutons, cut the bread into 1-inch cubes and mix together with the Herb Oil and sea salt flakes in a bowl. Spread onto a cookie sheet and toast in the oven for 15 minutes, turning them over about halfway through, until lightly golden on all sides.

Meanwhile, bring a saucepan of lightly salted water to a boil, add the eggs, and cook for 4 to 5 minutes (the yolks should be set but still quite soft). Remove from the heat, let stand for a minute, and then rinse under cold running water. Then peel off the shell while holding them under warm running water.

Bring another saucepan of lightly salted water to a boil, add the beans, and blanch for 2 to 3 minutes until tender. Rinse in cold running water and set aside to drain and cool.

Cut the eggs into quarters lengthwise and the lettuces into thick wedges. Toss the lettuce wedges in a large bowl with the avocado, beans, three-quarters of the shaved cheese, and the dressing. Divide the croutons and egg pieces evenly between serving plates and scatter with the rest of the cheese. Serve.

Like labneh (see page 43), ricotta is super-easy to make at home and doesn't require any fancy equipment except a little cheesecloth. In fact, when we were testing this recipe one quiet Sunday we found we didn't have any cheesecloth, so improvised and washed one of our cotton tote bags and used that instead! This recipe makes more ricotta than you will need, but don't worry! You'll find lots of uses for it. It's fantastic stirred through fresh pasta with a few spring vegetables, can be added to quiche fillings to give them an extra creamy, rich texture, and makes a delicious stuffing for fried zucchini flowers. Leftover ricotta will keep for up to 4 days in the refrigerator, sealed in a suitable container.

PRIMAVERA SALAD WITH HOMEMADE LEMON RICOTTA

SERVES 6 TO 8 AS AN APPETIZER

½ cup fava beans, defrosted if frozen
5oz sugar snap peas, trimmed
1 cup baby peas, defrosted if frozen
12 asparagus spears
olive oil
¼ cup Lemon Mint Dressing
  (*see* page 242)
1½oz pea shoots or watercress
sea salt flakes

For the Homemade Lemon Ricotta
4¼ pints milk
grated zest and juice of 1 large lemon
1 teaspoon salt

To make the ricotta, put the milk, grated lemon zest, and salt in a large saucepan and bring just to a boil. Add the lemon juice and remove from the heat, stirring gently, until curds start to form. Line a sieve with cleesecloth and set it over a bowl. Pour the curds and whey into the lined sieve, then tie the opposite ends of the cheesecloth together before tying the ends around a wooden spoon. Suspend the cloth in the air by hanging it across a sink or over a large plastic tub and let drain for 15 to 30 minutes (the longer it drains, the drier the ricotta becomes). Remove from the cheesecloth and store in an airtight container in the refrigerator until needed.

Preheat the oven to 400°F. Line a cookie sheet with nonstick parchment paper. Bring a saucepan of salted water to a boil, add the fava beans, and cook for 2 to 3 minutes, or until tender. Drain and refresh under cold running water. Remove the skins and set the beans aside. Steam the sugar snap and baby peas for 2 to 3 minutes, or until tender.

Snap the woody base off of the asparagus stalks. Lay the spears on the cookie sheet, sprinkle with sea salt flakes, and drizzle with olive oil. Roast for 5 to 10 minutes, or until tender but still firm. Let cool, then cut each spear in half. Add to a salad bowl with the dressing, pea shoots, and other vegetables and mix together, then spoon onto a serving plate. Crumble 3½oz of the ricotta over the top to serve.

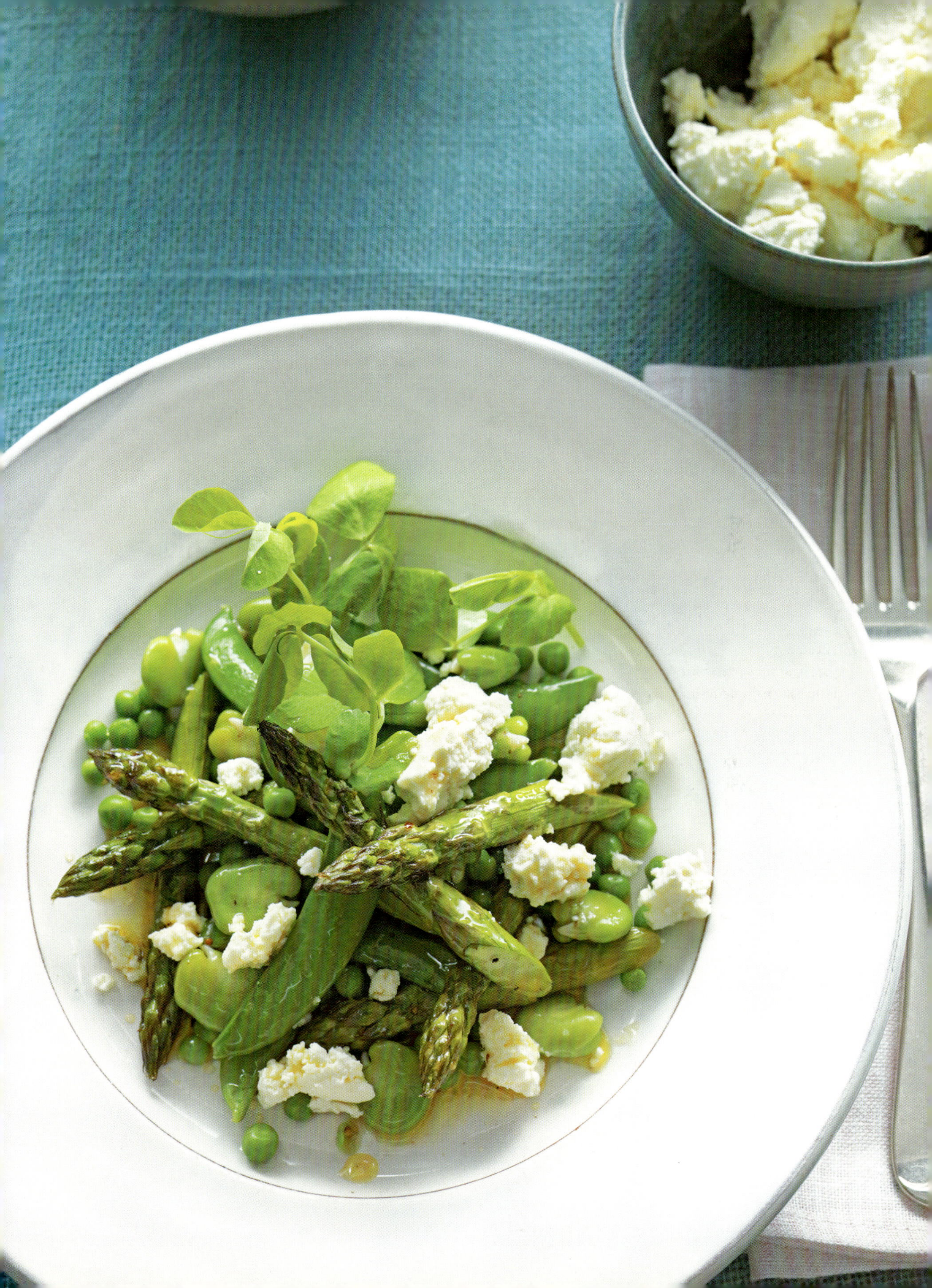

MAINS

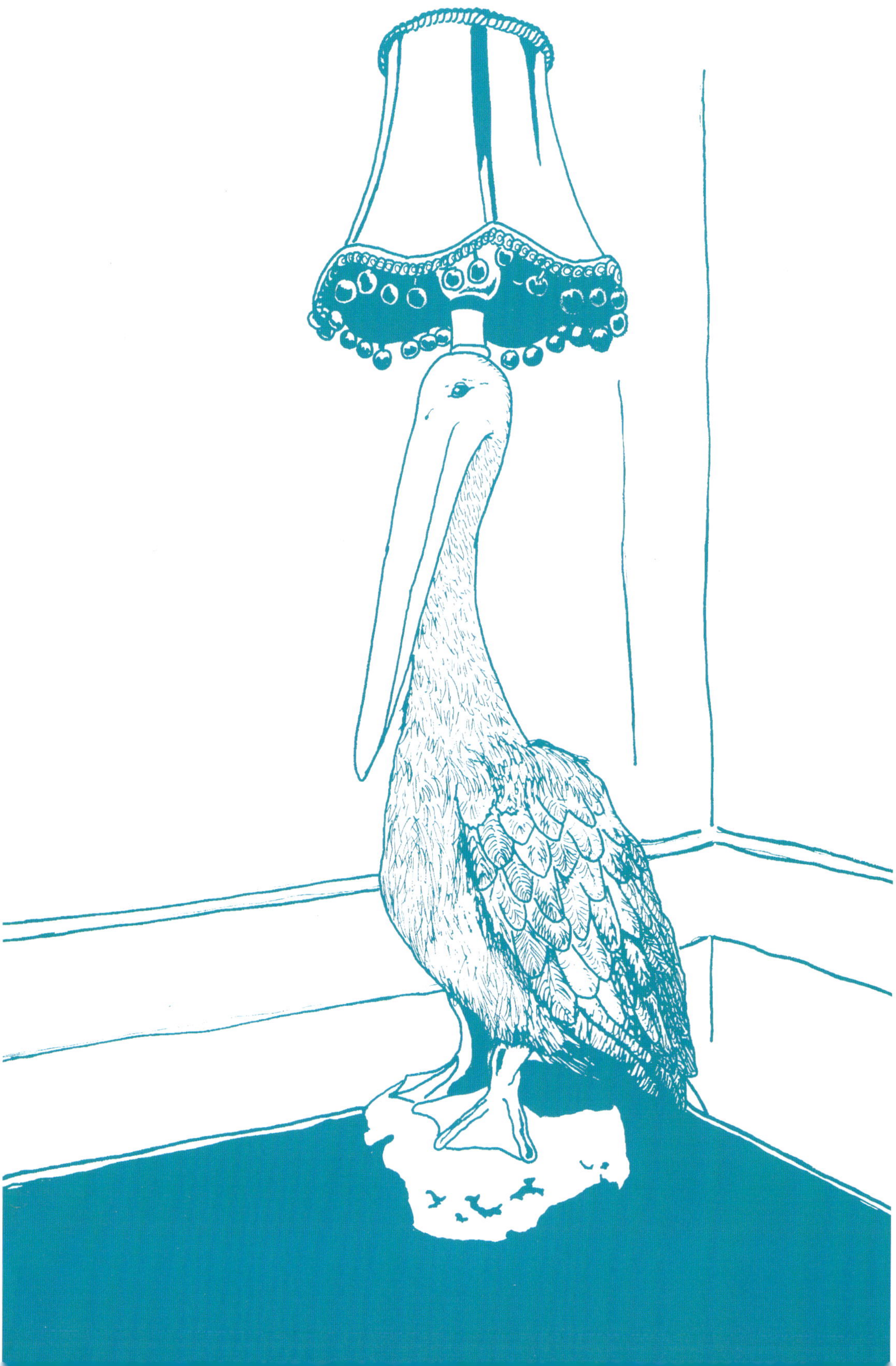

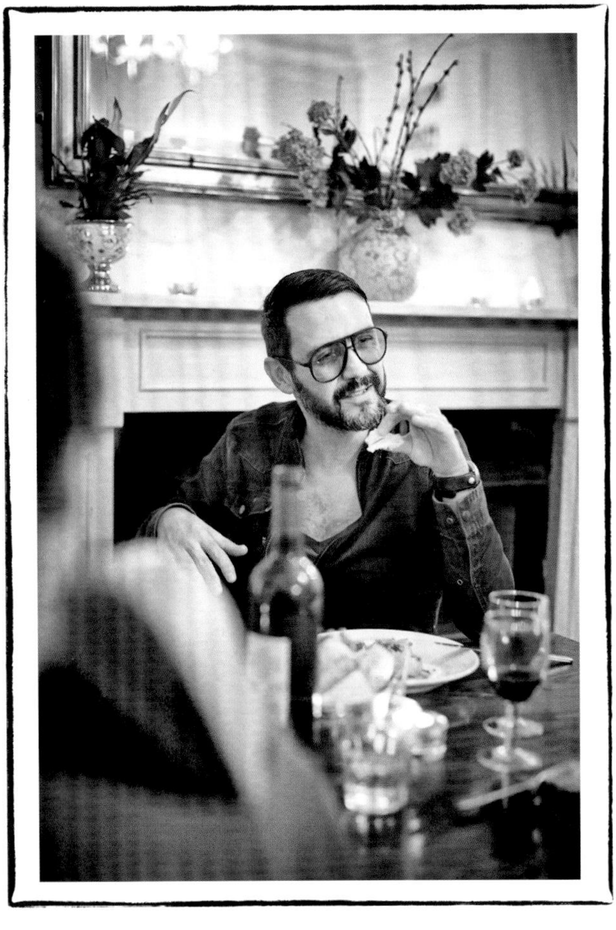

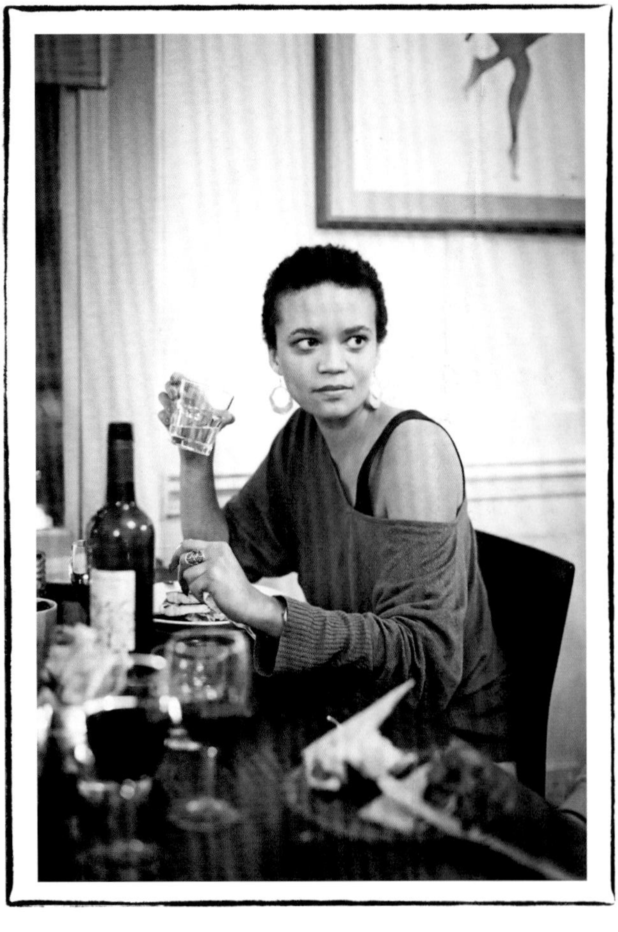

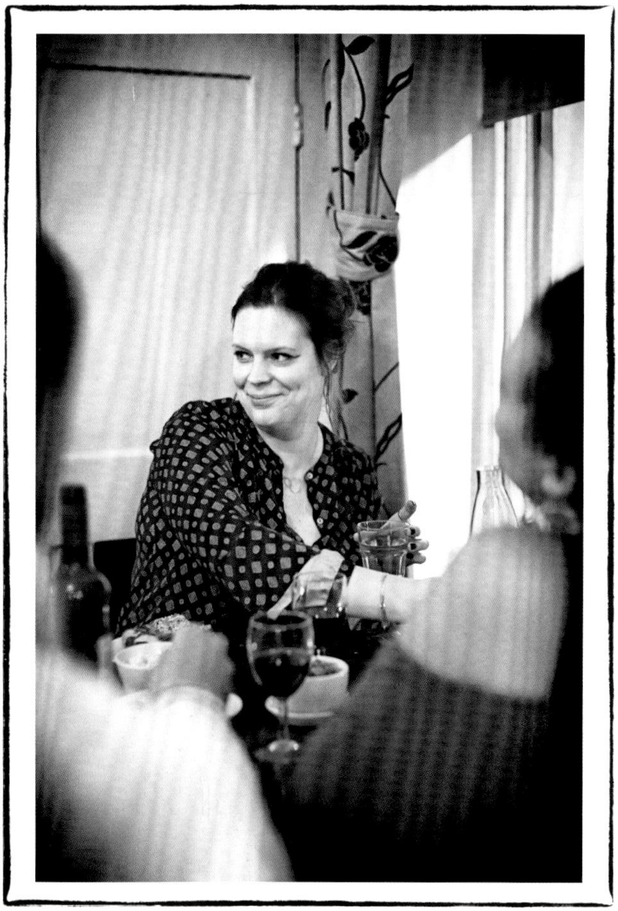

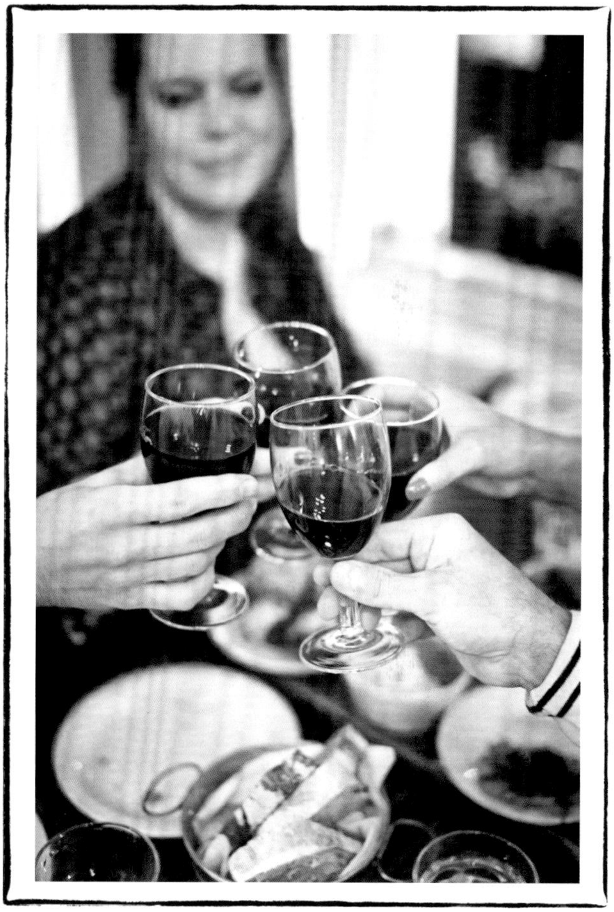

A great laksa is tricky to find, and a vegetarian version even more so, since a large part of a laksa's distinct flavor comes from the shrimp paste and fish sauce that are traditionally used. We've tried many ways to substitute these flavors, adding various fermented soybean sauces and pastes, but have come to prefer this simpler version, starring Thai hot mint and lime leaf. The tofu puffs act like a sponge, soaking up the flavors. They are available in Asian supermarkets.

PEA, CARROT, BELL PEPPER & TOFU LAKSA

SERVES 6

vegetable oil
3 x 14fl oz cans coconut milk
3½ cups vegetable stock
2½ tablespoons jaggery (palm sugar)
8oz rice noodles
2 carrots, thinly sliced
2 red bell peppers, cored, seeded, and diced
7oz sugar snap peas
1⅓ cups peas, defrosted if frozen
10oz tofu puffs

For the spice paste
6 lemon grass stalks
2-inch piece of fresh galangal or ginger root, peeled and minced
4 red chiles, seeded, and minced
6 garlic cloves, minced
½oz fresh turmeric, peeled or 2 teaspoons ground turmeric
15 lime leaves, middle stem removed
handful of Thai hot mint leaves
1 cup minced red Asian shallots or regular shallots
3 to 4 tablespoons vegetable oil

To serve
3 limes, halved
¼ cup crispy shallots
1 cup bean sprouts
handful of cilantro leaves, chopped

For the spice paste, remove the outer leaf of each lemon grass stalk, cut out the tough middle core, and finely slice the remainder. Add to a food processor with the chopped galangal and blend together for 5 minutes, then add the chilles, garlic, turmeric, lime leaves, mint, and minced shallots and continue to blend, adding the vegetable oil, to form a smooth paste.

Heat a splash of vegetable oil in a saucepan over low heat, add the paste, and cook for 15 minutes, or until it is toasted and lightly fragrant. Pour in the coconut milk and vegetable stock, stir in the jaggery, and bring to a simmer. Cook over a medium–low heat for 20 minutes, or until reduced to a fragrant, creamy broth.

Meanwhile, cook or soak the rice noodles in boiling water following the package instructions, then drain well and set aside. Blanch the vegetables in a saucepan of boiling water for no more than 1 minute, until just tender but still nice and crunchy. Drain.

Divide the noodles and tofu puffs between deep bowls, pour in the broth, and top each with a good handful of the blanched vegetables. Garnish with lime wedges, crispy shallots, bean sprouts, and chopped cilantro leaves. Serve.

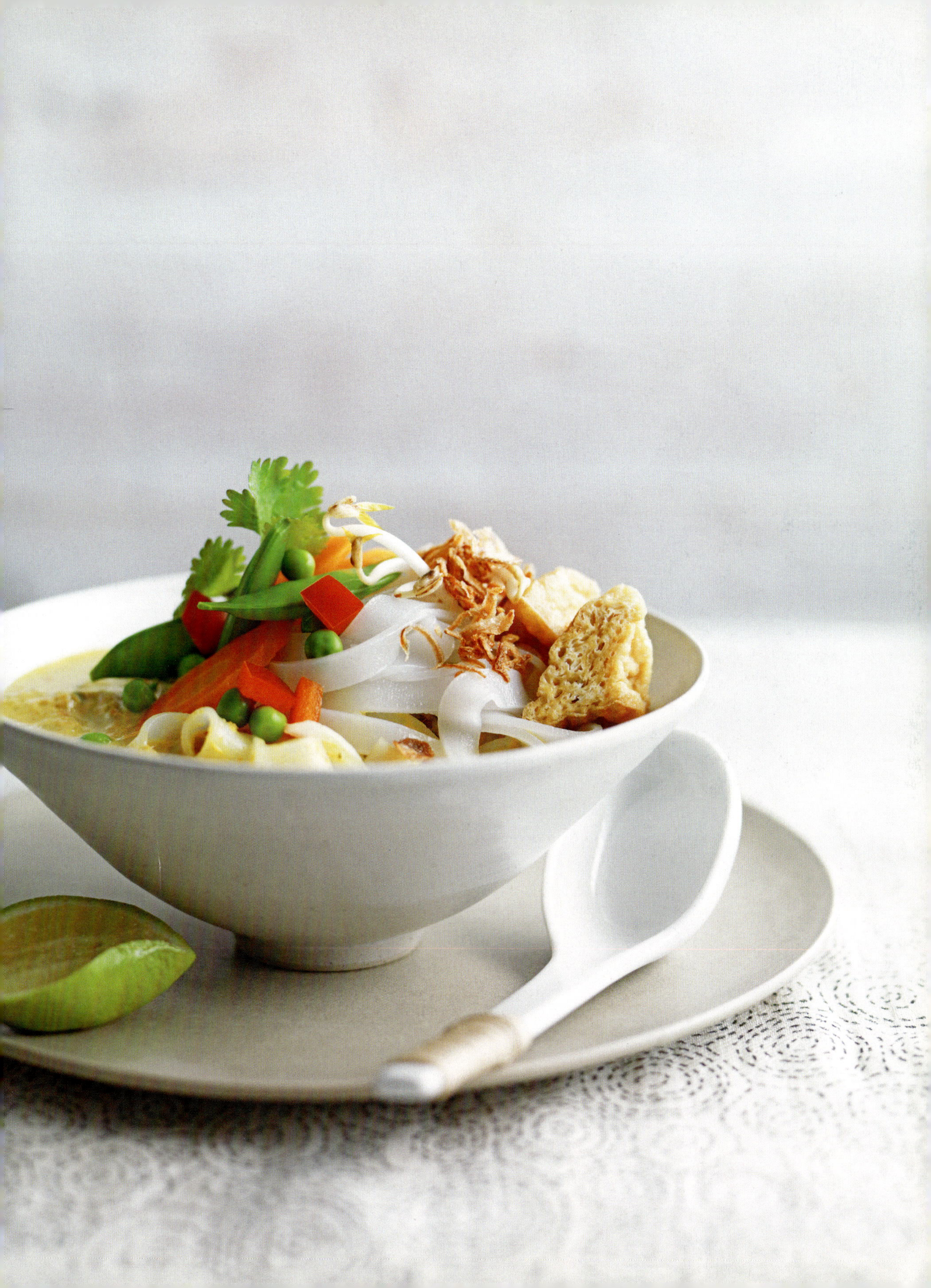

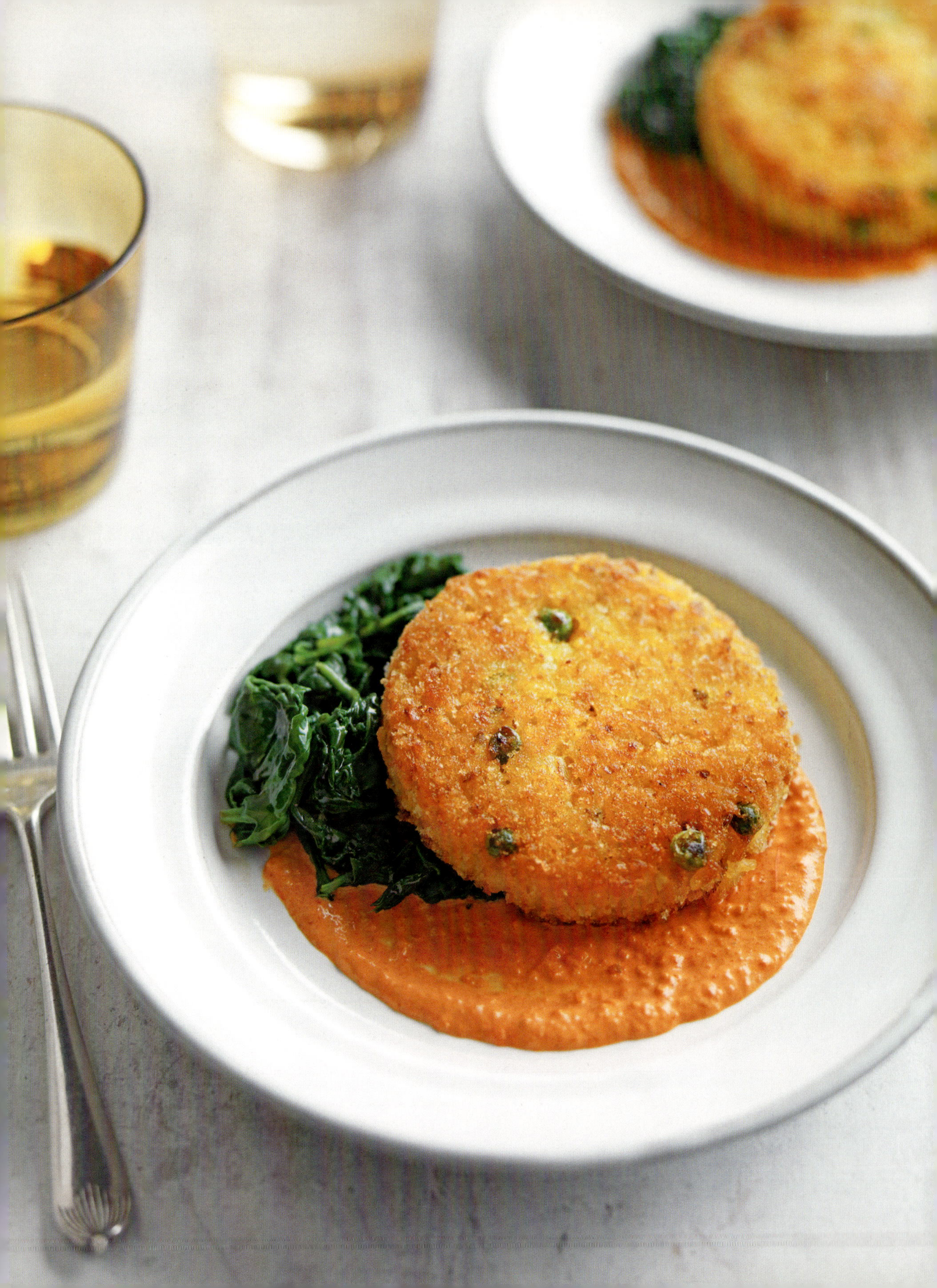

Risotto cakes are a great way to use up leftover risotto from a previous dinner, though they taste so good we make them from scratch like this. If you did want to make a simple risotto, just double the quantities and follow the basic rice-cooking method here, adding a little roasted pumpkin or squash. Enjoy it for dinner as a risotto and then use the extra to make these cakes the next day.

SAFFRON & PEA RISOTTO CAKES

SERVES 6

2 pints vegetable stock
light olive oil
1 onion, diced
6 garlic cloves, crushed
pinch of saffron threads
1 teaspoon fennel seeds
2 cups arborio rice
½ cup white wine
½ cup baby peas, defrosted if frozen
½ lb fresh or dried bread crumbs

To serve
Red Bell Pepper Sauce (*see* page 150)
wilted spinach

Bring the stock to a simmer in a saucepan. Heat a splash of oil in a separate saucepan, add the onion and garlic and cook, stirring, for 2 to 3 minutes, or until the onion has started to soften. Add the saffron, fennel seeds, and rice and sauté for another 2 minutes. Pour in the wine and let it bubble to reduce down until the pan is quite dry. Gradually add the stock, about a ladleful at a time, stirring frequently, until the rice is cooked but still firm.

Remove the rice from the heat and transfer to a small tray or large plate. Let cool for 10 minutes and then refrigerate for another 15 to 20 minutes, or until firm.

Once cool, remove the rice from the refrigerator and stir in the peas. Shape into cakes about 4 inches in diameter. Roll the cakes in the bread crumbs until evenly coated.

Heat a thin layer of oil in a wide skillet. Add the risotto cakes and fry for 2 to 3 minutes on each side until golden brown. Serve on individual plates with a spoonful or two of Red Bell Pepper Sauce and a little wilted spinach.

For a vegan alternative, pair this dish with **Tomato & Basil Sauce** (*see* page 151).

To make this gluten-free, coat the risotto cakes with **gluten-free breadcrumbs**.

One of our chefs, Alex Aimassi, first developed this as a lunchtime special. Now, it's one of our favorite dishes and flies out of the door whenever we make it. If you're using dried lasagne sheets, add a splash of water between layers of pasta when assembling this to stop it from drying out.

LONG-STEM BROCCOLI & ASPARAGUS WHITE LASAGNE

SERVES 8 TO 10

1½lb asparagus spears, trimmed and woody ends removed
1lb long-stem broccoli
1½lb fresh lasagne sheets
1 cup shredded vegetarian Parmesan-style hard cheese
1 cup sharp Cheddar cheese, shredded
salt

For the caramelized onion
a splash of light cooking oil (such as canola, peanut, or sunflower)
6 white onions, finely sliced
1 tablespoon superfine sugar

For the white sauce
3¼ quarts milk
1 white onion, cut into quarters
6 garlic cloves
3 bay leaves
1¾lb long-stem broccoli
2½ sticks butter
¾ cup all-purpose flour
2 bunches of basil leaves, chopped

For the caramelized onion, heat the oil in a saucepan over medium heat, add the onions, and cook for 15 minutes, stirring, until they begin to color. Add the sugar and continue to cook for 15 to 20 minutes, stirring occasionally, until the onions are dark golden brown and caramelized. Remove from the heat and set aside.

Meanwhile, for the white sauce, bring the milk, onion, garlic, and bay leaves to a simmer in a large saucepan over medium heat. Remove from the heat and set aside for 10 minutes so the flavors can infuse. Cook the broccoli in boiling water for 3 minutes, or until tender. Drain and coarsely chop. Melt the butter in a saucepan, add the flour, and stir together to form a roux. Strain the milk into the pan and whisk together to form a smooth sauce. Add the broccoli and basil to the sauce and blend with a stick blender until the sauce is smooth.

Bring a saucepan of salted water to a boil. Cut the asparagus widthwise into thirds and the broccoli widthwise in half, add to the water, and blanch for 2 minutes. Drain and set aside to cool.

Preheat the oven to 375°F. To make the lasagne, add a splash of water to the bottom of a 12 x 9-inch rectangular baking dish, then arrange a layer of lasagne sheets on top. Spoon half the caramelized onion, broccoli, asparagus, and half the grated cheeses evenly over the lasagne sheets, then ladle one-third of the white sauce evenly over the top. Repeat the layers of pasta, filling, and sauce, finishing with a third layer of pasta and a final layer of white sauce. Bake for 40 to 50 minutes, or until the pasta is cooked and the top is golden brown. If the lasagne is browning too much during cooking, cover it with foil.

Remove from the oven and let stand for 10 to 15 minutes to cool and set slightly before cutting into portions.

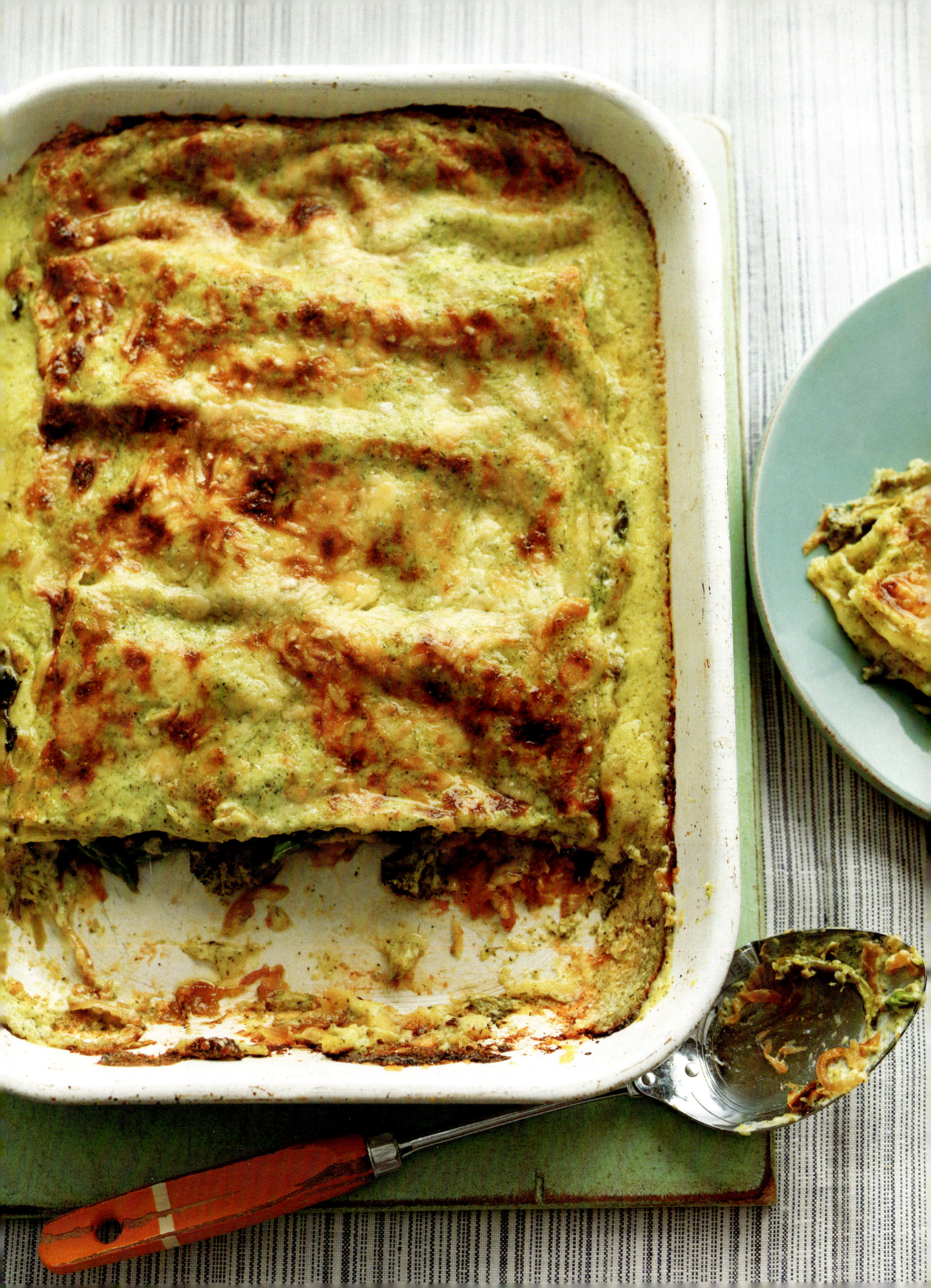

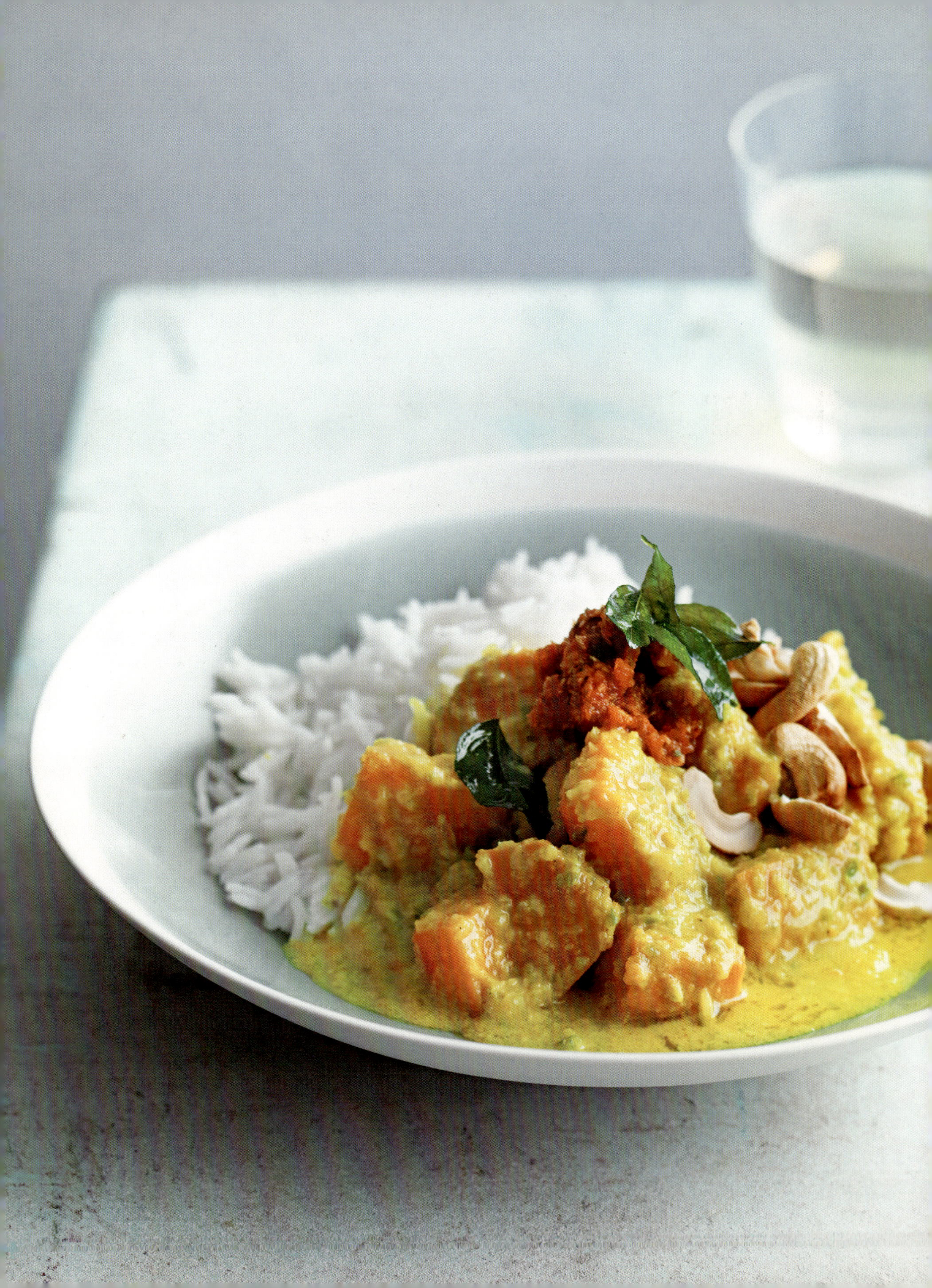

We partner this creamy, coconutty curry with our Garlic Rotis (see page 184) and Tomato & Coconut Sambal (see page 231). The curry powder recipe makes enough for future use. Just store the remainder in an airtight container in your spice collection. If you are short of time, 1 tablespoon of Madras curry powder can be used instead. Turmeric, Pea & Cardamom Basmati (see page 199) makes a nice alternative to plain basmati.

SRI LANKAN SWEET POTATO & CASHEW NUT CURRY

SERVES 6 TO 8

vegetable oil
3 large sweet potatoes, peeled and cut into 1½-inch chunks
1 large onion, diced
2-inch piece of fresh ginger root, peeled and chopped
3 garlic cloves
2 green chiles, trimmed and chopped
12 fresh or frozen curry leaves
2 teaspoons ground turmeric
1 cinnamon stick
4 x 14fl oz cans coconut cream
3½oz creamed coconut
1 tablespoon superfine sugar
2 cups basmati rice, washed thoroughly and strained
1¾ cups boiling water
salt
2 cups roasted cashew nuts, to garnish

For the curry powder
2 tablespoons coriander seeds
1 tablespoon fennel seeds
1 tablespoon cumin seeds
2 teaspoons fenugreek seeds
2 teaspoons black mustard seeds
¼oz fresh or frozen curry leaves

To serve (optional)
Garlic Rotis (*see* page 184)
Tomato & Coconut Sambal (*see* page 231)

First make the curry powder. Preheat the oven to 175°F. Roast the spices in the oven for 30–40 minutes, being careful not to burn them, until the curry leaves have dried out completely. Remove from the oven and grind to a powder using a mortar and pestle or spice/coffee grinder.

Increase the oven temperate to 400°F. Drizzle a little vegetable oil into a roasting pan. Add the sweet potato pieces, season with salt, and toss together thoroughly to coat. Roast for 15 minutes, or until cooked through, and set aside.

Blend the onion, ginger, garlic, and chiles together in a food processor to form a smooth paste. Heat a splash of oil in a large saucepan, add the curry leaves, and fry quickly for 10 to 15 seconds, being careful not to burn them. Add the paste and fry for 6 to 8 minutes over medium heat until toasted and fragrant. Add the turmeric and cinnamon and 1 tablespoon of the curry powder, season with salt, and fry for another 2 to 3 minutes. Then stir in the coconut cream, creamed coconut, and sugar. Bring to a simmer and cook for 15 minutes, or until the curry has thickened and reduced.

Now, cook the rice. Place the basmati in a saucepan, cover with the boiling water, bring back to a boil, and simmer, covered, for 10 to 12 minutes, or until the water has evaporated and the rice is tender.

Meanwhile, stir the cooked sweet potato into the curry and cook for another 6 to 8 minutes until heated through. Spoon the curry into bowls, garnish with roasted cashew nuts, and serve with the rice, and Garlic Rotis and Tomato & Coconut Sambal, if liked.

These escalopes are packed with rich flavors and benefit from being served with something fairly simple and fresh, like a chopped tomato and cucumber salad. While we have suggested pan-frying the escalopes here for the most crisp results, the more health-conscious among you might prefer to roast them in the oven for 10 to 15 minutes at 375°F. To make this recipe gluten-free, use gluten-free breadcrumbs.

FETA, CHILE & MINT-FILLED EGGPLANT ESCALOPE

SERVES 8

2 large eggplants
⅓ cup olive oil
¾ cup all-purpose flour
4 eggs, beaten
1¼lb fresh white bread crumbs
salt
mixed salad, to serve

For the filling
14½oz feta cheese, crumbled
2 red chiles, trimmed and minced
juice of 1 lemon
4 garlic cloves, minced
pinch of white pepper
1 bunch of mint leaves, finely chopped

Cut the tops off the eggplants and slice each lengthwise into 8 thin slices. Sprinkle the slices with salt and let stand in a colander set over a bowl for 20 minutes.

Preheat the oven to 350°F.

Rinse the eggplants to remove the salt and arrange them on 2 baking pans. Drizzle with 1 tablespoon of the oil and roast in the oven for 10 to 15 minutes, turning them over halfway through, until tender but not falling apart. Let cool on the baking pans.

For the filling, mix together all the ingredients in a bowl.

Take eight of the eggplant slices and spread a thin, even layer of the filling evenly over each of them. Press another eggplant slice on top to make a sandwich. Coat each of the eggplant escalopes with the flour, dusting off the excess, and dip first into the beaten egg and then into the bread crumbs.

Heat the remaining oil in a large nonstick skillet over low heat. Add a couple of the escalopes and gently fry for 4 minutes on each side until golden brown, then set aside on paper towels to drain. Repeat with the remaining escalopes and serve immediately with a mixed salad.

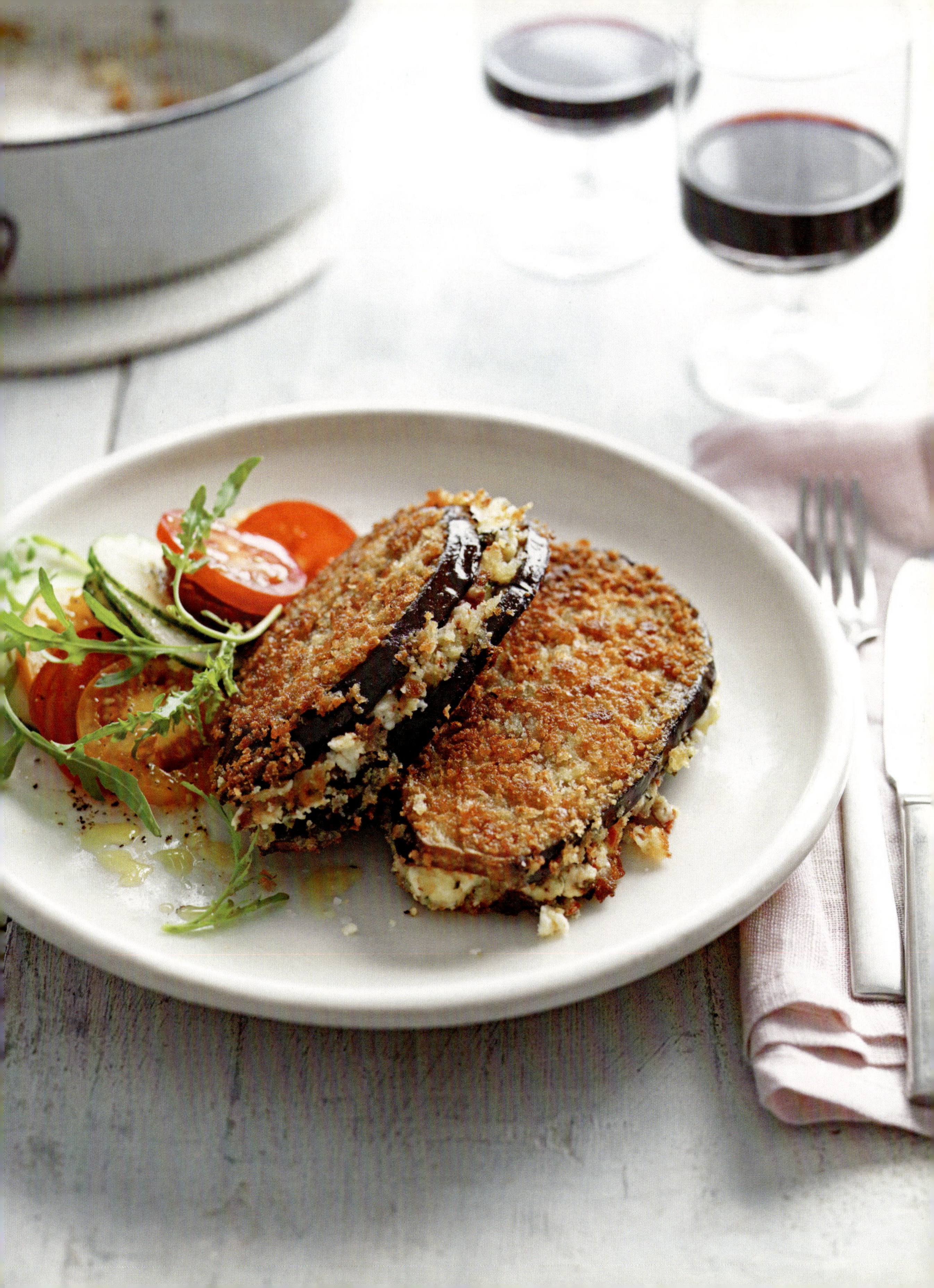

The Scotch egg is not, as its name suggests, from Scotland: it was invented by the London department store Fortnum & Mason in 1738. Despite its popularity, the egg's reputation has deteriorated over the years due to the proliferation of poor-quality supermarket varieties. It's a shame because, if cooked fresh with the yolks left slightly runny, they are unbeatable.

LEEK, CHIVE & CAPER SCOTCH EGGS
WITH MUSTARD BEURRE BLANC

SERVES 8

2lb potatoes, peeled and cut into even-sized pieces
2 tablespoons butter
2 large leeks, trimmed, cleaned, and finely diced
1 tablespoon Dijon mustard
1 tablespoon wholegrain mustard
1 bunch of chives, finely snipped
2½ tablespoons capers, coarsely chopped
8 large eggs, plus 3 eggs, beaten
¾ cup all-purpose flour
3½ cups panko bread crumbs
oil, for deep-frying
blanched asparagus, to serve
salt and pepper

For the Mustard Beurre Blanc
¾ cup white wine
3 large shallots, minced
2 tablespoons heavy cream
2¼ sticks cold butter, cut into cubes
1 tablespoon wholegrain mustard

Cook the potatoes in boiling water for 10 to 15 minutes, or until tender. Drain and mash until smooth. Melt the butter in a skillet, add the leeks, and cook, stirring, for 3 to 4 minutes, or until just tender. Let cool, then add to the mashed potatoes along with the mustards, chives, and capers. Stir to combine and let cool.

While the mixture is cooling, cook the whole eggs in a saucepan of boiling water for 4 minutes. Drain and refresh in cold water, then shell. Divide the cooled potatoes into eight equal portions. Arrange the flour, beaten egg, and bread crumbs in shallow bowls. Roll the eggs in the flour. Flatten a portion of mashed potatoes with your palm and fold it around the egg to form a ball. Roll this in the flour, then dip it into the beaten egg and roll it in the bread crumbs. Set on a platter, repeat with the remaining eggs, then let chill in the fridge.

For the beurre blanc, bring the wine and shallots to a boil in a saucepan. Cook for 3 to 5 minutes, or until reduced by two-thirds. Reduce the heat, add the cream, and slowly add the butter, whisking continuously, to form a smooth sauce. If it looks like the sauce is going to split at any point, add a little more cream. When all the butter is mixed through, remove from the heat, stir in the mustard, and season with salt and pepper to taste. Set aside in a warm place.

Half-fill a large saucepan or deep-fryer with vegetable oil and heat to 350°F, or until a cube of bread added to the oil browns in 30 seconds. Cook the eggs in batches for 5 minutes until golden brown. Serve with the blanched asparagus, drizzled with the Mustard Beurre Blanc.

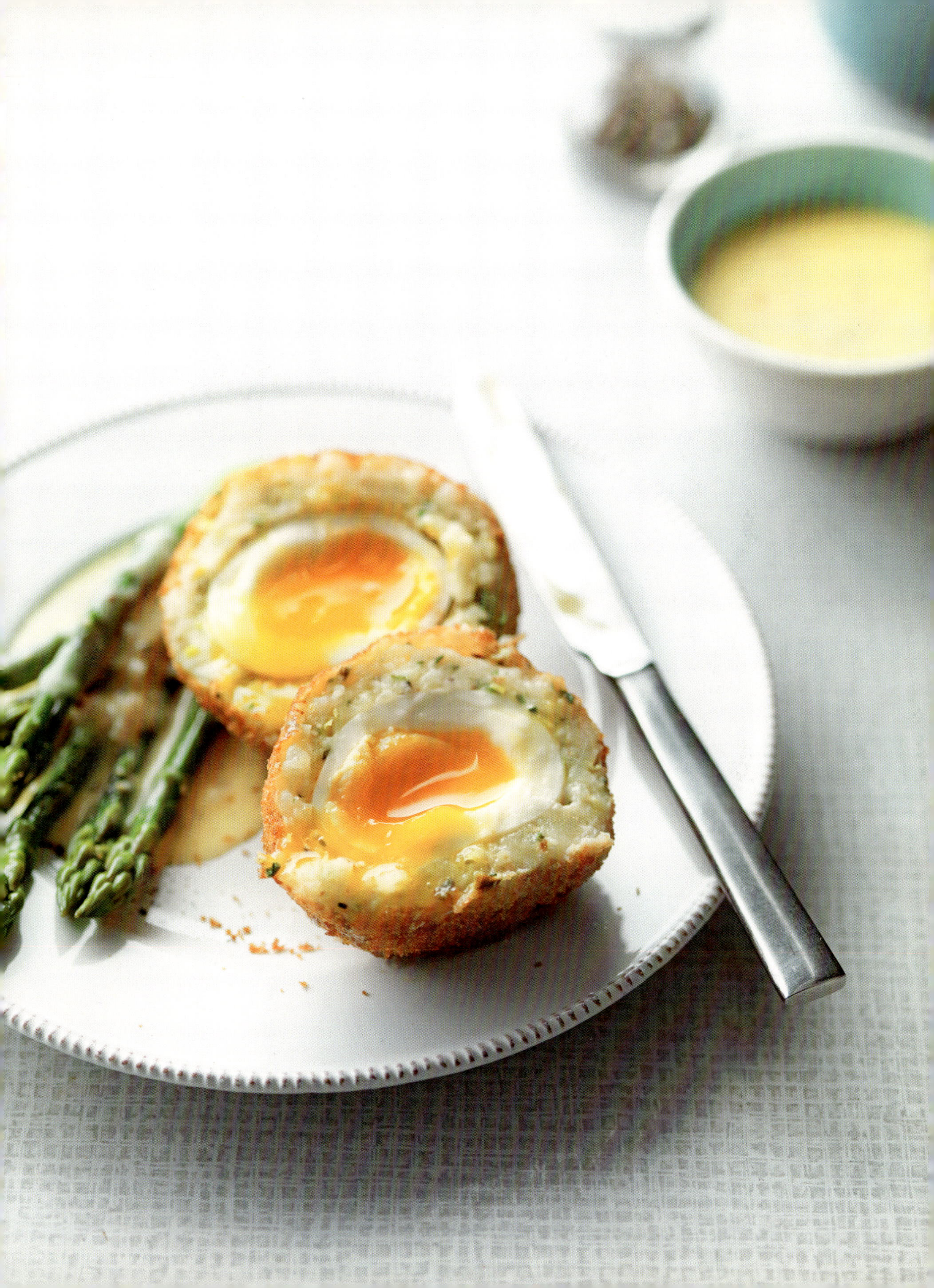

Definitely the sort of thing Jane would call a "winter warmer," this cozy, spicy, slightly sweet stew will keep the cold at bay on even the dullest and chilliest of days. If you're planning on entertaining then this is a great dish to prepare ahead of time and then simply reheat when your guests arrive, since the flavors will continue to develop long after cooking.

CINNAMON-SPICED
SQUASH & LIMA BEAN STEW

SERVES 6 TO 8

light oil (such as canola, peanut, or sunflower)
1 large butternut squash, peeled, seeded, and cut into 1-inch chunks
1 onion, diced
3 garlic cloves, minced
1 red bell pepper, cored, seeded, and diced
1 yellow bell pepper, cored, seeded, and diced
6 thyme sprigs
1 large rosemary sprig
2 bay leaves
1 cinnamon stick
1 teaspoon ground cinnamon
1 tablespoon smoked paprika
3 x 14oz cans diced tomatoes
¾ cup pitted kalamata olives
3 tablespoons maple syrup
1¾ cups water
3 x 14oz cans lima beans, drained and rinsed
salt and pepper

To serve
Chile Cornbread (*see* page 178)
fresh green salad

Preheat the oven to 400°F.

Splash a little oil into a roasting pan, add the squash pieces, season with salt, and toss together to coat thoroughly. Roast for 20 minutes, or until the pumpkin is soft and cooked through. Set aside.

Heat a drizzle of oil in a skillet, add the onion, garlic, and bell peppers and cook over very low heat, stirring, for 5 to 6 minutes, or until the onion has softened slightly. Add the herbs and spices, season with salt and pepper, and cook for another 5 minutes. Add the tomatoes, olives, maple syrup, and water, bring to a simmer, and cook over low heat for 30 minutes, stirring occasionally, until the sauce has thickened and reduced.

Stir in the roasted butternut squash and lima beans and cook for another 1 to 2 minutes, or until the squash is heated through. Spoon into bowls and serve with Chile Cornbread and a fresh green salad.

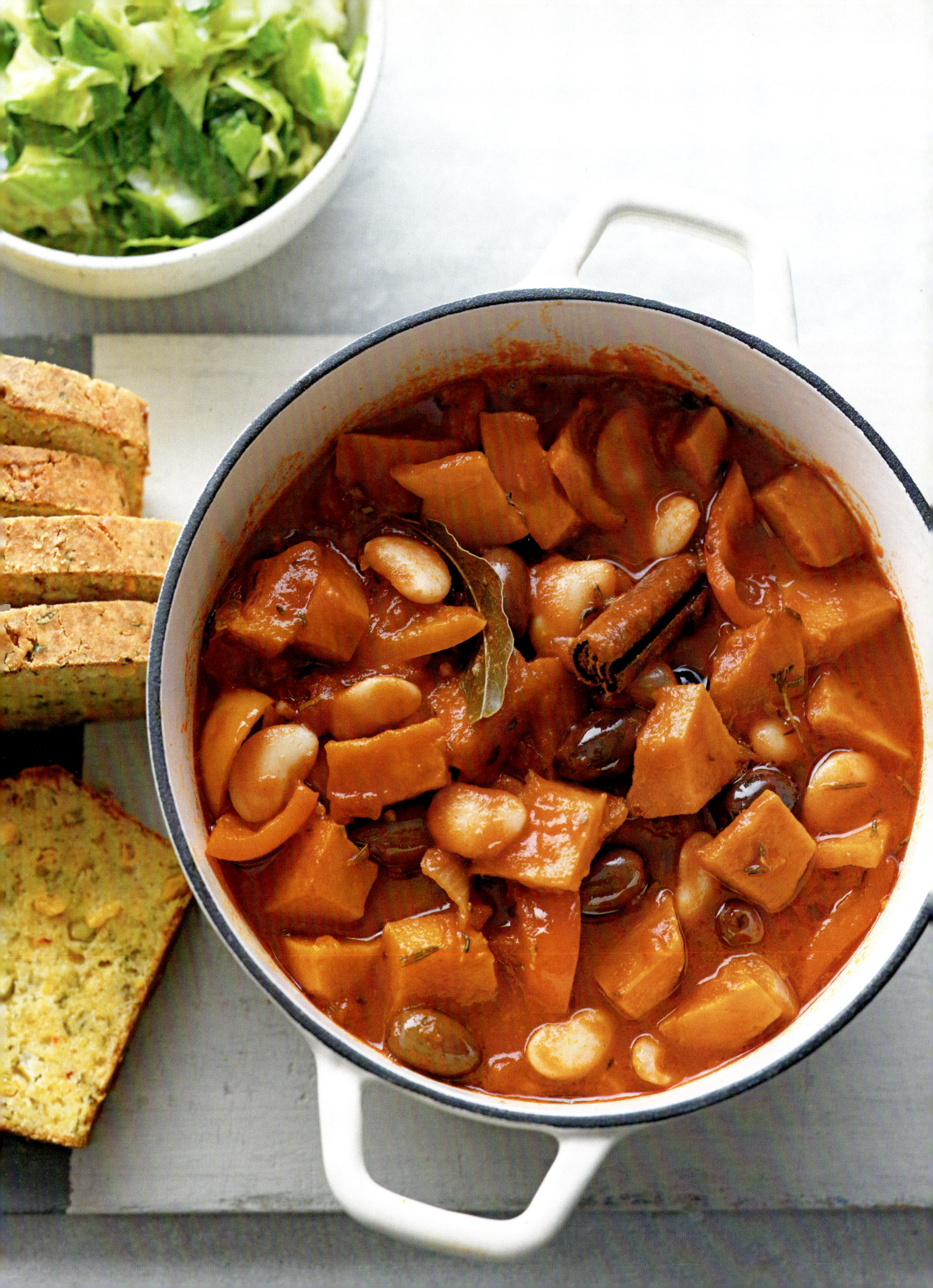

This classic Italian dish is just as good cold as hot, so can be made a day in advance and then served straight from the refrigerator alongside focaccia or with a simple arugula salad. While warm, it is great with our creamy Wet Polenta (see page 197). If you can't get baby eggplants you can substitute normal eggplants, cutting them first into half and then into wedges beforehand so they hold together in the sauce.

BABY EGGPLANT & ROAST BELL PEPPER CAPONATA

SERVES 6 TO 8

olive oil
2 red bell peppers
2 yellow bell peppers
1¾lb baby eggplants
1 large white onion, minced
6 garlic cloves, minced
handful of fresh basil leaves, chopped
4 celery stalks, trimmed, peeled, and sliced
1 tablespoon white wine vinegar
1 tablespoon superfine sugar
⅓ cup tomato paste
¾lb baby plum tomatoes or cherry tomatoes
10 pitted green olives
20 capers
1 small bunch of flat-leaf parsley, leaves picked and finely chopped
sea salt and pepper
Wet Polenta (*see* page 197), to serve

Preheat the oven to 475°F.

Drizzle a little olive oil into a roasting pan. Add the bell peppers and toss together thoroughly to coat. Roast for 15 minutes, or until the bell peppers have puffed up and are starting to split open. Transfer them to a bowl, cover with plastic wrap, and set aside to cool for 15 minutes. Once cool enough to handle, tear the bell peppers open, removing the cores and seeds. Peel off the skins and cut the flesh into strips ¾ inch thick. Set aside.

Peel half the skin off the eggplants in stripes and cut in half lengthwise. Rinse the eggplants under running water, drain, and sprinkle with a little sea salt. Heat a generous glug of olive oil in a large Dutch oven. Add the eggplants and sauté for 3 to 5 minutes, or until they begin to soften. Remove from the pan and set aside.

Add the onion and garlic to the Dutch oven and sauté for 5 minutes, or until the onion begins to soften. Add the basil and celery and cook, stirring, for another 2 minutes, then add the vinegar, sugar, and tomato paste. Cook, stirring, for 2 minutes then add all the remaining ingredients except the parsley. Bring to a simmer and cook, stirring occasionally, for 15 to 20 minutes until the sauce has thickened and reduced and the flavors have mingled.

Stir the parsley into the caponata and spoon onto plates. Serve with Wet Polenta.

A Ukrainian specialty, pampushki come in a number of different varieties. This savory version is an excellent, tasty way to use up leftover mashed potatoes; the raw grated pumpkin and potato create a wonderful crunchy contrast to the lovely, smooth mashed potatoes and melted cheese. Be sure to use a winter pumpkin with dense, firm flesh here and not a watery Jack-o'-lantern variety. A butternut squash will also work well.

PUMPKIN & POTATO PAMPUSHKI

SERVES 4 TO 6

1lb 2oz potatoes, peeled
14½oz pumpkin or butternut squash, peeled and seeded
olive oil
1 teaspoon finely chopped thyme
1 teaspoon finely chopped rosemary
gluten-free flour, for dusting (or regular flour, for non gluten-free)
salt and pepper

For the cheese filling
1 tablespoon of butter
1 teaspoon finely chopped rosemary
1 teaspoon finely chopped thyme
3 garlic cloves, minced
5oz soft goat cheese
1 tablespoon heavy cream or sour cream

To serve
wilted spinach
Tomato & Basil Sauce (*see* page 151)

For the cheese filling, melt the butter in a saucepan, add the herbs and garlic, and cook for 1 minute on low heat. Add to a bowl, crumble over the goat cheese, and mix well. Add the cream, season to taste, and stir together until smooth. Cover with plastic wrap and refrigerate.

Preheat the oven to 375°F. Cut a little less than half of the potatoes into even-sized pieces and add them to a saucepan of water. Bring to a boil and cook for 15 to 20 minutes until tender. Drain. While still hot, mash the potatoes and add to a bowl. Meanwhile, cut two-thirds of the pumpkin into even-sized chunks, add to a roasting pan, drizzle with oil, and roast for 25 to 30 minutes, or until very soft. Add to the bowl with the mashed potatoes and mash everything together.

Using the large side of your grater, grate the uncooked potato and pumpkin. Squeeze the grated vegetables with your hands to remove as much liquid as possible, then add to the mashed mixture along with the herbs. Season with salt and pepper to taste and stir well.

Divide the mashed mixture and the cheese filling into 4 to 6 portions, depending on the number of servings, and roll into balls. Take a ball of the mashed mixture, flatten it in your hand, and place a portion of cheese filling in the center. Wrap the mashed mixture around to seal it. Coat the pampushki in flour, dusting off any excess.

Heat some oil in a large nonstick skillet over low heat. Add the pampushki and fry for 5 minutes on each side until golden brown and crunchy. Serve with wilted spinach and warm Tomato & Basil Sauce.

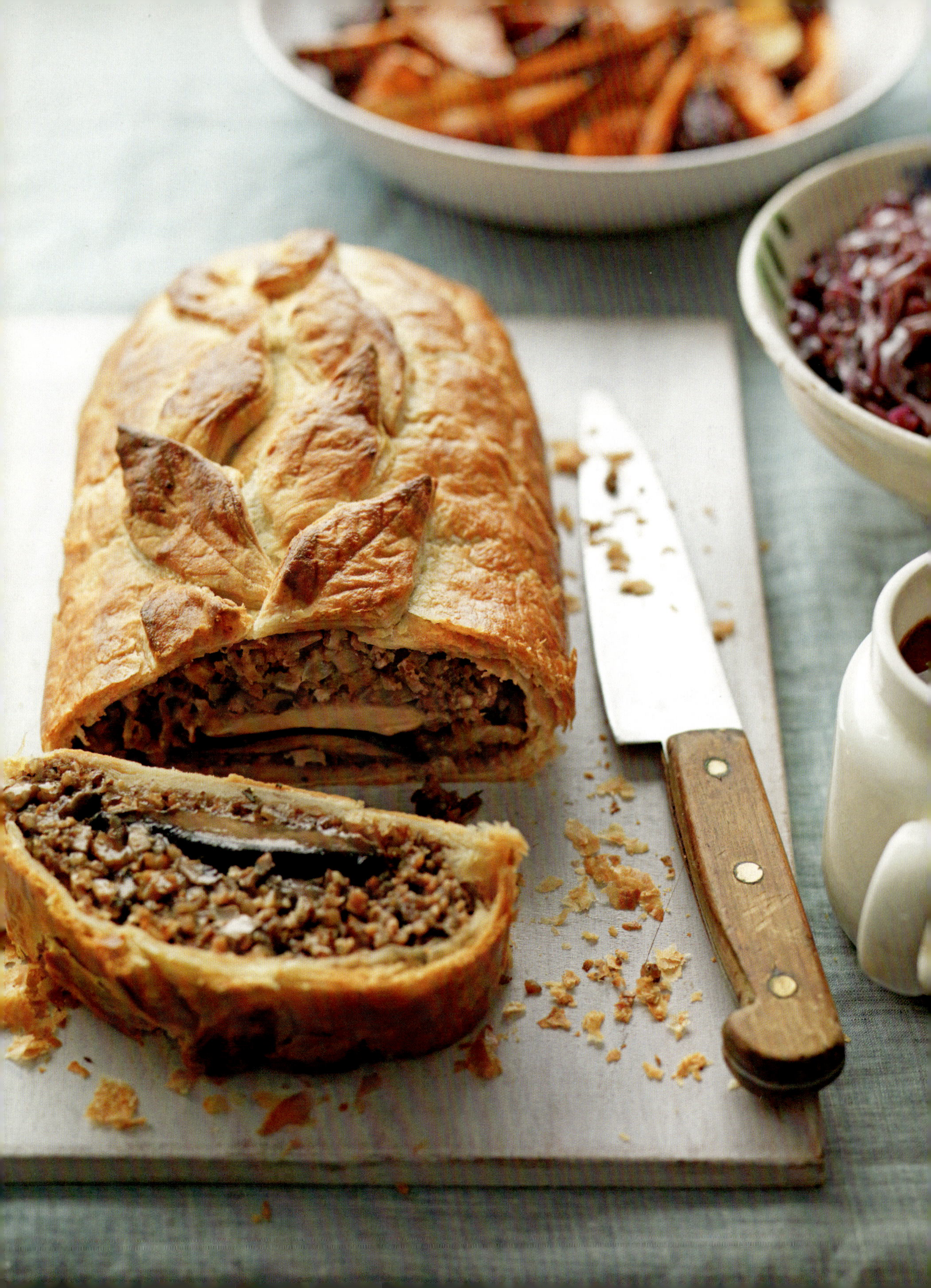

If you have an important meal that requires a centerpiece—Christmas dinner, for example—look no further. Slightly sweet and not overpoweringly rich, the filling can be made in advance, with the wellington assembled to bake later. While we like to make this vegan with the use of vegan puff pastry and soy cream to glaze, you can always use regular puff pastry and brush it with a little beaten egg, instead. We serve this with Braised Red Cabbage, Maple-roasted Root Vegetables, and Port Gravy (see pages 193, 188, and 236).

ROASTED PORTOBELLO MUSHROOM, PECAN & CHESTNUT WELLINGTON

SERVES 8 TO 10

light olive oil
1 large white onion, sliced
6 garlic cloves, minced
1 tablespoon chopped rosemary
1 teaspoon chopped thyme
2 tablespoons white wine
1 teaspoon dark brown sugar
1 cup pecans
7oz cooked and peeled chestnuts
1⅓ cups fresh white bread crumbs
truffle oil, to taste
1lb vegan puff pastry
2 tablespoons soy cream

For the roasted portobello mushrooms
1lb portobello mushrooms, trimmed
2 garlic cloves, sliced
1 thyme sprig, leaves picked
1 rosemary sprig, leaves picked
2 to 3 tablespoons olive oil

To serve
Braised Red Cabbage (*see* page 193)
Maple-roasted Root Vegetables
 (*see* page 188)
Port Gravy (*see* page 236)

Preheat the oven to 350°F. Line a cookie sheet with nonstick parchment paper.

To prepare the roasted portobello mushrooms, arrange the mushrooms on a baking pan, scatter with the garlic and herbs, and drizzle with the olive oil. Roast for 10 to 15 minutes, or until the mushrooms are tender but still holding their shape. Remove from the oven and set aside.

Warm a splash of olive oil in a small heavy saucepan, add the onion, garlic, and herbs and cook, stirring, for 15 minutes, or until the onion is caramelized. Pour in the white wine, stir in the sugar to dissolve, and cook for another 2 to 3 minutes. Remove from the heat and add to a large mixing bowl.

Put the pecans and chestnuts in a food processor and pulse into small pieces. Add to the mixing bowl along with the bread crumbs and mix everything together well.

Cut four of the portobello mushrooms in half and set aside (these will form the center of your wellington). Cut the remaining mushrooms into small chunks, add them to the mixing bowl, and mix everything together carefully using your fingers. Finally, add the truffle oil, a drop or two at a time, until you reach your desired strength of flavor.

Roll out the puff pastry onto a floured sheet of nonstick parchment paper into an 8 x 14-inch rectangle around $1/8$ inch thick. Trim the edges of the pastry to make it tidy and reserve the excess for decorating the top of the wellington.

Spoon half the mushroom and nut mixture lengthwise down the center of the pastry and spread out evenly, leaving a border of 2 to $2\frac{1}{2}$ inches down the longer sides. Arrange the portobello halves evenly over the mixture down the middle of the pastry then cover with the remainder of the mixture.

Brush the edges of the pastry with a little soy cream and fold over the ends and sides to roll the pastry around the filling. To do this, hold one side of the parchment paper and lift it so it starts to cover the filling. Peel the parchment paper back, leaving the pastry in place, then do the same with the other side. The pastry should overlap in the middle. Lift the wellington onto the prepared cookie sheet, turning it over so that the seam is on the bottom. Brush with some more soy cream and use the pastry trimmings to make stars, leaf shapes, or whatever you like, to decorate the top.

Bake the wellington for 1 to $1\frac{1}{4}$ hours, until puffed up, golden brown, and cooked through. Serve with Braised Red Cabbage, Maple-roasted Root Vegetables, and Port Gravy.

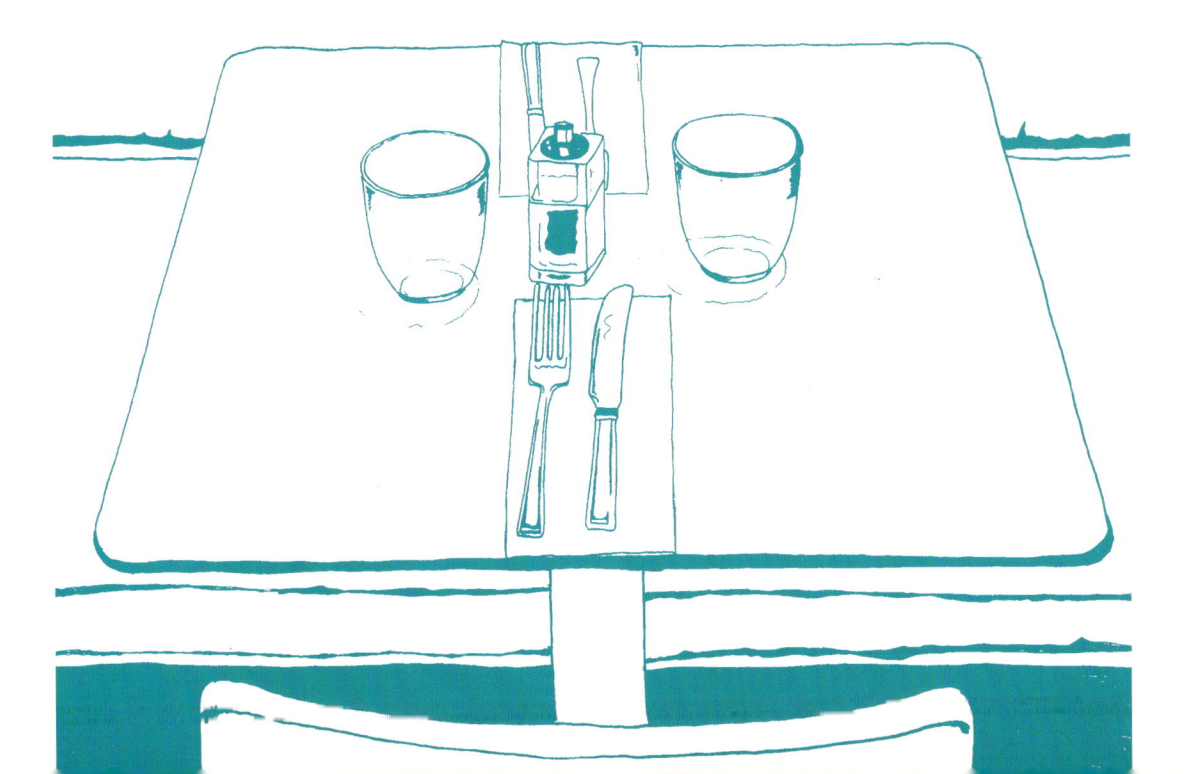

A vegetarian version of a classic steak and ale pie, our mushroom pie has been on the menu for more than a decade. It has all the winter's day appeal of the original, and is served with Roast Potato Wedges (see page 187) and mushy peas with mint for extra ballast.

WILD MUSHROOM & ALE PIES

MAKES 8 INDIVIDUAL PIES

3oz dried ceps
2lb mixed mushrooms (such as cremino or Portobello), trimmed, cleaned, and quartered
canola or light olive oil
4 small white onions, sliced
3 garlic cloves, minced
1 tablespoon light brown sugar
3 thyme sprigs, finely chopped
3 rosemary sprigs, finely chopped
1¼ cups brown ale
2½ tablespoons all-purpose flour
1 tablespoon wholegrain mustard
3 tablespoons dark soy sauce
2 pre-rolled vegan puff pastry sheets, thawed if frozen
soy cream, to glaze
pinch of dried basil
pinch of dried thyme

To serve
Roast Potato Wedges (*see* page 187)
mushy peas with mint

Preheat the oven to 350°F. Line a cookie sheet with nonstick parchment paper.

Rinse the ceps in warm water and strain to remove any sand or grit then add to a bowl and cover with boiling water. Soak for 15 minutes, then strain, reserving the soaking water, and coarsely chop.

Meanwhile, arrange the mushroom pieces on a baking pan, drizzle with oil, and roast for 15 minutes, or until just tender. Remove and set aside, adding any excess mushroom juices to the reserved cep water.

Heat a splash of oil in a large heavy saucepan. Add the onions and garlic and cook gently, stirring occasionally, for 10 to 12 minutes, until the onions begin to caramelize. Add the sugar, thyme, and rosemary and cook for another 10 minutes, until the onions are golden and sweet.

Pour in the ale, bring to a simmer, and cook for 5 to 10 minutes, or until the liquid is reduced by two-thirds. Sprinkle with the flour, stir it in until smooth, and then gradually add the mushroom juices, mustard, and soy sauce. Return to a simmer and cook, stirring frequently, for 20 to 25 minutes, or until thickened. Stir in the roasted mushrooms and ceps to heat them through. Keep warm.

While the pie mixture is cooking, cut the pastry into 5-inch squares. Place on the prepared cookie sheet and brush with soy cream. Scatter with the herbs and bake for 20 minutes, or until puffed and golden. Remove from the oven, let cool slightly, and then arrange on serving plates. Cut a square out of the top of each pastry, spoon the hot pie filling into the hole, and replace the lid. Serve with Roast Potato Wedges and mushy peas with mint.

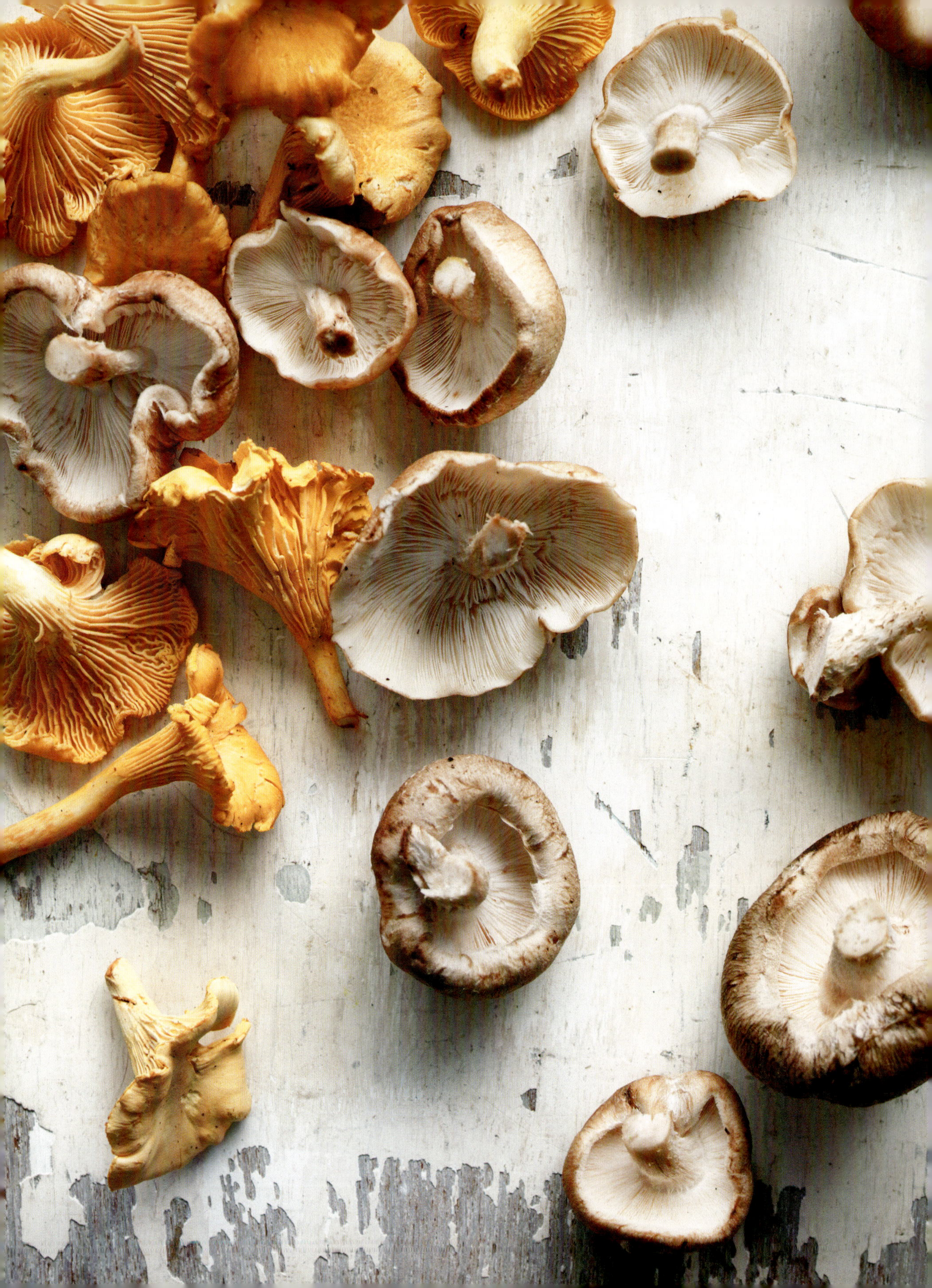

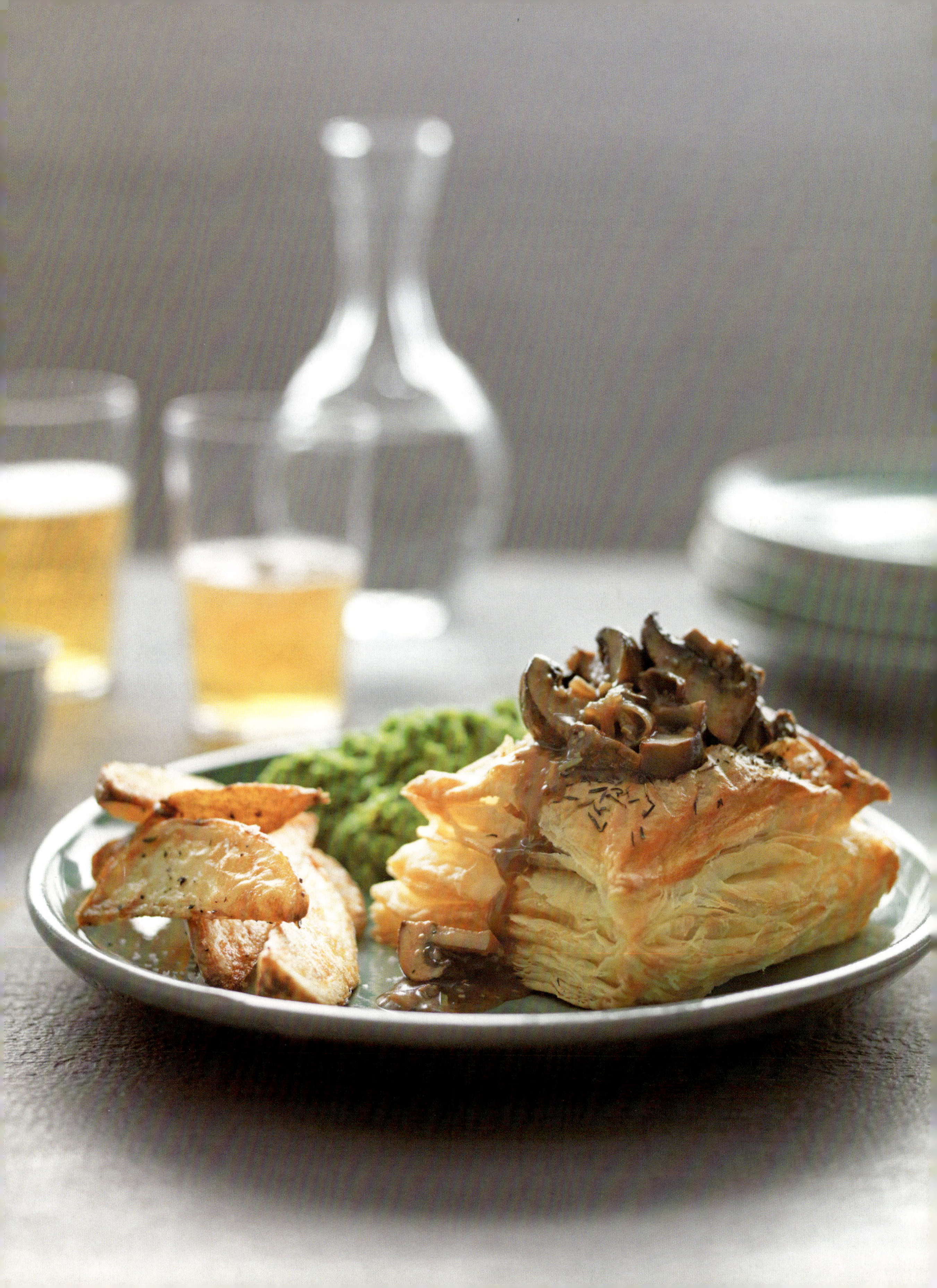

A filling and flavorful main course packed full of bright colors to cheer up your table in the fall. You can make the chili in advance to cut down on the labor involved here and, if you can't find baby pumpkins, you can always use the round bottom part of a butternut squash.

BLACK BEAN CHILI-FILLED BABY PUMPKINS
WITH TOASTED COCONUT RICE

SERVES 8

8 baby pumpkins or winter squash, scrubbed clean
light oil

For the Black Bean Chili
light oil
7oz pumpkin, cut into 1-inch cubes
1 zucchini, cut into 1-inch cubes
1 white onion, finely diced
3 garlic cloves, minced
2 celery stalks, minced
1 red chile, trimmed and minced
1 tablespoon chopped thyme leaves
3 tablespoons tomato paste
2 x 14oz cans diced tomatoes
1 tablespoon dark brown sugar
½ cinnamon stick
2 chipotle chiles, coarsely chopped or 3 tablespoons chipotle chile paste
½ teaspoon paprika
1¾ cups water
2 cups canned black beans
1 small bunch of cilantro, leaves picked and chopped

For the Toasted Coconut Rice
light oil
2 green chiles, minced
1lb basmati rice, washed
1¼ cups water
3 tablespoons coconut milk
1 cup desiccated coconut

Preheat the oven to 400°F.

For the black bean chili, drizzle a little oil into a roasting pan. Add the pumpkin pieces and toss together thoroughly to coat. Roast for 10 minutes. Add the zucchini and cook for another 5 to 10 minutes, or until the vegetables are tender. Set aside.

Heat a splash of oil in a large heavy saucepan, add the onion, and cook gently, stirring, for 5 minutes, until softened and translucent. Add the garlic, celery, chile, and thyme and cook for another 10 minutes, then add the tomato paste, tomatoes, sugar, cinnamon, chiles, paprika, and water and bring to a simmer. Cook for 20 minutes or so, stirring frequently, until the chili has thickened and reduced. Add the beans and cook for another 10 minutes. Then stir in the roasted vegetables and cilantro and keep the chili warm.

Meanwhile, roast the baby pumpkins. Cut the top off of each in a neat circle. Scoop out the seeds with a spoon. Place on a baking pan, drizzle with a little oil, and bake for 20 to 30 minutes, or until the flesh is cooked. Cover with foil to keep warm until needed.

For the toasted coconut rice, heat a drizzle of oil in a saucepan, add the chiles, and cook, stirring, for 2 minutes. Add the rice and cook, stirring, for 2 minutes, then cover with the water. Bring to a boil and simmer for 10 to 12 minutes, or until the water has evaporated and the rice is tender. Remove from the heat, pour in the coconut milk, and set aside, covered, for 5 minutes. Stir in the desiccated coconut to finish. To serve, place a large scoop of rice on each plate, fill the warm pumpkins with the chili, and place one on each plate beside the rice.

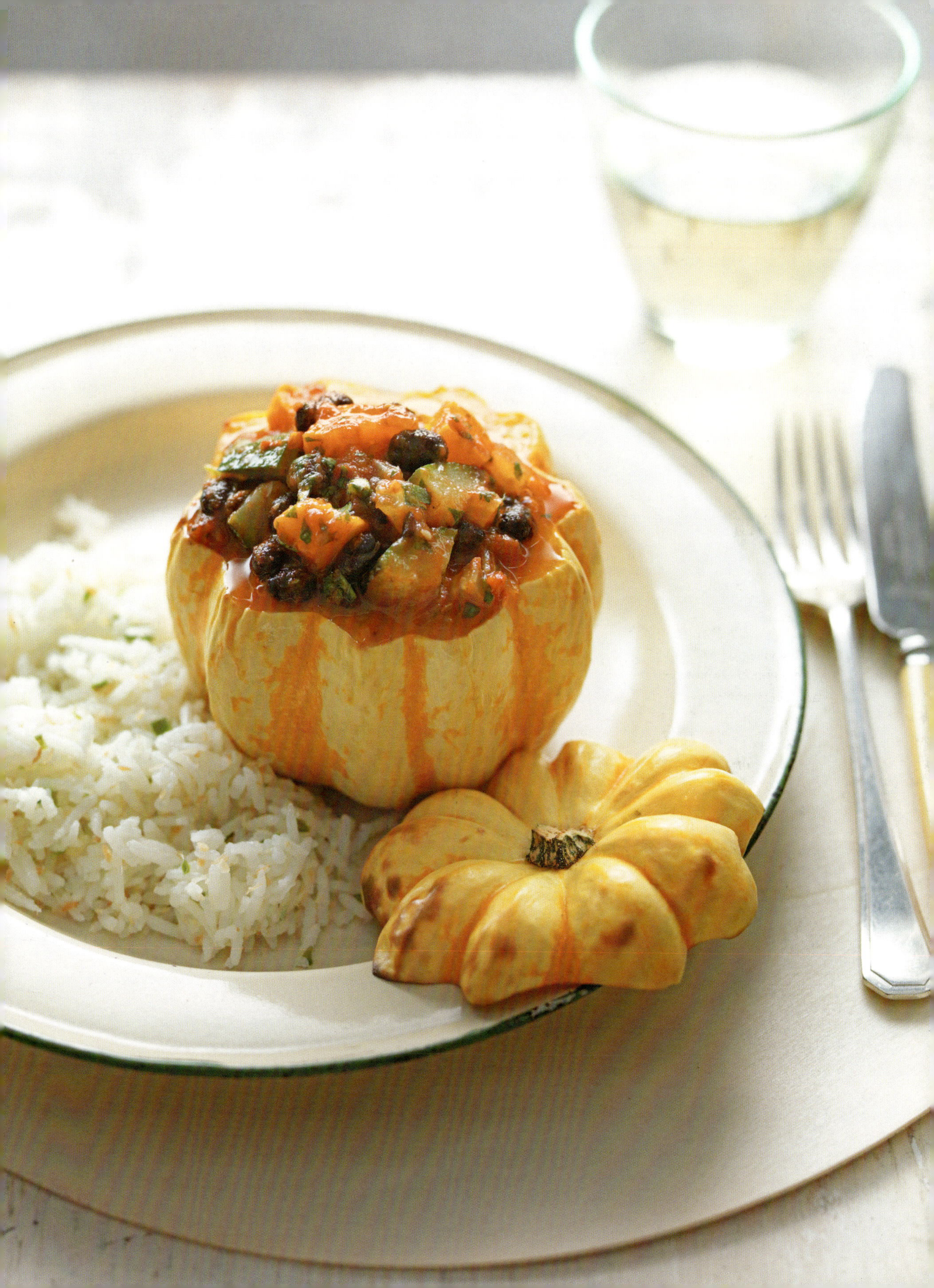

GF

Traditionally, this much-adapted Russian recipe is made with beef, but here we have changed the filling for a mixture of earthy mushrooms along with the rather unusual addition of lapsang souchong tea to give this dish a slightly smoky taste. Seeking out a variety of mushrooms including ceps, cremino, and meadow mushrooms will definitely help give the stroganoff more punch. We like to serve this with our Walnut & Leek Pilaf (see page 199).

LAPSANG-SCENTED MUSHROOM STROGANOFF

SERVES 6 TO 8

2lb mixed mushrooms (such as ceps, cremino, and meadow mushrooms), trimmed
light cooking oil (such as canola, peanut, or sunflower)
2 lapsang souchong tea bags
2½ cups boiling water
2 tablespoons butter
2 onions, finely sliced
6 garlic cloves, minced
1 tablespoon smoked paprika
2 tablespoons corn flour
1¾ cups heavy cream
2 tablespoons Dijon mustard
2 tablespoons tomato paste
1 cup sour cream
1 bunch of dill leaves, chopped
salt and pepper
Walnut & Leek Pilaf (*see* page 199), to serve

Preheat the oven to 375°F.

Cut the mushrooms into even, bite-size pieces. Drizzle a little oil into a roasting pan, add the mushrooms, and toss together thoroughly to coat. Roast for 10 to 15 minutes, or until the mushrooms are tender but have not yet begun to shrivel. Set aside.

Put the lapsang souchong tea bags into a bowl, cover with the boiling water, and let stand to infuse for 4 minutes. Remove and discard the tea bags and set the tea aside.

Melt the butter in a large saucepan over medium heat, add the onions, and cook, stirring, for 5 minutes, or until soft. Add the garlic and paprika and fry for another 2 to 3 minutes. Then add the corn flour and stir together well. Pour in the tea and heavy cream and stir in the mushrooms, mustard, and tomato paste. Bring to a simmer and cook gently for 15 minutes, stirring occasionally, until the sauce has begun to reduce and thicken slightly.

Add the sour cream and cook for another 5 minutes, or until the stroganoff is thick and creamy. Season with salt and pepper to taste. Divide between serving plates, scatter with the chopped dill, and serve with Walnut & Leek Pilaf.

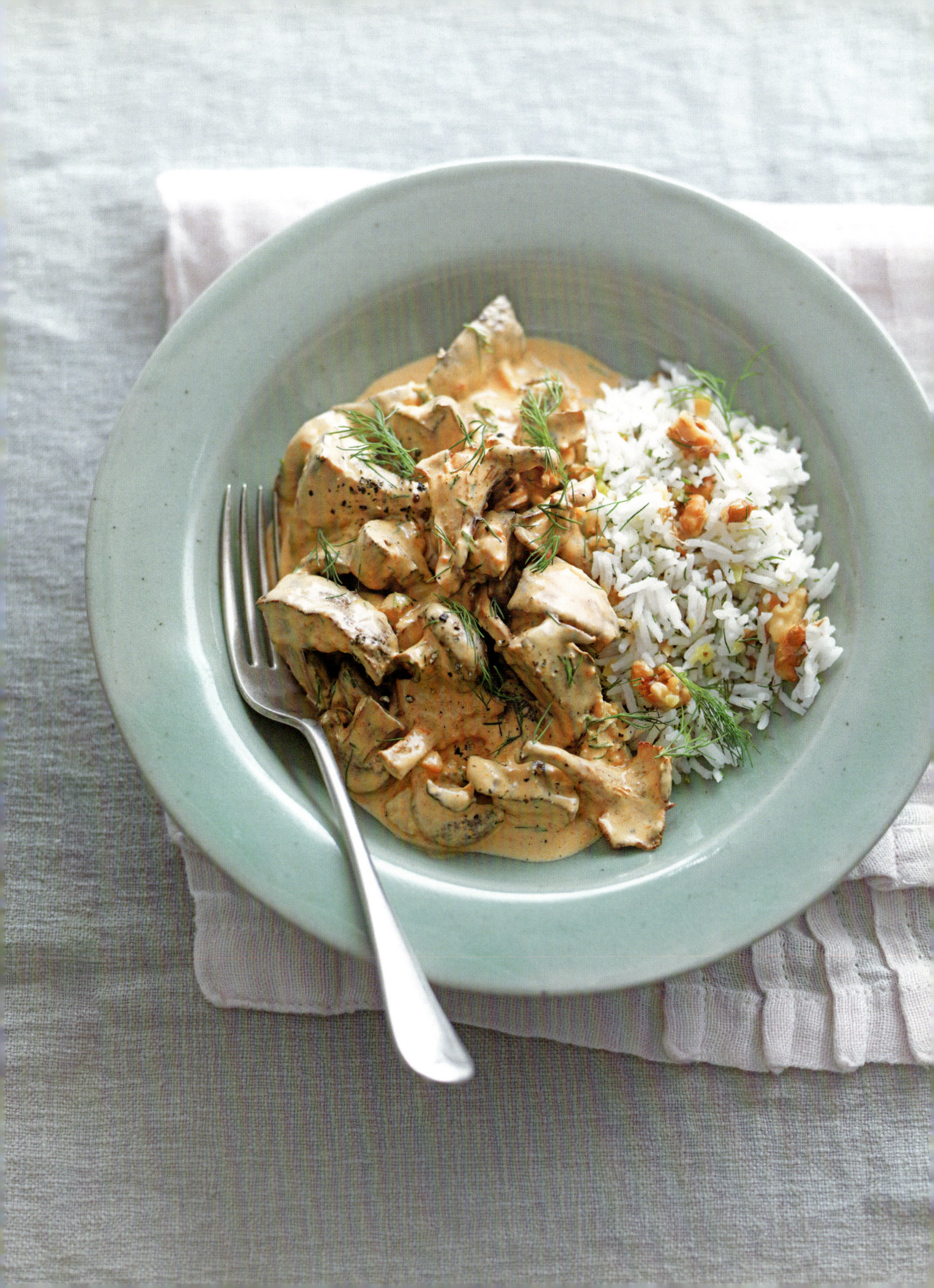

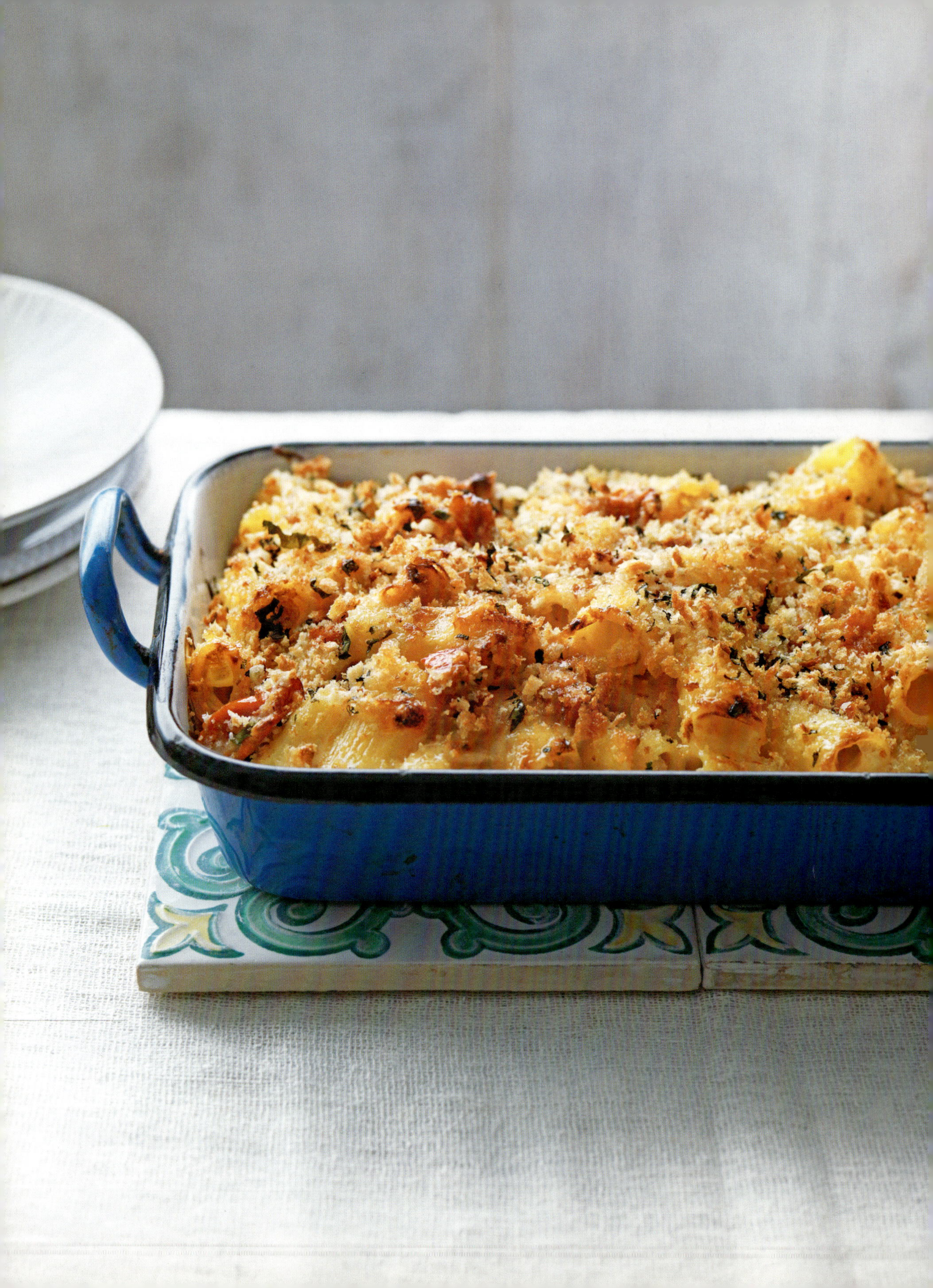

A simple, classic dish, which we've pimped up with the addition of sun-dried tomatoes, caramelized onions, and a basil crumb topping. When cooking something this simple, though, it's the basics that really need looking after. So, try to use a really good cheese here and don't skimp on the pasta either, because you will be able to taste the difference.

MACARONI & CHEESE WITH SUN-DRIED TOMATOES & BASIL CRUMB TOPPING

SERVES 8 TO 10

1lb macaroni
olive oil
1lb white onions, sliced
2 teaspoons turbinado sugar
½lb fresh bread crumbs
3 garlic cloves, minced
1 bunch of basil leaves, chopped
5oz sun-dried tomatoes in oil, chopped
salt and pepper

For the cheese sauce
3¼ pints milk, plus extra if needed
1 onion, sliced
3 bay leaves
1 stick butter, plus extra for greasing
1¼ cups all-purpose flour
7oz sharp Cheddar cheese, shredded
3½oz vegetarian Parmesan-style hard cheese, shredded

Preheat the oven to 375°F. Grease a 12 x 9-inch rectangular baking dish. Bring a saucepan of salted water to a boil, add the macaroni, and cook following the package instructions until al dente. Drain and set aside.

Heat a splash of oil in a saucepan over medium heat, add the onions, and cook, stirring occasionally, for 10 to 15 minutes, or until golden brown. Add the sugar, season with salt and pepper, and cook for another 10 minutes, or until the onions are dark golden. Remove from the heat.

Put the bread crumbs, garlic, and chopped basil into a food processor and blend together. Set aside.

For the cheese sauce, heat the milk in a saucepan over medium–low heat, add the onion and bay leaves, and bring to a simmer. Set aside for at least 10 minutes to allow the flavors to infuse. Melt the butter in a separate saucepan over low heat, add the flour, and stir together to make a roux. Using a strainer, gradually add the milk, stirring continuously with a whisk to stop it from becoming lumpy. Stir in the shredded cheeses, which will melt and help thicken the sauce. If the sauce is getting too thick, add another splash of milk to thin it down.

Pour the sauce into a large mixing bowl and stir in the cooked pasta, onions, and sun-dried tomatoes. Combine well then spoon it into the prepared baking dish, cover with the bread-crumb mixture, and drizzle a little olive oil evenly on top. Bake in the oven for 20 minutes, or until golden brown. Let cool for 10 minutes before serving.

V — **GF** *if served without couscous*

An underrated vegetable in our opinion, cauliflower is great for absorbing flavors while retaining a nice texture. If you can get it, romanesco cauliflower looks beautiful in this dish. This recipe was developed to accommodate people who don't eat onions or garlic, with the ginger, celery, carrot, and chile providing the base layers of flavor in their place. It's a good dish to make in advance because the flavors will deepen and develop.

CAULIFLOWER & GREEN OLIVE TAGINE

SERVES 6 TO 8

1 large cauliflower, separated into small florets
light cooking oil (such as canola, peanut, or sunflower)
2 celery stalks, trimmed and finely diced
5 carrots, cut into 1½-inch chunks
10oz fresh ginger root, peeled and finely chopped
2 red chiles, trimmed and minced
2 teaspoons ground cumin
2 teaspoons paprika
½ teaspoon ground turmeric
pinch of cayenne pepper
½ teaspoon vegetable bouillon powder
3 x 14oz cans diced tomatoes
3½ cups water
1¼ cups pitted green olives
2 preserved lemons, seeded and finely sliced
1 teaspoon superfine sugar
2 x 14oz cans chickpeas, drained and rinsed
1 bunch of cilantro, leaves picked and chopped
salt and pepper

To serve
Apricot & Pistachio Couscous (*see* page 192)

Bring a pan of salted water to a boil, add the cauliflower florets, and blanch for 2 to 3 minutes, or until just tender. Drain and set aside.

Add a splash of oil to a large saucepan or Dutch oven over medium heat, add the celery, carrot, ginger and chile, and sauté for 5 minutes, or until the celery is beginning to soften. Add the spices and bouillon powder, lower the heat, and cook, stirring, for another few minutes before adding the diced tomatoes, water, olives, preserved lemons, cauliflower, and sugar. Bring to a simmer and let cook for 20 minutes, stirring occasionally. Add the chickpeas and cook for another 10 minutes, or until the cauliflower is tender and all the flavors have come together. Season to taste with salt and pepper.

Remove from the heat and stir through the cilantro. Serve with Apricot & Pistachio Couscous.

If you don't really like cauliflower, this recipe also works well with large chunks of **roast eggplant** or, for a wintery version, **roast pumpkin**.

If you find the tagine too spicy, serve it with soy yogurt to cool it down.

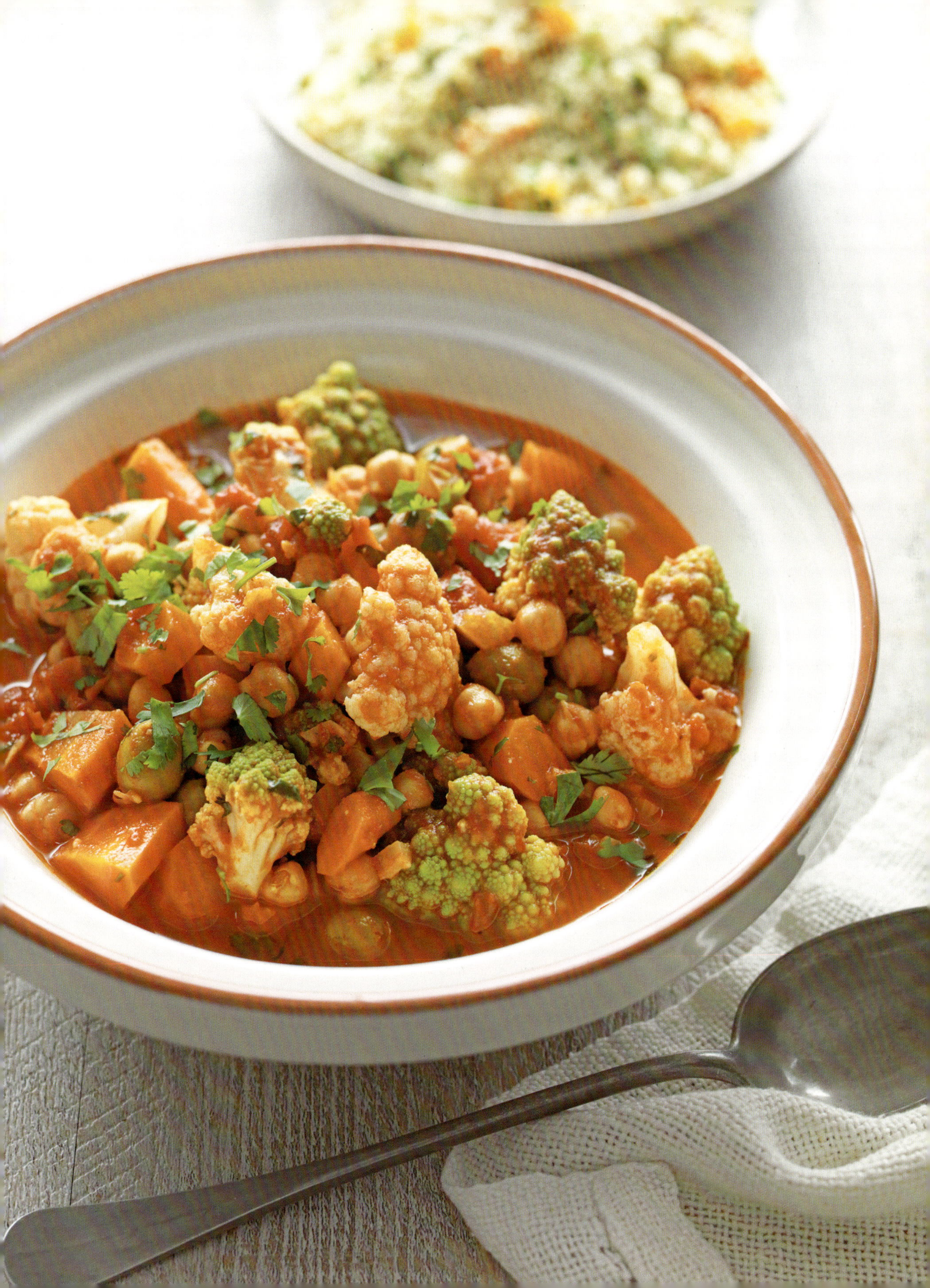

BURGERS

At Mildreds we make a different vegetarian burger just about every day. We use a huge range of different seasonal vegetables, herbs, spices, and beans, and regularly sell more than a hundred burgers daily. Once a customer asked us what machine we use to make them; he didn't believe us when we told him all of our burgers are made by hand.

The main binding agent used in our burgers is a dried soy protein mix, which can be found in most health food stores or ordered online. If you're finding this hard to get hold of, use a vegetarian sausage mixture instead.

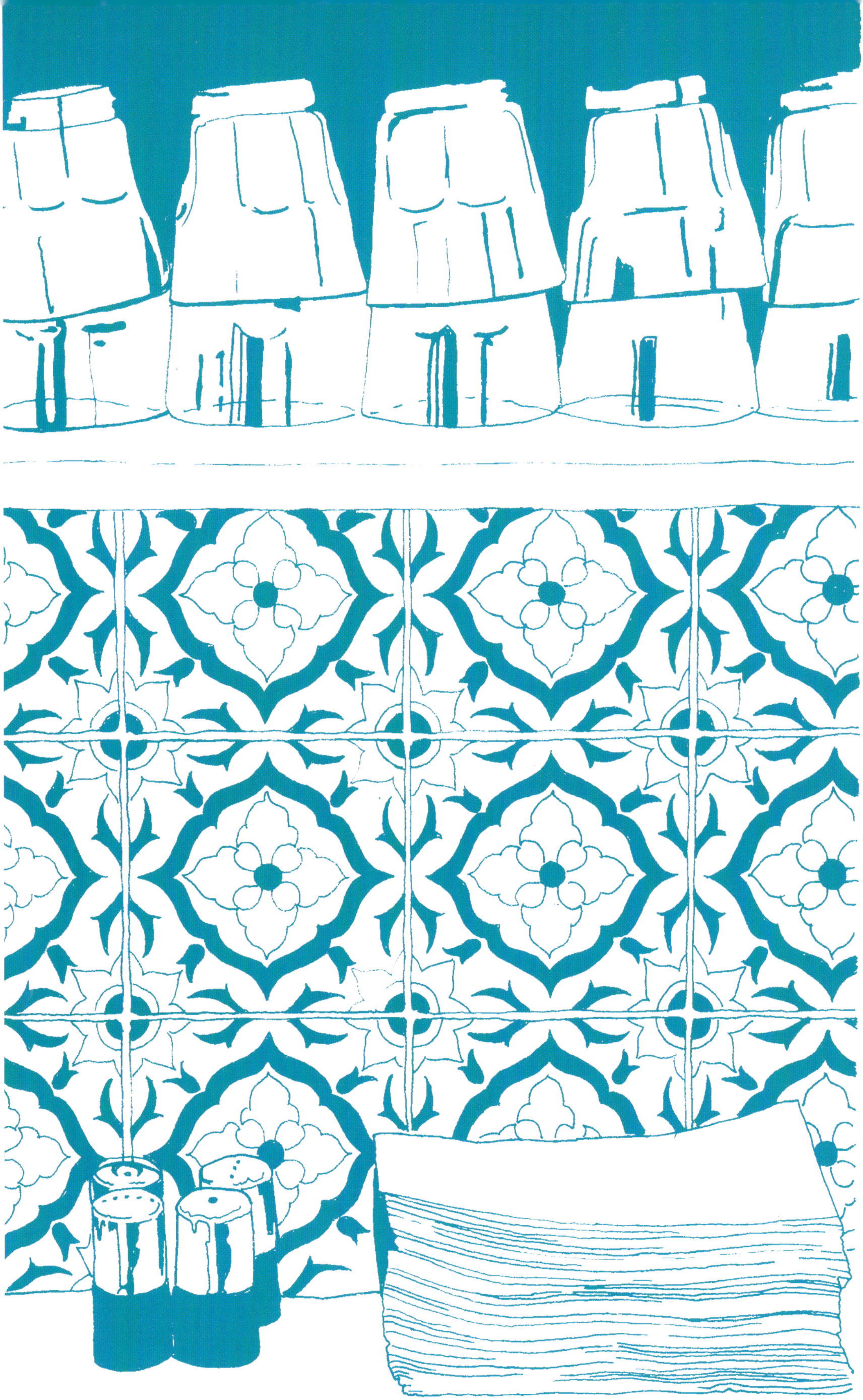

This Mediterranean burger goes really well with our Vegan Basil Mayonnaise (see page 232), slices of ripe tomato, red onion, arugula, and, for an extra treat, slices of melted buffalo mozzarella.

ITALIAN TOMATO, EGGPLANT & BLACK OLIVE BURGERS

MAKES 6 TO 10 BURGERS

light olive oil or other light cooking oil (such as canola, peanut, or sunflower)
1½ eggplants, cut into 1¼-inch cubes
1 white onion, finely diced
2 rosemary sprigs, leaves picked and finely chopped
4 garlic cloves, minced
14oz can diced tomatoes
½ cup tomato paste
1 chile, trimmed and minced
1½ tablespoons superfine sugar
1 bunch of basil leaves, chopped
1 cup pitted black olives, chopped
1¼lb dried soy protein mix, or other vegetarian dehydrated sausage mix

To serve
sourdough buns, split and toasted
arugula
tomato slices
red onion slices
Vegan Basil Mayonnaise (*see* page 232)
Carrot Relish (*see* page 237)
melted buffalo mozzarella cheese slices
Roast Potato Wedges (*see* page 187)

Preheat the oven to 400°F.

Drizzle a little oil into a roasting pan. Add the eggplant cubes and toss together to coat. Roast for 15 minutes, or until the eggplant is cooked through but not mushy. Set aside to cool.

Once cool, add the eggplant to a large mixing bowl along with all the other ingredients and, using your hands, knead for 5 minutes, or until everything is combined together. Cover with plastic wrap, transfer to the refrigerator, and let rest for 15 minutes.

Once rested, divide the mixture into 6 to 10 evenly sized pieces. (You may find at this point that the mixture is too solid to divide easily. If so, simply add a little water, ensuring that you stir it through thoroughly.) Shape the pieces into circular patties about ¾ to 1 inch in thickness.

Heat a splash of oil in a large skillet over medium heat. When hot, add the patties and fry for 10 minutes on each side.

Set the burgers into toasted sourdough buns and stuff with arugula, tomato and red onion slices, Vegan Basil Mayonnaise, Carrot Relish, and melted buffalo mozzarella, as you prefer. Serve with Roast Potato Wedges.

These always sell really fast when we put them on the menu. Lots of chunky colorful vegetables and beans make for a great-looking burger that pairs really well with Guacamole, slices of fresh avocado, and Sweet Potato Fries (see page 186).

MEXICAN KIDNEY BEAN, JALAPEÑO, ROASTED BELL PEPPER & CORN BURGERS

MAKES 6 TO 10 BURGERS

2 cups canned kidney beans, drained and rinsed
2 roasted red bell peppers in oil, drained and coarsely chopped
2/3 cup corn kernels
4 scallions, trimmed and coarsely chopped
1 bunch of cilantro, leaves picked and coarsely chopped
1 cup drained and coarsely chopped jalapeño chiles from a jar
14oz can diced tomatoes
1 tablespoon smoked paprika
1 teaspoon ground coriander
½ teaspoon chili powder
1¼lb dried soy protein mix, or other vegetarian dehydrated sausage mix
½ to 1 cup water
light olive oil or other light cooking oil (such as canola, peanut, or sunflower)

To serve
sourdough buns, split and toasted
Guacamole (*see* page 175)
avocado slices
arugula
tomato slices
red onion slices
Vegan Basil Mayonnaise (*see* page 232)
Carrot Relish (*see* page 237)
Sweet Potato Fries (*see* page 186)

Place all the solid ingredients in a large mixing bowl with ½ cup water. Knead together with your hands until the beans have broken up and the mixture has come together. Continue to knead, adding more water if necessary, until the mixture is dense but pliable. Cover with plastic wrap, transfer to the refrigerator, and let rest for 20 minutes.

Once rested, divide the mixture into 6 to 10 evenly sized pieces. (You may find at this point that the mixture is too solid to divide easily. If so, simply add a little water, ensuring that you stir it through thoroughly.) Shape the pieces into circular patties about ¾ to 1 inch in thickness.

Heat a splash of oil in a large skillet over medium heat. When hot, add the patties and fry for 10 minutes on each side.

Set the burgers into toasted sourdough buns and stuff with Guacamole and avocado slices, or our usual combination of arugula, tomato and red onion slices, Vegan Basil Mayonnaise, and Carrot Relish, as you prefer. Serve with Sweet Potato Fries.

A lovely purple burger with eastern European flavors, this is a consistent favorite at Mildreds and is excellent with our Beer-battered Onion Rings (see page 194). We serve all our burgers with arugula, tomatoes, red onion, Vegan Basil Mayonnaise (see page 232), and Carrot Relish (see page 237) but you could go full-on eastern European with these and serve them with sauerkraut or sour pickles instead.

BEET, FENNEL, APPLE & DILL BURGERS

MAKES 6 TO 10 BURGERS

3 small or 2 medium beets, peeled and coarsely grated
2 apples, coarsely grated
1 fennel bulb, trimmed and finely chopped
1 bunch of dill leaves, chopped
1 tablespoon fennel seeds, toasted and lightly ground
1¼lb dried soy protein mix, or other vegetarian dehydrated sausage mix
2 cups water, plus extra, if needed
light olive oil or other light cooking oil (such as canola, peanut, or or sunflower)

To serve
sourdough buns, split and toasted
arugula
tomato slices
red onion slices
Vegan Basil Mayonnaise (*see* page 232)
Carrot Relish (*see* page 237)
Beer-battered Onion Rings (*see* page 194)

To make the burgers, combine all the ingredients except the oil in a large mixing bowl and knead together with your hands for 5 minutes to form a dense but pliable burger mixture. Cover with plastic wrap and let chill in the fridge for 15 minutes.

Once rested, divide the mixture into 6 to 10 evenly sized pieces. (You may find at this point that the mixture is too solid to divide easily. If so, simply add a little water, ensuring that you stir it through thoroughly.) Shape the pieces into circular patties about ¾ to 1 inch in thickness.

Heat a splash of oil in a large skillet over medium heat. When hot, add the patties and fry for 10 minutes on each side.

Set the burgers into toasted sourdough buns and stuff with arugula, tomato and red onion slices, Vegan Basil Mayonnaise, and Carrot Relish, as you prefer. Serve accompanied by Beer-battered Onion Rings.

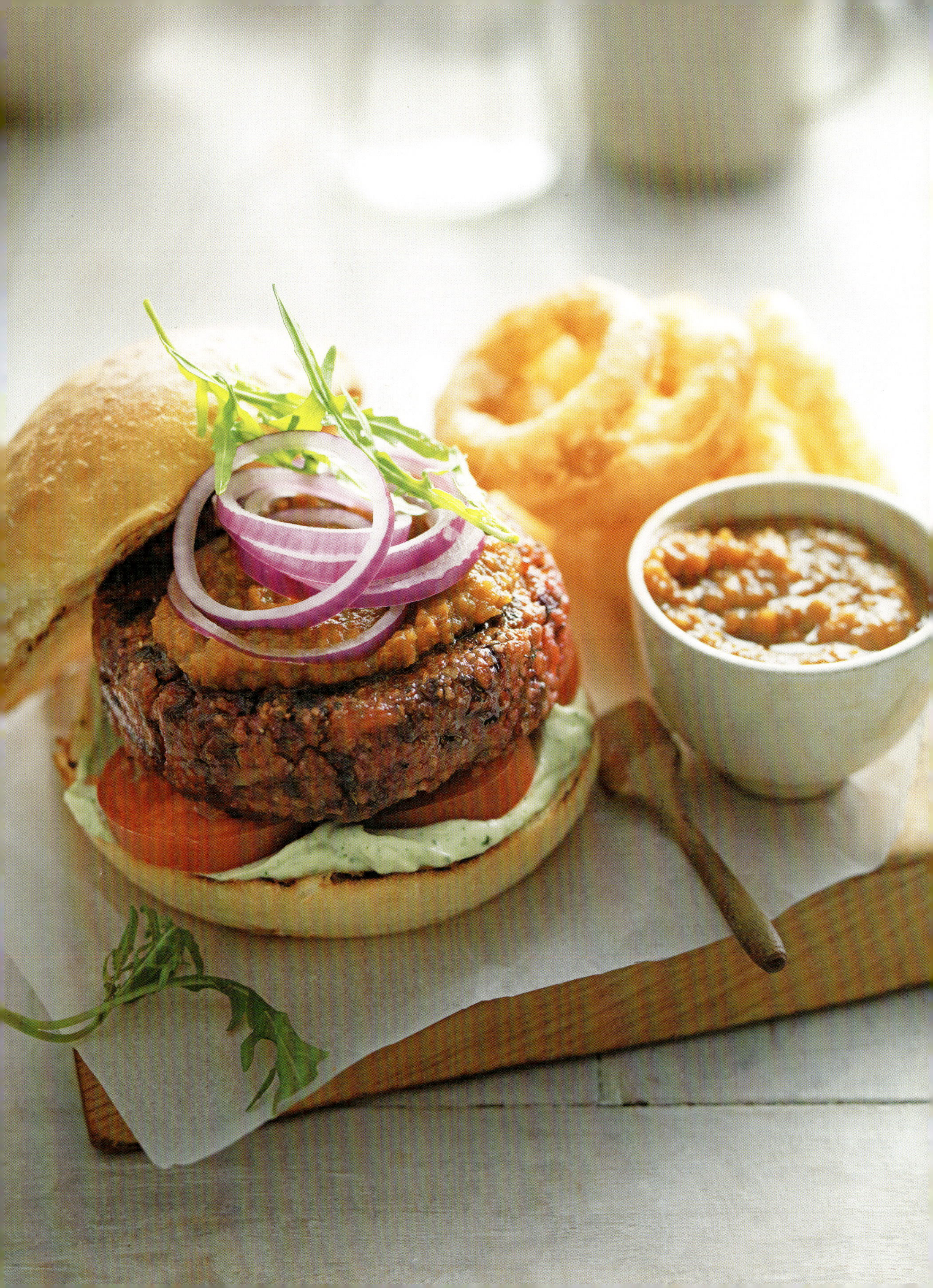

PASTA

Pasta, sadly, is often the only vegetarian option offered by a lot of mainstream restaurants, so we weren't sure whether to include pasta recipes in this book or not. However, our daily pasta specials are so popular we couldn't resist. Who doesn't love a delicious plate of this multifaceted carbohydrate (especially now that there are so many good gluten-free options for those people who had to avoid it previously)?

There are so many pasta sauces to choose from that we had a hard time narrowing it down. In the end, we've tried to include a little of everything, from a simple Tomato & Basil Sauce (*see* page 151) that's perfect as a base (and great for sneaking vegetables onto fussy children's plates), to summery Saffron & Goat Cheese Sauce (*see* page 148) and wintery Creamy Mushroom & Sherry Vinegar Sauce (see page 146)... and more. We've recommended pasta varieties to accompany the sauces but feel free to experiment and find your own favorites.

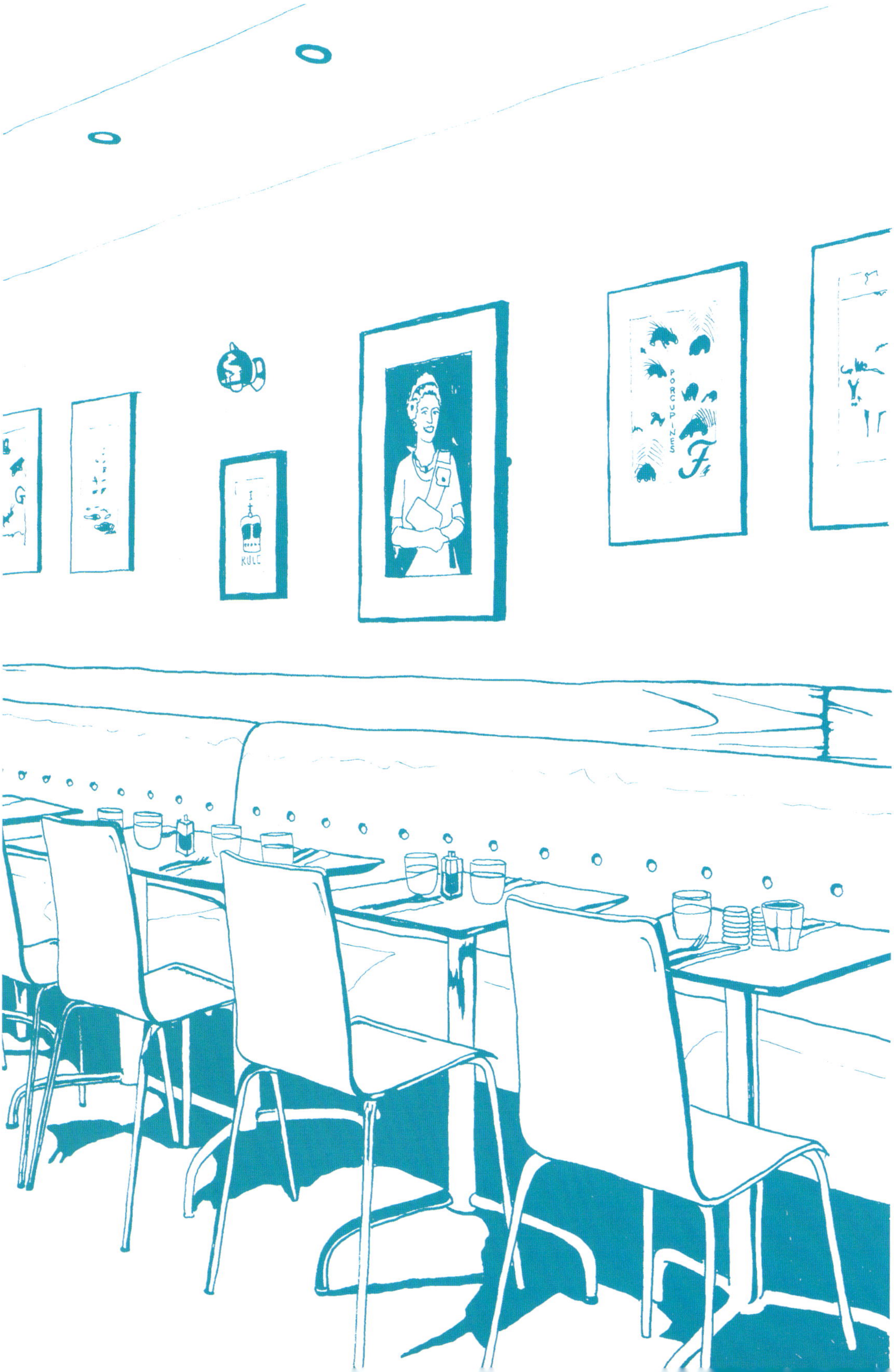
PORCUPINES

Sherry vinegar might seem like a strange thing to add to a cream sauce but trust us, it gives it a sweet, rich flavor that sets the whole thing off perfectly. While lovely with orecchiette, the "little ear" shaped pasta, it also pairs very well with potato gnocchi—just add a bottle of full-bodied red wine and some herby focaccia to mop up any leftover sauce for a deliciously rich, hearty meal.

CREAMY MUSHROOM & SHERRY VINEGAR ORECCHIETTE WITH GREEN STRING BEANS

SERVES 4 TO 6

1lb orecchiette
7oz green string beans, trimmed and cut in half

For the Creamy Mushroom & Sherry Vinegar Sauce
1lb cremino mushrooms, quartered
light cooking oil (such as canola, peanut, or sunflower)
2oz dried ceps
2 tablespoons butter
4 garlic cloves, finely sliced
1 large white onion, finely sliced
1 tablespoon turbinado sugar
handful of thyme sprigs, leaves picked
¼ cup sherry vinegar
2 cups heavy cream
salt and pepper

Preheat the oven to 375°F. For the sauce, arrange the mushrooms on a baking pan, drizzle with a little oil, and roast for 10 to 12 minutes, or until cooked but still firm. Remove from the oven and set aside. Rinse the ceps in warm water and strain to remove any sand or grit, then add to a bowl and cover with boiling water. Let soak for 15 minutes, and then strain, reserving the soaking water, and coarsely chop.

Melt the butter in a saucepan over medium heat, add the garlic and onion, and sauté for 5 to 8 minutes, stirring frequently, until the onion has softened and is starting to caramelize. Add the sugar and thyme and cook for 10 to 15 minutes, or until the onion is golden brown.

Strain any liquid that has escaped from the mushrooms while roasting and add it to the onions along with the ceps, cep soaking water, and sherry vinegar. Bring to a simmer and cook for about 10 to 15 minutes, or until the liquid has almost entirely evaporated. Add the cream and simmer gently for another 10 to 15 minutes, or until the sauce has thickened and reduced and is a deep caramel color.

Meanwhile, cook the pasta and beans. Bring a small saucepan of salted water to a boil, add the beans, and cook for 3 to 4 minutes, or until tender. Bring a separate saucepan of salted water to a boil, add the orecchiette, and cook following the package instructions. Drain. Stir the mushrooms through the sauce for a minute to warm. Season the sauce to taste with salt and pepper, pour onto the cooked pasta and beans, and mix everything together well to serve.

With its broad leaves, pretty little white flowers, and unmistakable garlicky aroma, wild garlic (also known as ramps) is a great seasonal food that grows happily in shady areas in deserted rural spots and urban parks alike. If you do find some in the wild, don't pick everything you see; just take a few leaves from several different plants so they can recover. Wild garlic is now available in season at many good supermarkets and gourmet food stores, though if you are struggling to get your hands on it, you can always use arugula here instead for a punchier, peppery alternative. Trofie is a little twisted pasta traditionally served with pesto. If you can't get hold of any, fusilli also works well here.

TROFIE WITH WILD GARLIC PESTO

SERVES 4 TO 6

1lb trofie or fusilli

For the Wild Garlic Pesto
3oz wild garlic (ramp) leaves
1 bunch of basil, leaves picked
½ bunch of flat-leaf parsley, leaves picked
1 cup light olive oil
1 teaspoon sea salt flakes
pinch of black pepper
¼ cup shredded vegetarian Parmesan-style hard cheese
2½ tablespoons pine nuts, toasted

Bring a pan of salted water to a boil, add the pasta, and cook following the package instructions.

While the pasta is cooking, make the wild garlic pesto. Wash the wild garlic leaves thoroughly and pat dry with a clean dish towel. Put them, along with the herbs, in a food processor, add a splash of the oil, and blend briefly together.

Add the sea salt flakes, pepper, cheese, and pine nuts and blend together, gradually adding the remaining olive oil until smooth. Taste and adjust the seasoning if necessary, then stir the mixture through the warm pasta. Serve.

This is a creamy, vibrant pasta dish that's perfect for a summer's lunch, with the thin zucchini ribbons cooked briefly in the heat of the pasta and sauce. We like to use both yellow and green zucchini here to give the dish a little extra color but, if you can't find the yellow ones, just using green will be fine. The saffron in the sauce adds a lovely golden color and a light, fragrant flavor that complements the goat cheese but, once again, this can be left out if you don't have any on hand—just add a teaspoon of picked thyme leaves instead.

SAFFRON & GOAT CHEESE TAGLIATELLE
WITH ZUCCHINI, CHERRY TOMATOES & BLACK OLIVES

SERVES 4 TO 6

1lb fresh tagliatelle

For the Saffron & Goat Cheese Sauce
2 tablespoons butter
1 red chile, seeded and minced
3 to 4 garlic cloves, minced
finely grated zest and juice of ½ lemon
1 cup white wine
large pinch of saffron threads
1 teaspoon superfine sugar
5 bay leaves
11½oz goat cheese
3 cups heavy cream
5 zucchini (3 green and 2 yellow), cut into thin ribbons using a vegetable peeler or mandoline
1⅓ cups good-quality pitted black olives
2 cups cherry tomatoes, quartered
salt and white pepper

To make the sauce, melt the butter in a saucepan over medium heat, add the chile, garlic, and grated lemon zest and cook, stirring, for 3 to 4 minutes, or until the garlic has softened and is fragrant. Add the lemon juice, white wine, saffron, sugar, and bay leaves, bring to a simmer, and cook, stirring occasionally, for 10 to 15 minutes, or until the liquid has reduced by half.

Remove and discard any rind from the goat cheese and crumble the cheese into pieces. Stir it into the sauce along with the cream and simmer gently for 5 to 10 minutes, stirring frequently, until the sauce has thickened and all the goat cheese has melted evenly into the sauce. Season to taste with salt and white pepper.

Meanwhile, bring a saucepan of salted water to a boil and cook the pasta following the package instructions.

Stir the zucchini, olives, and tomatoes into the sauce, add the cooked pasta, and stir to combine. Remove from the heat and serve.

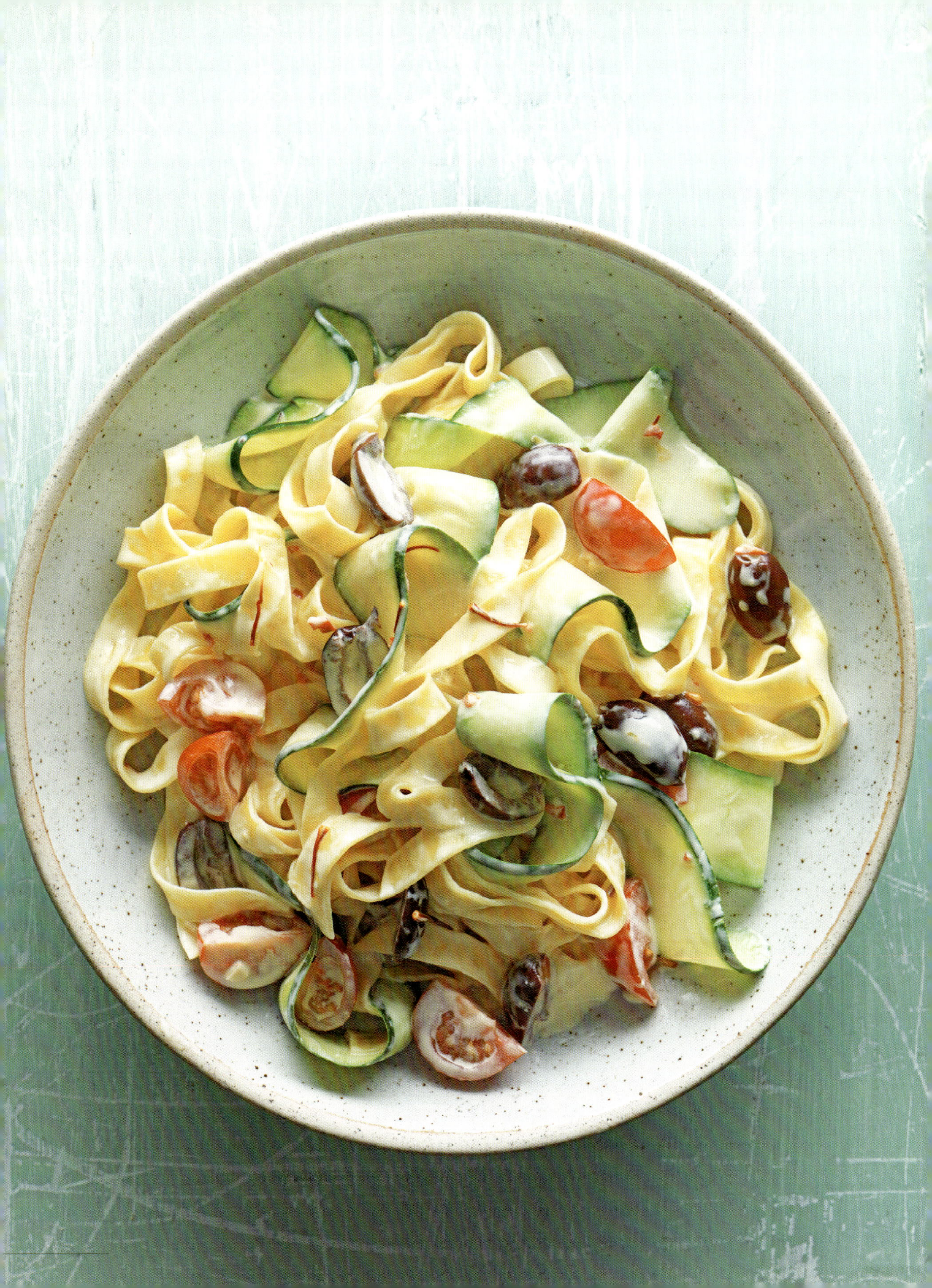

This smooth, sweet sauce is great served with our Saffron & Pea Risotto Cakes (see page 111) but is also excellent stirred through pasta. While other roasted red bell peppers can be used, we love the sweet finish that Spanish piquillo peppers lend to the sauce, so try and find them if you can.

PENNE WITH RED BELL PEPPER SAUCE

SERVES 4 TO 6

16 asparagus spears, trimmed
1¾ cups peas, defrosted if frozen
1lb penne
salt
2 cups shredded vegetarian Parmesan-style hard cheese, to serve

For the Red Bell Pepper Sauce
3 tablespoons light olive oil
1 onion, diced
2 garlic cloves, crushed
1 celery stalk, trimmed and diced
1 carrot, grated
¾ cup canned plum tomatoes
10oz roasted piquillo peppers in oil, drained
1 teaspoon superfine sugar
1 teaspoon salt
1 teaspoon tomato paste
pinch of black pepper
1¼ cups heavy cream, plus extra, if needed

Bring a saucepan of salted water to a boil. Break the woody ends off the asparagus spears and cut each into 2 to 3 pieces. Blanch for a minute, then add the peas and continue to blanch for another 20 seconds. Drain and rinse under cold water to refresh. Set aside.

For the red bell pepper sauce, heat the olive oil in a saucepan over medium heat, add the onion, garlic, celery, and carrot and cook for 5 minutes, stirring, until the onion is starting to soften. Add all the remaining ingredients except the heavy cream, bring to a simmer, and let cook gently, stirring occasionally, for 20 minutes, or until thickened and reduced. Stir in the heavy cream and continue to simmer gently for another 15 to 20 minutes until thick and creamy.

Remove the sauce from the heat and blend with a stick blender or in a food processor until smooth. If the sauce is looking a little thick, add an extra splash of heavy cream. Return the sauce to the saucepan and keep it warm.

Bring a saucepan of salted water to a boil. Cook the pasta following the package instructions then drain and add it to the sauce along with the blanched asparagus and peas. Stir to combine, divide between bowls, and scatter with the shredded cheese to serve.

Our resident Italian chef, Alex Aimassi, taught us this recipe and, while we had never put such a lot of different vegetables into a tomato sauce before, we have to admit it is undoubtedly much improved in both depth of flavor and texture. The sweetness of the sauce contrasts well with the salty tapenade, with the roasted eggplants and baby spinach adding a wonderful splash of color.

RIGATONI WITH TOMATO & BASIL SAUCE
& BLACK OLIVE TAPENADE

SERVES 4 TO 6

4 large eggplants
light olive oil
1lb rigatoni
3oz baby spinach
salt
2 cups shredded vegetarian Parmesan-style hard cheese, to serve

For the Tomato & Basil Sauce
light olive oil
1 onion, diced
2 garlic cloves, minced
1 celery stalk, diced
1 carrot, grated
1 bunch of basil
½ small red chile, trimmed, seeded, and diced
2 x 13oz cans plum tomatoes
1 teaspoon superfine sugar
1 cup water
salt and pepper

For the Black Olive Tapenade
1¼ cups pitted kalamata olives
large handful of parsley, chopped
2 garlic cloves, crushed
¼ cup olive oil
juice of ½ lemon
2 tablespoons capers in brine, drained and rinsed

To make the black olive tapenade, put all the ingredients into a food processor and blend to a smooth paste. Set aside until needed.

For the sauce, heat a splash of olive oil in a large saucepan over medium heat, add the onion, garlic, celery, carrot, basil, and chile and cook, stirring, for about 8 minutes, or until the onions are softened and lightly colored. Add the canned plum tomatoes, sugar, and water and season with salt and pepper. Bring to a simmer and cook gently, stirring occasionally, for 25 to 30 minutes, or until the sauce has thickened and reduced by half.

Meanwhile, preheat the oven to 350°F. Cut the eggplants into 1-inch cubes and rinse under running water. Drain well and place on a baking pan. Drizzle with olive oil, season with salt, and toss together well to coat. Roast for 15 minutes, or until the eggplant cubes are golden and cooked through. Set aside.

Remove the sauce from the heat and blend with a stick blender or in a food processor until smooth. Return the sauce to the pan to keep warm.

Bring a saucepan of salted water to a boil and cook the pasta following the package instructions. Drain the pasta, add it to the sauce with the eggplant cubes and baby spinach, and stir well to combine. Divide between bowls, drizzle with the tapenade, and scatter with the shredded cheese to serve.

This recipe is all about the sauce. The recipe here will make about three times the amount you need for this stir-fry. This is no bad thing, however, because the sauce is exceptionally tasty and can be easily frozen in portions for later use. Simply store it in freezer bags or use it to fill an ice cube tray and you'll have a sauce ready to whip up a delicious, authentic stir-fry at a moment's notice. You can use just about any vegetables you like for this dish and, if you're in a real hurry, even the ready-chopped bags of vegetables for stir-fries you can buy in the supermarkets will work fine.

SHIITAKE MUSHROOM & CHINESE VEGETABLE STIR-FRY

SERVES 4 TO 6

vegetable oil
4 carrots, sliced thinly into disks
12 baby corn, left whole or sliced in half
1 red bell pepper, cored, seeded, and sliced
1 red chile, trimmed and minced
4 garlic cloves, minced
¾lb choy sum (Chinese flowering cabbage), shredded
¾lb napa cabbage, shredded
5 scallions, trimmed and sliced into 2-inch batons
steamed jasmine rice, to serve

For the shiitake mushroom sauce
light cooking oil (such as canola, peanut, or sunflower)
3½oz shiitake mushrooms, trimmed
½ cup shaoxing rice wine or sherry
3 tablespoons light soy sauce
3 tablespoons kecap manis (sweet soy sauce)
1 star anise
1¼ cups water
1 tablespoon cornstarch

For the shiitake mushroom sauce, heat a drizzle of oil in a saucepan, add the mushrooms, and cook for 3 to 5 minutes, stirring, until soft. Deglaze the pan with the rice wine, and then add the soy sauce, kecap manis, star anise, and water and bring to a simmer. Continue to cook, stirring occasionally, for 10 to 15 minutes, or until reduced by one-third. Then remove from the heat and purée with a stick blender or in a food processor until smooth.

Return the sauce to the pan. Mix the cornstarch with a few tablespoons of water, add to the sauce, and cook for 3 to 5 minutes, stirring frequently, until thickened. Remove the pan from the heat and set aside.

Heat a wok over high heat, add a splash of vegetable oil, and stir-fry the carrots, baby corn, and bell pepper for 2 minutes, adding a splash of water along the way to steam the vegetables slightly. Add the chile, garlic, choy sum, and napa cabbage and stir-fry for 2 minutes more, adding another splash of water if necessary. Add the scallions and ½ cup of the shiitake sauce and cook, stirring, for a few minutes until the sauce coats the ingredients evenly. Serve with fragrant jasmine rice.

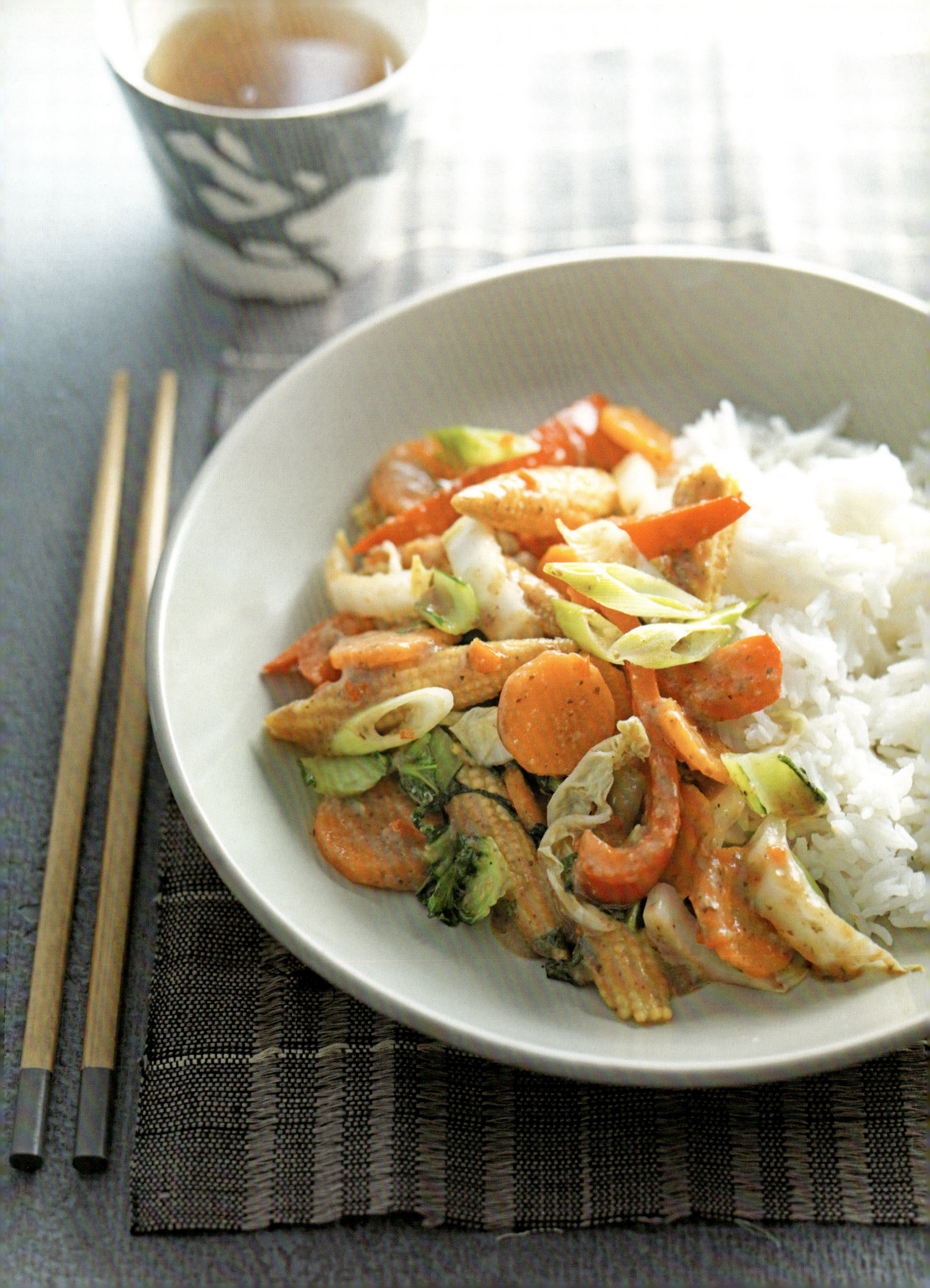

This vegetarian version of a traditional beef pho—the famous dish from the north of Vietnam—is a delicious, fragrant noodle and vegetable broth topped with bean sprouts and mint. If you don't like mushrooms or seaweed this will still work without them, and you can substitute any vegetables you like. Vietnamese mint is different from regular garden mint because it is stronger and has a more peppery taste. You can find it in Asian supermarkets. If you can't get hold of it, garden mint makes a suitable substitute.

SHIITAKE MUSHROOM & SEAWEED PHO

SERVES 6 TO 8

2 large white onions, unpeeled
6-inch piece of fresh ginger root
3 tablespoons sesame oil
1 red chile, coarsely chopped
3 garlic cloves
5 shiitake mushrooms, trimmed
finely grated zest of ½ orange and juice of 2 oranges
2 tablespoons tamarind paste
6 star anise
1 cinnamon stick
2 quarts water
½ cup tamari
½ cup maple syrup
2 nori seaweed sheets, cut into strips, or 2oz dried kelp soaked in 1¼ cups hot water

To finish
3 tablespoons sesame oil
10 shiitake mushrooms, trimmed and thinly sliced
1 red chile, trimmed and thinly sliced, plus extra to garnish
10oz wild rice noodles
1lb bean sprouts
2 handfuls of cilantro leaves
2 handfuls of Vietnamese mint leaves
2 nori seaweed sheets, cut into thin strips

Place the whole onions and ginger on a hot ridged grill pan or barbecue and cook for 10 to 15 minutes, turning occasionally, until the onion and ginger skins have blackened and the onions have softened and caramelized. Set aside to cool, then peel off the skins and cut into large chunks.

Warm the sesame oil in a large saucepan over medium heat, add the onion, ginger, chile, whole garlic cloves, shiitake mushrooms, and grated orange zest and sauté for 5 to 10 minutes, or until the mixture is fragrant and the flavors have melded together. Add the orange juice, tamarind paste, star anise, and cinnamon and cook, stirring, for a few more minutes, then stir in the water, tamari, and maple syrup. Bring the mixture to a boil then reduce the heat and simmer gently for 20 minutes, or until the liquid has reduced by about half. Strain into a bowl and add the nori seaweed or soaked kelp.

To finish, return the pan to the heat with the sesame oil, add the shiitake mushrooms and chile, and cook for 2 to 3 minutes, or until the mushrooms are warmed through.

Return the strained broth to the pan and bring to a simmer. Add the rice noodles and cook for 3 to 5 minutes, or until the noodles are just done. Ladle into bowls and scatter with the bean sprouts, herbs, nori seaweed strips, and a few extra slices of chile. Serve.

The smoked tofu ragù used here is rich and full of deep, complex flavors that contrast well with the creamy béchamel and tangy feta cheese.

EGGPLANT MOUSSAKA WITH SMOKED TOFU RAGÙ

SERVES 8 TO 10

3lb eggplant, cut into ¼-inch disks
7½oz smoked tofu, crumbled
½ teaspoon fennel seeds
½ teaspoon cumin seeds
½ teaspoon smoked paprika
½ teaspoon vegetable bouillon powder
½ tablespoon chili oil
2oz feta cheese
salt

For the tomato sauce
splash of light cooking oil
1 white onion, finely diced
3 garlic cloves
1 carrot, finely diced
½ small leek, trimmed, cleaned, and diced
½ red chile, trimmed and minced
½ fennel bulb, trimmed and finely diced
1¼lb diced tomatoes
1½ tablespoons tomato paste
1 cup water
1½ tablespoons superfine sugar
½ cinnamon stick

For the béchamel sauce
2 cups milk
pinch of grated nutmeg
¼ white onion
1 bay leaf
pinch of white pepper
2½ tablespoons butter, plus extra for greasing
⅓ cup all-purpose flour

To garnish
handful of fresh mint leaves, chopped
2 red chiles, chopped

Preheat the oven to 350°F. Grease a 12 x 9-inch rectangular baking dish with butter. Sprinkle the eggplant disks with salt, add to a colander set over a bowl, and let stand for 20 minutes. Meanwhile, combine the tofu in a bowl with the spices, bouillon powder, and chili oil. Spread the mixture across a cookie sheet and roast for 20 minutes, turning the tofu over a few times during cooking, until it begins to crisp. Rinse the eggplants and arrange on oiled baking pans. Roast for 8 minutes on each side until soft. Remove from the oven and reduce the heat to 325°F.

For the tomato sauce, heat the oil in a saucepan over low heat, add the onion and garlic, and cook, stirring, for 8 to 10 minutes, or until translucent. Add the carrot, leek, chile, and fennel and cook for another 5 minutes until beginning to soften. Add the tomatoes, paste, water, sugar, and cinnamon and simmer gently for 20 minutes, stirring occasionally. Let cool then stir in the roasted tofu and set aside.

Meanwhile, make the béchamel. Heat the milk in a saucepan, add the nutmeg, onion, bay leaf, and pepper, bring to a simmer and remove from the heat. Set aside for at least 10 minutes to allow the flavors to infuse. Melt the butter in another saucepan, add the flour, and stir together. Using a strainer, gradually add the milk, stirring continuously with a whisk to stop it from getting lumpy. Continue to stir, over low heat, until the sauce is thick, glossy, and custardlike.

To assemble, arrange one-third of the eggplant in the prepared baking dish. Spoon half the tofu and tomato sauce evenly over them, and then add a second layer of eggplant and the remaining tofu sauce. Lay the remaining eggplants on top and cover with the béchamel. Crumble the feta evenly over the top. Bake for 45 minutes until bubbling and lightly brown. If the moussaka looks like it is coloring too quickly, cover it with foil to stop it from burning. Remove from the oven and let cool for 10 minutes. Garnish with chopped mint and chiles to serve.

Mee Goreng is a spicy, dry, stir-fried noodle dish found in Malaysia, Indonesia, and Singapore. Here's our vegetarian version. We use a couple of ingredients you might not be familiar with, such as kecap manis, a thick, sweet Indonesian soy sauce widely available in Asian supermarkets. It is key to the flavor of this dish so we urge you to look for it, though you could substitute hoisin sauce (just add half the quantity). Kai-lan is also known as Chinese broccoli or Chinese kale, and has a similar flavor to broccoli. If you struggle to find it use long-stem broccoli instead. For best results and to avoid the stir-fry releasing too much liquid, cook in two batches.

MEE GORENG

SERVES 4 TO 6

vegetable oil
4 eggs, lightly beaten
1 onion, sliced
6 garlic cloves, minced
1½oz fresh ginger root, peeled and minced
1 red chile, trimmed and minced
2 yellow bell peppers, cored, seeded, and diced
1¼lb kai-lan (Chinese broccoli) or choy sum (Chinese cabbage), shredded
3 carrots, halved and finely sliced
1 teaspoon chili flakes or sambal paste
1 teaspoon ground coriander
1 teaspoon ground cumin
1lb package of cooked egg noodles
4 scallions, trimmed and sliced
3 cups bean sprouts
¼ cup dark soy sauce
½ cup kecap manis (sweet soy sauce)

To garnish
4 limes, cut into wedges
1¼ cups roasted peanuts
handful of fresh cilantro leaves

In a medium-sized, skillet heat a splash of oil, pour in the beaten eggs, quickly stir, and shake the pan to distribute them evenly. Cook until set. Slip the omelet onto a plate, roll it up into a large cigar shape, and slice into strips. Set aside.

Heat a large wok or skillet over high heat until very hot, then add a splash of oil, swirling to coat the surface evenly. Add the onion and stir-fry for 2 to 3 minutes, or until just beginning to color. Then add the garlic, ginger, chile, bell peppers, kai-lan or choy sum, carrots, and a splash of water. Stir-fry for 2 to 3 minutes, or until the vegetables are just tender.

Add the chili flakes, ground coriander, and cumin and stir-fry for 20 to 30 seconds, adding another splash of water to stop them from burning. Add the noodles, scallions, and bean sprouts and stir in the soy sauce and kecap manis. Spoon onto serving plates, top with the omelet slices, and garnish with lime wedges, roasted peanuts, and fresh cilantro leaves.

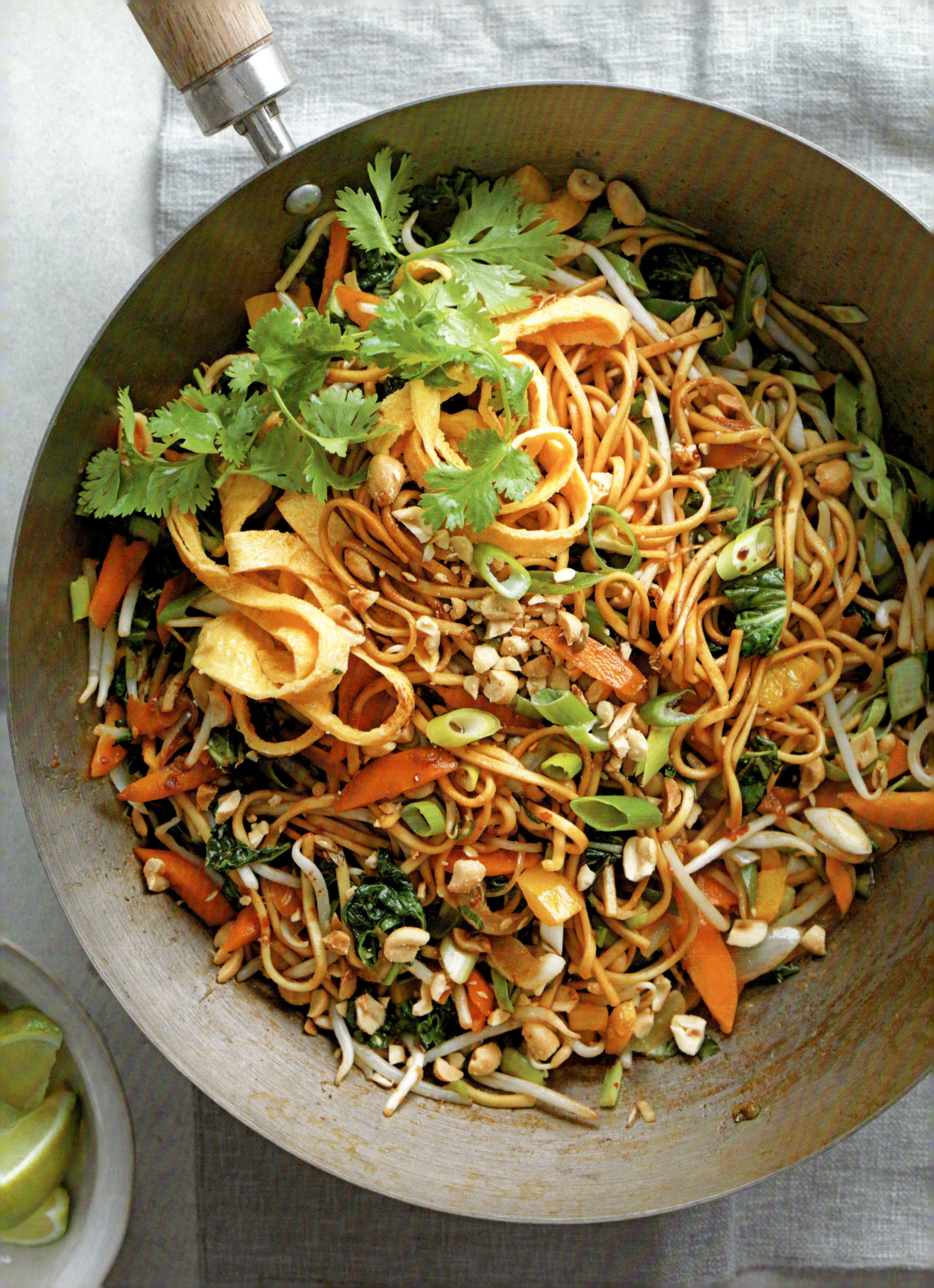

LATIN

At Mildreds we are passionate about Latin food. Here we've put together a great spread of Latin treats, taking influences from Argentina, Chile, Mexico, and Peru, among other countries. Fresh, spicy, and zesty—this is perfect party food that's great fun to make and eat.

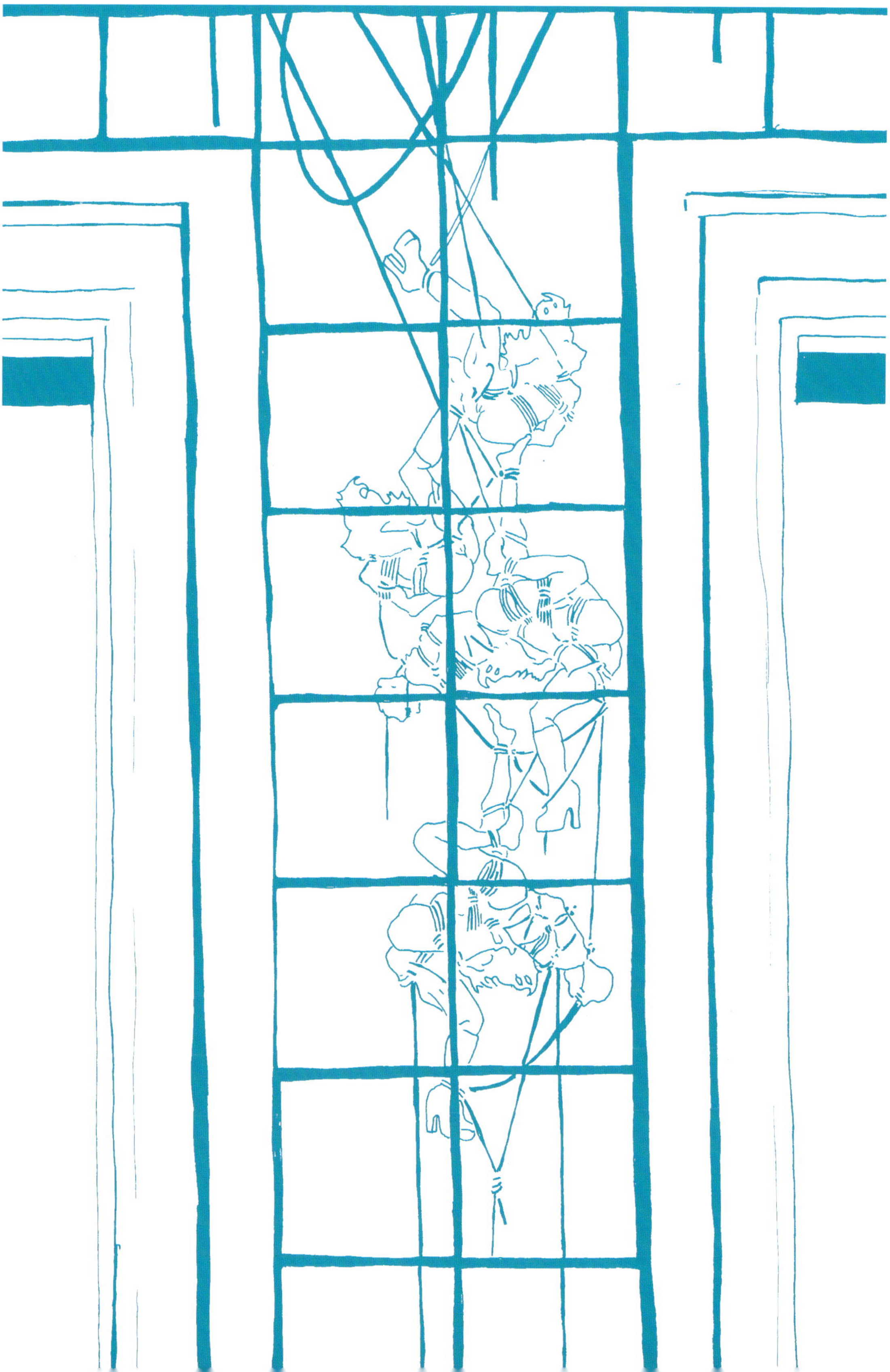

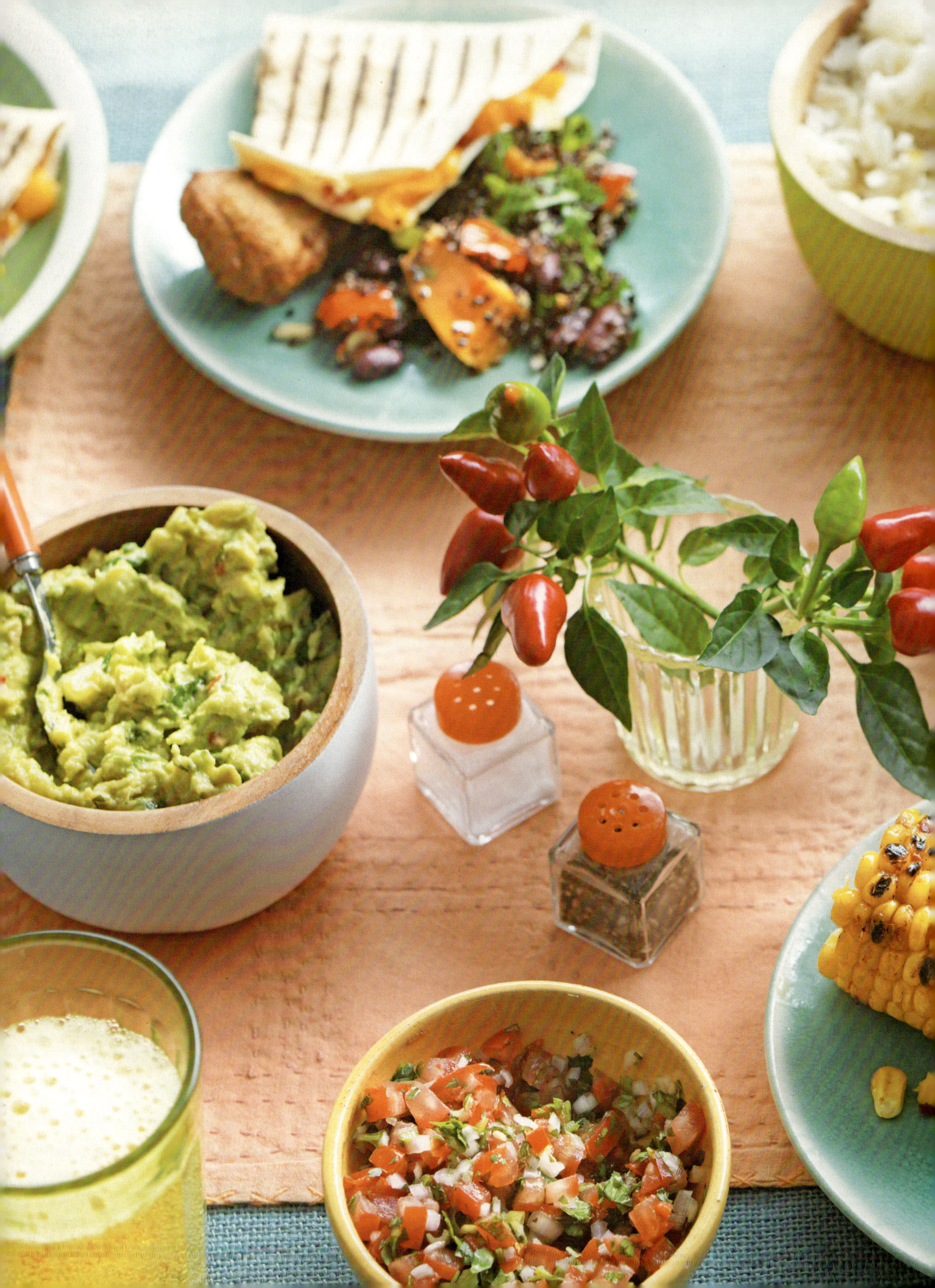

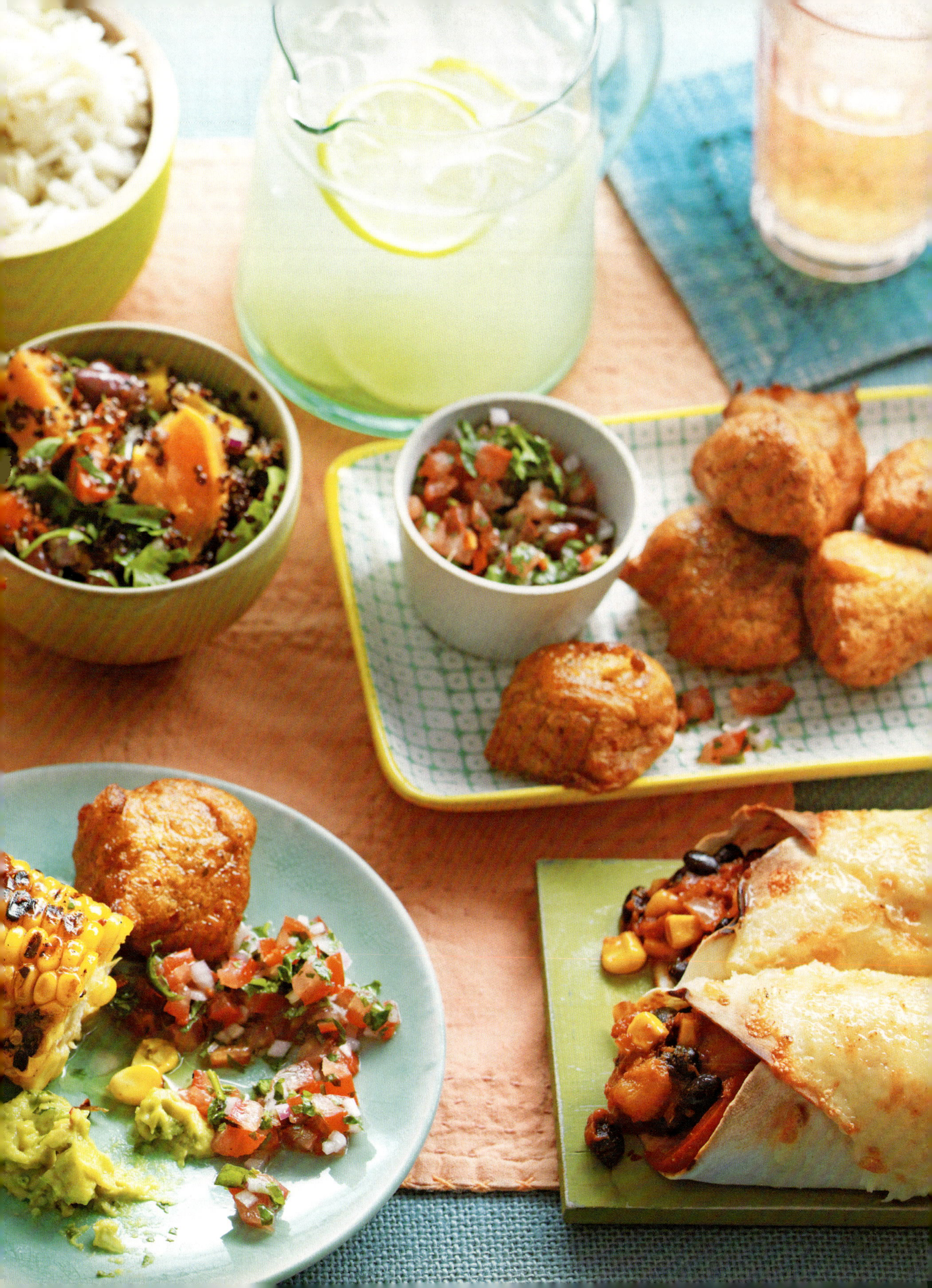

While the other salads in this section can all be served as appetizers or main courses, this is really intended as an accompaniment to Mexican or Latin dishes, such as our Black Bean and Pumpkin Burritos (see page 165). Fresh, crunchy, and slightly spicy, it works well as a side, though if you do want to make it more substantial, add some shredded cheese and a few handfuls of tortilla chips.

MEXICAN SALAD WITH AVOCADO, BABY GEM, SCALLION & JALAPEÑO

SERVES 6 TO 8 AS A SIDE DISH

6 baby gem lettuces, trimmed
2 large ripe avocados, sliced or just scooped out into chunks with a spoon
3 jalapeño chiles, sliced
1½ cups red cherry tomatoes, halved
1½ cups yellow cherry tomatoes, halved
6 scallions, trimmed and finely sliced diagonally
handful of cilantro leaves
½ cup Chipotle Lime Dressing (*see* page 240)

Separate the lettuce leaves and place in a large bowl along with all the remaining ingredients. Toss together well to combine and serve on plates alongside a main dish.

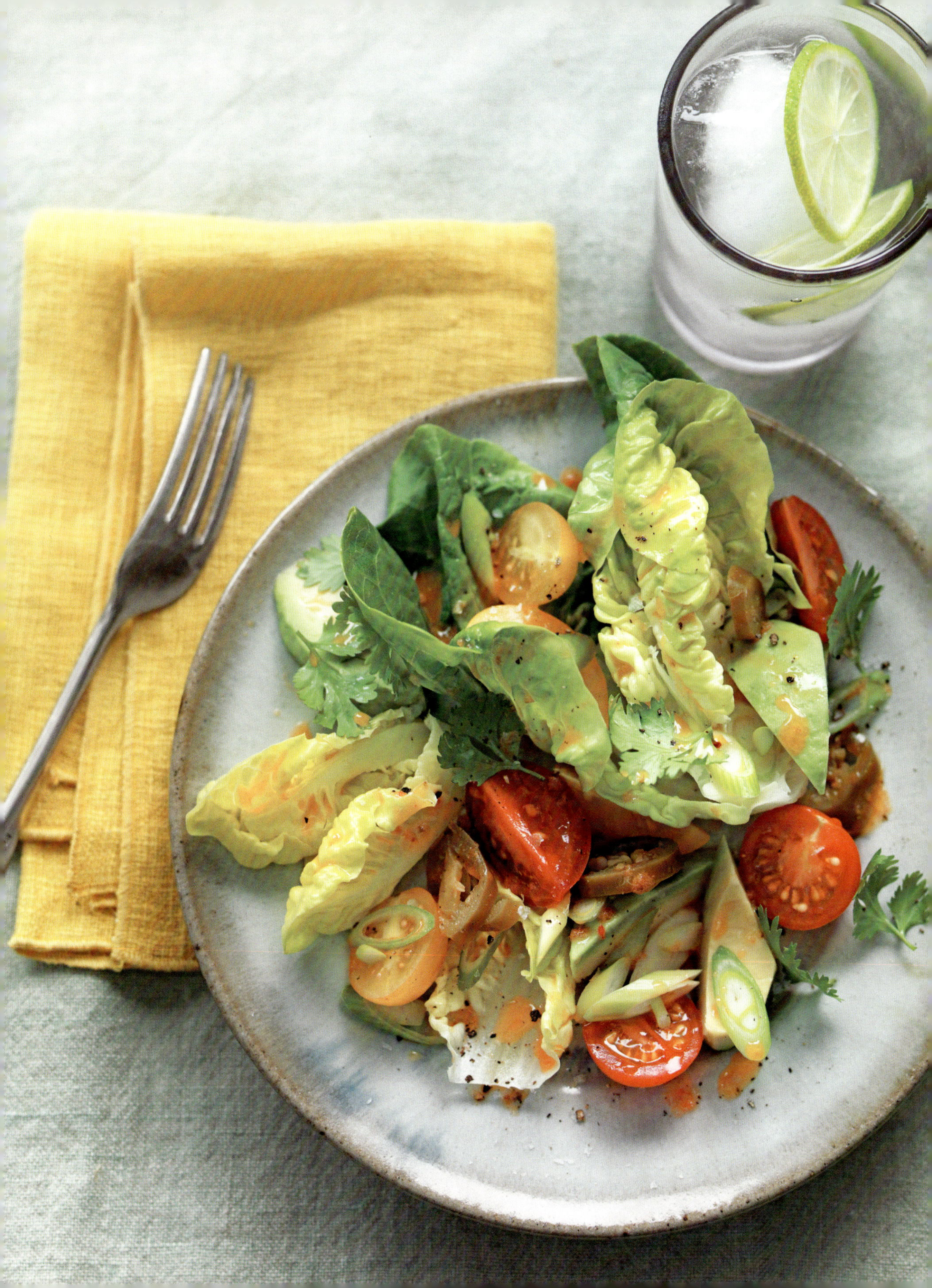

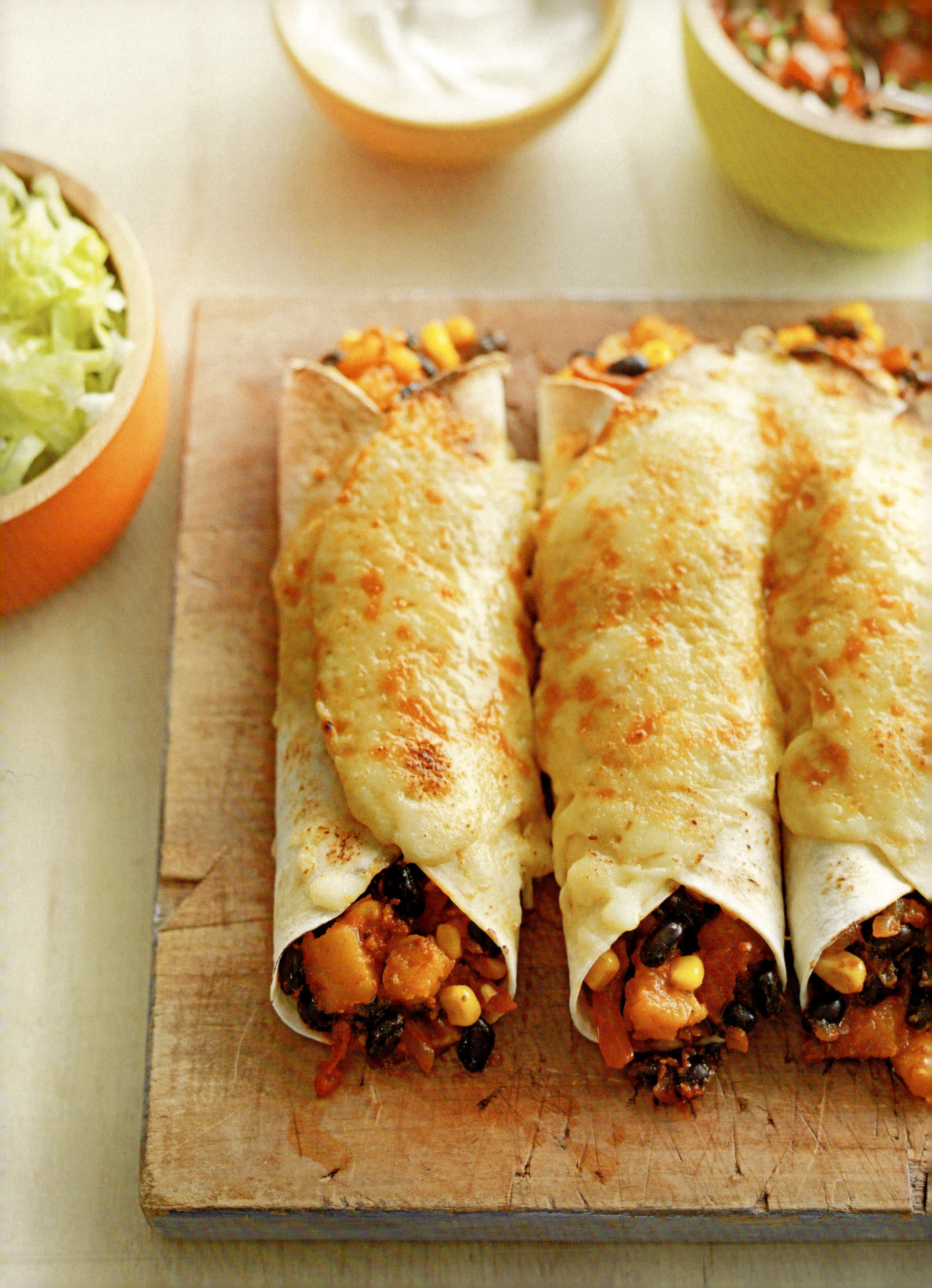

While Mexican ingredients are easier to get hold of these days, you may have trouble finding some of the ingredients below in your local supermarket. A quick look online for a specialist supplier will help root out the more unusual ones. Likewise, if you can't find dried chipotle, just use regular chili flakes instead. This is great served with Guacamole (see page 175) and Tomatillo Rice (see page 198).

BLACK BEAN & PUMPKIN BURRITOS

SERVES 6 TO 8

light cooking oil
13oz pumpkin or butternut squash, peeled, seeded, and cut into 1-inch chunks
1½ cups dried black turtle beans
1 teaspoon chopped epazote
2 pints water
½ teaspoon baking soda
1 onion, finely diced
1 red bell pepper, cored, seeded, and sliced
3 garlic cloves, minced
¼ teaspoon cayenne pepper
1 teaspoon paprika
1 teaspoon smoked paprika
2 teaspoons ground cumin
1 teaspoon crushed dried chipotle chile or dried hot chili flakes
14oz can diced tomatoes
2 tablespoons tomato paste
1¼ cups corn kernels
2½ cups shredded Cheddar cheese
6 to 8 flour tortillas
salt

To serve
shredded iceburg lettuce
Pico de Gallo (see page 22)
sour cream

Preheat the oven to 375°F. Drizzle a little oil into a roasting pan. Add the pumpkin pieces, season with salt, and toss together thoroughly to coat. Roast for 15 minutes, or until cooked through. Set aside.

Meanwhile, place the beans, epazote, water, and baking soda in a medium saucepan and bring to a simmer. Cook, stirring occasionally to stop the beans from sticking to the bottom of the pan, for 30 to 40 minutes, or until the beans have begun to break down and become mushy.

Heat a splash of oil in a separate saucepan, add the onion, and sauté for 5 minutes, or until the onion begins to color. Add the bell pepper and garlic and cook for another 2 to 3 minutes, and then add the cayenne pepper, paprikas, cumin, and chile and cook over low heat for a few minutes to release their flavors; be careful not to let them burn. Add the diced tomatoes, tomato paste, and corn. Season with salt and bring to a simmer. Lower the heat and cook gently, stirring occasionally, for 25 to 30 minutes, or until the sauce has thickened and reduced and the flavors have melded together.

Stir the pumpkin and beans into the sauce and heat gently to warm through. Remove from the heat. Divide the black bean and pumpkin chili between the tortillas, roll them tightly, cover in the cheese, and place under a hot broiler for 2 to 3 minutes, until the cheese has melted. Serve with shredded lettuce, *Pico de Gallo*, and sour cream.

Brie may not be the first cheese that springs to mind when you think of quesadillas but it does work fantastically well at sandwiching the tortillas together. These are great served as an appetizer with a little Guacamole (see page 175) and sour cream, or as something to snack on for a party. If you can't get your hands on Mexican oregano then just use normal oregano instead.

MANGO, BRIE & JALAPEÑO QUESADILLAS

MAKES 6 QUESADILLAS

1 mango, peeled and finely diced
5½oz Brie, sliced
¼ teaspoon dried Mexican oregano
1 small jalapeño chile, trimmed and diced
6 tortillas, 6 inches in size
Guacamole (*see* page 175), to serve

Mix the mango, Brie, oregano, and chile together in a bowl.

Lay the tortillas out on a flat work surface and fill one half of each with a generous tablespoon of the filling mixture. Fold the tortillas in half, pressing down on them gently with your fingertips to ensure they hold their shape during cooking.

Heat a skillet or ridged grill pan over medium heat, add the quesadillas, and cook for 1 to 2 minutes on each side until they are golden brown and the cheese has started to melt. Serve with Guacamole.

A good alternative to Brie would be **smoked Cheddar** or **mozzarella cheese**.

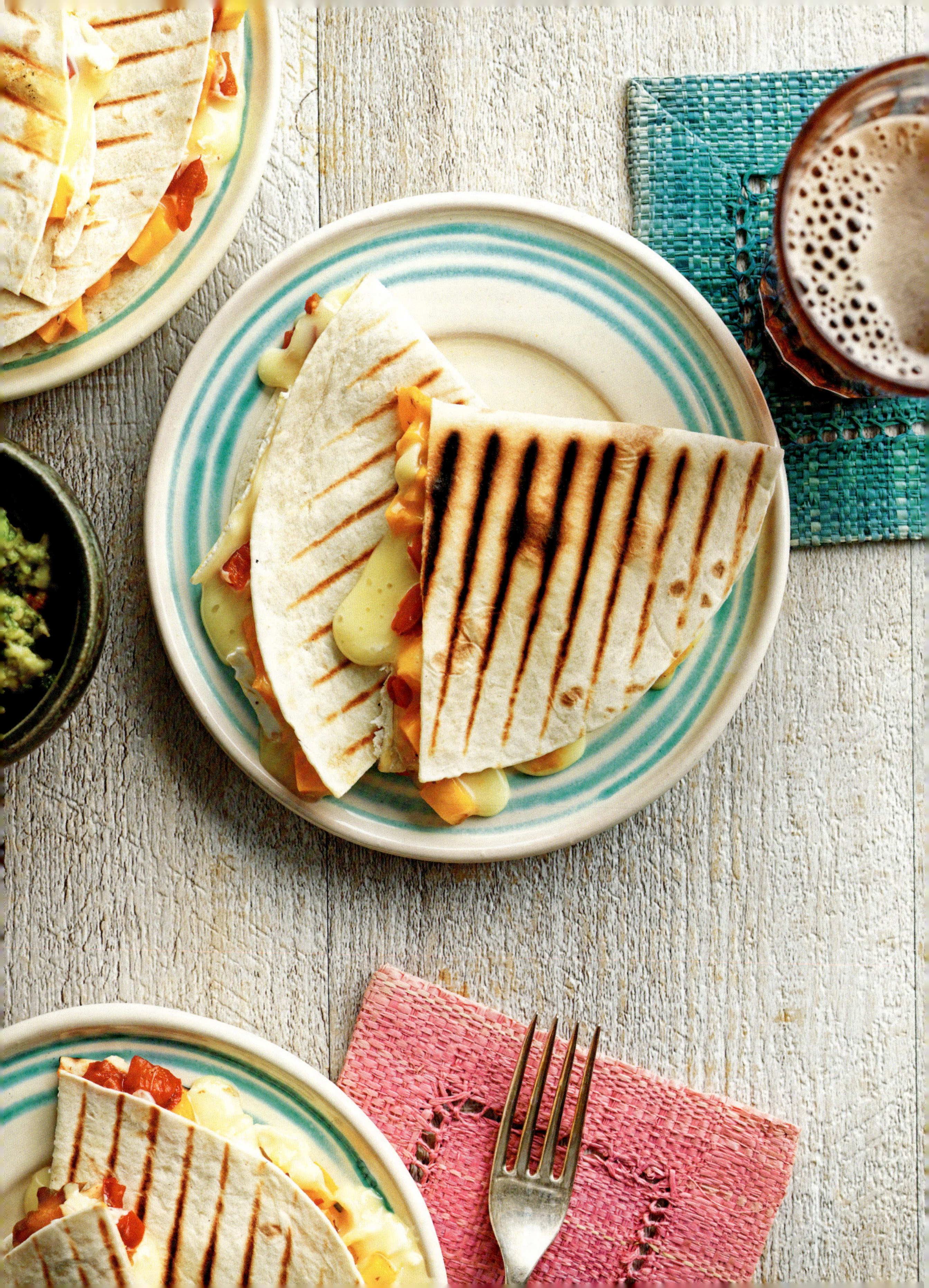

Empanadas are to Latin America what pasties are to Cornwall in the far west of England, and can be found almost everywhere. Typical vegetarian versions feature a mixture of cheese and spinach or sweet potato but we like to load ours with a variety of cheeses. These are delicious served with Pebre (see page 176), the tang of the tomato and vinegar acting as the perfect foil to the rich, cheesy, flaky empanadas. The calorie count of these empanadas can be reduced slightly by oven-baking rather than deep-frying; just note that you will need to make the dough a little thicker if doing so.

TRIPLE CHEESE EMPANADAS

MAKES 20 FRIED OR 15 BAKED EMPANADAS

1 cup diced mozzarella cheese
1¼ cups shredded sharp Cheddar cheese
1¼ cups shredded smoked Cheddar cheese
8 scallions, trimmed and finely chopped
2 red chiles, trimmed and minced
beaten egg, to glaze
sunflower oil, for deep-frying (optional)

For the dough
2 cups all-purpose flour, plus extra for dusting
3 tablespoons butter
1 teaspoon salt
½ teaspoon baking powder
½ teaspoon baking soda
1 tablespoon superfine sugar
½ teaspoon ground turmeric
½ teaspoon chili powder
¾ cup milk
½ cup water

For the dough, mix together all the solid ingredients in a bowl. Heat the milk and water together to just below boiling point. Then remove from the heat and stir into the bowl with the solid ingredients to form a dough. Let cool. Once cool, knead the dough until smooth and elastic, cover it with plastic wrap, and place it in the refrigerator for at least 30 minutes to rest.

Mix the cheeses, scallions, and chiles together well in a bowl.

Once the dough has rested, separate it into 20 balls for frying or 15 balls for baking. Roll out the dough on a lightly floured surface into circles around 10 inches in diameter. Brush the edges with beaten egg, place a tablespoon of filling in the center of each, and fold them together to make a half-moon shape. Finally, press the edges together with a fork to make sure they are well sealed and there are no weak points where the cheese can escape.

Depending on whether you are deep-frying or baking your empanadas, either fill a large saucepan or deep-fryer with the sunflower oil and heat to 350°F, or until a cube of bread added to the oil browns in 30 seconds, or preheat the oven to 375°F.

Deep-fry the empanadas for 3 to 5 minutes, or until lightly golden, remove with a slotted spoon, and drain on paper towels. Or, bake the empanadas in the oven or 15 to 20 minutes until golden. Serve.

The chile we use for the chile butter in this recipe is found in a lot of our Mexican recipes. It comes in a rich sauce and is usually found canned. While very easy to get hold of in the US and Latin America, it is slightly harder for us to obtain here in Europe (though this is getting easier as Mexican food becomes more widely available generally). If you haven't got any on hand, a few crushed chili flakes combined with a little smoked paprika makes a good substitute.

LIME & CHILE CORN

SERVES 8 TO 10 AS PART OF A LATIN PARTY

½ stick salted butter
grated zest of 1 lime
1 chipotle chile in adobo, minced
6 to 8 corn cobs, husks removed
sea salt flakes

Melt the butter in a small saucepan or a microwave, add the grated lime zest and chopped chile, and mix together well.

Place the corn in a large saucepan of boiling water and cook for 3 to 4 minutes, or until the kernels are just tender.

Remove the corn from the water using long-handled tongs and place them on a hot ridged grill pan or preheated barbecue. Brush the corn with half the chipotle butter and cook, turning every few minutes, until nicely colored on all sides. Remove from the heat, brush with the remaining butter, and season with salt to serve.

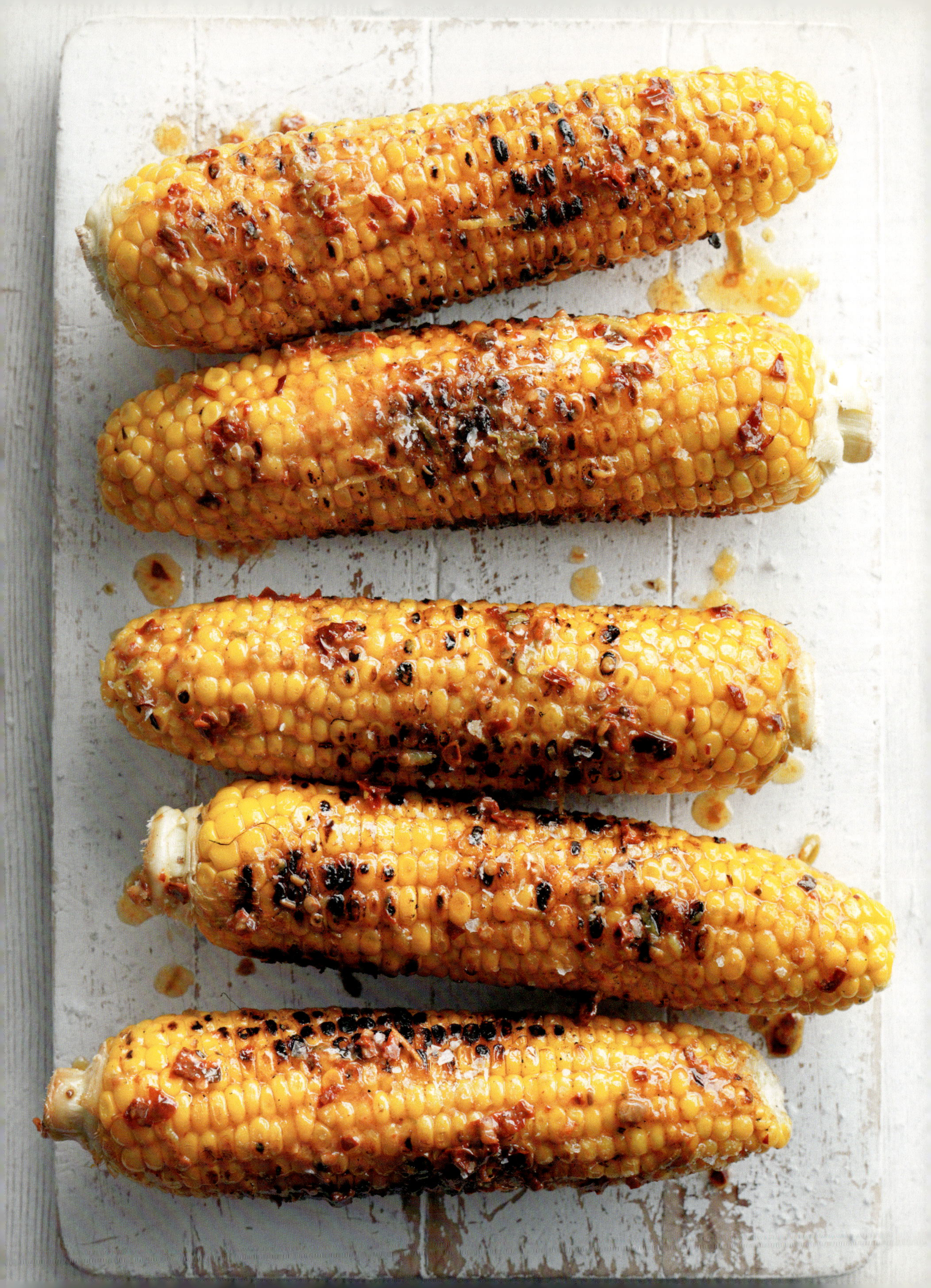

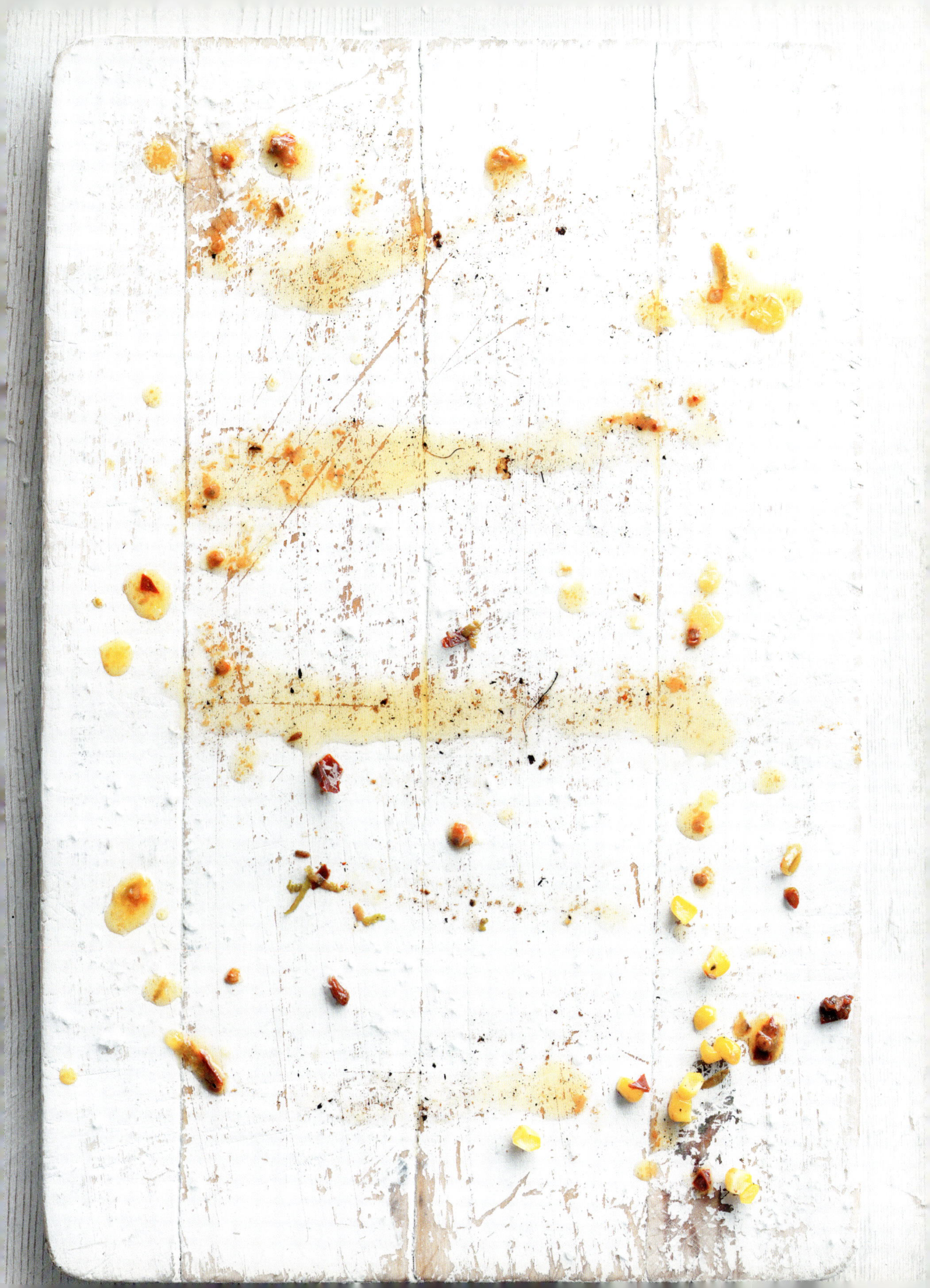

Plantains are one of those things that can seem a little intimidating to use if you've never cooked with them before. They look like big versions of normal bananas, but they need to be cooked before you can eat them. You can cook with both the green and yellow plantains, however, for this recipe you will need the ripe yellow ones (but not the ones that are so ripe they are almost black). If you can't find plantains you can substitute slightly under-ripe normal bananas. Serve immediately after cooking to enjoy them at their best.

PLANTAIN FRITTERS

SERVES 8 TO 10 AS PART OF A LATIN PARTY

sunflower oil, for deep-frying
3 ripe plantains, peeled and coarsely chopped
2 red chiles, trimmed and minced
1 small white onion, chopped
handful of cilantro leaves
grated zest and juice of 1 lime
1 tablespoon peanut butter
pinch of salt
pinch of chili powder
¾ cup all-purpose flour sifted with ¾ teaspoon baking powder
Pebre (*see* page 176), to serve

Fill a large saucepan or deep-fryer with sunflower oil and heat to 350°F, or until a cube of bread added to the oil browns in 30 seconds.

Put all the remaining ingredients except the flour and baking powder mixture into a food processor and blend together until smooth and creamy. Then add the flour mixture and blend together again until well combined.

Working in batches, carefully drop small spoonfuls of the batter into the hot oil and cook for 5 minutes, or until the fritters have puffed up and are golden brown. Remove from the pan with a slotted spoon and drain on paper towels. Serve immediately accompanied by Pebre.

Serve these as an appetizer before **Cinnamon-spiced Squash & Lima Bean Stew** (*see* page 120), or serve them alongside the stew as an alternative to the **Chile Cornbread** (*see* page 178).

To turn these into a main course, serve with **Mexican Salad with Avocado, Baby Gem, Scallion & Jalapeño** (*see* page 162), **Pebre** (*see* page 176), and **Guacamole** (*see* page 175).

MAINS

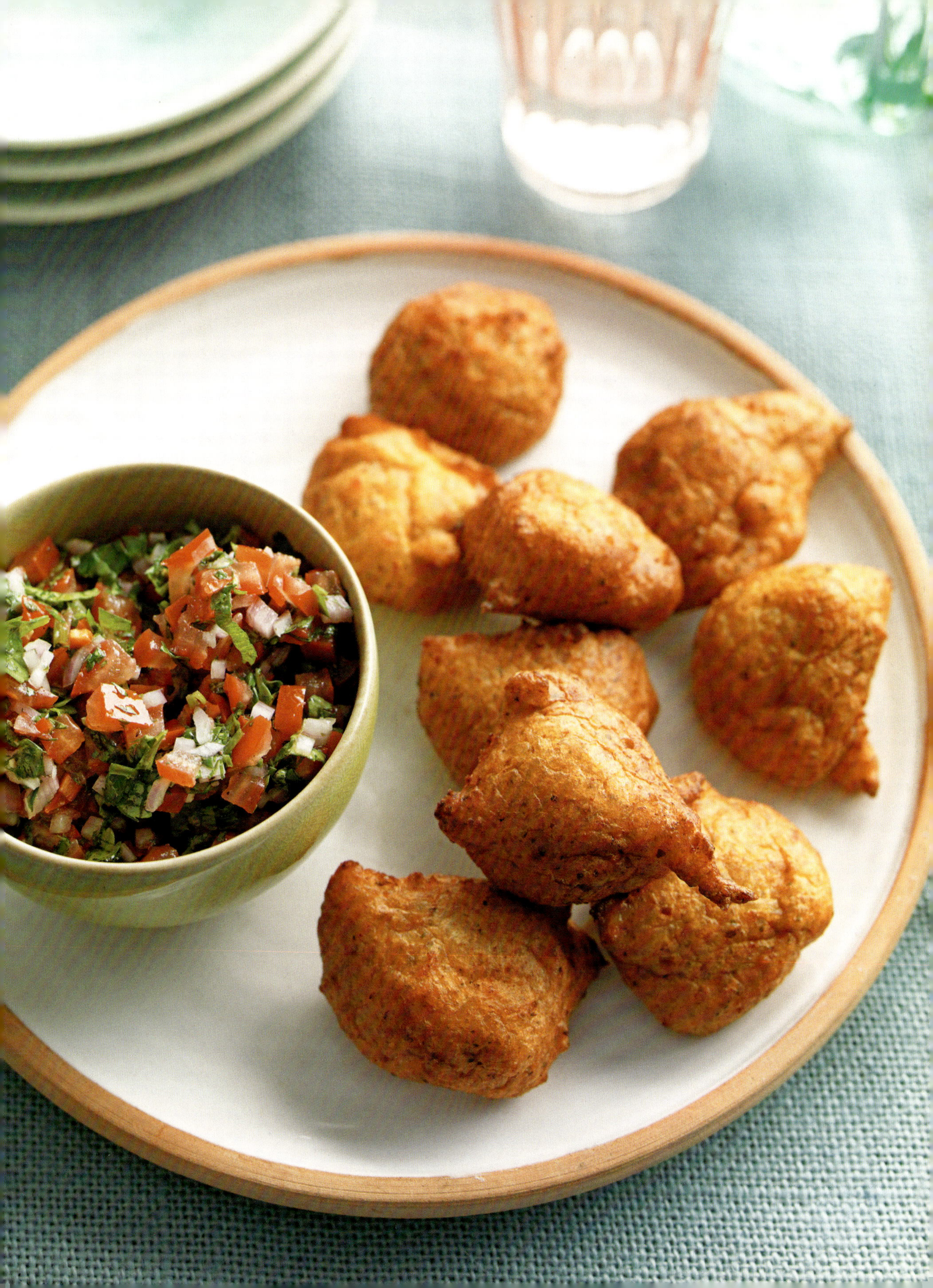

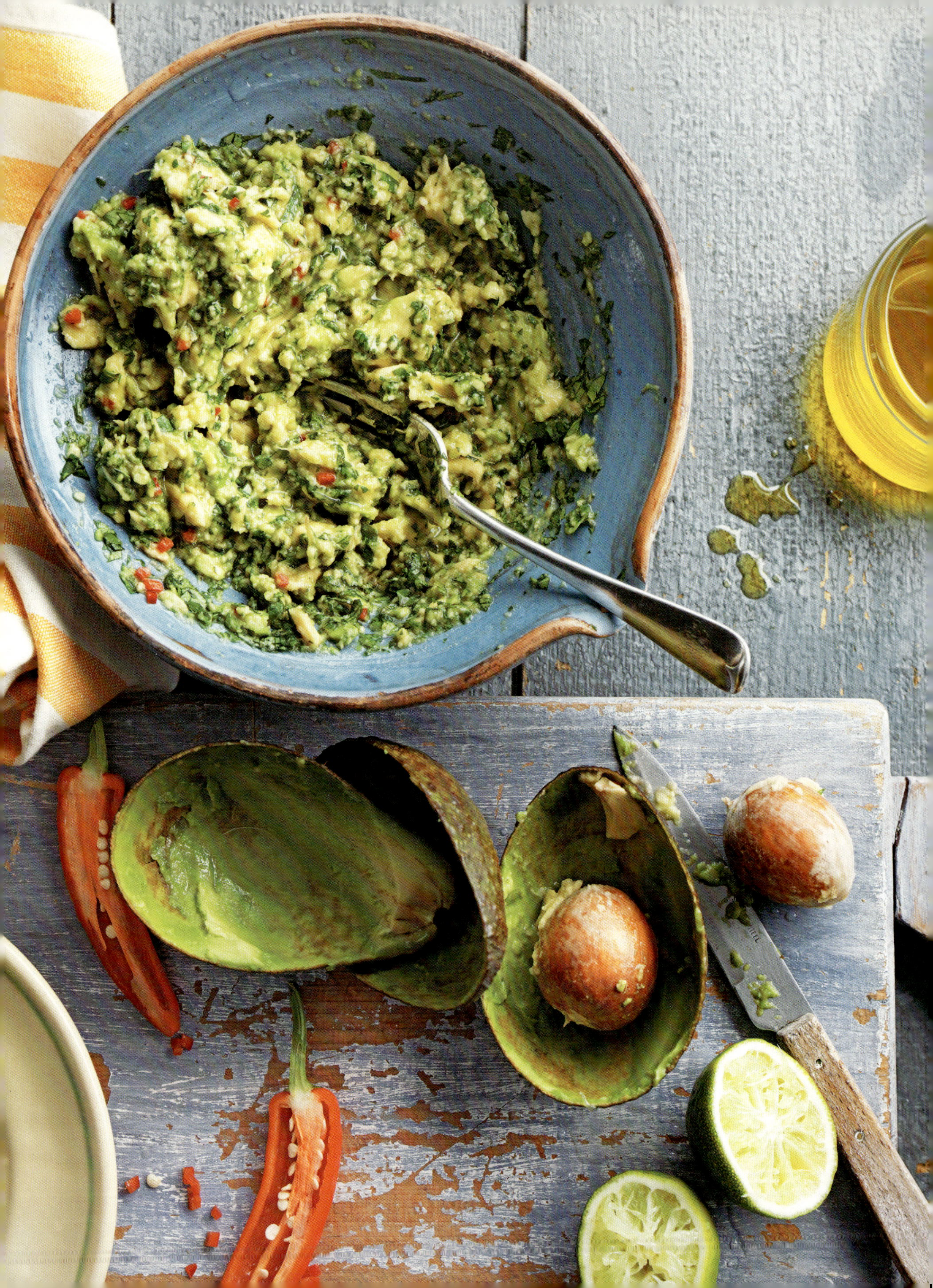

Guacamole can be used as a dip or condiment to go with a variety of dishes. The addition of finely diced tomato or fresh red bell peppers is a nice variation. We like to make guacamole super smooth when serving it for parties, because this makes it easier for dipping. However, we leave it chunkier when making it to be served as a side or condiment for burritos or tacos.

GUACAMOLE

SERVES 4

3 ripe avocados
½ small red chile, trimmed, seeded, and finely diced
2 tablespoons extra virgin olive oil
juice of 1 lime
handful of cilantro leaves, chopped
salt and white pepper

Peel and seed the avocados, place them in a mixing bowl or food processor, and add the remaining ingredients. Either mash with a fork to a coarse-textured purée or mix well in the food processor to a smooth paste, depending on your preference. Season with salt and pepper to taste and serve.

Use ripe hass avocados for guacamole (they are the blacker, thick-skinned knobbly ones).

To stop guacamole from discoloring if you are making it in advance, don't allow any air to make contact with it. Keep it in a bowl and press plastic wrap right onto the surface of the guacamole, as well as covering the bowl.

Pebre is a Chilean condiment served alongside almost every dish that is eaten at the dinner table in that country. It is similar to Pico de Gallo (see page 22), or Mexican tomato salsa, but it differs in that it is wetter and more vinegary. This makes it a great accompaniment to empanadas and other Latin dishes, and it is good with a dash or two of Tabasco sauce for a little extra kick. If you can't find very ripe tomatoes, just add a pinch of sugar to the mixture.

PEBRE

SERVES 4

5 large ripe tomatoes
1 small banana shallot, minced
2 garlic cloves, minced
1 small red chile, trimmed and minced
1 bunch of cilantro, leaves picked and chopped
½ cup olive oil
2 tablespoons water
1 tablespoon red wine vinegar or lemon juice
2 teaspoons Tabasco sauce (optional)
salt and pepper

Cut the tomatoes in half and remove the cores. Then dice the tomato flesh into small chunks. Add to a mixing bowl with the rest of the ingredients and stir well to combine. Season with salt and pepper to taste, and serve.

V (if sour cream is omitted) *GF*

Beans, beans are good for your heart, the more you eat, the… better they are! A staple of Mexican and Tex-Mex cuisine, this recipe calls for dried black beans but dried pinto or red beans can also be used; if you do so, they should be soaked overnight before cooking. Epazote is a Mexican herb often combined with bean dishes because of its antiflatulent properties. So, while this herb isn't essential to this recipe, it's recommended if you can find it! This dip is great served with a side of corn chips.

BLACK BEAN DIP

SERVES 4 TO 6

1 cup dried black beans
1 teaspoon epazote
1 teaspoon salt
2½ pints water, plus extra if needed
½ teaspoon baking soda
1 bunch of cilantro, leaves picked and chopped
2 tablespoons sour cream, to garnish (optional)

For the sauce
light oil (such as canola, peanut, or sunflower)
½ onion, minced
1 small red chile, trimmed and minced
2 garlic cloves, minced
2 teaspoons ground coriander
½ teaspoon ground cumin
2 teaspoons paprika
½ teaspoon cayenne pepper
1 cup chopped tomatoes
1 tablespoon tomato paste

Put the beans, epazote, and salt in a saucepan, cover with the water, and bring to a simmer. Add the baking soda and continue to simmer over low heat for 30 to 40 minutes, stirring occasionally. Add a little more water if necessary to stop the beans from sticking to the bottom of the pan, and cook until the beans have begun to break down and become mushy.

Meanwhile, for the sauce, heat a splash of oil in a separate saucepan, add the onion, chile, and garlic and sauté for 5 minutes, or until the onion has softened. Add the spices and fry for another few minutes, stirring, then pour in the chopped tomatoes and tomato paste and bring to a simmer. Cook over low heat, stirring occasionally, for 15 to 20 minutes, or until the mixture is creamy in texture and the flavors have melded together.

Once the beans are ready, add them to the sauce and stir in the chopped cilantro. Spoon into a bowl and garnish with sour cream, if you like.

Gluten-free and deliciously moist, cornbread is well known as being a staple food of the Southern states, but is also popular in Latin America and the Caribbean. It goes really well with our Cinnamon-spiced Squash & Lima Bean Stew (see page 120) and our Cranberry Bean Soup with Smoked Tofu & Pico de Gallo (see page 22).

CHILE CORNBREAD

SERVES 8 TO 10 AS PART OF A LATIN PARTY

butter, for greasing, plus extra for spreading on the bread
1½ cups cornmeal, plus extra for sprinkling
1 cup corn kernels
½ red chile, trimmed and minced
2 scallions, trimmed
3½oz smoked Cheddar cheese
¾ cup gluten-free all-purpose flour
¼ cup superfine sugar
1 bunch of cilantro, leaves picked and chopped
pinch of cayenne pepper
1 teaspoon salt
½ teaspoon baking powder
¼ teaspoon baking soda
2 eggs
2 cups milk
½ cup sour cream
3 tablespoons sunflower oil

Preheat the oven to 400°F. Line the bottom of a 12 x 4-inch loaf pan with nonstick parchment paper. Grease the sides with butter and sprinkle with 2 to 3 tablespoons of cornmeal.

Place the remaining cornmeal and all the other solid ingredients in a bowl and mix together thoroughly. Add the eggs, milk, sour cream, and sunflower oil and stir together to combine.

Spoon the cornbread mixture into the prepared loaf pan and bake for 45 to 50 minutes, or until lightly golden and the point of a skewer inserted into the center of the loaf comes out clean. Let cool for a few minutes in the pan before turning out onto a wire rack to cool further. Serve smothered with butter.

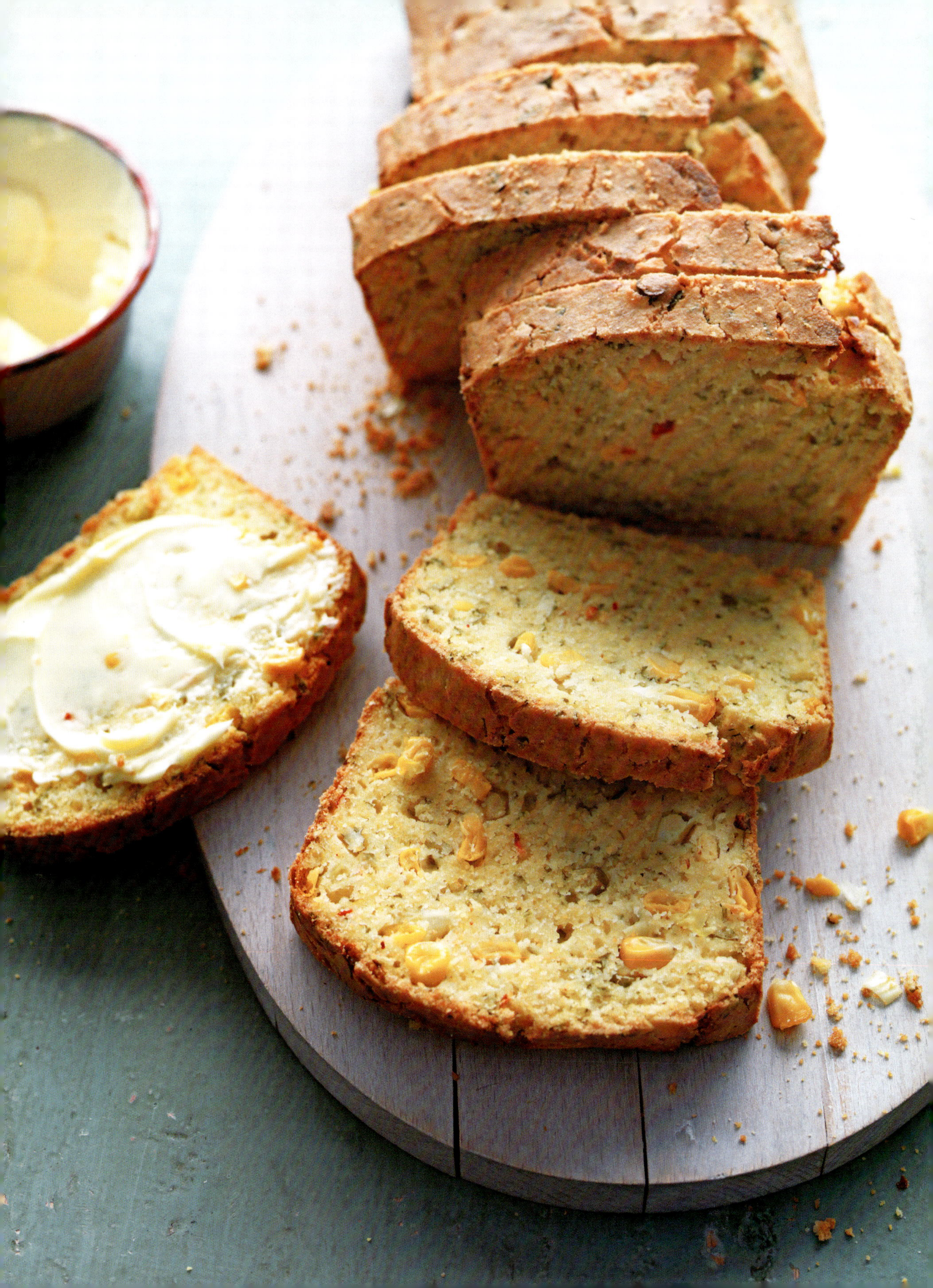

SIDES

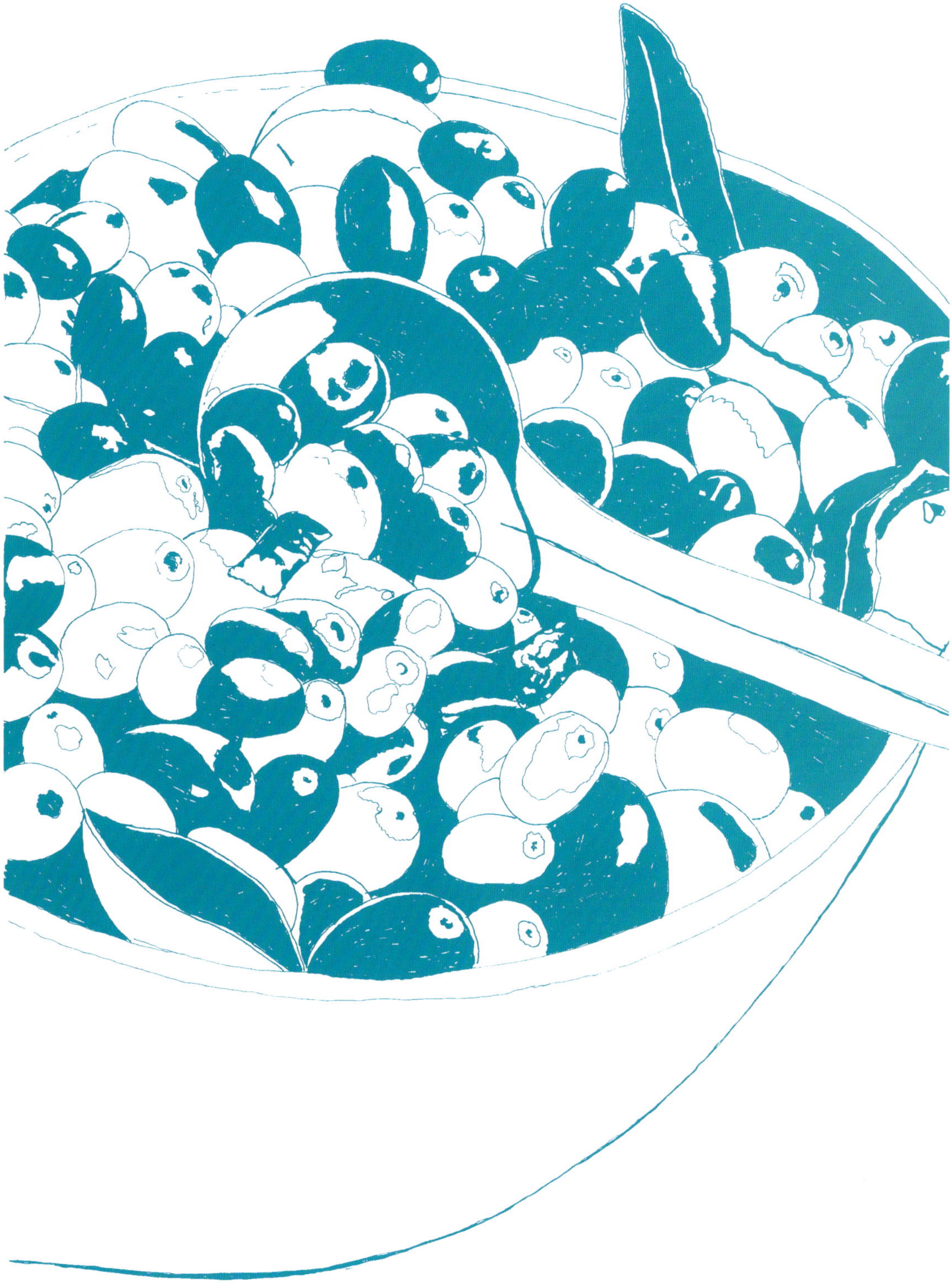

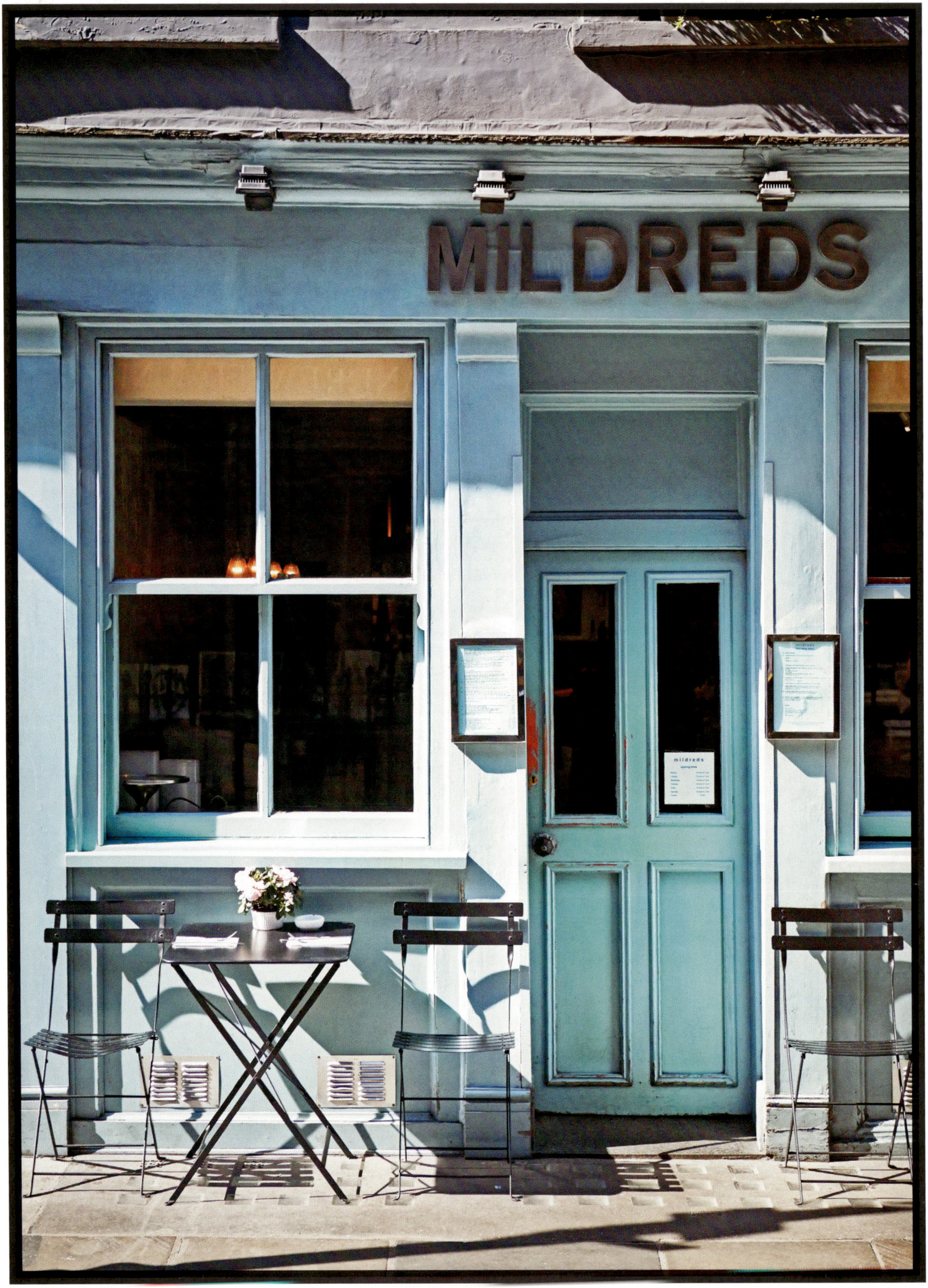
MILDREDS

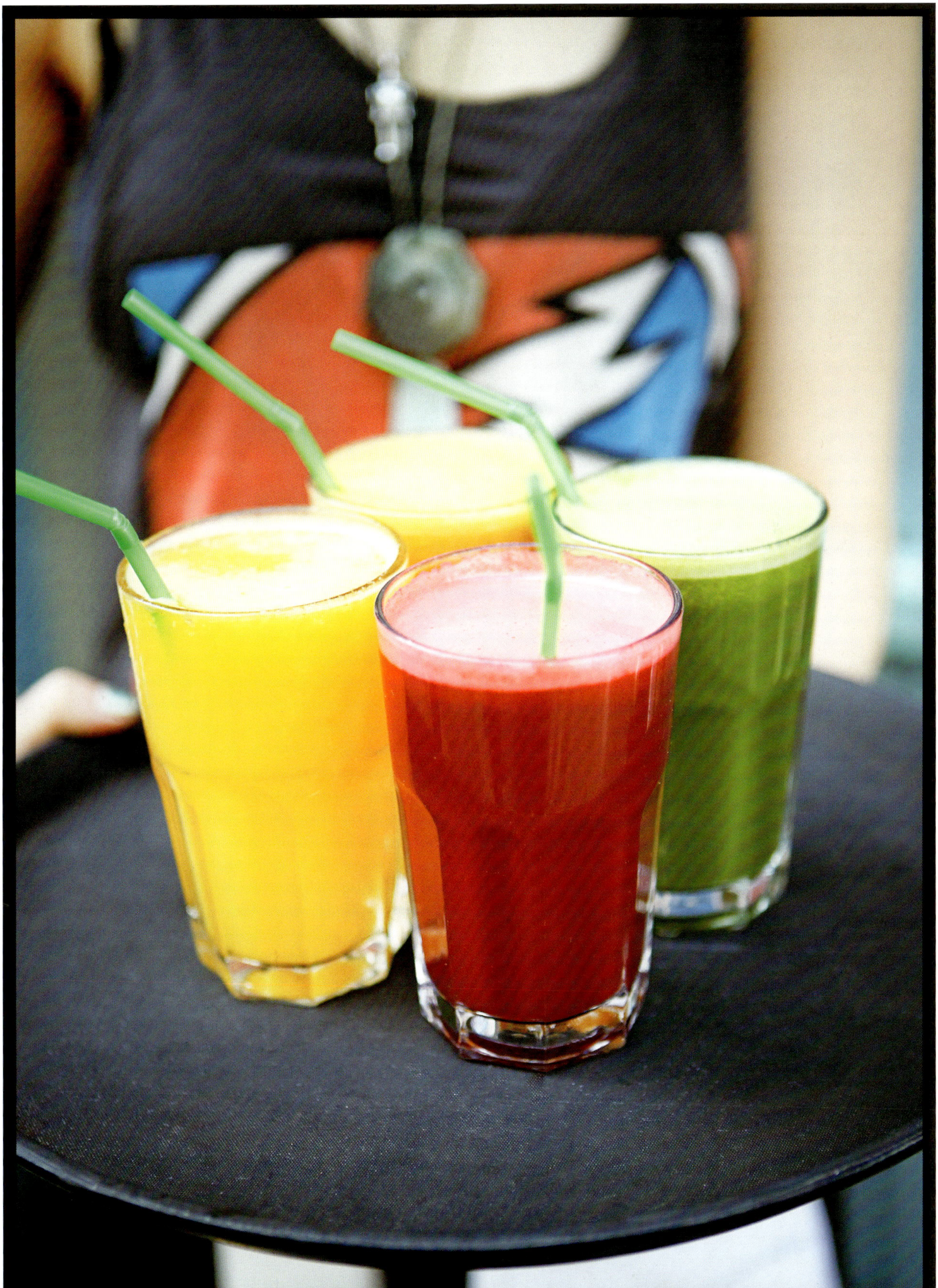

These very simple yeast-free flatbreads make a great accompaniment to curries and are also excellent filled with spicy pickles and salads.

GARLIC ROTIS

MAKES 8 ROTIS

1½ tablespoons butter
3 garlic cloves, minced
½ teaspoon dried chili flakes
1¾ all-purpose flour, plus extra for dusting
½ cup whole-wheat flour
2 teaspoons baking powder
⅓ to ½ cup water
vegetable oil

Warm the butter in a small saucepan over low heat, add the garlic and chili flakes, and cook, stirring, for 1 minute, or until the garlic has begun to release its flavor but has not yet colored. Sift the flours and baking powder into a mixing bowl, add the butter mixture, and gradually stir in the water using a wooden spoon to form a moist (but not sticky) dough. Knead the dough for a few minutes until smooth, cover with a clean damp cloth, and let stand for 30 minutes to rise until nearly doubled in size.

Divide the risen dough into 8 pieces and form into balls. Dust with a little flour, then roll out on a lightly floured work surface into thin circles about ¼ inch thick. Wipe a heavy skillet with just enough oil to grease the bottom, place over medium heat, and cook the rotis one at a time for 2 to 3 minutes on each side, until puffed up and brown. Serve immediately, or cover with a clean dish towel and reheat in the oven at a low temperature when needed.

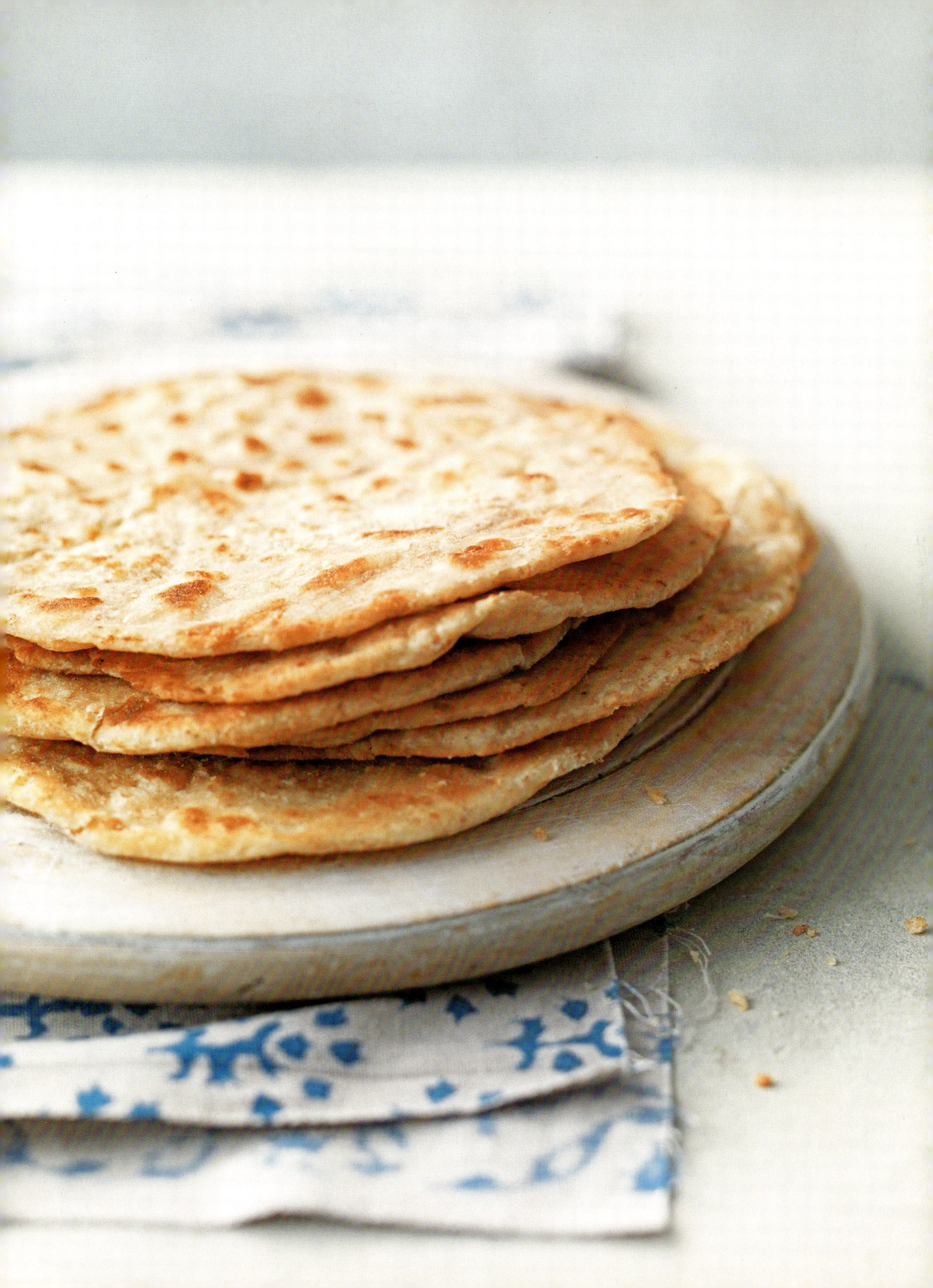

These fries are very popular at Mildreds and are great served with our Mexican Kidney Bean, Jalapeño, Roasted Bell Pepper & Corn Burgers and a little Vegan Basil Mayonnaise (see pages 141 and 232). While they are straightforward to make they do require deep-frying, so be careful when using hot oil.

SWEET POTATO FRIES

SERVES 4 TO 6 AS A SIDE

3 large sweet potatoes, ends trimmed
sunflower oil for deep-frying
sea salt flakes
3 scallions, finely chopped (optional)

Scrub the sweet potatoes to remove any dirt but do not peel. Slice into sticks about 3/4 inch thick.

Fill a large saucepan or deep-fryer with the sunflower oil and heat it to 325°F, or until a cube of bread added to the oil browns in 40 seconds. To avoid overcrowding the pot, cook the sweet potatoes in batches and fry for 4 to 6 minutes, or until just cooked through but not beginning to color. Remove with a slotted spoon and transfer to paper towels to drain.

Increase the heat of the oil to 350°F, or until a cube of bread added to the oil browns in 30 seconds. Fry the sweet potato fries once again for 2 to 3 minutes, or until crisp and golden. Sprinkle with sea salt flakes and scatter with a few chopped scallions, if using. Serve.

We like to serve these wedges with our Wild Mushroom & Ale Pies (see page 127) and our burgers. In the restaurant we often serve these deep-fried, but they are just as delicious, healthier, and a lot less fiddly when roasted like this.

ROAST POTATO WEDGES

SERVES 4 TO 6 AS A SIDE

6 to 8 round red or round white potatoes
½ cup Herb Oil (*see* page 238)
1 to 2 teaspoons sea salt flakes
5 thyme sprigs, leaves picked

Preheat the oven to 400°F.

Scrub the potatoes, cut them in half and then into wedges about ¾ inch thick. Put them in a large saucepan, and cover with water, and then drain (this will remove excess starch). Return the potatoes to the pan, cover with water, and bring to a boil. Simmer for 30 seconds and then drain.

Pour the herb oil into a large roasting pan and place it in the preheated oven for a few minutes. When the oil is hot, remove the pan from the oven. Carefully place the parboiled potatoes into the hot oil, scatter with the sea salt flakes and thyme, and shuffle them around to ensure the potato wedges are evenly coated in oil. Roast for 30 minutes, turning them over halfway through cooking, until crispy and golden brown. Serve.

V **GF**

While we've included these deliciously sweet root vegetables here in our sides section, they also make a fantastic warm salad when mixed with a few balsamic pickled onions, maple roast pecans, and some baby spinach.

MAPLE-ROASTED ROOT VEGETABLES

SERVES 6 TO 8 AS A SIDE

1lb parsnips, peeled and quartered lengthwise

13oz carrots, peeled and quartered lengthwise

13oz butternut squash or pumpkin, peeled and cut into bite-size pieces

11½oz beets, peeled and cut into ½-inch wedges

2 tablespoons maple syrup

½ cup Herb Oil (*see* page 238)

Preheat the oven to 400°F. Place a roasting pan in the oven to warm (this will prevent the potatoes from sticking while roasting).

Put the vegetables in a large mixing bowl, pour in the maple syrup and Herb Oil, and toss everything together, ensuring that the vegetables are well coated. Carefully remove the hot roasting pan from the oven and place the vegetables in it, spreading them out evenly. Roast for about 25 minutes, or until the vegetables are golden brown and cooked through. Serve.

If you aren't vegan, **honey** also works well as an alternative to maple syrup here.

These vegetables are a nice accompaniment to the **Wild Mushroom & Ale Pies** (*see* page 127).

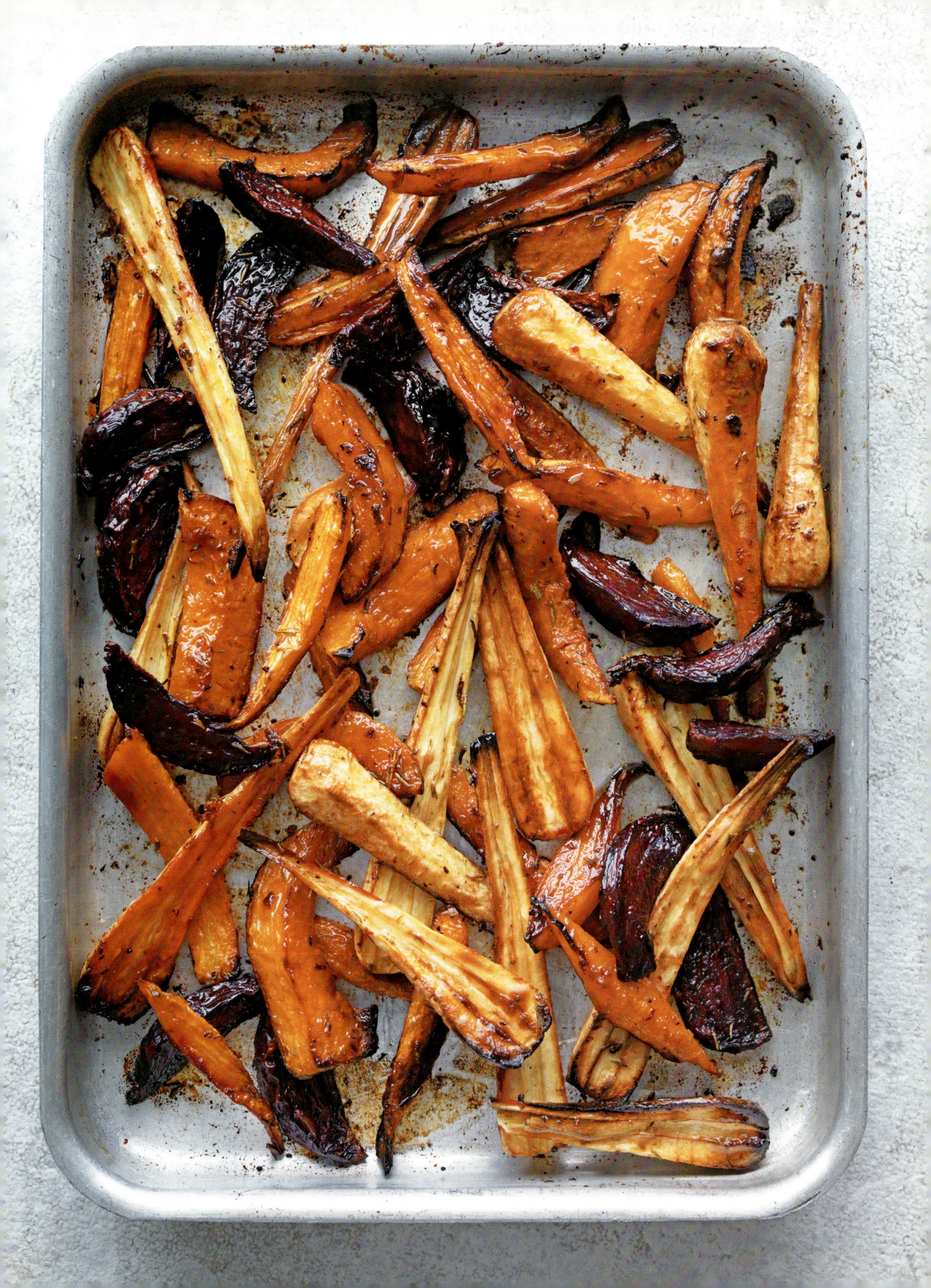

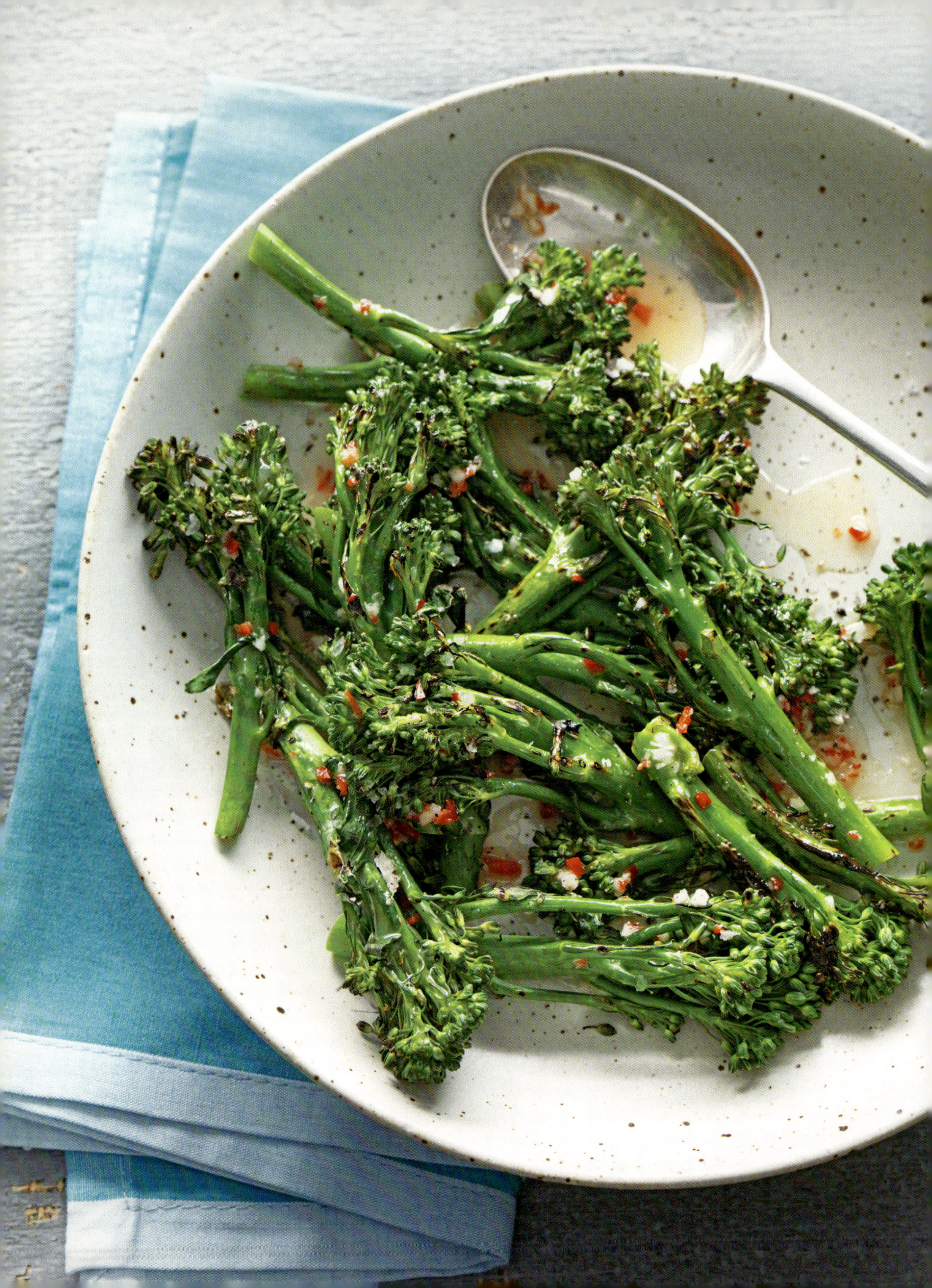

Lovely and colorful, this is a great summer side. We really recommend making the chilli lemon oil in advance by a day or so, to allow the flavors to mellow and blend together well. This recipe makes quite a lot of oil, but it's so great for dressing vegetables, adding to salads, or drizzling over bread before chargrilling we're sure you'll use it all up. It will keep refrigerated for at least a week in a sealed container.

CHARGRILLED LONG-STEM BROCCOLI
WITH CHILE LEMON OIL

SERVES 4 TO 6 AS A SIDE

13oz long-stem broccoli or purple sprouting broccoli
sea salt

For the Chile Lemon Oil
1 red chile, trimmed and coarsely chopped
4 garlic cloves, coarsely chopped
juice of ½ lemon
pinch of sea salt flakes
1¼ cups light olive oil

For the chile lemon oil, put all the ingredients in a large measuring cup or pitcher and blend using a stick blender for 1 to 2 minutes. Alternatively, mince the chile and garlic and then combine with the lemon juice, salt, and oil.

Bring a large saucepan of salted water to a boil, add the broccoli spears, and blanch for 2 to 3 minutes, or until cooked but still slightly firm. Drain.

Heat a ridged grill pan over high heat, add the broccoli, and chargrill for 2 to 3 minutes, turning halfway through cooking, until nicely charred and cooked through. Remove from the heat, drizzle with 2 to 3 tablespoons of the chile lemon oil, and scatter with a little sea salt. Serve.

We use this couscous as an accompaniment for our Cauliflower & Green Olive Tagine (see page 136), though it is also very good served with Maple-roasted Root Vegetables (see page 188) and Harissa (see page 228) as a light lunch.

APRICOT & PISTACHIO COUSCOUS

SERVES 6 TO 8 AS A SIDE

1¼ cups pistachios
1½ cups couscous
2 tablespoons olive oil
grated zest and juice of 1 lemon
¾ cup chopped dried apricots
1¼ cups boiling water
1 small bunch of flat-leaf parsley, leaves picked and chopped
salt and pepper

Toast the pistachios in a dry skillet over low heat for 3 to 4 minutes, or until beginning to color. Remove from the heat and set aside.

Add the couscous, olive oil, grated lemon zest, lemon juice, and chopped apricots to a mixing bowl and stir to combine. Season with salt and pepper. Pour in the boiling water, cover with plastic wrap, and let stand for 10 minutes, or until the couscous is fluffy.

Put the pistachios in a food processor and pulse them briefly into small pieces. Stir the nuts through the couscous with the chopped parsley and serve.

This is a lovely, warming winter side dish. Try making it several hours in advance of the rest of your meal (or even the day before) and reheating it before serving, to allow the flavors to develop even more.

BRAISED RED CABBAGE

SERVES 6 TO 8 AS A SIDE

2lb red cabbage, finely shredded
1 red onion, diced
¾ cup golden raisins
½ cinnamon stick
2 bay leaves
2 tablespoons balsamic vinegar
12 juniper berries
¼ cup dark brown sugar
1 cup water, plus extra if needed
salt and pepper

Put all the ingredients in a saucepan over medium heat. Bring to a boil and then reduce to a simmer. Cover and cook over low heat for 45 minutes, stirring occasionally, until the cabbage is tender and the flavors have melded together. Add a little extra water, if necessary, to stop the cabbage from drying out. Serve.

These onion rings are delicious served with our Beet, Fennel, Apple & Dill Burgers (see page 142). Gluten-free flour makes the onion batter really light and less oily and, if you want to make these into an entirely gluten-free treat, just use gluten-free beer instead of the regular kind.

BEER-BATTERED ONION RINGS

SERVES 4 TO 6 AS A SIDE

vegetable oil, for deep-frying
2 cups gluten-free self-rising flour
pinch of sea salt flakes
2 cups gluten-free golden ale
  (or golden ale, for non gluten-free)
2 large yellow onions, cut into ½-inch
  slices, rings separated

Half-fill a large saucepan or deep-fryer with vegetable oil and heat to 350°F, or until a cube of bread added to the oil browns in 30 seconds.

Add the flour to a bowl with the sea salt flakes and gradually beat in the ale to form a batter. Drop a handful of the onion rings into the batter and stir to coat them generously.

Using long-handled tongs, drop the battered rings carefully into the hot oil and cook for 3 to 4 minutes, or until crisp and lightly golden. Remove from the oil with a slotted spoon and drain on paper towels. Repeat with the remaining onion rings. Serve immediately.

These are great served as an appetizer before our **Wild Mushroom & Ale Pies** (*see* page 127) or for a Sunday lunch on a winter's day.

You can spice up the batter with **coursely ground mixed pepper** for a spicier finish or even **cumin and chili flakes** for a taste of India, in which case you should serve the onion rings with a **mint yogurt dip**.

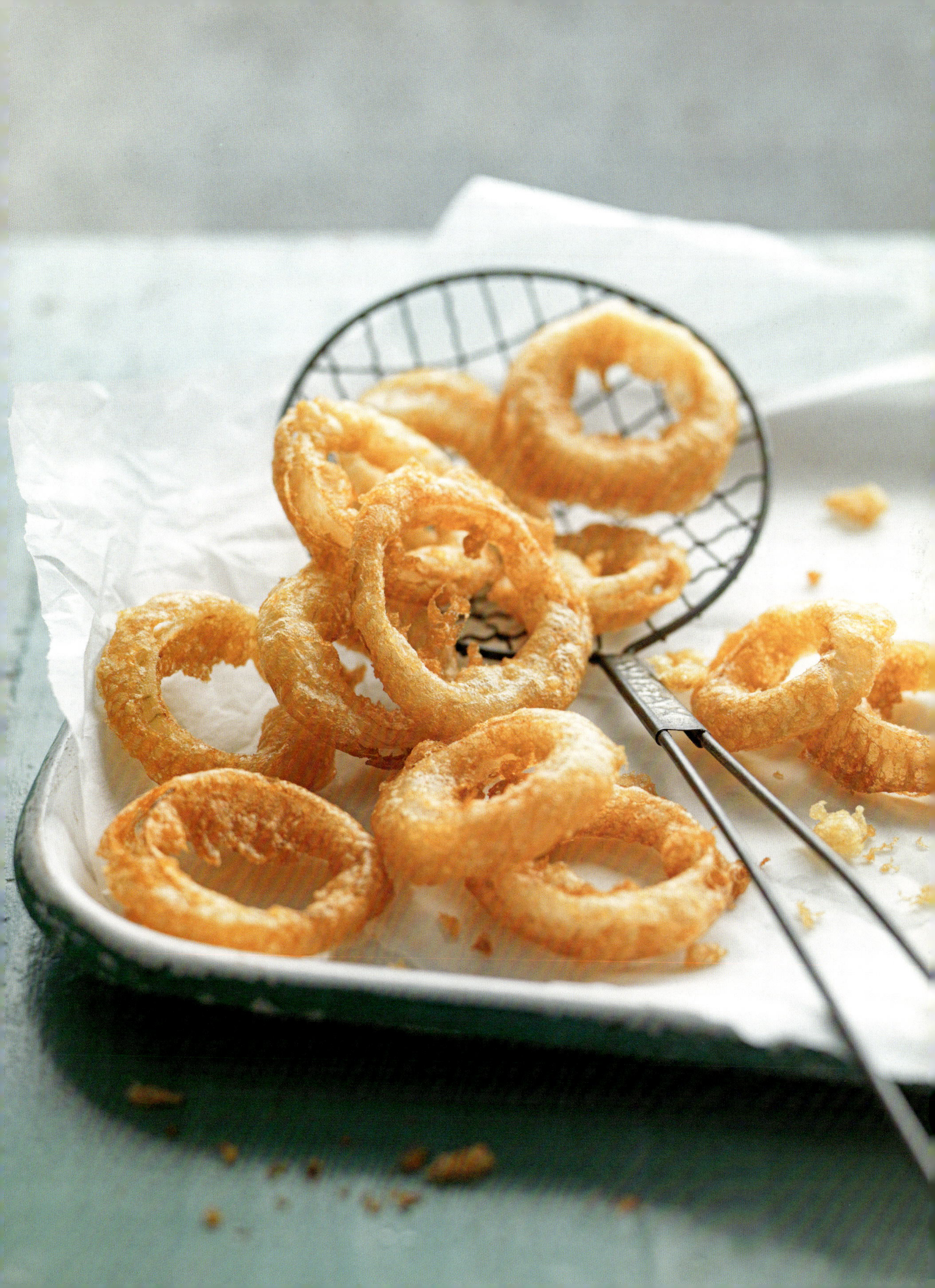

A really hearty, wintery side dish packed full of vegetables, this is wonderful served with baked potatoes and sautéed greens as a main meal, or spooned over toasted buttery sourdough bread as a light supper. If you want to save time, you can use canned beans here; just reduce both the water used for cooking and the time the beans simmer for by half.

MOLASSES-BAKED BEANS

SERVES 8 TO 10 AS A SIDE

- 1 cup dried great Northern, navy, or cannellini beans
- 3 tablespoons light olive oil or other light cooking oil (such as canola, peanut, or sunflower)
- 1 red chile, trimmed and minced
- 6 garlic cloves, finely sliced
- 2 white onions, finely diced
- 1 small fennel bulb, trimmed, cored, and finely diced
- 2 celery sticks, trimmed, peeled, and finely diced
- 2 carrots, peeled and finely diced
- ½ cinnamon stick
- 1 teaspoon smoked paprika
- 6 bay leaves
- 2 x 14oz cans diced tomatoes
- ½ cup tomato paste
- 1 tablespoon dark brown sugar
- 2 tablespoons molasses
- 2 cups water
- salt

Put the beans in a bowl, cover them with water, and let them soak overnight.

The next day, drain and rinse the beans. Bring a saucepan of salted water to a boil, add the beans, and cook for 40 to 60 minutes, or until they are tender but still holding their shape.

Meanwhile, preheat the oven to 350°F.

Heat the oil in a large saucepan over medium heat, add the chile, garlic, and onions and sauté for 5 to 8 minutes, or until the onions are soft and translucent. Add the fennel, celery, and carrots and cook for another 8 to 10 minutes, stirring, until the vegetables are beginning to soften. Add the cinnamon stick, paprika, and bay leaves and cook for another minute before adding the tomatoes, tomato paste, sugar, molasses, and water. Simmer for 20 to 25 minutes, or until all the vegetables are tender and the sauce has thickened.

Spoon the beans and sauce into a Dutch oven or large baking dish with a lid and stir to combine. Cover and bake for 1 hour, or until the beans are soft and the flavors have melded together. Serve.

Cooked in the classic style, wet polenta is an excellent accompaniment to Italian dishes such as Baby Eggplant & Roast Bell Pepper Caponata (see page 122).

WET POLENTA

SERVES 6 TO 8 AS A SIDE

4 cups vegetable stock
1 cup instant polenta
2oz vegetarian Parmesan-style hard cheese, shredded
2oz mascarpone
salt and pepper

Pour the vegetable stock into a large saucepan, season with salt and pepper, and bring to a boil. Add the polenta, whisking continuously to prevent lumps from forming, and simmer for 2 to 3 minutes, or until the polenta has thickened and all the stock has been absorbed.

Remove from the heat, stir in the cheeses, and season to taste with salt and pepper. Serve.

Coming from the same family as the cape gooseberry, tomatillos originate in Mexico, where they are a staple of the cuisine. They give this rice a slightly sour taste, which works nicely as a balance to burritos and other Mexican foods.

TOMATILLO RICE

SERVES 6 TO 8 AS A SIDE

light cooking oil (such as canola, peanut, or sunflower)
1 teaspoon ground coriander
7oz tomatillos, stalks removed, coarsely chopped
2 cups basmati rice, washed thoroughly and strained
1¾ cups boiling water
salt

Heat a splash of oil in a medium-sized saucepan and lightly fry the ground coriander for 30 to 40 seconds over low heat. Add the tomatillos and rice and season with salt.

Pour in the water and bring to a boil. Then reduce to a simmer and cook, covered, for 8 to 10 minutes, or until the rice is fluffy and cooked through. Remove from the heat and let sit, covered, for another 2 to 3 minutes to steam and fluff up further before serving.

We serve this with our Lapsang-scented Mushroom Stroganoff (see page 132). If walnuts aren't your thing, crushed hazelnuts or pecans can be used in their place.

WALNUT & LEEK PILAF

SERVES 8 TO 10 AS A SIDE

1 cup walnut pieces
2 tablespoons butter
1 leek, trimmed, cleaned, and diced
1 celery stalk, trimmed and diced
1½lb basmati rice, washed thoroughly and strained
3½ cups boiling water
1 bunch of dill, leaves picked and chopped

Preheat the oven to 350°F. Place the walnut pieces on a baking pan and toast in the oven for 8 to 10 minutes, or until just beginning to color. Remove from the oven and set aside.

In a small saucepan, melt the butter, add the leek and celery, and sauté for 5 to 8 minutes until soft. Add the washed rice and boiling water, cover, and simmer over low heat for 8 to 10 minutes, or until the rice has absorbed all the water and is tender. Remove from the heat and let cool a little in the pan, then stir in the walnuts and dill. Serve.

This simple pea pilaf adds a flash of color to curries and is fragrant without being overpowering.

TURMERIC, PEA & CARDAMOM BASMATI

SERVES 6 TO 8 AS A SIDE

vegetable oil
6 cardamom pods, seeds removed and lightly crushed
½ cinnamon stick
¼ teaspoon ground turmeric
½ teaspoon salt
1½ cups basmati rice, washed thoroughly and strained
1¾ cups boiling water
1¼ cups peas, defrosted if frozen

Heat a splash of oil in a small saucepan, add the cardamom, and cook for 1 minute, stirring, over medium heat. Add the cinnamon, turmeric, and salt and fry for another minute. Then add the basmati rice and boiling water. Bring to a gentle simmer and cook, covered, for 8 to 10 minutes, or until the rice is cooked through. Remove from the heat, stir in the peas, cover with a clean dish towel, and set aside for 10 minutes to steam and fluff up further.

DESSERTS

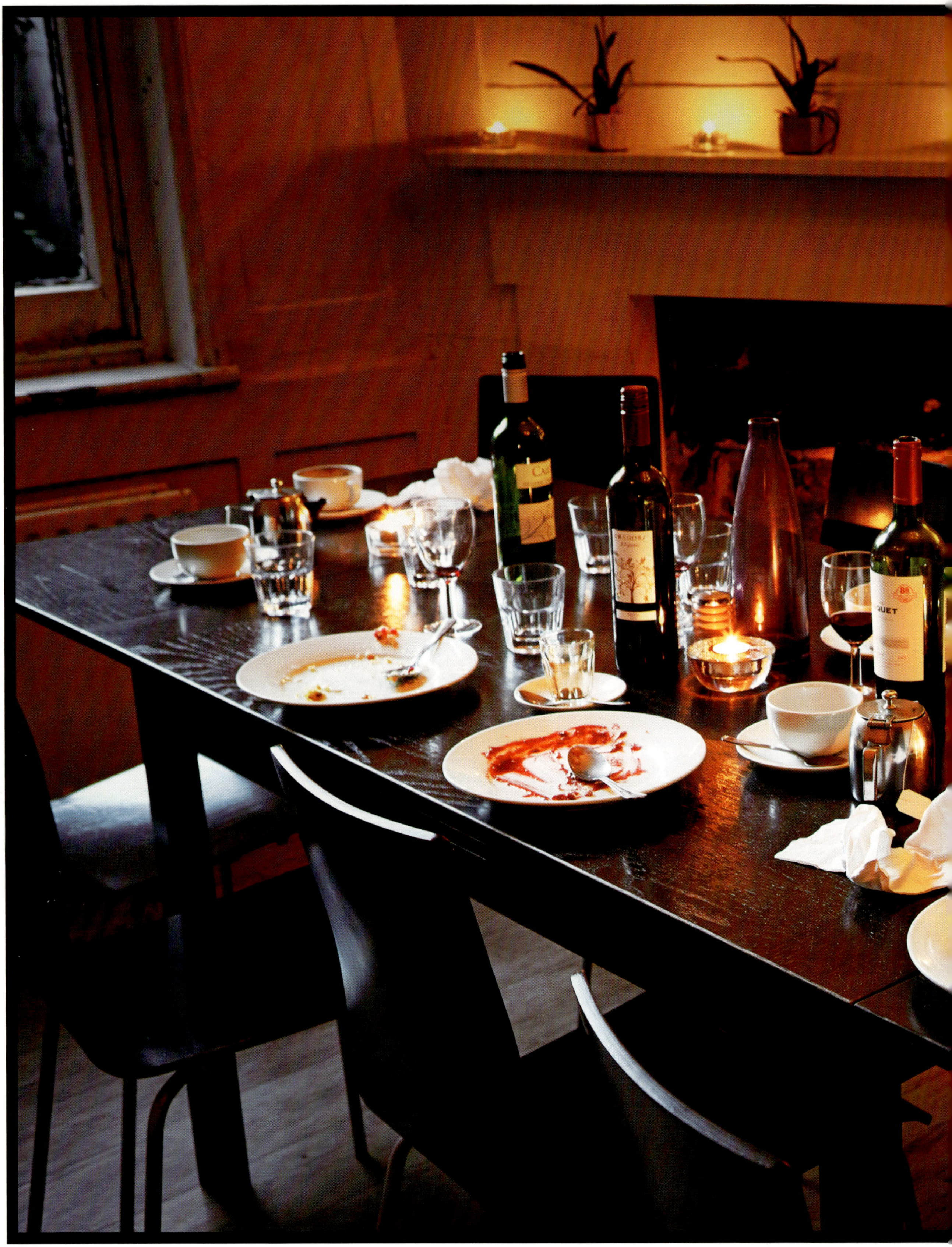

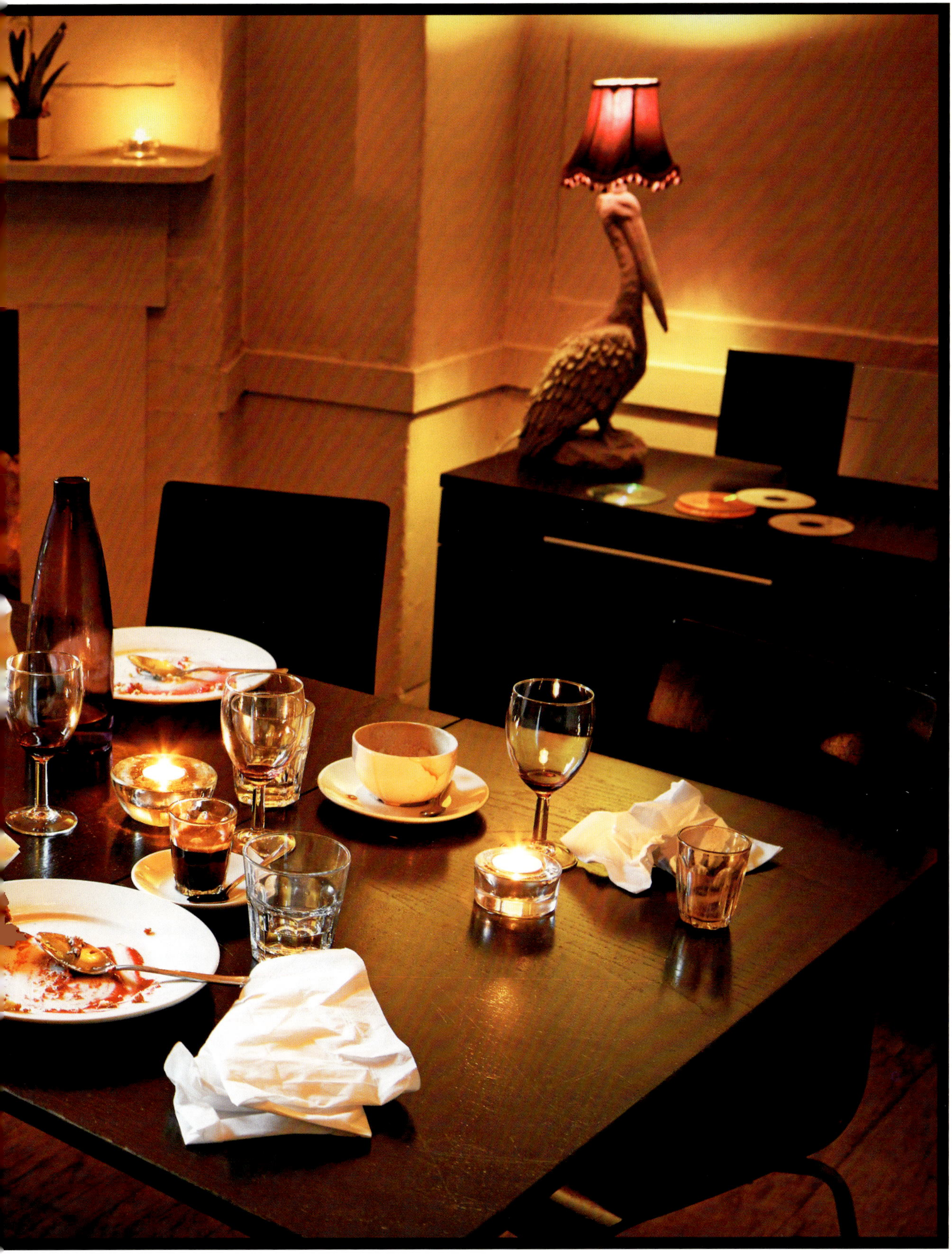

This surprisingly light cheesecake can easily be made gluten-free by using gluten-free crackers for the ginger-flavored crust. If you're short of time, a less labor-intensive version of the cake can be made using fresh raspberries instead; just fold 1½ cups of raspberries into the cheesecake filling before spooning it over the crust.

WHITE CHOCOLATE & RASPBERRY RIPPLE CHEESECAKE

SERVES 8 TO 10

For the raspberry compote
3 cups raspberries
½ cup superfine sugar
1 teaspoon cornstarch
2 tablespoons lemon juice

For the crust
7oz gluten-free graham crackers (or regular graham crackers, for non gluten-free)
¼ teaspoon ground ginger
2 tablespoons turbinado sugar
pinch of sea salt flakes
1 piece crystallized or preserved ginger (optional)
¼ cup butter, melted

For the filling
1½lb cream cheese
2½ tablespoons cornstarch
½ teaspoon vanilla extract
finely grated zest of ½ lemon
1 cup superfine sugar
2 eggs, plus 1 yolk
¾ cup sour cream
5oz white chocolate chips or white chocolate broken into small pieces

Preheat the oven to 375°F. Line a 9-inch springform cake pan with nonstick parchment paper. For the compote, heat half of the raspberries with the superfine sugar in a small saucepan and cook for 5 to 8 minutes over very low heat, stirring occasionally, until the sugar has dissolved. Mix the cornstarch and lemon juice together in a bowl, add to the raspberries, and cook until the mixture is thick enough to coat the back of a spoon. Take off the heat and mash with a fork or blend with a stick blender until smooth, then pass through a sieve to remove the seeds. Stir the remaining raspberries into the mixture and set aside to cool.

For the crust, put the dry ingredients into a food processor with the ginger, if using, and blend until the mixture resembles fine bread crumbs. Stir in the butter, then add to the prepared cake pan and press down into an even layer. Bake for 10 minutes, or until lightly toasted, then remove and set aside to cool. Reduce the heat to 325°F.

For the filling, beat the cheese, cornstarch, vanilla extract, and lemon zest together in a stand mixer or in a bowl using a spoon. Add the sugar, eggs, and egg yolk, one at a time, beating together briefly between each addition. Fold in the sour cream and chocolate chips.

To assemble, pour one-third of the compote onto the crust. Spoon in half the filling, spread it evenly, then add another third of the compote. Add the rest of the filling and spoon over the remaining compote in three parallel lines. Drag a knife through the lines to create a marbled effect. Bake for 1¼ hours, or until the filling is starting to color at the edge and is beginning to get firm but still wobbles. Remove from the oven and let chill for at least 3 hours in the fridge before serving.

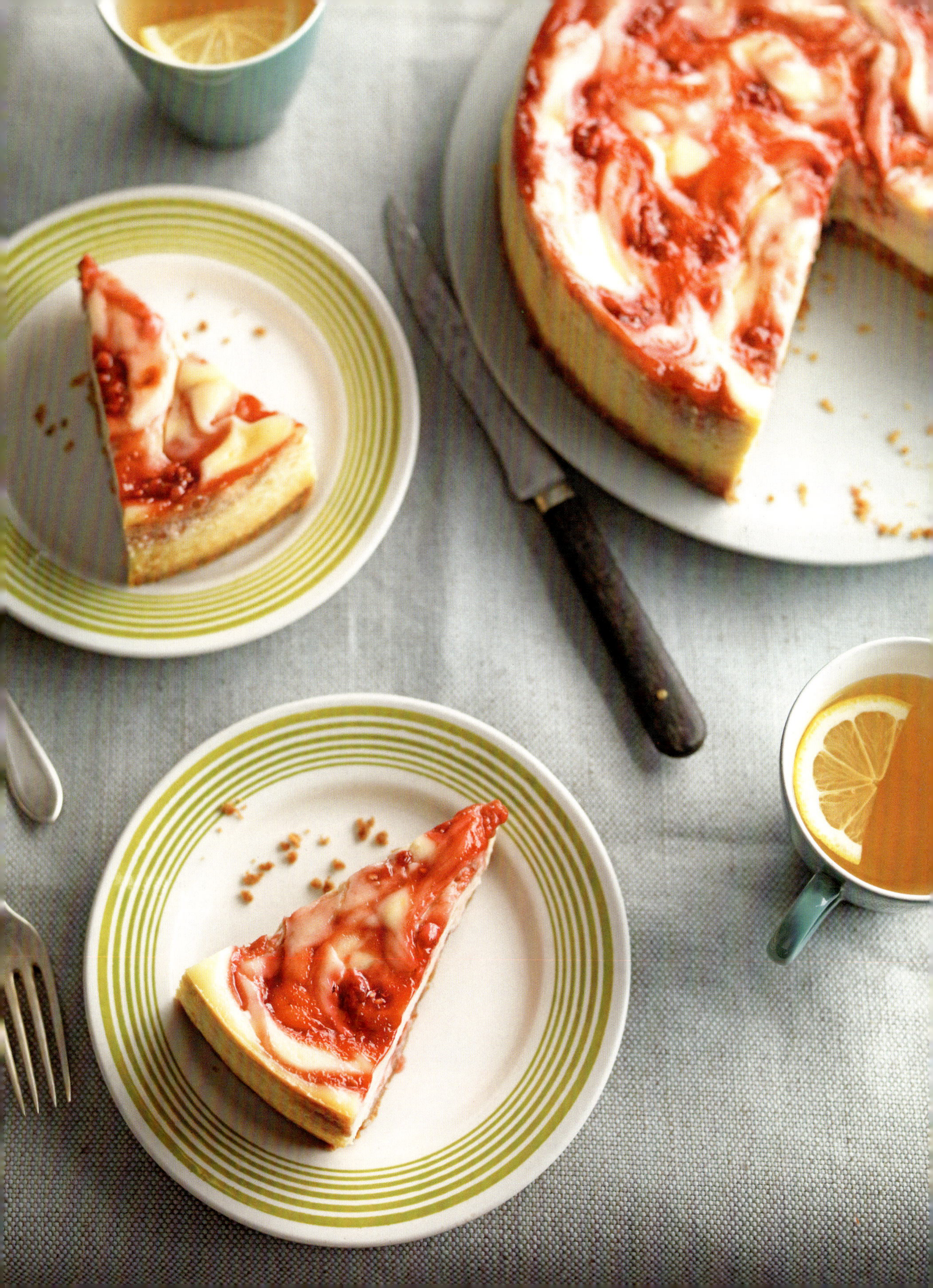

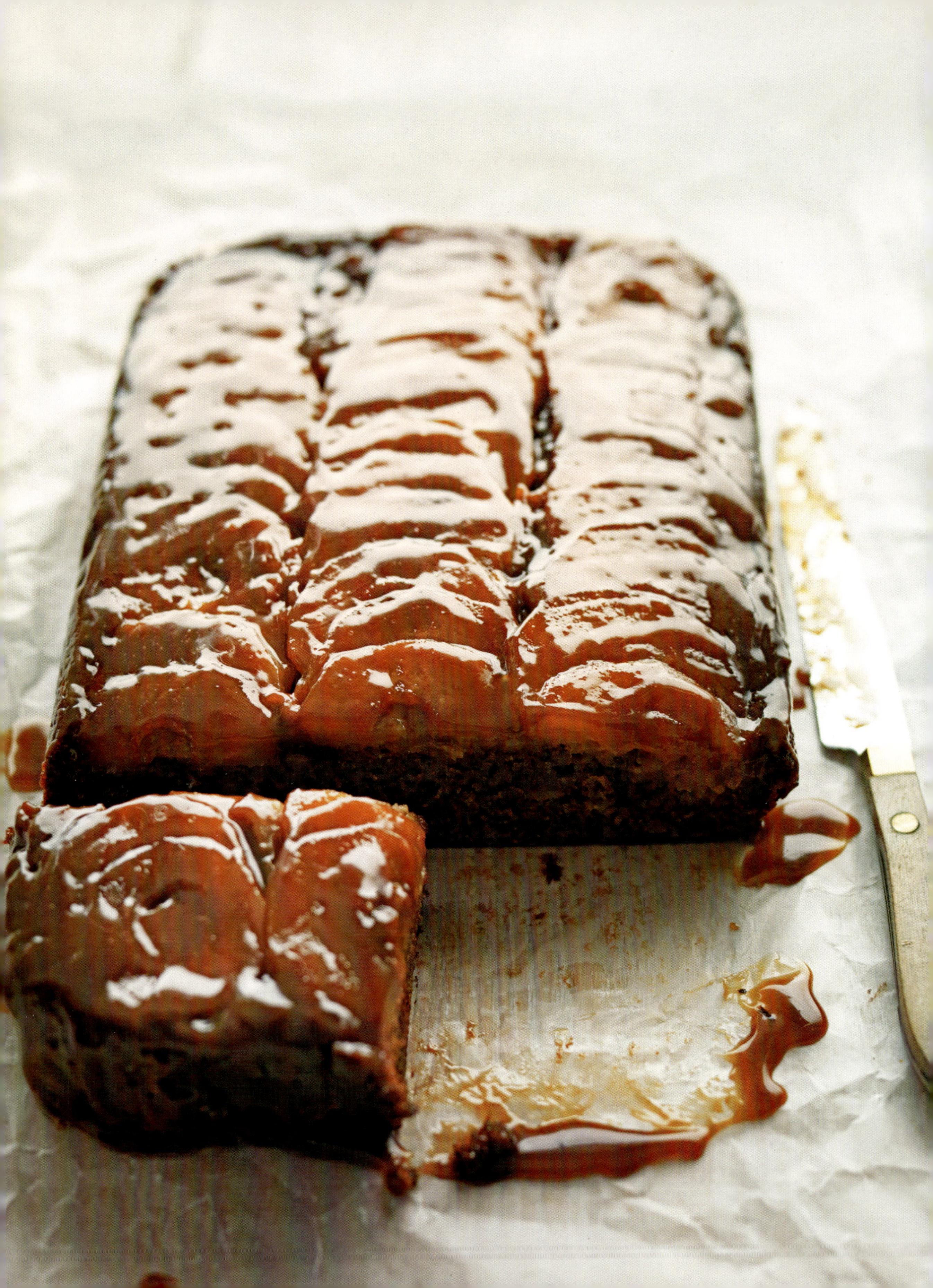

This is a twist on the classic, with apples and ginger cutting through the sweetness and adding extra layers of flavor to this much-loved dessert. This pudding works particularly well with gluten-free flour, though you'll get exactly the same results with regular all-purpose flour if you don't have any gluten-free flour. If you like a straightforward sticky toffee pudding, simply omit the ginger and apples.

APPLE & GINGER STICKY TOFFEE PUDDING

SERVES 8 TO 12

10oz dates
1¼ cups boiling water
4 crisp apples, such as Winesap or Cortland, peeled and cored
2 to 3 pieces preserved ginger in syrup
¼ cup butter
1¾ cups dark brown sugar
1 teaspoon vanilla extract
5 eggs
2½ cups gluten-free self-rising flour or 2½ cups all-purpose flour sifted with 2½ teaspoons baking powder
1 teaspoon baking soda
1 teaspoon baking powder
1 teaspoon ground ginger
whipped cream, to serve (optional)

For the toffee sauce
1 stick butter
2 cups dark brown sugar
1 tablespoon vanilla extract
1 tablespoon preserved ginger syrup
½ teaspoon lemon juice
1¾ cups heavy cream

Preheat the oven to 375°F and line a 12 x 9-inch baking dish with nonstick parchment paper. Add the dates to a bowl, cover with the boiling water, and let soak.

For the toffee sauce, put all the ingredients except the cream into a saucepan and gently simmer for 5 minutes, stirring occasionally, until the sugar has dissolved and the mixture is a deep caramel color. Stir in the cream and cook for another minute. Remove from the heat.

Cover the bottom of the prepared pan with a thin layer of the sauce. Cut two of the apples into thin rounds and use these to cover the botttom of the dish. Drizzle them with a little more toffee sauce and set aside the remainder (you should have about half left). Coarsely chop the remaining apples, add them to a food processor, and pulse to small pieces. Remove and set aside. Put the dates and water in the processor with the stem ginger and blend into chunky pieces.

Cream together the butter, sugar, and vanilla extract in a bowl until pale and fluffy. Beat in the eggs one at a time until fully incorporated, then fold in the date mixture. In a separate bowl, mix together the flour, baking soda, baking powder, ginger, and apple pieces. Fold the egg and date mixture into the dry mixture and pour into the dish. Bake for 35 minutes, or until evenly risen and a skewer inserted into the center comes out clean. Remove from the oven and let cool for 5 to 10 minutes.

Meanwhile, warm the remaining toffee sauce in the microwave or a small saucepan over low heat. Invert the pudding onto a plate and serve with the warmed toffee sauce and whipped cream, if liked.

This show-stopping celebration cake will delight vegans and nonvegans alike. It can be made in stages in advance to cut down on the work, while the ganache can also be omitted if you would like something lighter and simpler.

CHOCOLATE, COCONUT & BANANA MOUSSE CAKE

SERVES 10 TO 12

For the crust
10oz gluten-free graham crackers (or regular graham crackers, for non gluten-free)
3½oz good-quality semisweet chocolate chips or semisweet chocolate squares broken into small pieces (about 50% cocoa solids)
⅓ cup vegan margarine, melted

For the filling
1 cup apple juice
1 cup maple syrup
½ cup turbinado sugar
1 tablespoon (¼oz) aga
1 x 7oz creamed coconut block
5 bananas
1lb firm silken-style tofu

For the ganache
1 cup soy cream
1 tablespoon light corn syrup
11½oz good-quality semisweet chocolate chips or semisweet chocolate squares broken into small pieces (about 50% cocoa solids)

To decorate
handful of lightly toasted coconut flakes

Line a 10-inch springform cake pan with nonstick parchment paper.

For the crust, put the crackers and dark chocolate chips or pieces in a food processor and blend together until the mixture resembles fine bread crumbs. Stir in the melted margarine, then add the mixture to the prepared cake pan and press down into an even layer. Let chill in the refrigerator until needed.

For the filling, heat the apple juice, maple syrup, sugar, and agar in a saucepan and bring to a boil. Reduce the heat and simmer for at least 10 minutes, stirring continuously with a whisk, until the agar is fully dissolved.

Warm the creamed coconut in a microwave and add to the food processor with the juice and syrup mixture, 2 of the bananas, and the tofu. Blend together well to a purée consistency.

Slice the remaining bananas and arrange evenly on the chilled crust. Then pour in the tofu mixture. Chill in the refrigerator for at least 4 hours to set then remove from the pan and transfer to a wire rack.

For the ganache, heat the soy cream and light corn syrup together in a saucepan until just beginning to bubble. Remove from the heat and stir in the chocolate pieces, then blend together with a stick blender for 2 to 3 minutes, or until glossy and smooth. Let cool for 2 to 3 minutes, then spoon into the center of the cake and smooth over the top and sides with a spatula into an even layer. Chill for at least 1 hour to allow the ganache to set. Decorate with toasted coconut flakes before serving.

Surprisingly simple to make but impressive to serve, this dessert is a perfect summer dinner party finale. Having tested many different versions using agar flakes as a setting agent in the past, this is by far the easiest we've found and gives the best results, too.

PANNA COTTA WITH POACHED NECTARINES

SERVES 6

2½ cups heavy cream
1½ cups skim milk
¾ cup superfine sugar
½ vanilla bean, split lengthwise and seeds scraped
3 tablespoons agar flakes

For the Poached Nectarines
6 nectarines
zest of ½ lemon
½ cup superfine sugar
¾ cup rosé wine

Preheat the oven to 350°F. Lightly grease 6 individual ramekins.

For the poached nectarines, cut the nectarines in half along the seams, twist to open and prise out the stones. Place the nectarine halves, cut-side down, in a baking dish. Add the lemon zest and sugar, pour in the wine, and bake in the oven for 15 to 20 minutes, or until the skins of the nectarines are starting to loosen and wrinkle. Remove from the oven, add to a bowl, and cover with plastic wrap. Let cool, then remove the nectarine skins and cut into thirds. Strain the nectarine juices and reserve for later.

To make the panna cotta, warm all the ingredients together in a pan. Bring to a boil then immediately lower the heat and cook gently, whisking continuously, for 5 minutes, or until the mixture has thickened and can coat the back of a spoon.

Strain the mixture through a fine sieve and pour into the prepared ramekins. Chill in the refrigerator for at least 3 hours.

To serve, run a knife around the inside of the ramekins and invert the panna cotta onto individual plates. Spoon a little roasted nectarine around each panna cotta and drizzle with a little of the reserved nectarine juices to finish.

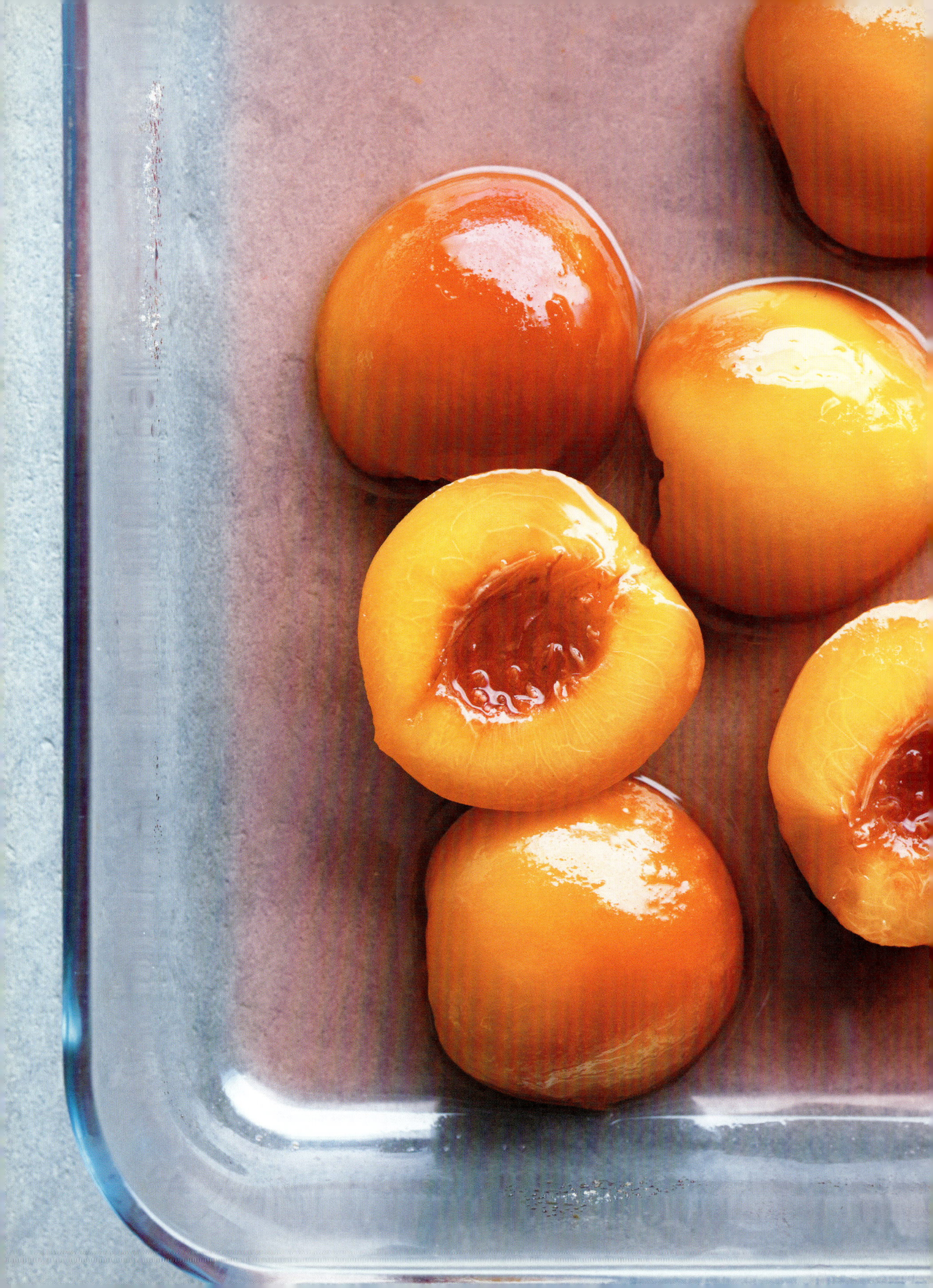

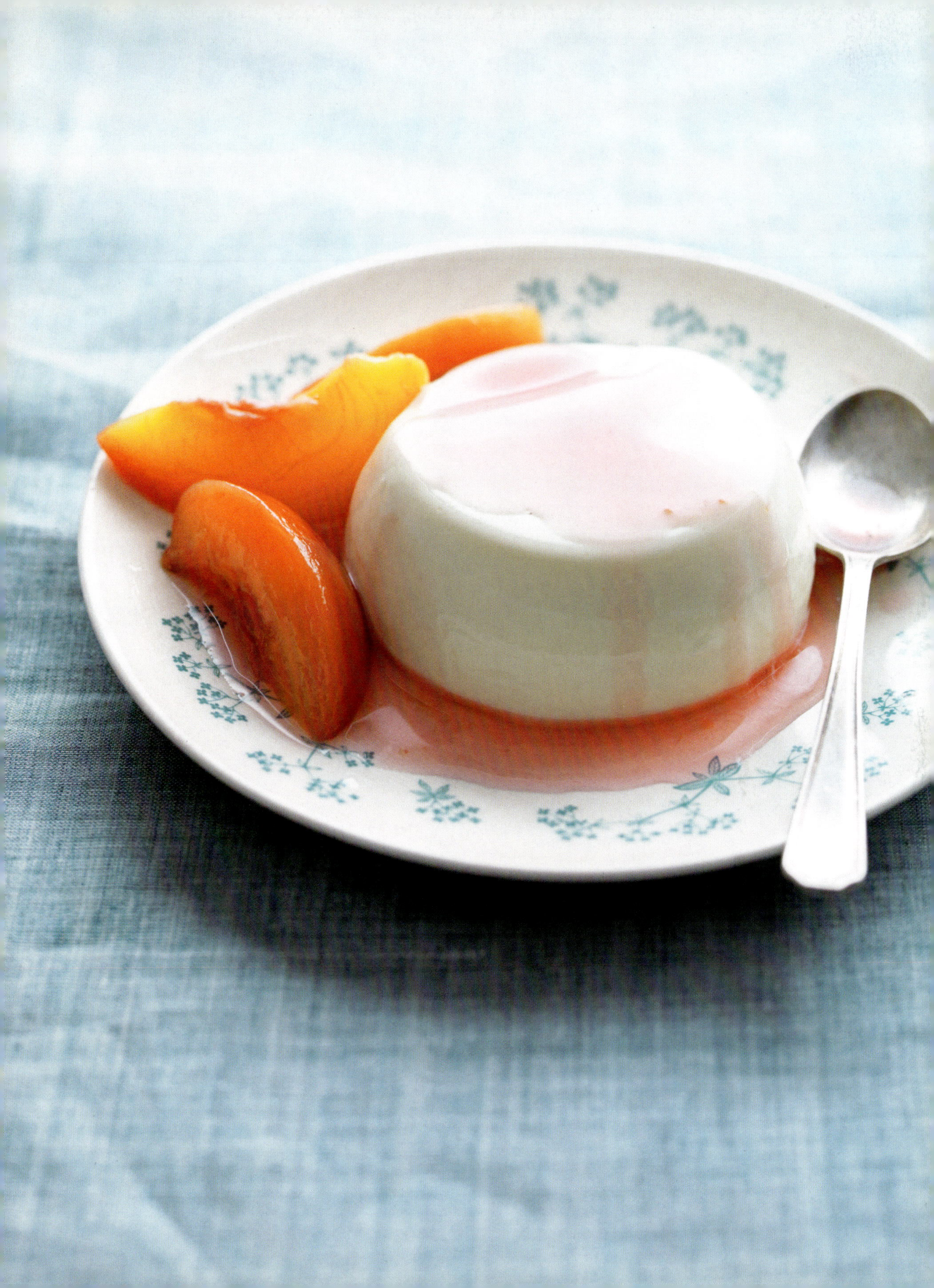

This no-bake cake really couldn't be any simpler to make, though the result is a rich vegan dessert that is perfect for a dinner party. It has featured regularly on our menu with various different fruits for so many years that its origins have been lost in the mists of time—apologies to whoever first came up with it but, rest assured, it is an absolute Mildreds classic. While you do need to use a good-quality semisweet chocolate to make this cake, don't try using one that is too high in cocoa solids, because anything more than 55% will cause the mixture to separate.

DARK CHOCOLATE & RASPBERRY TRUFFLE CAKE

SERVES 10 TO 12

3¼ cups soy cream, plus extra to serve
2lb good-quality semisweet chocolate chips or semisweet chocolate squares broken into small pieces (about 50% cocoa solids)
1lb raspberries, plus an extra handful to decorate
unsweetened cocoa powder, to dust

Line the bottom and sides of a 9-inch springform cake pan with nonstick parchment paper.

Pour the soy cream into a large saucepan and bring to a boil. Remove from the heat and stir in the chocolate pieces with a spoon. Beat the mixture briskly by hand for 5 minutes or blend with a stick blender for 3 to 4 minutes until glossy and smooth, then carefully fold in the raspberries. Spoon the mixture into the prepared pan and smooth the surface (banging the pan carefully on the counter once will help do this). Then refrigerate for at least 3 hours until firm and cool.

When ready to serve, unlatch the pan and remove the parchment from the sides. Take a large serving plate and place it over the cake, then turn the cake and plate over and remove the bottom part of the pan along with the layer of parchment paper. Dust the cake with the cocoa powder and add a few more raspberries, to decorate. Cut into slices and serve with soy cream.

A favorite at Mildreds since it was introduced by Daniel Strutt, this dessert has a creamy texture that marries well with the tartness of the passion fruit. If you can find passion fruit purée it will cut down on the work here. Decorate with homemade gingersnap cookies, or omit these for a gluten-free option.

PASSION FRUIT CRÈME CARAMEL
WITH GINGERSNAP COOKIES

SERVES 8

1¾ cups superfine sugar
2 cups heavy cream
⅔ cup skim milk
6 large eggs
seeds of 1 passion fruit, to decorate

For the passion fruit juice
either use 1 cup of passion fruit purée or 8 to 10 passion fruit (making 1 cup of seeds and flesh)
2½ tablespoons superfine sugar
½ cup water

For the Gingersnap Cookies
3½ tablespoons butter
2½ tablespoons light corn syrup
⅓ cup dark brown sugar
½ cup all-purpose flour
½ teaspoon ground ginger

Preheat the oven to 375°F. Line a cookie sheet with nonstick parchment paper. For the passion fruit juice, scoop out the seeds and flesh from the passion fruit and add to a saucepan. Add the sugar and water and bring to a boil. Lower the heat and simmer for 3 to 5 minutes, or until the sugar has dissolved. Strain and set aside.

For the gingersnap cookies, melt the butter, syrup, and sugar in a saucepan and stir until the sugar is dissolved. Remove from the heat and beat in the flour and ginger. Place teaspoonfuls of the mixture onto the prepared baking sheet 4 inches apart. Bake for 10 minutes, or until they are golden brown with bubbles on the surface. Remove from the oven and let cool on the cookie sheet, then store until needed in an airtight container, separated by nonstick parchment paper to stop them from sticking together. Reduce the heat to 300°F.

Arrange 8 x 7-fl oz dariole molds or standard ramekins in a deep roasting pan. Put ¾ cup of the sugar in a small saucepan on high heat, cover with water, but do not stir it. When the sugar starts to stick, swirl it in the pan, turn down the heat, and cook until it is a dark caramel color. Spoon 2 tablespoons of the caramel into each mold, working quickly because the caramel will keep cooking.

In a bowl, beat together the remaining sugar with the juice, cream, milk, and eggs until combined. Strain into a large measuring cup or pitcher, then use to fill the molds. Half-fill the roasting pan with water and bake the caramels in the middle of the oven for 1 hour, or until risen slightly. Remove from the pan and refrigerate for at least 2 hours or until fully set. To serve, run a small knife around the edge of each caramel and invert onto serving plates. Decorate with passion fruit seeds.

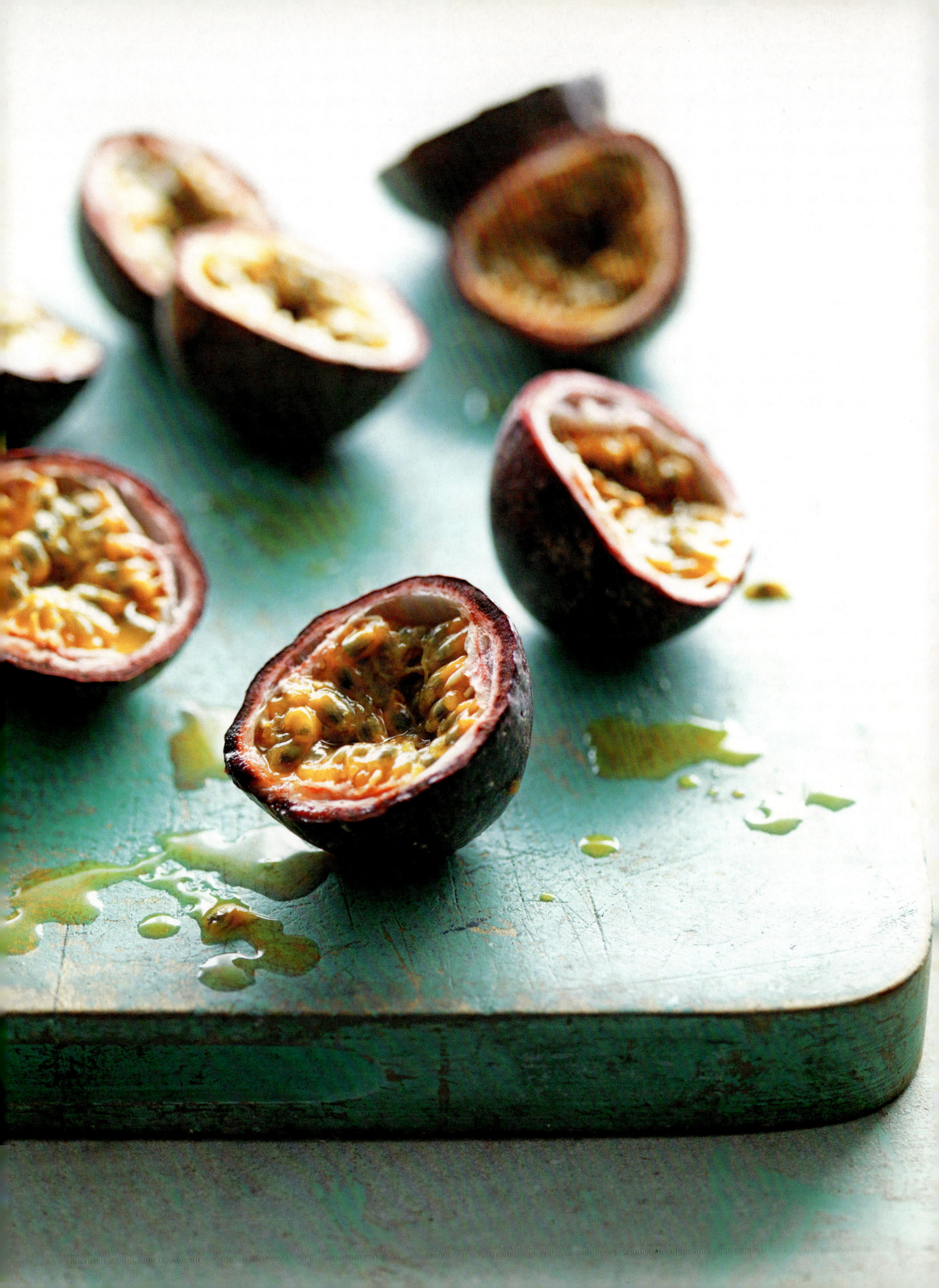

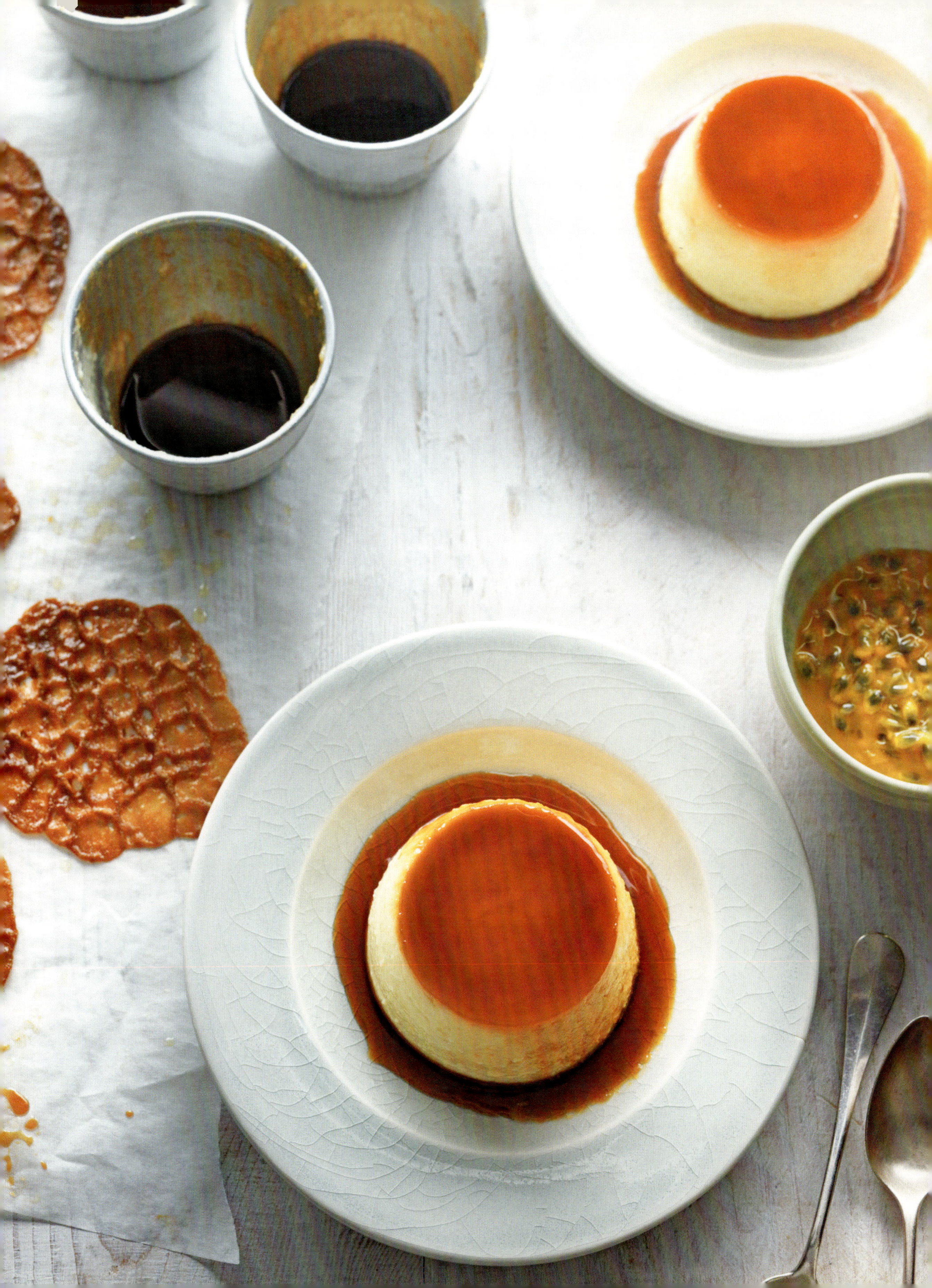

This delicious gluten-free cake, with its beautiful jeweled topping of pomegranates, rose petals, and pistachios, takes inspiration from two places—a Persian walnut cake in Claudia Rodin's Jewish Food, *as well as the classic River Café lemon polenta cake. It is filled with the Middle Eastern flavors of the former and has all the moistness of the latter, though only about half the fat.*

PERSIAN-SPICED ALMOND, PISTACHIO & POLENTA CAKE WITH ROSE PETAL & POMEGRANATE SYRUP

SERVES 8 TO 10

1¼ cups shelled pistachio nuts, plus a handful to decorate
1¾ sticks butter
2 cups superfine sugar
grated zest of 4 lemons, plus juice of 2
5 eggs, separated
2¾ cups ground almonds
1¾ cups polenta
1 teaspoon baking powder
pinch of salt

For the Rose Petal and Pomegranate Syrup
juice of 3 lemons
½ cup water
1 tablespoon rosewater
1 cup superfine sugar
2 cardamom pods
2 star anise
½ cinnamon stick
1 tablespoon rose petals
handful of pistachios kernels, coarsely chopped
1 pomegranate, seeds removed

Preheat the oven to 375°F. Line a 9-inch cake pan with nonstick parchment paper. Cut out a piece of parchment paper to match the top of the pan and set aside.

Add the pistachios to a food processor and blend them to a fine powder. Set aside.

Cream the butter, sugar, and lemon juice together in an electric stand mixer, or in a bowl using a spoon, until pale and fluffy. Beat in the egg yolks a couple at a time. Fold in the ground almonds, ground pistachios, polenta, grated lemon zest, baking powder, and salt, being careful not to overmix the batter.

Beat the egg whites until fairly stiff then fold them into the batter. Pour the batter into the prepared pan and cover with the loose piece of parchment paper. Bake on the lower shelf of the oven for 1¼ hours, remove the parchment paper, and bake for another 15 minutes, or until the cake has risen and springs back when lightly pressed with a finger.

To make the syrup, put the lemon juice, water, rosewater, sugar, and spices in a pan and cook over medium heat for 3 to 5 minutes, or until the sugar has dissolved and the syrup has thickened and reduced slightly. Strain to remove the spices, add the rose petals and pistachios, and set aside to cool. Once cool, stir in the pomegranate seeds.

Prick the cake all over with a toothpick and cover with the syrup. Scatter with a few whole pistachios to decorate and serve.

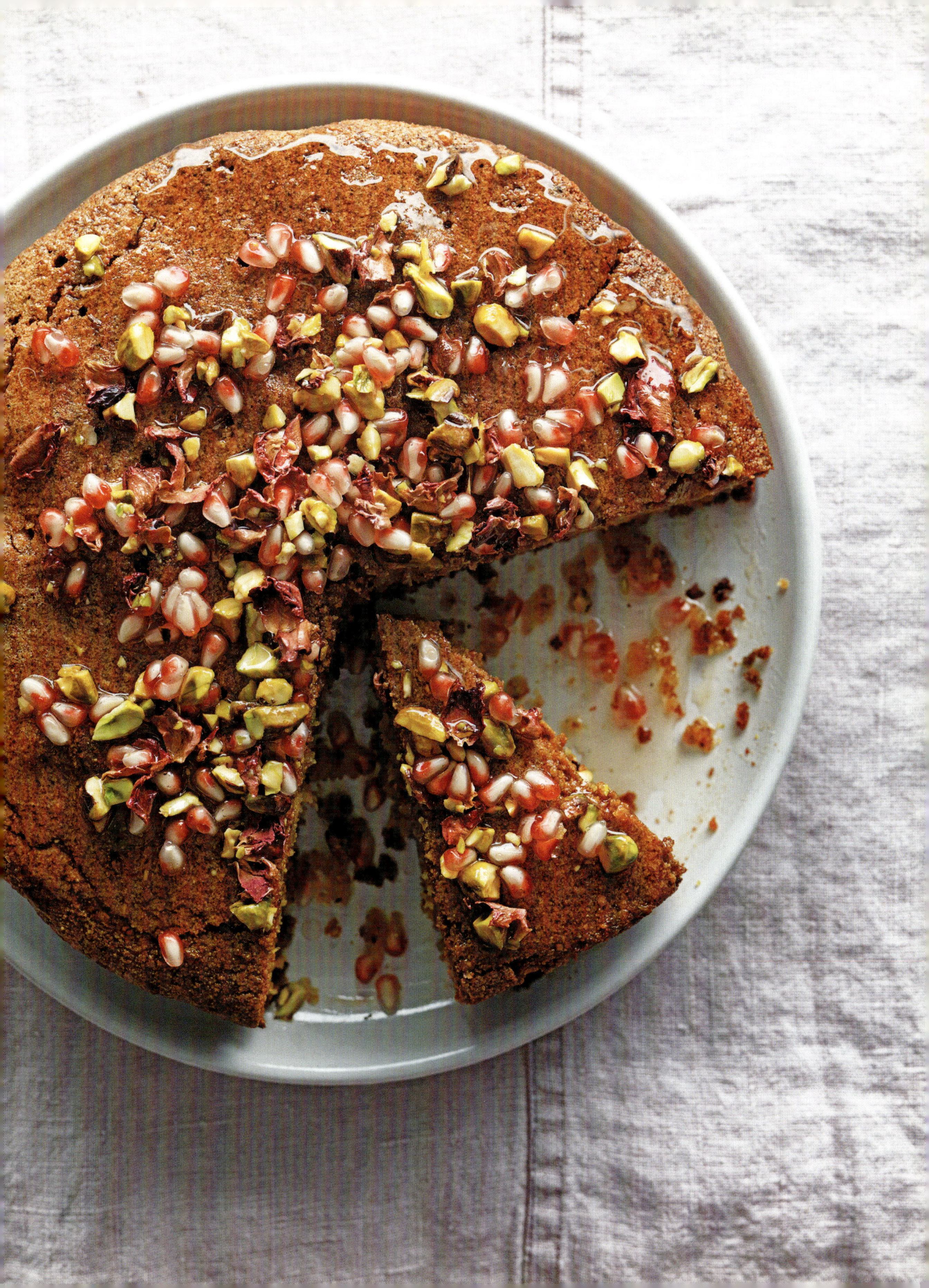

If you're hunting for a pudding with pizzazz to add to your repertoire that requires very little time and even less skill to put together, then look no further. This is a lovely summer dessert full of bright colors and fresh flavors.

MANGO FOOL WITH MINT SUGAR & BLACK SESAME BRITTLE

SERVES 6 TO 8

⅔ cup water
½ cup superfine sugar
juice of 1 lime
2 small ripe Mexican Ataúlfo mangoes or 1 large ripe mango, peeled and chopped, plus extra cubes to decorate
1 teaspoon cornstarch
1½ cups heavy cream

For the Black Sesame Brittle
2 tablespoons black sesame seeds
1 cup superfine sugar

For the Mint Sugar
5 mint leaves
¼ cup turbinado sugar
grated zest of ½ lime

Add the water, sugar, and lime juice to a saucepan and bring to a boil. Lower the heat to a simmer, add the mango, and cook for 2 to 3 minutes, or until the mango begins to break down. Mix the cornstarch with a little water to form a smooth paste and add it to the saucepan. Simmer gently for 3 minutes. When the mixture is thick enough to coat the back of a spoon, remove it from the heat and blend to a smooth purée using a stick blender. Let cool.

Whip the cream in a bowl to soft peaks. Carefully fold in two-thirds of the mango purée. Refrigerate the fool and remaining mango purée until ready to assemble.

For the black sesame brittle, line a baking pan with nonstick parchment paper. Gently toast the sesame seeds in a saucepan over low heat for 1 to 2 minutes, or until fragrant. Remove the seeds from the pan and set aside. Add the sugar to the pan and heat gently, without stirring, until melted and light caramel in color. Add the sesame seeds and cook for another minute. Then pour the mixture onto the prepared baking pan, spread it as thinly as possible. Let cool, then snap into shards about 2 to 4 inches in length.

To make the mint sugar, blend the ingredients together with a hand-held blender using the mixer attachment, or in a spice grinder.

To assemble the fools, coat the rims of 6 to 8 martini or margarita glasses with the mint sugar. Spoon a layer of fool into the bottom of each glass, top with a layer of mango purée, and finish with another layer of fool. Scatter with the cubes of mango and decorate with the sesame brittle shards. Serve.

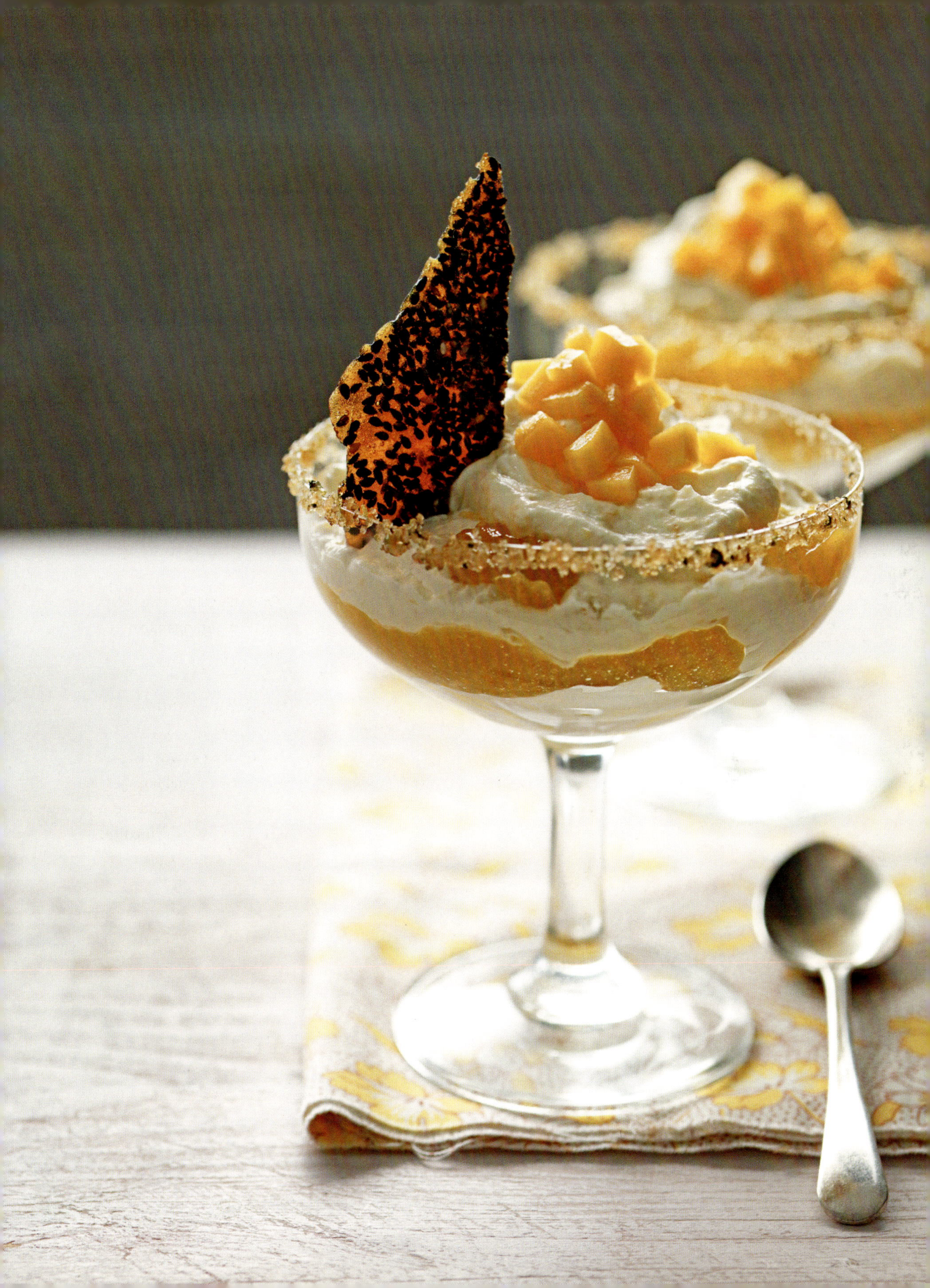

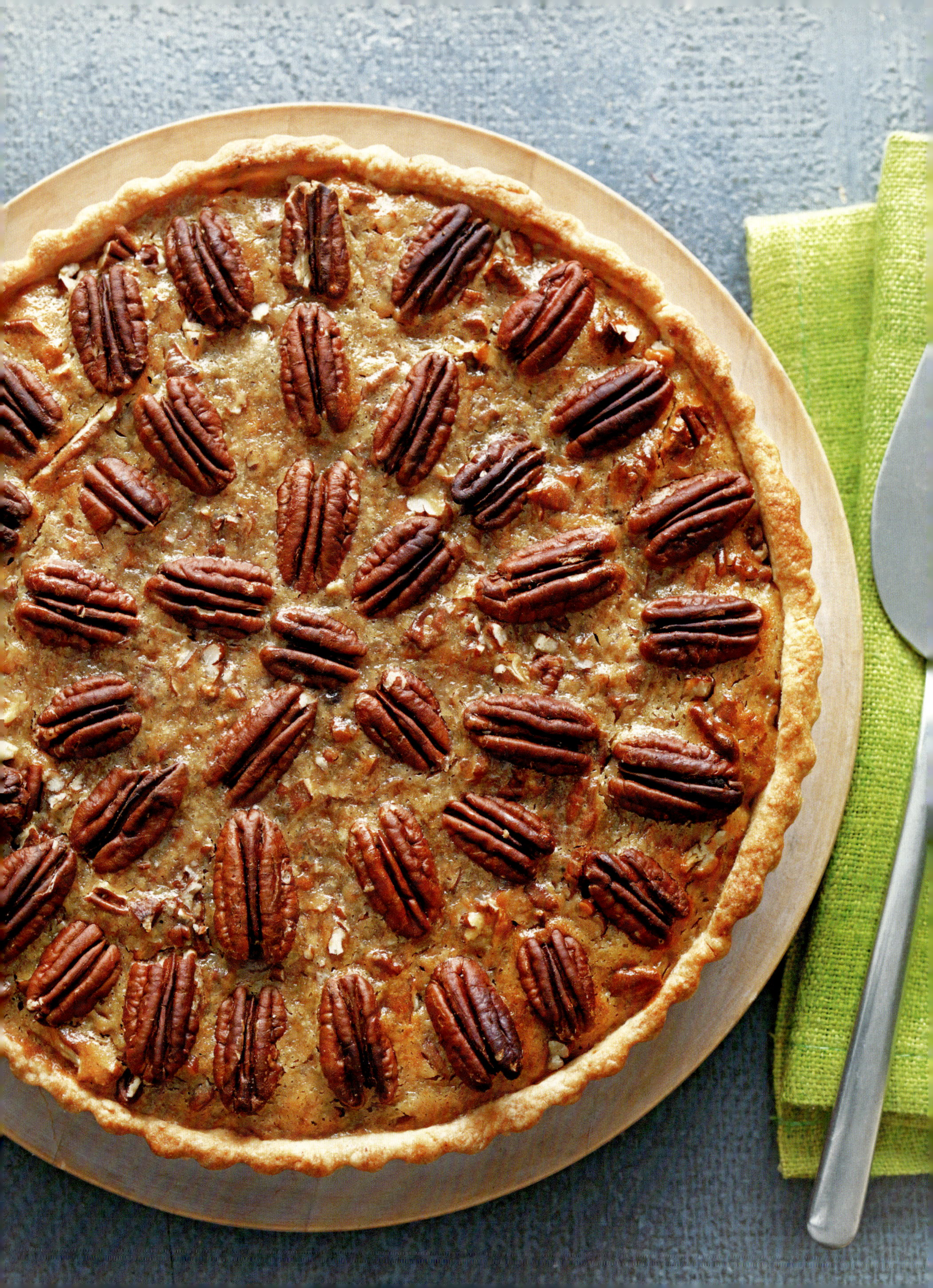

This is our vegan take on pecan pie. We've reduced the sweetness and added more nuts, while the traditional creamy filling has been transformed through the addition of silken tofu. To give it a boozy, rich flavor, add some bourbon to the caramel after taking it off the heat.

MAPLE PECAN PIE WITH VEGAN SWEET PASTRY

SERVES 8 TO 10

½ cup maple syrup
1¾ cups light brown sugar
1 teaspoon vanilla extract
grated zest of ½ small orange and juice of 1 orange
½ cup vegan margarine
½ teaspoon salt
⅓ cup bourbon (optional)
8oz silken tofu
3½ tablespoons cornstarch
pinch of ground cinnamon
½ vanilla bean, split lengthwise and seeds scraped
½ cup unsweetened soy milk
2¼ cups pecans, plus 25 halves for topping
cream or ice cream, to serve (optional)

For the Vegan Sweet Pie Crust
2 cups all-purpose flour, plus extra for dusting
¼ cup light brown sugar
pinch of salt
pinch of ground cinnamon
grated zest and juice of 1 orange
½ cup vegan margarine, chilled
1 tablespoon iced water
2 teaspoons apple cider vinegar

Preheat the oven to 325°F. Line a 9-inch loose-bottomed pie pan with nonstick parchment paper. Cut another piece of parchment paper slightly larger than the top of the pan and set aside.

For the crust, place the flour, sugar, salt, cinnamon, and grated orange zest in a bowl, add the margarine, and rub in with your fingertips until the mixture resembles fine bread crumbs. Add the water, vinegar, and orange juice and bring together to form a dough. Roll into a ball, seal in plastic wrap, and chill in the refrigerator for at least 30 minutes.

Roll out the dough on a lightly floured surface to a ¼-inch thickness and use it to line the pan. Cover the dough with the parchment paper and fill with baking beans. Bake for 20 to 25 minutes (remove the beans for the final 5 minutes), until lightly golden and cooked.

Put the syrup, sugar, vanilla, and orange zest and juice in a saucepan. Bring to a boil, lower the heat, and simmer, stirring, for about 3 minutes, or until the mixture has reduced to a thick, light caramel. Remove from the heat and stir in the margarine, salt, and bourbon, if using.

Blend together the tofu, cornstarch, cinnamon, and vanilla seeds in a food processor until smooth. Continue to blend, gradually adding the soy milk, until the mixture has the consistency of heavy cream. Add the caramel and blend, then add the pecans and pulse for a few seconds until the pecans are just coarsely chopped.

Pour the filling into the pie crust and spread evenly. Top with the pecan halves and bake for 1 to 1¼ hours, or until the filling is soft but set, the top is slightly raised and a crust has formed. Let cool slightly and then serve warm with cream or ice cream, if you like.

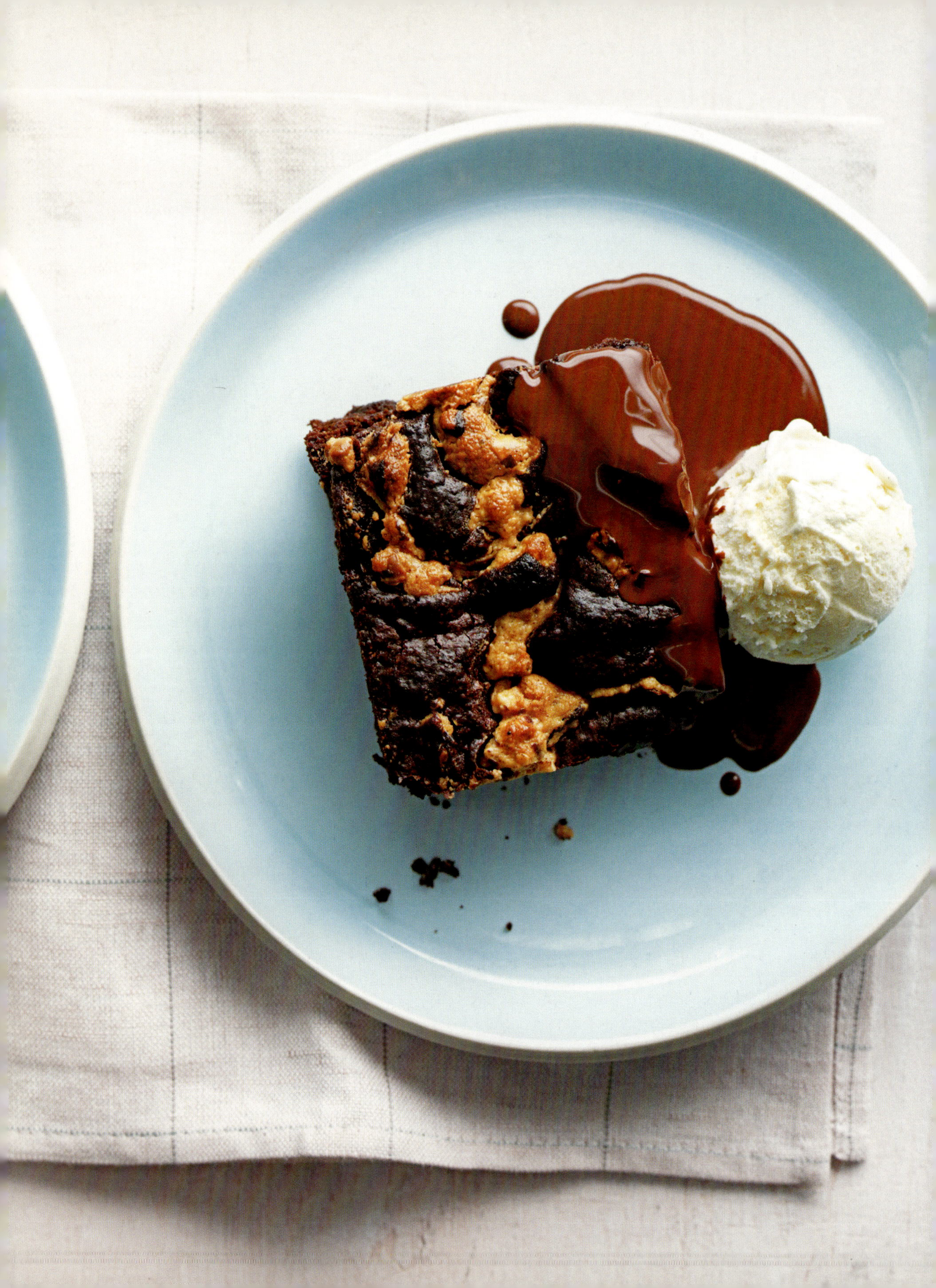

We have tried tons of different brownie recipes over the years, vegan and otherwise, but this simple version is one of the best we've found. If you don't tell, no one will know these brownies are vegan; they are rich, squishy, and chocolatey and everything a brownie should be. You don't have to bother serving the brownies with the chocolate sauce, though it does give them a little something extra.

PEANUT BUTTER BROWNIES
WITH HOT CHOCOLATE SAUCE

SERVES 8 TO 12

11oz wheat-free flour
1¾ cups dark brown sugar
1¾ cups light brown sugar
1½ cups unsweetened cocoa powder
1 teaspoon baking powder
pinch of salt
¾ cup good-quality chunky peanut butter
1 cup water
1 cup vegetable oil
2 tablespoons good-quality vanilla extract
2½oz good-quality semisweet chocolate chips or semisweet chocolate squares broken into small pieces (about 50% cocoa solids)
vanilla ice cream, to serve

For the Hot Chocolate Sauce
1 cup soy cream
1 tablespoon light corn syrup
4oz good-quality semisweet chocolate chips or semisweet chocolate squares broken into small pieces (about 50% cocoa solids)
3½ tablespoons dark brown sugar
1 cup unsweetened cocoa powder
1 cup water, plus extra if needed

Preheat the oven to 325°F. Line an 8 x 12-inch baking pan with nonstick parchment paper.

Put the flour, sugars, cocoa powder, baking powder, and salt into a bowl and mix together thoroughly to remove any lumps. Add a tablespoon of the peanut butter, the water, oil, vanilla extract, and chocolate and beat for 2 to 3 minutes to combine. The batter should be the texture of whipped cream; if it looks too thick, add a little more water. Pour the batter into the prepared pan and level the top.

Put the remaining peanut butter in a pastry bag and pipe lines over the brownie batter, ensuring you pipe all the way to the edges. Drag a knife through the top layer of the batter in the opposite direction to the piped lines to create a marbled effect. Bake for 45 to 50 minutes (or until semifirm in the center). Set aside to cool.

For the sauce, heat the cream and syrup in a saucepan over medium heat until they begin to boil, then remove from the heat and stir in the chocolate. Whisk the sugar, cocoa and water together in a bowl and pour into the chocolate mixture. Beat well and return to the heat to warm through. Beat briskly together for 5 minutes or blend with a stick blender for 3 minutes, or until glossy and smooth.

Cut the brownies into squares with a sharp knife and serve with the warm chocolate sauce and vanilla ice cream, if liked.

DIPS, SAUCES & DRESSINGS

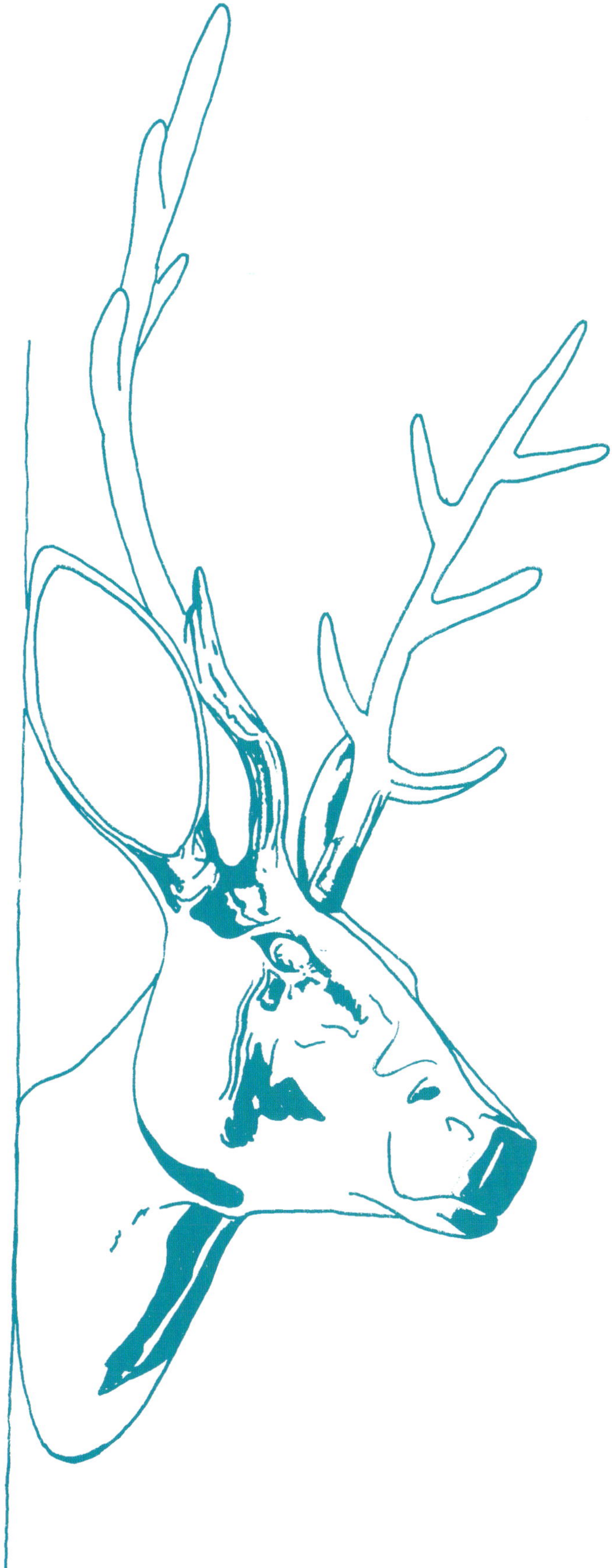

BOUSQUET
BOUSQUET
BOUSQUET
CALOR
CALOR
ST-GERMAIN
PASSOA
CAMPA
BACARDI
Tanqueray
EXPORT STRENGTH
LONDON DRY GIN
DRÁGORA
DRÁGORA
CALOR
ORGANIC TEMPRANILLO
HENDERSON'S
RELISH
RADNOR
HILLS
SPARKLING
39% vol

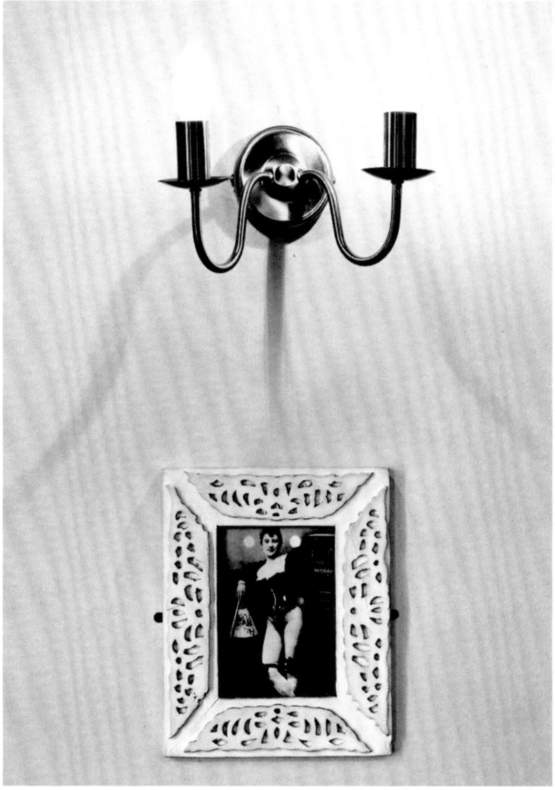
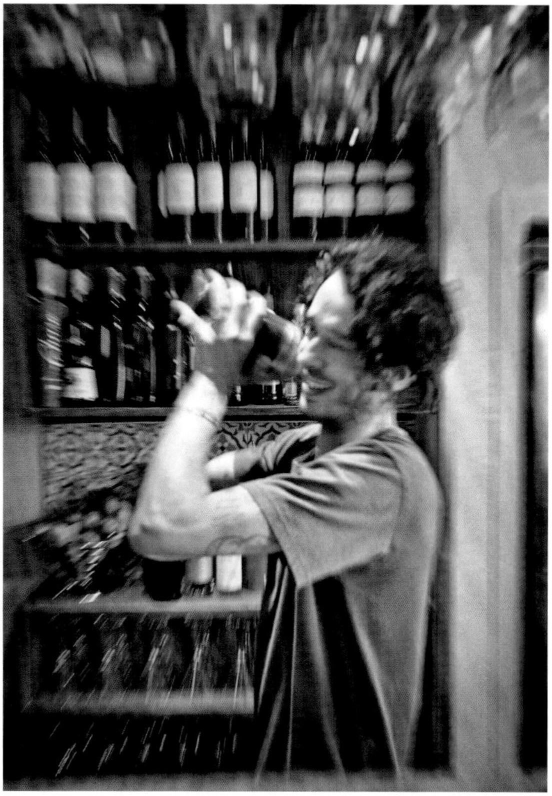

There are lots of decent ready-made varieties of harissa available but, if you haven't made it from scratch before, give this a try because harissa is one of those things that really benefits from being homemade. As with a lot of spiced sauces, the flavors will deepen and develop, so it's a good thing to make a day or two in advance. You might find this harissa quite mild so, if you really like heat, just add a couple more chiles.

HARISSA

MAKES APPROXIMATELY 1¼ CUPS

¼ cup light olive oil, divided
3 red bell peppers
2 red chiles, trimmed
1½ tablespoons cumin seeds
1½ tablespoons smoked paprika
2 teaspoons tomato paste
2 garlic cloves, peeled
handful of cilantro leaves

Preheat the oven to 475°F.

Drizzle one-third of the olive oil into a roasting pan. Add the bell peppers and chiles and toss together to coat thoroughly. Roast for 15 minutes, or until the bell peppers and chiles have puffed up and are starting to split open. Transfer them to a bowl, cover with plastic wrap, and set aside to cool for 15 minutes. Once cool enough to handle, tear the bell peppers and chiles open and discard the cores and seeds. Peel off and discard the skins and set the flesh aside.

Toast the cumin seeds in a dry skillet over medium heat for about 1 minute, or until fragrant. Using a mortar and pestle, grind the toasted cumin together with the smoked paprika.

Combine all the ingredients in a large measuring cup or pitcher and blend with a stick blender until smooth. For a really smooth harissa, pass the mixture through a sieve or chinois.

This spicy paste packed with Middle-Eastern flavors is similar to the commonly found harissa made with red bell pepper, though it is considerably less spicy, with the green vegetables and mint giving it a much fresher finish. It can be used as a dressing or as an accompaniment to dishes, such as tagine.

GREEN HARISSA

MAKES APPROXIMATELY 1¾ CUPS

6 green chiles, trimmed
1 teaspoon cumin seeds
1 teaspoon fennel seeds
1 teaspoon sumac
2 teaspoons chili flakes
1¾ cups light olive or canola oil
handful each of mint, flat-leaf parsley, and cilantro leaves
grated zest and juice of 2 lemons
2 cups peas, defrosted if frozen
4 scallions, trimmed
6 garlic cloves, peeled

Preheat the oven to 475°F.

Arrange the chiles on a baking pan and roast for 15 minutes, or until they have puffed up and are starting to split open. Transfer them to a bowl, cover with plastic wrap, and set aside to cool for 15 minutes. Once cool enough to handle, tear the chiles open and discard the cores and seeds. Peel off the skins and set the chile flesh aside.

Toast the cumin and fennel seeds in a dry skillet over medium heat for about 1 minute, or until fragrant. Using a mortar and pestle, grind the toasted spices together with the sumac and chili flakes.

Combine all the ingredients in a large measuring cup or pitcher and blend with a stick blender until smooth. For a really smooth harissa, pass the mixture through a sieve or chinois.

A lot of the success of this Mediterranean dip depends on the quality of the haricot beans used. We use a Spanish variety that are softer than usual and work particularly well here; quite often the type that come in jars are slightly better than the ones in cans.

POTATO & WHITE BEAN DIP

SERVES 4 TO 6

¾lb round white or round red potatoes, peeled and halved
4 garlic cloves
½ cup ground almonds
13oz can or jar haricot beans, drained and rinsed
½ cup extra virgin olive oil, plus extra to garnish
pinch of white pepper
juice of 1 lemon
1 tablespoon apple cider vinegar
pinch of sweet paprika, to garnish

Put the halved potatoes in a large saucepan, cover with water, and bring to a boil. Reduce the heat and simmer for 15 to 20 minutes, or until cooked through.

Drain the cooked potatoes and add to a food processor along with the rest of the ingredients. Blend until smooth. Serve garnished with a drizzle of olive oil and a sprinkling of paprika and accompanied by warm pitta bread.

Sambal is a hot, spicy condiment served alongside various dishes of Southeastern Asia and India. With the addition of fresh herbs and spices, this version has a sweet yet powerful kick that shouldn't overload your mouth with heat. However, it's worth adding the raw chile a little at a time at the end to achieve a spice level that you are comfortable with.

TOMATO & COCONUT SAMBAL

MAKES APPROXIMATELY 3 CUPS

light cooking oil (such as canola, peanut, or sunflower)
12 fresh or frozen curry leaves
2 small onions, diced
1 teaspoon chili powder
1 teaspoon salt
14oz can diced tomatoes
3 tablespoons tomato paste
2 tablespoons superfine sugar
2 green chiles, trimmed and minced
handful of cilantro leaves, chopped
¾oz fresh ginger root, peeled and chopped
⅓ cup desiccated coconut

Heat a splash of oil in a small saucepan, add the curry leaves, and fry briefly for 10 to 15 seconds, being careful not to burn them. Add the onions and cook, stirring, for 5 minutes, or until they have started to soften. Add the chili powder and cook for a few minutes more, then add the salt, diced tomatoes, tomato paste, and sugar and simmer over low heat for 15 to 20 minutes, or until the sambal has thickened and reduced and the flavors have melded together.

Remove from the heat and blend the sauce to a smooth consistency using a stick blender or food processor. Set aside and let cool.

Once cool, stir the chiles, cilantro leaves, ginger, and desiccated coconut through the sambal and combine thoroughly. Transfer to a suitable container and refrigerate for up to a week.

V **GF**

This is our classic vegan mayo. It accompanies all of our burgers and fries, though it is also good mixed into a potato salad or thinned a little and used as a salad dressing. It will keep for up to two weeks in a sealed jar in the refrigerator.

VEGAN BASIL MAYONNAISE

MAKES APPROXIMATELY 2 CUPS

1 small bunch of basil leaves
2 garlic cloves
1 tablespoon Dijon mustard
⅔ cup unsweetened soy milk
1¾ cups light oil (such as canola, vegetable, or sunflower)
salt and pepper

Put all the ingredients in a large measuring cup or pitcher and season with salt and pepper. Blend with a stick blender until all the oil is incorporated. If it looks too thick, add a little more soy milk or water. Transfer to a suitable container and refrigerate until needed.

You can substitute other herbs for the basil in this recipe; for example **chervil** or **tarragon** or a **mixture of green herbs**.

If you don't eat soy products, use **almond milk** instead of soy milk.

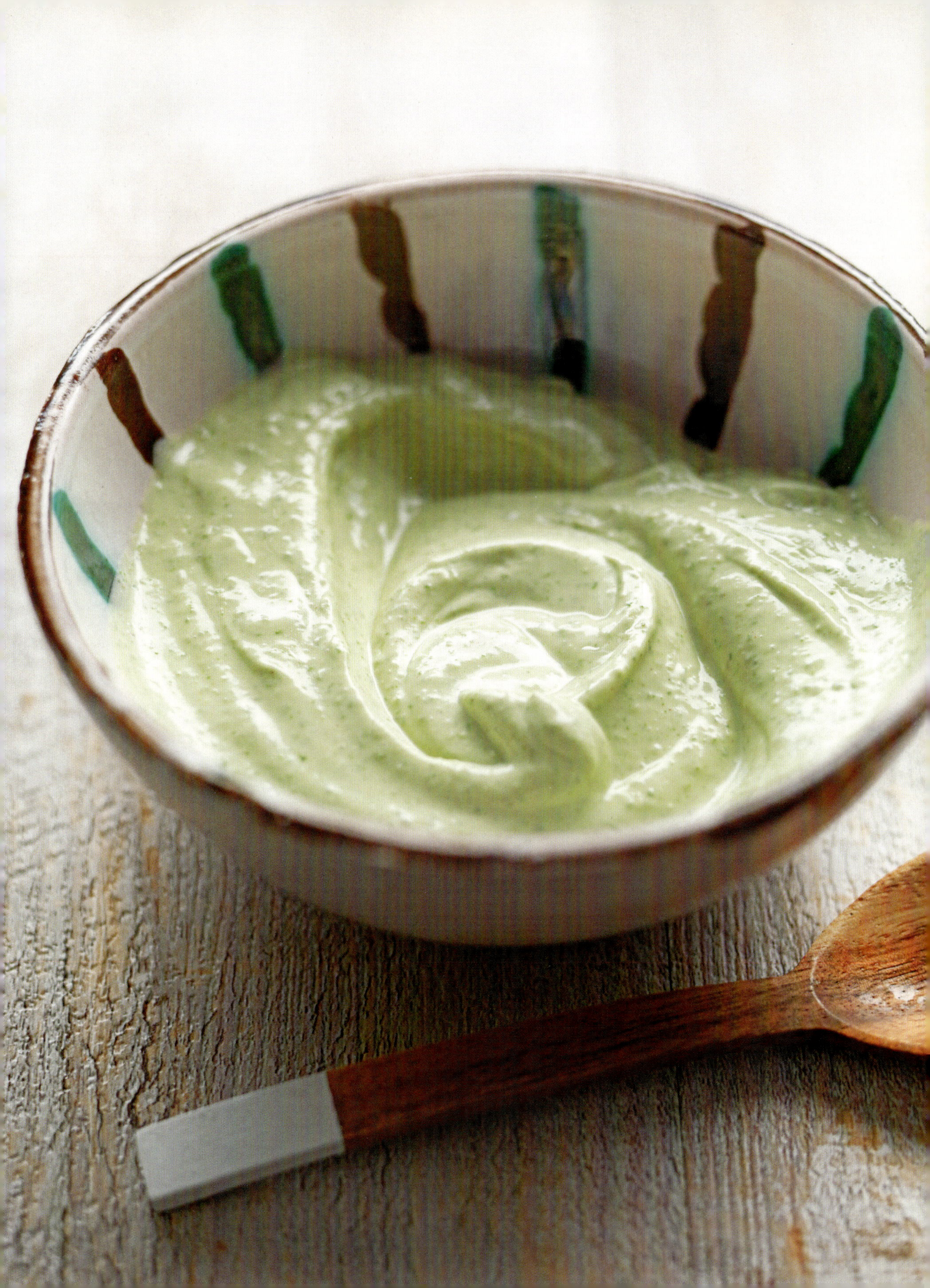

GF

This is a mild aïoli that pairs wonderfully with grilled vegetables, warm salads, roast potato wedges, and our Artichoke Crostini (see page 52). It will keep in the refrigerator for up to a week.

ROAST GARLIC & LEMON AIOLI

MAKES APPROXIMATELY 1¾ CUPS

7 garlic cloves, peeled
1¼ cups light olive oil, plus extra for drizzling
2 egg yolks
juice of ½ lemon
1 tablespoon Dijon mustard
½ teaspoon white pepper
3 tablespoons boiling water
salt

Preheat the oven to 350°F.

Place the garlic cloves in the center of a small of sheet of aluminum foil, drizzle with a little oil, and seal to form a parcel. Roast in the oven for 15 minutes, or until the garlic is just beginning to brown. Set aside to cool.

Place the cooled garlic cloves, egg yolks, lemon juice, mustard, and white pepper in a food processor and blend together until puréed. With the motor running, add the oil in a thin, steady stream, gradually adding the boiling water as you go to prevent the mixture from splitting. Season to taste with salt. Transfer to a suitable container, seal with a lid, and refrigerate until needed.

Truffle oil varies so hugely in strength that we haven't put an exact quantity here; instead we suggest you add a little, taste, and adjust the amount until you are satisfied it's strong enough. Remember that the flavor will develop and deepen, so it's better to err on the side of caution than end up with something that's overpowering.

TRUFFLE MAYONNAISE

MAKES APPROXIMATELY 1¼ CUPS

3 tablespoons light oil (such as canola, peanut or sunflower), plus extra if needed
½ cup light olive oil
truffle oil, to taste
½ cup soy cream
juice of ½ lemon
1 teaspoon Dijon mustard
salt and pepper

Mix the sunflower and olive oils together in a large measuring cup or pitcher. Stir in the truffle oil a few drops at a time, tasting and continuing to add more until the oil mixture has a light truffle flavor.

Place the soy cream, lemon juice, and mustard in a food processor, season to taste with salt and pepper, and blend together. With the motor running, add the oil in a thin, steady stream until you get a thick, creamy mayonnaise, adding a little extra sunflower oil if needed. Transfer to a suitable container and refrigerate until needed (the mayonnaise will keep for a week or two).

We serve this rich gravy with our Roasted Portobello Mushroom, Pecan & Chestnut Wellington (see page 125).

PORT GRAVY

MAKES APPROXIMATELY 2½ PINTS

2 tablespoons olive oil
½ small white onion, coarsely chopped
½ carrot, coarsely chopped
1 celery stalk, trimmed and coarsely chopped
2 garlic cloves
1 thyme sprig
1 rosemary sprig
2 pints water
1 teaspoon vegetable bouillon powder
2 cups vegetarian port
2 tablespoons gluten-free all-purpose flour (or regular all-purpose flour, for non gluten-free)
1½ tablespoons tomato paste
1½ tablespoons tamari (gluten-free soy sauce)

Heat the oil in a large saucepan over medium–high heat. Add the onion, carrot, celery, garlic, and herbs and fry for 5 minutes or so, stirring, until the vegetables soften and start to color. Add the water and bouillon powder and bring to a boil. Reduce the heat to a simmer and cook gently for 20 minutes. Remove the stock from the heat and strain, discarding the vegetables and herbs.

Pour the port into another large saucepan and simmer until reduced to just a couple of tablespoons of liquid. Add the flour and whisk together to form a roux. Stir in the tomato paste and tamari.

Whisking continuously to prevent lumps, gradually add the stock. Simmer gently until the gravy is thickened and glossy.

We've served this relish with our vegetable burgers at Mildreds for more than 15 years. It's a recipe that has been handed down to us by former head chef Gillian Snowball. It adds a delicious sweet piquancy to burgers and sandwiches, or when served with cheese and crackers. This is a preserve, so you can store it in sterilized jars for a couple of weeks.

CARROT RELISH

MAKES APPROXIMATELY 3 X 14-FL OZ JARS

1¼lb carrots, grated
1½lb apples, peeled, cored, and quartered
⅔ cup dark brown sugar
2 cups apple cider vinegar
⅓ cup tomato paste
1¾ cups golden raisins
1 cup apple juice

Place all the ingredients in a large saucepan, cover, and bring to a simmer. Then lower the heat and cook gently, stirring occasionally, for 25 to 30 minutes, or until the relish has thickened and reduced.

Remove from the heat and blend well in a food processor or with a stick blender to form a smooth paste. Decant into sterilized jars, and seal. This will keep for up to two weeks in the refrigerator.

It's great to have a jar of this on hand. It adds loads of flavor to roasted vegetables, and making a batch up to use whenever you need it will save chopping herbs and garlic later. It should keep for well about a week in the refrigerator.

HERB OIL

**MAKES APPROXIMATELY
2 CUPS**

2 cups light oil (such as canola, peanut, or sunflower)
4 garlic cloves
3 rosemary sprigs, leaves picked
3 thyme sprigs, leaves picked
salt

Put the oil, garlic, rosemary, and thyme in a large measuring cup or a pitcher, season with salt, and blend with a stick blender until smooth. Alternatively, chop the garlic, rosemary, and thyme leaves and add them to a jar or bottle with a screw-top lid along with the salt and oil. Fasten the lid securely, and shake well to combine.

Purple basil, also confusingly called red basil, has leaves that are a wonderful dark purple color, though when they are blended into a mixture such as this, the color changes to a lovely dark pink. If you can't find purple basil, just use regular green basil. The flavor will be the same, if not the color.

PURPLE BASIL OIL

**MAKES APPROXIMATELY
1 CUP**

1 large bunch of purple basil leaves
grated zest and juice of 1 lemon
1 cup light olive oil
salt and pepper

Place all the ingredients in a large measuring cup or pitcher, season with salt and pepper, and blend with a stick blender until smooth.

238 DIPS, SAUCES & DRESSINGS

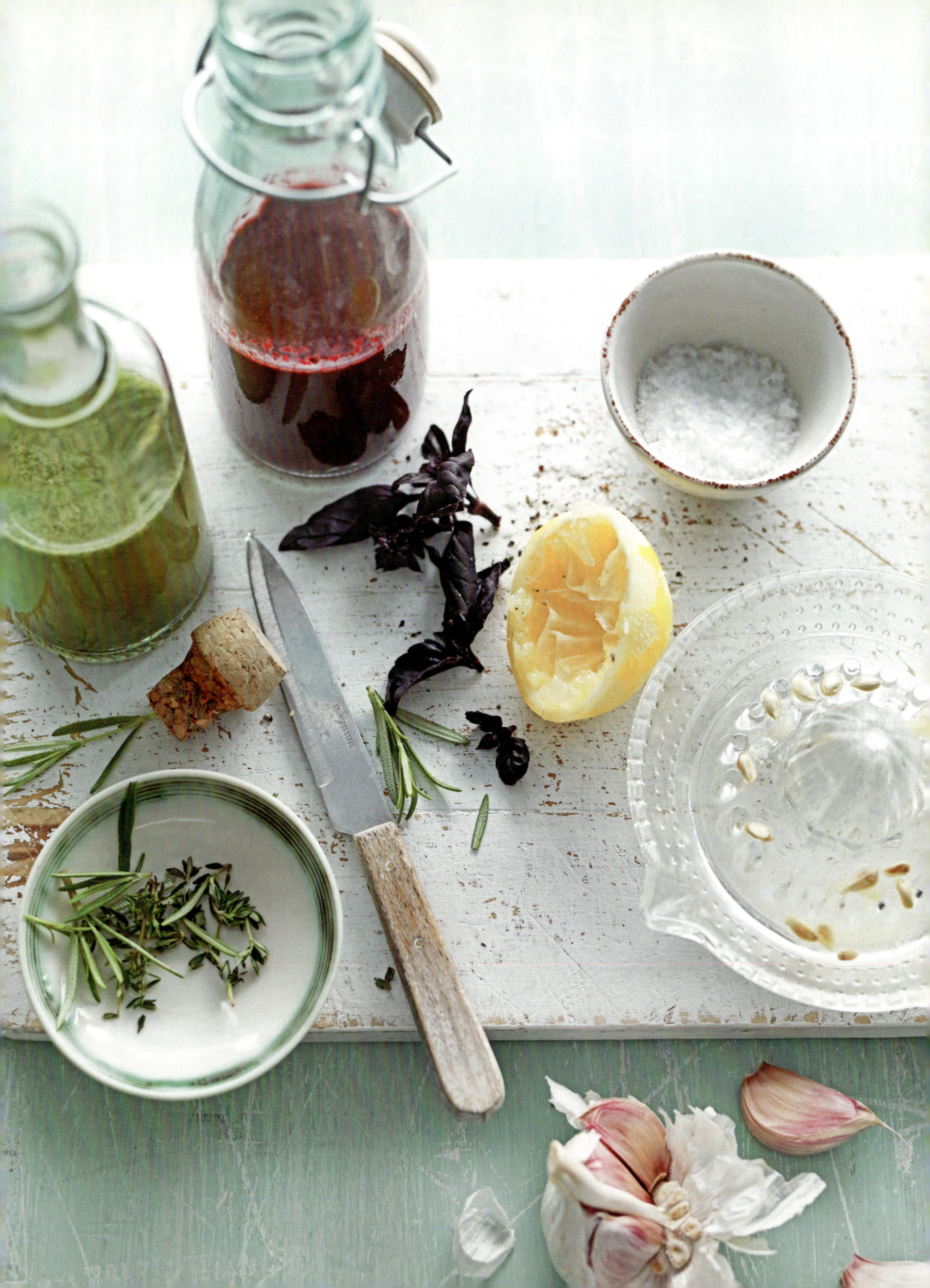

This Vegetarian Caesar Dressing tastes just as good as the original, which many people wrongly assume to be vegetarian (it contains anchovies, so it isn't). Henderson's Relish works nicely to give this dressing the tang it needs, but it is a condiment that can be tricky to find outside the north of England. However, a vegetarian Worcestershire sauce from your local health food shop will do very well instead.

VEGETARIAN CAESAR DRESSING

Put all the ingredients except the oil in a food processor along with a splash of water and blend until smooth. With the motor running, add the oil in a steady stream until the dressing is thick and shiny, adding a little extra splash of water if it thickens too much.

MAKES APPROXIMATELY 1¾ CUPS

1 cup soy cream
1 garlic clove
juice of 1 lemon
1 teaspoon Henderson's Relish or vegetarian Worcestershire sauce
½ teaspoon Tabasco sauce
pinch of white pepper
pinch of cayenne pepper
pinch of salt
1 teaspoon Dijon mustard
2oz vegetarian Parmesan-style hard cheese, shredded
⅔ cup light olive or canola oil

This zesty and slightly spicy dressing is great for Latin salads. Chipotle chiles are mild, smoky chiles usually sold canned.

CHIPOTLE LIME DRESSING

Place all the ingredients in a large measuring cup or a pitcher and blend with a stick blender until smooth. Alternatively, chop the chiles, add to a jar or bottle with a screw-top lid along with all the other ingredients, fasten the lid securely, and shake well to combine.

MAKES APPROXIMATELY 1½ CUPS

2 chipotle chile peppers
grated zest and juice of 1 lime
juice of 1 lemon
1 cup olive or canola oil
1 teaspoon tomato paste
2 teaspoons powdered sugar

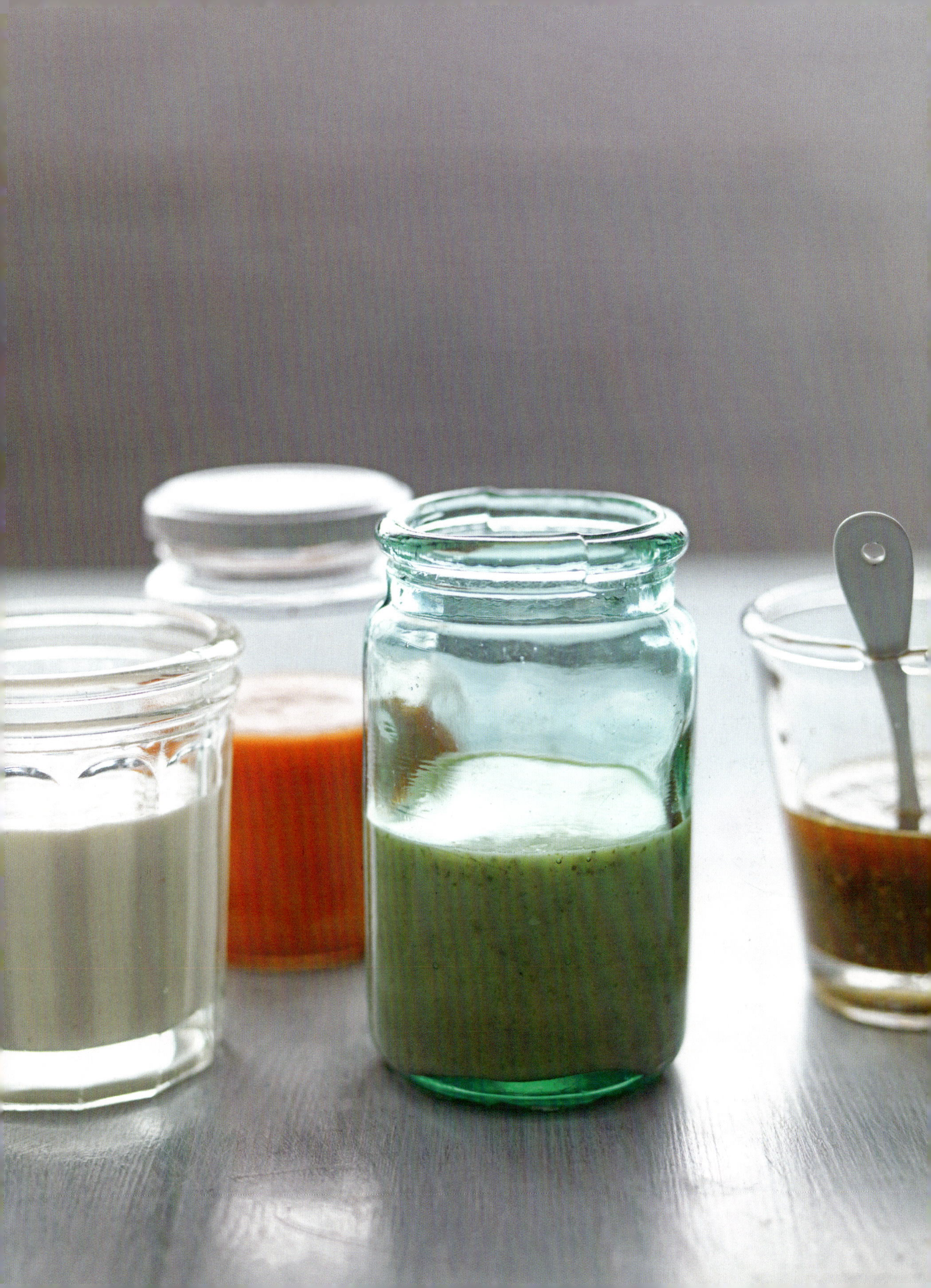

A very easy dressing to make, it has simple fresh flavors that pair well with lots of different kinds of salads, and is also really tasty tossed with fresh green vegetables.

LEMON MINT DRESSING

MAKES APPROXIMATELY 1½ CUPS

handful of mint leaves
1 garlic clove
grated zest of 1½ lemons and juice of 3 lemons
⅔ cup light olive oil
1 garlic clove
salt and pepper
1 teaspoon Dijon mustard
1 teaspoon powdered sugar

Place all the ingredients in a large measuring cup or a pitcher and blend with a stick blender until smooth. Alternatively, chop the mint and garlic and add them to a jar or bottle with a screw-top lid along with all the other ingredients. Fasten the lid securely, and shake well to combine.

This tangy Asian dressing is perfect for noodle dishes and salads that feature Asian vegetables. It can also be used as a stir-fry sauce.

SESAME CHILE DRESSING

MAKES APPROXIMATELY 1 CUP

1 red chile, trimmed
2 garlic cloves
handful of cilantro leaves
¼oz fresh ginger root, peeled
grated zest and juice of 1 lime
1 teaspoon tamarind paste
1 tablespoon sesame seeds, lightly toasted
3 tablespoons gluten-free sweet chili sauce
⅔ cup sesame oil
2 tablespoons tamari (gluten-free soy sauce)

Place all the ingredients in a large measuring cup or a pitcher and blend with a stick blender until smooth. Alternatively, chop the chile, garlic, cilantro, and ginger and add them to a jar or bottle with a screw-top lid along with all the other ingredients. Fasten the lid securely, and shake well to combine.

Another simple dressing to make, this goes very well with salad but is also delicious served with warm roast vegetables.

ORANGE MAPLE DRESSING

MAKES APPROXIMATELY 1½ CUPS

2 garlic cloves
3 thyme sprigs, leaves picked
2 rosemary sprigs, leaves picked
juice of 2 oranges plus grated zest of 1
3 tablespoons maple syrup
½ cup olive oil
½ teaspoon Dijon mustard
½ teaspoon wholegrain mustard

Place all the ingredients in a large measuring cup or pitcher and blend with a stick blender until smooth. Alternatively, chop the garlic, thyme, and rosemary and add them to a jar or bottle with a screw-top lid along with all the other ingredients. Fasten the lid securely, and shake well to combine.

This rich, nutty, Middle Eastern dressing is a great addition to salads and vegetable dishes.

TAHINI DRESSING

MAKES APPROXIMATELY ¼ PINT

⅓ cup tahini paste
juice of 1 lemon
¼ teaspoon sumac
2 tablespoons maple syrup

Put the tahini paste, lemon juice, sumac, and maple syrup into a food processor and season with salt and pepper. Blend together, gradually adding water as you go, until the dressing has the consistency of heavy cream. (You can do this by hand using a whisk if you like, but you may get a few lumps.) Taste and adjust the seasoning as necessary.

GLUTEN-FREE MENU IDEAS

MENU ONE

MENU TWO

244 GLUTEN-FREE MENU IDEAS

MENU THREE

MENU ONE

PRIMAVERA SALAD WITH
HOMEMADE LEMON RICOTTA
(SEE PAGE 102)

LAPSANG-SCENTED
MUSHROOM STROGANOFF
(SEE PAGE 132)

PANNA COTTA WITH
POACHED NECTARINES
(SEE PAGE 209)

MENU TWO

SPRING VEGETABLE PAKORA WITH
MANGO YOGURT DIP
(SEE PAGE 49)

SRI LANKAN SWEET POTATO
& CASHEW NUT CURRY
(SEE PAGE 115)

PERSIAN SPICED ALMOND,
PISTACHIO & POLENTA CAKE
WITH ROSE PETAL &
POMEGRANATE SYRUP
(SEE PAGE 216)

MENU THREE

MANGO SUMMER ROLLS
WITH SPICY PEANUT SAUCE
(SEE PAGE 37)

PEA, CARROT, BELL PEPPER
& TOFU LAKSA
(SEE PAGE 108)

MANGO FOOL WITH MINT
SUGAR & BLACK
SESAME BRITTLE
(SEE PAGE 218)

VEGAN MENU IDEAS

MENU ONE

MENU TWO

246 VEGAN MENU IDEAS

MENU THREE

MENU ONE

PUY LENTIL SALAD WITH ROAST VEGETABLES (SEE PAGE 87)

ROASTED PORTOBELLO MUSHROOM, PECAN & CHESTNUT WELLINGTON (SEE PAGE 125)

MAPLE-ROASTED ROOT VEGETABLES (SEE PAGE 188)

BRAISED RED CABBAGE (SEE PAGE 193)

DARK CHOCOLATE & RASPBERRY TRUFFLE CAKE (SEE PAGE 212)

MENU TWO

ARTICHOKE CROSTINI WITH VEGAN BASIL MAYONNAISE (SEE PAGES 52 & 232)

BLACK BEAN CHILI-FILLED BABY PUMPKINS WITH TOASTED COCONUT RICE (SEE PAGE 130)

MAPLE PECAN PIE WITH VEGAN SWEET PASTRY (SEE PAGE 221)

MENU THREE

STUFFED BABY EGGPLANTS WITH TAHINI DRESSING (SEE PAGES 67 & 243)

CAULIFLOWER & GREEN OLIVE TAGINE (SEE PAGE 136)

APRICOT & PISTACHIO COUSCOUS (SEE PAGE 192)

PEANUT BUTTER BROWNIES WITH HOT CHOCOLATE SAUCE (SEE PAGE 223)

VEGAN MENU IDEAS

SUPPLIERS

Even though supermarkets stock a wider range of specialty products these days, you can still find yourself running around to 2 or 3 different grocery stores trying to find all the ingredients you're looking for in order to execute that special dinner. I recommend putting some trust into your local Italian deli, Middle Eastern grocery store, or Asian/Oriental supermarket, if you're lucky enough to have one nearby.

If you find your local stores don't sell specialty items, the list of the following online suppliers will hopefully save you some time when you are hunting down the right ingredients. You can also try the Grocery and Gourmet section of Amazon, which carries an astonishing range of products.

www.wholefoodsmarket.com

With stores located across the US, Whole Foods Markets offers a great selection of products including gluten-free flours, vegetable bouillon powders, vegan margarine, agar flakes, soy milk, soy cream, and various other soy, gluten-free, and vegan products, as well as a good selection of grains, beans, and legumes. They also offer a selection of organic and gluten-free breads as well as heirloom varieties of fresh vegetables, which will be useful when you want to find organic pumpkins and squash. They also stock vegetarian cheeses. Check their site for a Whole Foods Market near you, or order online. Other stores that emphasize organic ingredients include Albertson's www.albertsons.com

www.hotpaella.com

This retailers has been importing a comprehensive range of top-quality Spanish foods into the US for forty years, including piquillo peppers, lima beans, Spanish paprika, and chickpeas, as well as high-quality cooked Spanish beans and legumes.

www.savoryspiceshop.com
www.mexgrocer.com

For all your chile needs, whether whole, crushed, and powdered, savoryspiceshop.com is also the place to find Mexican oregano. Epazote can be purchased online from www.mexgrocer.com

www.morinu.com

Mori-nu, based in Torrance, California, offer a range of tofu made without preservatives and using Non-GMO soybeans. You can find organic tofu at Whole Foods Markets, either in a store near you or online, as outlined above.

www.bobsredmill.com
www.glutenfreemall.com
www.igourmet.com

These sites offer a very wide range of non-wheat and gluten-free flours, as well as gluten-free baking ingredients, which can be ordered online if you cannot find what you need locally. In addition, Bob's Red Mill products are available in hundreds of stores in a number of US states. The website can tell you if there is a supplier near you.

www.asianfoodgrocer.com
www.marukaiestore.com
If authentic Japanese, Chinese, Thai, or Korean products are difficult to get hold of near you, try the grocery and gourmet section of Amazon, or the two online providers listed here. Note that both also sell organic versions of Asian foods.

www.titanfoods.net
www.christosmarket.com
These are online suppliers of all traditional Greek and contemporary Mediterranean products, with a great selection of products. They have everything from good-quality olive oils, feta, and halloumi cheeses, to olives, pita bread, grape leaves, and so much more.

www.zamourispices.com
For a great selection of Middle Eastern spices along with rose water, rose petals, and various other specialty ingredients.

www.olivenation.com
As well as a range of organic spices, oils, vinegars, grains, rice, pasta, and sugar, you can order pomegranate molasses from this site.

www.veganessentials.com
Located in Wisconsin, this online retailer sells vegan Parmesan cheese, agar, and a range of gluten- and wheat-free products.

If you cannot find ready-made vegan puff pastry, there is a recipe for making your own on *www.veganbaking.net*. The site also gives a list of every known vegan bakery worldwide.

INDEX

A

ale
  Wild Mushroom & Ale Pies 127
almonds
  Homemade Labneh Cheese with Grilled Peaches, Almonds, Arugula & Pomegranate Molasses 43
  Persian Spiced Almond, Pistachio & Polenta Cake with Rose Petal & Pomegranate Syrup 216
apples
  Apple & Ginger Sticky Toffee Pudding 207
  Beet, Apple & Red Cabbage Borscht 27
  Beet, Fennel, Apple & Dill Burgers 142
  Carrot Relish 237
  Spiced Carrot, Apple & Parsnip Latkes with Cucumber Ribbon Salad 51
Apricot & Pistachio Couscous 192
Artichoke Crostini with Roast Garlic and Lemon Aïoli 52
arugula
  Homemade Labneh Cheese with Grilled Peaches, Almonds, Arugula & Pomegranate Molasses 43
asparagus
  Heirloom Potato & Roast Asparagus Salad with Truffle Mayonnaise 93
  Long-stem Broccoli & Asparagus White Lasagne 112
  Penne with Red Bell Pepper Sauce 150
  Primavera Salad with Homemade Lemon Ricotta 102
  Roasted Asparagus with Poached Eggs & Orange Hollandaise 38
avocados
  Caesar Salad with Avocado & Green String Beans 101
  Guacamole 175
  Mexican Salad with Avocado, Baby Gem, Scallion & Jalapeño 162

B

Baby Eggplant & Roast Bell Pepper Caponata 122
bananas
  Chocolate, Coconut & Banana Mousse Cake 208
basil
  Macaroni & Cheese with Sun-dried Tomatoes & Basil Crumb Topping 135
  Oyster Mushroom Fusilli Salad with Purple Broccoli, Basil & Pine Nuts 94
  Purple Basil Oil 238
  Rigatoni with Tomato & Basil Sauce & Black Olive Tapenade 151
  Vegan Basil Mayonnaise 232
beans
  Black Bean & Pumpkin Burritos 165
  Black Bean Chili-filled Baby Pumpkins with Toasted Coconut Rice 130
  Black Bean Dip 177
  Caesar Salad with Avocado & Green String Beans 101
  Cinnamon-spiced Squash & Lima Bean Stew 120
  Cranberry Bean Soup with Smoked Tofu & Pico de Gallo 22
  Creamy Mushroom & Sherry Vinegar Orecchiette with Green String Beans 146
  Mexican Kidney Bean, Jalapeño, Roasted Bell Pepper & Corn Burgers 141
  Molasses-baked Beans 196
  Peruvian Quinoa Salad with Kidney Beans, Bell Peppers & Chipotle Lime Dressing 88
  Potato & White Bean Dip 230
  Primavera Salad with Homemade Lemon Ricotta 102
  Pumpkin, Cavolo Nero & Haricot Bean Broth 28
Beer-battered Onion Rings 194
beets
  Beet & Dill Dip 76
  Beet, Apple & Red Cabbage Borscht 27
  Beet, Fennel, Apple & Dill Burgers 142
  Detox Salad 89
  Maple-roasted Root Vegetables 188
  Warm Ruby & Golden Beet Salad with Roast Hazelnuts, Blood Oranges & Labneh 92
Black Bean & Pumpkin Burritos 165
Black Bean Chili-filled Baby Pumpkins with Toasted Coconut Rice 130
Black Bean Dip 177
Braised Red Cabbage 193
Cranberry Bean Soup with Smoked Tofu & Pico de Gallo 22
bell peppers
  Baby Eggplant & Roast Bell Pepper Caponata 122
  Harissa 228
  Mexican Kidney Bean, Jalapeño, Roasted Bell Pepper & Corn Burgers 141
  Pea, Carrot, Bell Pepper & Tofu Laksa 108
  Penne with Red Bell Pepper Sauce 150
  Peruvian Quinoa Salad with Kidney Beans, Bell Peppers & Chipotle Lime Dressing 88
  Pumpkin, Feta & Piquillo Pepper Pie 55
  Roast Bell Pepper & Black Olive Lahmacuns 66
  Thai-spiced Roasted Red Bell Pepper, Sweet Potato, Ginger & Coconut Milk Soup 18
  Peruvian Quinoa Salad with Kidney Beans, Bell Peppers & Chipotle Lime Dressing 88
broccoli
  Chargrilled Long-stem Broccoli with Chile Lemon Oil 191
  Long-stem Broccoli & Asparagus White Lasagne 112
  Oyster Mushroom Fusilli Salad with Purple Broccoli, Basil & Pine Nuts 94
brownies
  Peanut Butter Brownies with Hot Chocolate Sauce 223
  Bubble & Squeak Cakes Filled with Welsh Rarebit 40
bulgur
  Ruby Jeweled Tabbouleh 96
burgers 138
  Beet, Fennel, Apple & Dill Burgers 142
  Italian Tomato, Eggplant & Black Olive Burgers 140
  Mexican Kidney Bean, Jalapeño, Roasted Bell Pepper & Corn Burgers 141
butter
  Leek, Chive & Caper Scotch Eggs with Mustard Beurre Blanc 118

C

cabbage
  Beet, Apple & Red Cabbage Borscht 27
  Braised Red Cabbage 193
  Korean Hot & Sour Soup 23
  Pumpkin, Cavolo Nero & Haricot Bean Broth 28
Caesar Dressing, Vegetarian 240
Caesar Salad with Avocado & Green String Beans 101
capers
  Leek, Chive & Caper Scotch Eggs with Mustard Beurre Blanc 118
cardamom
  Turmeric, Pea & Cardamom Basmati 199
carrots
  Carrot Relish 237
  Detox Salad 89
  Maple-roasted Root Vegetables 188
  Pea, Carrot, Bell Pepper & Tofu Laksa 108
  Spiced Carrot, Apple & Parsnip Latkes with Cucumber Ribbon Salad 51
cashews
  Sri Lankan Sweet Potato & Cashew Nut Curry 115
Cauliflower & Green Olive Tagine 136
Chargrilled Long-stem Broccoli with Chile Lemon Oil 191
cheese
  Bubble & Squeak Cakes Filled with Welsh Rarebit 40
  Chili Flake & Feta Dip 78

Chile Cornbread 178
Crispy Polenta with Slow-roast Cherry Tomatoes & Lemon Mascarpone 59
Eggplant Moussaka with Smoked Tofu Ragù 155
Feta, Chile & Mint-filled Eggplant Escalopes 116
Figs with Blue Cheese Mousse & Roasted Hazelnuts 44
Halloumi, Zucchini & Mint Fritters 64
Homemade Labneh Cheese with Grilled Peaches, Almonds, Arugula & Pomegranate Molasses 43
Macaroni & Cheese with Sun-dried Tomatoes & Basil Crumb Topping 135
Mango, Brie & Jalapeño Quesadillas 166
Minestrone Verde with Saffron Arborio Rice 21
Penne with Red Bell Pepper Sauce 150
Primavera Salad with Homemade Lemon Ricotta 102
Pumpkin & Potato Pampushki 123
Pumpkin, Feta & Piquillo Pepper Pie 55
Rigatoni with Tomato & Basil Sauce & Black Olive Tapenade 151
Saffron & Goat Cheese Tagliatelle with Zucchini, Cherry Tomatoes & Black Olives 148
Savory Hazelnut Pancakes Filled with Chanterelle Mushrooms & Mascarpone 54
Spanakopita 70
Sun-dried Tomato & Mozzarella *Arancini* with Warm Grilled Eggplant & Zucchini Salad 34
Triple Cheese Empanadas 168
Trofie with Wild Garlic Pesto 147
Warm Ruby & Golden Beet Salad with Roast Hazelnuts, Blood Oranges & Labneh 92
Wet Polenta 197

cheesecake
White Chocolate & Raspberry Ripple Cheesecake 204

chestnuts
Roasted Portobello Mushroom, Pecan & Chestnut Wellington 125–6

chickpeas
Falafel 72
Hummus 77

chiles/chili flakes
Chargrilled Long-stem Broccoli with Chile Lemon Oil 191
Chile Cornbread 178
Chili Flake & Feta Dip 78
Chipotle Lime Dressing 240
Cranberry Bean Soup with Smoked Tofu & *Pico de Gallo* 22
Feta, Chile & Mint-filled Eggplant Escalopes 116

Green Harissa 229
Lime & Chile Corn 169
Mango, Brie & Jalapeño Quesadillas 166
Mexican Kidney Bean, Jalapeño, Roasted Bell Pepper & Corn Burgers 141
Mexican Salad with Avocado, Baby Gem, Scallion & Jalapeño 162
Peruvian Quinoa Salad with Kidney Beans, Bell Peppers & Chipotle Lime Dressing 88
Sesame Chile Dressing 242
Tempura Vegetables with Noodle, Mango & Cucumber Salad & Chile Dipping Sauce 56
Chipotle Lime Dressing 240

chives
Leek, Chive & Caper Scotch Eggs with Mustard Beurre Blanc 118

chocolate
Chocolate, Coconut & Banana Mousse Cake 208
Dark Chocolate & Raspberry Truffle Cake 212
Peanut Butter Brownies with Hot Chocolate Sauce 223
White Chocolate & Raspberry Ripple Cheesecake 204
Cinnamon-spiced Squash & Lima Bean Stew 120

coconut
Black Bean Chili-filled Baby Pumpkins with Toasted Coconut Rice 130
Chocolate, Coconut & Banana Mousse Cake 208
Sri Lankan Sweet Potato & Cashew Nut Curry 115
Sweet Potato & Coconut Blinis with Pan-fried Okra & Jerk Dressing 50
Tomato & Coconut Sambal 231

coconut milk
Thai-spiced Roasted Red Bell Pepper, Sweet Potato, Ginger & Coconut Milk Soup 18

corn
Chile Cornbread 178
Lime & Chile Corn 169
Mexican Kidney Bean, Jalapeño, Roasted Bell Pepper & Corn Burgers 141

couscous
Apricot & Pistachio Couscous 192

cream
Creamy Mushroom & Sherry Vinegar Orecchiette with Green String Beans 146
Lapsang-scented Mushroom Stroganoff 132
Mango Fool with Mint Sugar & Black Sesame Brittle 218
Panna Cotta with Poached Nectarines 209
Passion Fruit Crème Caramel with Gingersnap Cookies 213
Crispy Polenta with Slow-roast Cherry Tomatoes & Lemon Mascarpone 59

croutons
Caesar Salad with Avocado & Green String Beans 101

cucumber
Roast Eggplant, Cucumber & Baby Plum Tomato Salad with Tahini Dressing 100
Spiced Carrot, Apple & Parsnip Latkes with Cucumber Ribbon Salad 51
Tempura Vegetables with Noodle, Mango & Cucumber Salad & Chile Dipping Sauce 56

D

Dark Chocolate & Raspberry Truffle Cake 212
Detox Salad 89

dill
Beet & Dill Dip 76
Beet, Fennel, Apple & Dill Burgers 142

E

eggplant
Baby Eggplant & Roast Bell Pepper Caponata 122
Eggplant Moussaka with Smoked Tofu Ragù 155
Feta, Chile & Mint-filled Eggplant Escalopes 116
Italian Tomato, Eggplant & Black Olive Burgers 140
Rigatoni with Tomato & Basil Sauce & Black Olive Tapenade 151
Roast Eggplant, Cucumber & Baby Plum Tomato Salad with Tahini Dressing 100
Stuffed Baby Eggplants 67
Sun-blushed Tomato & Mozzarella *Arancini* with Warm Grilled Eggplant & Zucchini Salad 34

eggs
Feta, Chile & Mint-filled Eggplant Escalopes 116
Leek, Chive & Caper Scotch Eggs with Mustard Beurre Blanc 118
Mee Goreng 156
Passion Fruit Crème Caramel with Gingersnap Cookies 213
Roasted Asparagus with Poached Eggs & Orange Hollandaise 38
epazote 165, 177

F

Falafel 72
fennel
Beet, Fennel, Apple & Dill Burgers 142
Detox Salad 89
Feta, Chile & Mint-filled Eggplant Escalopes 116
Figs with Blue Cheese Mousse & Roasted Hazelnuts 44

G

garlic
  Artichoke Crostini with Roast Garlic and Lemon Aïoli 52
  Garlic Rotis 184
  Roast Garlic & Lemon Aïoli 234

garlic, wild (ramps)
  Trofie with Wild Garlic Pesto 147

Gazpacho 29

ginger
  Apple & Ginger Sticky Toffee Pudding 207
  Passion Fruit Crème Caramel with Gingersnap Cookies 213
  Thai-spiced Roasted Red Pepper, Sweet Potato, Ginger & Coconut Milk Soup 18

gluten-free dishes 13
  Apple & Ginger Sticky Toffee Pudding 207
  Baby Eggplant & Roast Bell Pepper Caponata 122
  Beer-battered Onion Rings 194
  Beet & Dill Dip 76
  Beet, Apple & Red Cabbage Borscht 27
  Bubble & Squeak Cakes Filled with Welsh Rarebit 40
  Black Bean Chili-filled Baby Pumpkins with Toasted Coconut Rice 130
  Black Bean Dip 177
  Braised Red Cabbage 193
  Bubble & Squeak Cakes Filled with Welsh Rarebit 40
  Carrot Relish 237
  Chargrilled Long-stem Broccoli with Chile Lemon Oil 191
  Chile Cornbread 178
  Chili Flake & Feta Dip 78
  Chipotle Lime Dressing 240
  Chocolate, Coconut & Banana Mousse Cake 208
  Cinnamon-spiced Squash & Lima Bean Stew 120
  Cranberry Bean Soup with Smoked Tofu & *Pico de Gallo* 22
  Crispy Polenta with Slow-roast Cherry Tomatoes & Lemon Mascarpone 59
  Dark Chocolate & Raspberry Truffle Cake 212
  Detox Salad 89
  Falafel 72
  Gazpacho 29
  Green Harissa 229
  Guacamole 175
  Harissa 228
  Heirloom Potato & Roast Asparagus Salad with Truffle Mayonnaise 93
  Herb Oil 238
  Homemade Labneh Cheese with Grilled Peaches, Almonds, Arugula & Pomegranate Molasses 43

Hummus 77
Korean Hot & Sour Soup 23
Lapsang-scented Mushroom Stroganoff 132
Lemon Mint Dressing 242
Lime & Chile Corn 169
Mango Fool with Mint Sugar & Black Sesame Brittle 218
Mango Summer Rolls with Spicy Peanut Sauce 37
Maple-roasted Root Vegetables 188
Marinated Mushrooms 73
menu ideas 244–5
Mexican Salad with Avocado, Baby Gem, Scallion & Jalapeño 162
Minestrone Verde with Saffron Arborio Rice 21
Molasses-baked Beans 196
Orange Maple Dressing 243
Panna Cotta with Poached Nectarines 209
Pea, Carrot, Bell Pepper & Tofu Laksa 108
Peanut Butter Brownies with Hot Chocolate Sauce 223
Pebre 176
Persian Spiced Almond, Pistachio & Polenta Cake with Rose Petal & Pomegranate Syrup 216
Port Gravy 236
Peruvian Quinoa Salad with Kidney Beans, Bell Peppers & Chipotle Lime Dressing 88
Potato & White Bean Dip 230
Primavera Salad with Homemade Lemon Ricotta 102
Pumpkin & Potato Pampushki 123
Pumpkin, Cavolo Nero & Haricot Bean Broth 28
Purple Basil Oil 238
Puy Lentil Salad with Roasted Vegetables 87
Roast Eggplant, Cucumber & Baby Plum Tomato Salad with Tahini Dressing 100
Roast Garlic & Lemon Aïoli 234
Roast Potato Wedges 187
Roasted Asparagus with Poached Eggs & Orange Hollandaise 38
Sesame Chile Dressing 242
Shiitake Mushroom & Chinese Vegetable Stir-fry 152
Spiced Carrot, Apple & Parsnip Latkes with Cucumber Ribbon Salad 51
Spiced Okra with Cherry Tomatoes, Baby Spinach & Mint 99
Spring Vegetable Pakora with Mango Yogurt Dip 49
Sri Lankan Sweet Potato & Cashew Nut Curry 115

Stuffed Baby Eggplants 67
Sun-dried Tomato & Pine Nut Stuffed Grape Leaves 75
Sweet Potato & Coconut Blinis with Pan-fried Okra & Jerk Dressing 50
Sweet Potato Fries 186
Thai-spiced Roasted Red Bell Pepper, Sweet Potato, Ginger & Coconut Milk Soup 18
Tomatillo Rice 198
Tomato & Coconut Sambal 231
Tomato & Mushroom Tom Yum 24
Truffle Mayonnaise 235
Turmeric, Pea & Cardamom Basmati 199
Vegan Basil Mayonnaise 232
Vegetarian Caesar Dressing 240
Walnut & Leek Pilaf 199
Warm Ruby & Golden Beet Salad with Roast Hazelnuts, Blood Oranges & Labneh 92
Wet Polenta 197
White Chocolate & Raspberry Ripple Cheesecake 204
Wild Rice Salad with Peas, Pea Shoots & Green Harissa 84

grape leaves
  Sun-dried Tomato & Pine Nut Stuffed Grape Leaves 75

Green Harissa 229
Guacamole 175

H

Halloumi, Zucchini & Mint Fritters 64

Harissa 228
  Green Harissa 229
  Wild Rice Salad with Peas, Pea Shoots & Green Harissa 84

hazelnuts
  Figs with Blue Cheese Mousse & Roasted Hazelnuts 44
  Savory Hazelnut Pancakes Filled with Chanterelle Mushrooms & Mascarpone 54
  Warm Ruby & Golden Beet Salad with Roast Hazelnuts, Blood Oranges & Labneh 92

Heirloom Potato & Roast Asparagus Salad with Truffle Mayonnaise 93
Henderson's Relish 240
Herb Oil 238
Homemade Labneh Cheese with Grilled Peaches, Almonds, Arugula & Pomegranate Molasses 43
Hummus 77

I

Italian Tomato, Eggplant & Black Olive Burgers 140

252 INDEX

K

kecap manis 156
Korean Hot & Sour Soup 23

L

Lapsang-scented Mushroom Stroganoff 132

LEEKS
Leek, Chive & Caper Scotch Eggs with Mustard Beurre Blanc 118
Walnut & Leek Pilaf 199

LEMONS
Artichoke Crostini with Roast Garlic and Lemon Aïoli 52
Chargrilled Long-stem Broccoli with Chile Lemon Oil 191
Crispy Polenta with Slow-roast Cherry Tomatoes & Lemon Mascarpone 59
Lemon Mint Dressing 242
Primavera Salad with Homemade Lemon Ricotta 102
Roast Garlic & Lemon Aïoli 234

LENTILS
Puy Lentil Salad with Roasted Vegetables 87

LETTUCE
Mexican Salad with Avocado, Baby Gem, Scallion & Jalapeño 162

LIMES
Chipotle Lime Dressing 240
Lime & Chile Corn 169
Peruvian Quinoa Salad with Kidney Beans, Peppers & Chipotle Lime Dressing 88
Long-stem Broccoli & Asparagus White Lasagne 112

M

Macaroni & Cheese with Sun-dried Tomatoes & Basil Crumb Topping 135

MANGOES
Mango Fool with Mint Sugar & Black Sesame Brittle 218
Mango Summer Rolls with Spicy Peanut Sauce 37
Mango, Brie & Jalapeño Quesadillas 166
Spring Vegetable Pakora with Mango Yogurt Dip 49
Tempura Vegetables with Noodle, Mango & Cucumber Salad & Chile Dipping Sauce 56

MAPLE SYRUP
Maple Pecan Pie with Vegan Sweet Pastry 221
Maple-roasted Root Vegetables 188
Orange Maple Dressing 243
Marinated Mushrooms 73
Mee Goreng 156

MENU IDEAS
gluten-free dishes 244–5
vegan dishes 246–7
Mexican Kidney Bean, Jalapeño, Roasted Bell Pepper & Corn Burgers 141
Mexican Salad with Avocado, Baby Gem, Scallion & Jalapeño 162
Minestrone Verde with Saffron Arborio Rice 21

MINT
Feta, Chile & Mint-filled Eggplant Escalopes 116
Halloumi, Zucchini & Mint Fritters 64
Mango Fool with Mint Sugar & Black Sesame Brittle 218
Spiced Okra with Cherry Tomatoes, Baby Spinach & Mint 99
Vietnamese mint 154
Molasses-baked Beans 196

MUSHROOMS
Creamy Mushroom & Sherry Vinegar Orecchiette with Green String Beans 146
Lapsang-scented Mushroom Stroganoff 132
Marinated Mushrooms 73
Oyster Mushroom Fusilli Salad with Purple Broccoli, Basil & Pine Nuts 94
Roasted Portobello Mushroom, Pecan & Chestnut Wellington 125–6
Savory Hazelnut Pancakes Filled with Chanterelle Mushrooms & Mascarpone 54
Shiitake Mushroom & Chinese Vegetable Stir-fry 152
Shiitake Mushroom & Seaweed Pho 154
Tomato & Mushroom Tom Yum 24
Wild Mushroom & Ale Pies 127

MUSTARD
Leek, Chive & Caper Scotch Eggs with Mustard Beurre Blanc 118

N

NECTARINES
Panna Cotta with Poached Nectarines 209

NOODLES
Mango Summer Rolls with Spicy Peanut Sauce 37
Mee Goreng 156
Shiitake Mushroom & Seaweed Pho 154
Tempura Vegetables with Noodle, Mango & Cucumber Salad & Chile Dipping Sauce 56

O

OKRA
Spiced Okra with Cherry Tomatoes, Baby Spinach & Mint 99
Sweet Potato & Coconut Blinis with Pan-fried Okra & Jerk Dressing 50

OLIVE OIL
Artichoke Crostini with Roast Garlic and Lemon Aïoli 52
Chargrilled Long-stem Broccoli with Chile Lemon Oil 191
Roast Garlic & Lemon Aïoli 234

OLIVES
Cauliflower & Green Olive Tagine 136
Italian Tomato, Eggplant & Black Olive Burgers 140
Rigatoni with Tomato & Basil Sauce & Black Olive Tapenade 151
Roast Bell Pepper & Black Olive Lahmacuns 66
Saffron & Goat Cheese Tagliatelle with Zucchini, Cherry Tomatoes & Black Olives 148

ONIONS
Beer-battered Onion Rings 194
Spanakopita 70

ORANGES
Orange Maple Dressing 243
Roasted Asparagus with Poached Eggs & Orange Hollandaise 38
Warm Ruby & Golden Beet Salad with Roast Hazelnuts, Blood Oranges & Labneh 92
Oyster Mushroom Fusilli Salad with Purple Broccoli, Basil & Pine Nuts 94

P

Panna Cotta with Poached Nectarines 209

PARSNIPS
Maple-roasted Root Vegetables 188
Spiced Carrot, Apple & Parsnip Latkes with Cucumber Ribbon Salad 51
Passion Fruit Crème Caramel with Gingersnap Cookies 213

PASTA 144
Creamy Mushroom & Sherry Vinegar Orecchiette with Green String Beans 146
Long-stem Broccoli & Asparagus White Lasagne 112
Macaroni & Cheese with Sun-dried Tomatoes & Basil Crumb Topping 135
Oyster Mushroom Fusilli Salad with Purple Broccoli, Basil & Pine Nuts 94
Penne with Red Bell Pepper Sauce 150
Rigatoni with Tomato & Basil Sauce & Black Olive Tapenade 151
Saffron & Goat Cheese Tagliatelle with Zucchini, Cherry Tomatoes & Black Olives 148
Trofie with Wild Garlic Pesto 147

PEA SHOOTS
Wild Rice Salad with Peas, Pea Shoots & Green Harissa 84

peaches
  Homemade Labneh Cheese with Grilled Peaches, Almonds, Arugula & Pomegranate Molasses 43

peanut butter
  Mango Summer Rolls with Spicy Peanut Sauce 37
  Peanut Butter Brownies with Hot Chocolate Sauce 223

peas
  Pea, Carrot, Bell Pepper & Tofu Laksa 108
  Primavera Salad with Homemade Lemon Ricotta 102
  Saffron & Pea Risotto Cakes 111
  Turmeric, Pea & Cardamom Basmati 199
  Wild Rice Salad with Peas, Pea Shoots & Green Harissa 84

Pebre 176

pecans
  Maple Pecan Pie with Vegan Sweet Pastry 221
  Roasted Portobello Mushroom, Pecan & Chestnut Wellington 125–6

Penne with Red Bell Pepper Sauce 150

pine nuts
  Oyster Mushroom Fusilli Salad with Purple Broccoli, Basil & Pine Nuts 94
  Spanakopita 70
  Sun-dried Tomato & Pine Nut Stuffed Grape Leaves 75

pistachios
  Apricot & Pistachio Couscous 192
  Persian Spiced Almond, Pistachio & Polenta Cake with Rose Petal & Pomegranate Syrup 216

Plantain Fritters 172

polenta
  Crispy Polenta with Slow-roast Cherry Tomatoes & Lemon Mascarpone 59
  Persian Spiced Almond, Pistachio & Polenta Cake with Rose Petal & Pomegranate Syrup 216
  Polenta Crackers 45
  Wet Polenta 197

pomegranate molasses
  Homemade Labneh Cheese with Grilled Peaches, Almonds, Arugula & Pomegranate Molasses 43

pomegranates
  Persian Spiced Almond, Pistachio & Polenta Cake with Rose Petal & Pomegranate Syrup 216

Port Gravy 236

potatoes
  Bubble & Squeak Cakes Filled with Welsh Rarebit 40
  Heirloom Potato & Roast Asparagus Salad with Truffle Mayonnaise 93
  Potato & White Bean Dip 230
  Pumpkin & Potato Pampushki 123
  Roast Potato Wedges 187

Primavera Salad with Homemade Lemon Ricotta 102

pumpkin
  Black Bean & Pumpkin Burritos 165
  Black Bean Chili-filled Baby Pumpkins with Toasted Coconut Rice 130
  Maple-roasted Root Vegetables 188
  Pumpkin & Potato Pampushki 123
  Pumpkin, Cavolo Nero & Haricot Bean Broth 28
  Pumpkin, Feta & Piquillo Pepper Pie 55

Purple Basil Oil 238
Puy Lentil Salad with Roasted Vegetables 87

Q

quinoa
  Peruvian Quinoa Salad with Kidney Beans, Bell Peppers & Chipotle Lime Dressing 88

R

raspberries
  Dark Chocolate & Raspberry Truffle Cake 212
  White Chocolate & Raspberry Ripple Cheesecake 204

rice
  Black Bean Chili-filled Baby Pumpkins with Toasted Coconut Rice 130
  Minestrone Verde with Saffron Arborio Rice 21
  Saffron & Pea Risotto Cakes 111
  Sun-dried Tomato & Mozzarella *Arancini* with Warm Grilled Eggplant & Zucchini Salad 34
  Sun-dried Tomato & Pine Nut Stuffed Grape Leaves 75
  Tomatillo Rice 198
  Turmeric, Pea & Cardamom Basmati 199
  Walnut & Leek Pilaf 199
  Wild Rice Salad with Peas, Pea Shoots & Green Harissa 84

Rigatoni with Tomato & Basil Sauce & Black Olive Tapenade 151
Roast Bell Pepper & Black Olive Lahmacuns 66
Roast Eggplant, Cucumber & Baby Plum Tomato Salad with Tahini Dressing 100
Roast Garlic & Lemon Aïoli 234
Roast Potato Wedges 187
Roasted Asparagus with Poached Eggs & Orange Hollandaise 38
Roasted Portobello Mushroom, Pecan & Chestnut Wellington 125–6

rose petals
  Persian Spiced Almond, Pistachio & Polenta Cake with Rose Petal & Pomegranate Syrup 216

Ruby Jeweled Tabbouleh 96

S

saffron
  Minestrone Verde with Saffron Arborio Rice 21
  Saffron & Goat Cheese Tagliatelle with Zucchini, Cherry Tomatoes & Black Olives 148
  Saffron & Pea Risotto Cakes 111
  Savory Hazelnut Pancakes Filled with Chanterelle Mushrooms & Mascarpone 54

scallions
  Mexican Salad with Avocado, Baby Gem, Scallion & Jalapeño 162
  Spring Vegetable Pakora with Mango Yogurt Dip 49

seaweed
  Shiitake Mushroom & Seaweed Pho 154

sesame oil
  Sesame Chile Dressing 242
  Sesame Chile Dressing 242

sesame seeds
  Mango Fool with Mint Sugar & Black Sesame Brittle 218

sherry vinegar
  Creamy Mushroom & Sherry Vinegar Orecchiette with Green String Beans 146
  Shiitake Mushroom & Chinese Vegetable Stir-fry 152
  Shiitake Mushroom & Seaweed Pho 154

soy cream
  Vegetarian Caesar Dressing 240

Spanakopita 70

spices
  Cinnamon-spiced Squash & Lima Bean Stew 120
  Pea, Carrot, Bell Pepper & Tofu Laksa 108
  Persian Spiced Almond, Pistachio & Polenta Cake with Rose Petal & Pomegranate Syrup 216
  Saffron & Goat Cheese Tagliatelle with Zucchini, Cherry Tomatoes & Black Olives 148
  Saffron & Pea Risotto Cakes 111
  Spiced Carrot, Apple & Parsnip Latkes with Cucumber Ribbon Salad 51
  Spiced Okra with Cherry Tomatoes, Baby Spinach & Mint 99
  Sweet Potato & Coconut Blinis with Pan-fried Okra & Jerk Dressing 50
  Thai-spiced Roasted Red Bell Pepper, Sweet Potato, Ginger & Coconut Milk Soup 18
  Turmeric, Pea & Cardamom Basmati 199

spinach
  Spanakopita 70
  Spiced Okra with Cherry Tomatoes, Baby Spinach & Mint 99

squash
- Cinnamon-spiced Squash & Lima Bean Stew 120
- Maple-roasted Root Vegetables 188
- Pumpkin & Potato Pampushki 123
- Sri Lankan Sweet Potato & Cashew Nut Curry 115
- Stuffed Baby Eggplants 67
- Sun-blushed Tomato & Mozzarella *Arancini* with Warm Grilled Eggplant & Zucchini Salad 34
- Sun-dried Tomato & Pine Nut Stuffed Grape Leaves 75

sweet potatoes
- Sri Lankan Sweet Potato & Cashew Nut Curry 115
- Sweet Potato & Coconut Blinis with Pan-fried Okra & Jerk Dressing 50
- Sweet Potato Fries 186
- Thai-spiced Roasted Red Bell Pepper, Sweet Potato, Ginger & Coconut Milk Soup 18

T

tahini
- Hummus 77
- Roast Eggplant, Cucumber & Baby Plum Tomato Salad with Tahini Dressing 100
- Tahini Dressing 243
- Tempura Vegetables with Noodle, Mango & Cucumber Salad & Chile Dipping Sauce 56
- Thai-spiced Roasted Red Bell Pepper, Sweet Potato, Ginger & Coconut Milk Soup 18

toffee
- Apple & Ginger Sticky Toffee Pudding 207

tofu
- Cranberry Bean Soup with Smoked Tofu & *Pico de Gallo* 22
- Eggplant Moussaka with Smoked Tofu Ragù 155
- Pea, Carrot, Bell Pepper & Tofu Laksa 108
- Tomatillo Rice 198

tomatoes
- Baby Eggplant & Roast Bell Pepper Caponata 122
- Crispy Polenta with Slow-roast Cherry Tomatoes & Lemon Mascarpone 59
- Eggplant Moussaka with Smoked Tofu Ragù 155
- Gazpacho 29
- Italian Tomato, Eggplant & Black Olive Burgers 140
- Korean Hot & Sour Soup 23
- Macaroni & Cheese with Sun-blushed Tomatoes & Basil Crumb Topping 135
- Pebre 176
- Rigatoni with Tomato & Basil Sauce & Black Olive Tapenade 151
- Roast Eggplant, Cucumber & Baby Plum Tomato Salad with Tahini Dressing 100
- Saffron & Goat Cheese Tagliatelle with Zucchini, Cherry Tomatoes & Black Olives 148
- Spiced Okra with Cherry Tomatoes, Baby Spinach & Mint 99
- Sun-dried Tomato & Mozzarella *Arancini* with Warm Grilled Eggplant & Zucchini Salad 34
- Sun-dried Tomato & Pine Nut Stuffed Grape Leaves 75
- Tomato & Coconut Sambal 231
- Tomato & Mushroom Tom Yum 24
- Triple Cheese Empanadas 168
- Trofie with Wild Garlic Pesto 147

truffle oil
- Heirloom Potato & Roast Asparagus Salad with Truffle Mayonnaise 93
- Truffle Mayonnaise 235
- Turmeric, Pea & Cardamom Basmati 199

V

vegan dishes 13
- Apricot & Pistachio Couscous 192
- Baby Eggplant & Roast Bell Pepper Caponata 122
- Beer-battered Onion Rings 194
- Black Bean Chili-filled Baby Pumpkins with Toasted Coconut Rice 130
- Black Bean Dip 177
- Braised Red Cabbage 193
- Carrot Relish 237
- Chargrilled Long-stem Broccoli with Chile Lemon Oil 191
- Chipotle Lime Dressing 240
- Chocolate, Coconut & Banana Mousse Cake 208
- Cinnamon-spiced Squash & Lima Bean Stew 120
- Cranberry Bean Soup with Smoked Tofu & *Pico de Gallo* 22
- Dark Chocolate & Raspberry Truffle Cake 212
- Detox Salad 89
- Falafel 72
- Gazpacho 29
- Green Harissa 229
- Guacamole 175
- Harissa 228
- Heirloom Potato & Roast Asparagus Salad with Truffle Mayonnaise 93
- Herb Oil 238
- Hummus 77
- Korean Hot & Sour Soup 23
- Lemon Mint Dressing 242
- Mango Summer Rolls with Spicy Peanut Sauce 37
- Maple Pecan Pie with Vegan Sweet Pastry 221
- Maple-roasted Root Vegetables 188
- Marinated Mushrooms 73
- menu ideas 246–7
- Mexican Salad with Avocado, Baby Gem, Scallion & Jalapeño 162
- Molasses-baked Beans 196
- Orange Maple Dressing 243
- Pea, Carrot, Bell Pepper & Tofu Laksa 108
- Peanut Butter Brownies with Hot Chocolate Sauce 223
- Pebre 176
- Peruvian Quinoa Salad with Kidney Beans, Bell Peppers & Chipotle Lime Dressing 88
- Plantain Fritters 172
- Potato & White Bean Dip 230
- Pumpkin, Cavolo Nero & Haricot Bean Broth 28
- Purple Basil Oil 238
- Puy Lentil Salad with Roasted Vegetables 87
- Roast Eggplant, Cucumber & Baby Plum Tomato Salad with Tahini Dressing 100
- Roast Bell Pepper & Black Olive Lahmacuns 66
- Roast Potato Wedges 187
- Roasted Portobello Mushroom, Pecan & Chestnut Wellington 125–6
- Ruby Jeweled Tabbouleh 96
- Sesame Chile Dressing 242
- Spiced Okra with Cherry Tomatoes, Baby Spinach & Mint 99
- Sri Lankan Sweet Potato & Cashew Nut Curry 115
- Stuffed Baby Eggplants 67
- Sun-dried Tomato & Pine Nut Stuffed Grape Leaves 75
- Sweet Potato Fries 186
- Thai-spiced Roasted Red Bell Pepper, Sweet Potato, Ginger & Coconut Milk Soup 18
- Tomatillo Rice 198
- Tomato & Coconut Sambal 231
- Tomato & Mushroom Tom Yum 24
- Truffle Mayonnaise 235
- Turmeric, Pea & Cardamom Basmati 199
- Vegan Basil Mayonnaise 232
- Wild Mushroom & Ale Pies 127
- Wild Rice Salad with Peas, Pea Shoots & Green Harissa 84

vegetables
- Maple-roasted Root Vegetables 188
- Mee Goreng 156
- Puy Lentil Salad with Roasted Vegetables 87
- Shiitake Mushroom & Chinese Vegetable Stir-fry 152

Spring Vegetable Pakora with Mango Yogurt Dip 49
Tempura Vegetables with Noodle, Mango & Cucumber Salad & Chile Dipping Sauce 56
Vegetarian Caesar Dressing 240

W

Walnut & Leek Pilaf 199
Warm Ruby & Golden Beet Salad with Roast Hazelnuts, Blood Oranges & Labneh 92
Wet Polenta 197
White Chocolate & Raspberry Ripple Cheesecake 204
Wild Mushroom & Ale Pies 127
Wild Rice Salad with Peas, Pea Shoots & Green Harissa 84
Worcestershire Sauce, vegetarian 240

Y

yogurt
  Spring Vegetable Pakora with Mango Yogurt Dip 49

Z

zucchini
  Halloumi, Zucchini & Mint Fritters 64
  Saffron & Goat Cheese Tagliatelle with Zucchini, Cherry Tomatoes & Black Olives 148
  Sun-dried Tomato & Mozzarella *Arancini* with Warm Grilled Eggplant & Zucchini Salad 34

ACKNOWLEDGMENTS

A massive thank you to Eleanor and Yasia from Octopus, and Dan and Sarah who between them took this from the back burner and brought it to a rolling boil.

To Jonathan and Patrick whose photography and design brought the Mildreds mojo to life.

To Martin, whose generosity and belief in Mildreds has kept us afloat when the chips were down.

To my three sons, Ambrose, Flinn, and Milo, just because.

To Kathy, the absolute stalwart of Mildreds.

To everyone else behind the scenes, especially Annie and Tabitha, whose creative talent has made this book happen.

And last but not the least, to Diane—we had the dream, Lambie.